Struggle
Against History

U.S. FOREIGN POLICY
IN AN AGE
OF REVOLUTION

EDITED BY

Neal D. Houghton

With an Introduction by

ARNOLD J. TOYNBEE

A CLARION BOOK
Published by Simon and Schuster

A Clarion Book
Published by Simon and Schuster
Rockefeller Center, 630 Fifth Avenue
New York, New York 10020

Reprinted by arrangement with Washington Square Press, Inc.

THIRD PAPERBACK PRINTING

Library of Congress Catalog Card Number: 68-20580
Manufactured in the United States of America
By Murray Printing Co., Forge Village, Mass.

The following papers are the result of a seminar held 19–23 March 1967 in Estes Park, Colorado. There have been numerous meetings in recent times throughout the United States — indeed throughout the world — in an attempt to express a *concern* for United States involvements in Southeast Asia and elsewhere. The purpose of this meeting was to examine the *basic historical causes* of overall United States posture, in an "Age of Multirevolution on all Continents." And to examine the consequences of this posture. The holding of this seminar and the preparation of its resulting book were indispensably facilitated by Professor Maurice L. Albertson of Colorado State University and the Center for Research and Education at Estes Park.

This volume is respectfully dedicated to the seventy percent of the people of the world who live in the underdeveloped areas of Asia, Africa, and Latin America — to the people who bear the burden of what has come to be called the "American Century."

N. D. H.

Contents

Foreword
Foreign Policy and Social
Blindness in the United States

NEAL D. HOUGHTON

I

**Basic Concepts of this Great
Convulsive Transition Period**

Perhaps no other people in modern history has ever been in
more urgent need of a working understanding of its *era* than
we now are. And, frankly, I see too little evidence that even
our highest and most responsible political and intellectual
leadership has that basic understanding. In the fall of 1966,
one alert newsman reported, just as a matter of *news*, that
our people are "simply . . . confused; they know we are in a
mess and they don't know what to do."[1]

There is, of course, plenty of official assertion and reasser-
tion of good intention and dedication to the pursuit of goals,
in foreign policy and international politics, which are largely
unattainable. They are unattainable because they are just not
compatible with the great human technological forces which,
currently and prospectively, are reshaping the world.

The position of the United States in Vietnam, for example,
as of the mid-1960s and prospectively, is untenable, simply
because the policy upon which it rests is in defiance of those
same forces. This policy, in Asia and elsewhere, rests on our
officially proclaimed purpose to "shape the course of history"
in those vast areas, "in our favor."[2]

---

[1] Carl T. Rowan, "Crisis of Leadership," *Arizona Daily Star,* October
5, 1966.

[2] See *Department of State 1963: A Report to the Citizen,* Department
of State Publication 7530, General Foreign Policy Series 187, May, 1963.
For sale by Superintendent of Documents (Washington, D.C.: U.S.

And, even if the Vietnam involvement of the 1960s should be fortunately "settled" in some way we should still be faced with the prospect of becoming involved in at least twenty other "Vietnams" in Asia and elsewhere — if Washington persists in resisting and liquidating all basic social revolutions of which it may disapprove.

As indicated by the title, basic emphasis here will be upon *this great convulsive transition period.*

At this point, may it be said, oversimply, that the contemporary period in world history is a *normal* — basically understandable and explainable but remarkably not understood and unexplained — era of rapid social change. Our understanding of contemporary regional and world developments is limited by our lack of understanding of their origins.

This lack of understanding is neither new to us nor confined to us. The point is that (1) until the twentieth century, we did not imperatively *need* to understand. We were not in a position to make vastly significant mistakes in foreign policy prior to the late 1890s. During the first 100 years of our national existence, our territorial expansionism was generally confined to what I have called elsewhere "continental imperialism."[3] And (2) the dominant imperial "powers" of the nineteenth century — whose confident, high-riding leadership also lacked profound, functional understanding of the forces, which were soon to emerge so explosively in their imperial domains — have all gone down the drain of history. They *were* in positions to make significant mistakes, and they continued to

---

Government Printing Office). Price, $1.50. See specifically pp. 23-25. See also Dean Rusk, "The U.S. Defense Commitments," *Department of State Newsletter*, September, 1966.

And, for a report upon the launching, in the summer of 1966, of a vast State Department indoctrination program, aimed at beefing up "teaching" and "research," at all levels, of international relations and American foreign policy, see "1300 Educators Attend Department Conference," *Department of State Newsletter*, July, 1966, and "1400 Discuss World Affairs Education," Department of State *Foreign Policy Briefs*, July 11, 1966. For a fuller report, see *Department of State Bulletin* (Special Issue), July 18, 1966.

[3] See Neal D. Houghton, "Social Structure and Foreign Policy of the United States," *Year Book of World Affairs, 1961*, XV (London: London Institute of World Affairs, University of London), 93–134.

make them — fatally, during the first half of the twentieth century — until they finally went the way of all the great empires of all history, into *imperial oblivion*.

II

Power-Dependent, Perspective-Resistant Leadership

Now comes the United States — lacking both extensive experience as a world imperialist power and functioning historical perspective for understanding this period of traumatic global convulsive change — to move into that vast imperialistic void. In fact, Washington — in confidence and relative social blindness, perhaps even in unawareness — has launched an unprecedentedly ambitious new kind of *world imperialism*.[4] Or it may prove to be an unexampled kind of isolationism, consisting of the United States self-appointed as the "leader" of the so-called "free world," whom anticipated "allies" may just not follow.[5]

The confidence of our top-level leadership is grounded, admittedly, upon unprecedented military *power* and national *wealth* — and upon officially proclaimed willingness to *use* our presumed overwhelmingly superior *firepower* wherever, whenever, and to whatever extent it may appear to be needed. But, tragically, these are just not the remedies for what ails the

---

[4] See Stringfellow Barr, "Consulting the Romans — An Analogy Between Ancient Rome and Present-Day America," (Santa Barbara: Center for the Study of Democratic Institutions, January, 1967). See also, D. F. Fleming, "Can *Pax Americana* Succeed?" see p. 271 in this volume; and Arnold J. Toynbee, "The Failure of American Foreign Policy," *Fact*, September–October, 1965.

[5] For perhaps the most penetratingly critical and constructively readable analysis of the matter yet to appear, see Edmund Stillman and William Pfaff, *Power and Impotence — The Failure of America's Foreign Policy* (New York: Vintage Books, 1967). See also J. William Fulbright, *The Arrogance of Power* (New York: Vintage, 1967); Norman A. Graeber, *The New Isolationism* (New York: Ronald, 1956); "Commager Declares U.S. Overextends World Role," *The New York Times*, February 21, 1967; David Horowitz, *The Free World Colossus* (New York: Hill & Wang, 1965); and Frederick L. Schuman, "Toward National Suicide," *Monthly Review*, XVIII (February, 1967), 40–41.

world. Military firepower, however delivered, just won't feed increasing billions of hungry and distressed people. Nor can even enormous economic "aid" do that job, in a cold war context of "containment" of basic social revolution, with the ill-concealed purpose of restoring or creating opportunities for Americans to make profits — in Asia, Africa, and Latin America.[6] No combination of modern war-making — and "other wars" — by Western whites may be expected effectively to "pacify" the nationalistically and racially minded peoples of these vast areas who are in basic social revolution against both traditional native upper-class abuses and white and/or *yanqui* "imperialism."

Yet, in the mid-1960s, one of the observable characteristics of our highest official foreign policy functionaries, the Johnson Team first stringers — certainly Johnson, Rusk, McNamara, and Humphrey — was their apparent *unconcern* with deepening and broadening their own functional understanding of this world in multi-revolution.[7] Being politically sensitive, however, in the Texas tradition, to criticism of our foreign policies and tactics — most notably, our Vietnam involvements and tactics — the White House issued a dramatic public statement on February 3, 1964:

> President Johnson today called on the Nation's top scholars, thinkers, writers, teachers, and specialists in all fields to generate fresh, new, and imaginative ideas for the benefit of the government. . . . The President wants to insure a "wide-open window for ideas" in the White House.

---

[6] See J. P. Morray, "Aid Without Tears," *California Law Review,* XLVI (December, 1958), 665–98.

[7] See Clayton Fritchey, "The Politicians vs. the Foreign Service," *Harper's,* (January, 1967), 90–94. See also, McGeorge Bundy, "The End of Either/Or," *Foreign Affairs,* XLV (January, 1967), 189–201; Thomas L. Hughes, "Policy-Making in a World Turned Upside Down," *The New York Times,* February 24, 1967; James Deakin, "How Johnson Sees the World," *War/Peace Report,* VII (January, 1967); and Smith Simpson, "Who Runs the State Department? — The Rusk Enigma," *The Nation,* March 6, 1967.

And, in what was declared to be a "unique approach to channel the Nation's best thinking" through that "open window for ideas," Eric F. Goldman, Princeton Professor of History, was designated to serve as a "coordinator for the reception of the work of the Nation's scholars and specialists." He was directed to "help keep a continuous flow of specific proposals, general approaches and opinions from a wide range of experts outside the Government."[8]

Presumably, that "flow" would be *toward* our highest government policy-makers.[9] Yet, when one reads the fine print in the statement, one finds no promise that the whole grandiose design was to have any effective enlightening or restraining influence upon those high priests of foreign policy or their policies.

And, of course, no such impact was discernible. In fact, though Professor Goldman was assigned office space in the White House — and allowed to use White House stationery — he served on only a part-time $75-per-day-worked basis. And, after two and a half years of it, he resigned in some degree of obvious frustration, purportedly to publish a critical book, within a year or so, about the Johnson administration.[10]

---

[8] For press buildup of the Goldman assignment, see Tom Wicker, "Princeton Historian Named 'Idea Man' at the White House," *The New York Times,* February 4, 1964; "Torrents of Suggestions Swamp LBJ's Idea Man," *Arizona Daily Star,* February 12, 1964; James Reston, "The Part-Time Brain Hunt at Princeton," *The New York Times,* February 21, 1964; Max Freedman, "Professor Goldman's Task," *Arizona Daily Star,* February 23, 1964; and Bernard Gauzer, "LBJ Advisor Serves as Funnel for Ideas," *ibid.,* April 26, 1964.

[9] Mr. Goldman's appointment was by no means an isolated matter in the spectacular 1964 Johnson pre-election and post-election gestures toward lining up respectable "cold war"-minded academic and intellectual support for the "Johnson Team." See, for example, Nan Robertson, "Douglas Cater Begins His Chores of 'Thinking Ahead' for LBJ," *Arizona Daily Star,* May 22, 1964; Robert B. Semple, Jr., "President Names His 16 Advisors," *The New York Times,* September 10, 1964; "President Picks 16 Advisors on Foreign Affairs," *Department of State Newsletter,* October, 1964; Tad Szulc, "11 Groups Shape Johnson Program," *The New York Times,* October 1, 1964; and "Blueprint for Foreign Policy" (ed.), *ibid.,* October 15, 1964.

[10] *The New York Times,* September 8, 1966. See also "Former Advisor Condemns LBJ: Conduct of Viet Nam War Draws Attack by Ex-

The immediate White House down-talk reaction, Bill Moyers speaking (only some three months before Moyers also resigned), characterized Goldman as having been only:

> a part-time peripheral figure who had had a mere dozen meetings with the President in 30 months . . . who had missed most of the staff's regular meetings with the academic world . . . and who had worked most of the time on cultural matters with Mrs. Johnson's press aide.[11]

Obviously, the Johnson Team had learned little and/or forgotten little during Goldman's incumbency as front man for this "open window for ideas" play. Nor, could the White House press release credibly saddle him with responsibility for the failure of his mission.[12] Certainly, by that summer and fall (1966), there had come a discernible concern among "intellectuals" about the alleged *unconcern* of Johnson Team management for the *concerns* of "thinking men," in matters of foreign policy.[13]

In a prompt move to:

> "supplant the defector [Goldman] with a new (full-time) consultant from the world of scholarship," there was little ballyhoo about White House hunger for "ideas." There was no implication that critical policy-changing enlightenment was to be sought.[14] It was simply announced that

---

Speech Writer, Richard Goodwin" (*The New York Times* News Service), *Arizona Daily Star*, September 18, 1966.

[11] Specifically, "Dr. Goldman was said to have worked 148 days in 1964, 117 days in 1965, and 66 days in 1966." See Max Frankel, "New Presidential Consultant Gets Added Duties," *ibid.*, September 10, 1966.

[12] See "Failure of a Mission" (ed.), *The Nation*, September 19, 1966.

[13] See, for example, Saul Friedman, "Idea Men Leaving LBJ," *Denver Post*, July 12, 1966; James Reston, "Washington: The Man Power Problem at State," *The New York Times*, July 27, 1966; "Thinking Men Grumbling Because LBJ Won't Permit Them to Think: Ivy Leaguers Fume as Professor Quits," *Arizona Daily Star*, September 13, 1966; Evans and Novak, "Goldman's Stumbling Exit," *ibid.*, September 15, 1966; and Reston, "Washington: Moving Day Along the Dog Run," *The New York Times*, September 23, 1966.

[14] See, for example, Benjamin Welles, "Civilians Will Aid on Foreign Policy," *The New York Times*, October 10, 1966.

"Professor John P. Roche of Brandeis University, a former national chairman of Americans for Democratic Action, comes with the attractive credentials of domestic liberalism and support of the President's foreign policy in Viet Nam."[15]

And, in the considerable shuffling of foreign policy personnel in the summer and fall of 1966 (along with "supplanting the defector," Goldman), it appeared that, dominantly, hardline cold warriors were being recruited, from whom rationalizing support — rather than clarifying perspective — for enlightened foreign policies might be expected.[16] Our self-confident moguls of policy were certainly not arranging to be disturbed by enlightening perspective.

III

Search for Enlightenment Toward Social Statesmanship

Thus any prospect for turning our cold war mentality toward rationality, based upon an understanding of our foreign policy challenges, may depend largely on our reading public.

How, then, may anyone, anywhere go about the quest for more adequate perspective?

First, let it be said that no adequate perspective can be obtained merely by looking *out our windows* upon current conditions and situations. This is not to deny the obvious and imperative need for constant, alert, and discriminating obser-

---

15 See Frankel, *op. cit.*

16 See Walt W. Rostow, "Hawk-Eyed Optimist," *Time*, July 15, 1966; Chalmers Roberts, "Rostow: Proposal Becomes Policy," *Denver Post*, July 17, 1966; Max Frankel, "LBJ Shuffles 'Team,'" *Arizona Daily Star*, September 22, 1966; "New Team in State" (ed.), *The New York Times*, September 22, 1966; "A Thinker and Doer: Eugene Victor Debs Rostow," *ibid.;* Tom Wicker, "State Department Shifts: Administration Critics Doubt That New Aids Will Alter Established Policy," *ibid.*; Robert Richardson Bowie, "Tough Adviser to Rusk," *ibid.*, September 28, 1966; William S. White, "LBJ's Cabinet Reshuffle," *Arizona Daily Star*, September 29, 1966; and Marquis Childs, "Walt Rostow, LBJ Advisor," *ibid.*, October 24, 1966.

vation of the current local, regional, and world happenings.

There is nothing fundamentally wrong with professorial efforts and devices to inject objectivity into our current observations so long as they do not purport to replace essential historical perspective. I refer especially to the increasing numbers of academic tomes on analysis and theory of international relations[17] and to "simulation" and related mechanized cerebration.[18] Let them become as creatively and readably helpful as possible.

But more is needed to make our current "through-a-porthole" observations functional. And, no factor is more essential than history — pertinent wisdom accumulated from the experiences of mankind.

For some years I have been working to provide some help in this matter, and I propose to offer some of it here.

We need to know something about our national proclivities for reacting at home to foreign and international goings-on.[19] We need to learn about the experiences of peoples in previous *convulsive transition periods*.[20] We must realize that currently observable conditions, attitudes, and developments on other continents are long-term *products* of the deeply rooted social structures of those areas affected by centuries of European colonial imperialism and private corporate profit-seeking operations there.

[17] See, for example, Stanley H. Hoffman (ed.), *Contemporary Theory in International Relations* (Englewood Cliffs: Prentice-Hall, 1960); J. David Singer (ed.), *Human Behavior and International Politics* (Chicago: Rand McNally, 1965); and Charles A. McClelland, *Theory and the International System* (New York: Macmillan, 1966).

[18] See the very competent symposium by Chadwick Alger, Richard Brody, Harold Guetzkow, Robert Noel, and Richard C. Snyder, *Simulation in International Relations: Developments for Research and Teaching* (Englewood Cliffs: Prentice-Hall, 1963). See also Mordecai Roshwald, "The Cybernetics of Blunder," *The Nation*, March 13, 1967.

[19] See Neal D. Houghton, "The Challenge to Political Scientists in Recent American Foreign Policy: Scholarship or Indoctrination," *American Political Science Review*, 52 (September, 1958), 678–88. and "Some Domestic and International Implications of the 1964 Elections in the United States," *Background*, IX (Summer, 1965), 153–62.

[20] See Neal D. Houghton, "Perspective for Foreign Policy Objectives in Areas — and in an Era — of Rapid Social Change," *Western Political Quarterly*, XVI (December, 1963) 844–84.

We must also be aware that the United States, both as government and as private business enterprise, was a "Johnny come lately" to that period of collapsing European imperialism, riding obliquely and awkwardly into the Asian and European picture late in the nineteenth century and in the early decades of the twentieth with British encouragement. We were unaware that we had joined the British-French balance-of-power system, near the time of its impending collapse — soon enough to find ourselves involved in its final (and fatal) two world wars.[21]

We need to know that, "By far the most basic of all basic factors influencing the foreign policy of the United States has been economic."[22] During the nineteenth century our "continental imperialism" was primarily based on the modest, natural desires of emigrating families to acquire homes and the less modest desires of businessmen and corporations to make money, in North American continental areas not yet under control of the United States. Even then, secondarily, we were involved in a number of foreign trading operations — with varying kinds of government support. As those private money-making pursuits have become increasingly extended and more complex, they have become correspondingly more dependent upon government support. During the twentieth century this relationship between business and government has been spectacularly observable (a) in the Mexican, Caribbean, and Central American parts of Latin America,[23] (b) in our involvement in World War I,[24] and (c) in our post-World War II cold war policies, tactics, and prospective operations.[25]

---

[21] See Neal D. Houghton, "Social Structure and Foreign Policy of the United States," *op. cit.*

[22] *Ibid.*, p. 93, and *passim*; and William A. Williams, *The Tragedy of American Diplomacy* (New York: World Publishing Company, 1959).

[23] See, minimally, Benjamin H. Williams, *Economic Foreign Policy of the United States* (New York: McGraw-Hill, 1929); Dana G. Munro, *The United States and the Caribbean Area* (Boston: World Peace Foundation, 1934); and J. Fred Rippy, *The Capitalists in Colombia* (New York: Vanguard, 1931).

[24] See H. C. Peterson, *Propaganda for War* (Norman; University of Oklahoma Press, 1939).

[25] Neal D. Houghton, "Perspective for Foreign Policy Objectives . . . in an Era of Rapid Social Change," *op. cit.* See also Fred J. Cook,

And we need to know that the roots of the so-called cold war — in fearsome pursuit of which our foreign policy has now become so awesomely dangerous — lie much farther back in history than 1945. It was not precipitated by the Soviet Union[26] but was inherent in the unwarranted wartime London-Washington illusion that, following the war, pre-1914 Europe and European capitalist imperialism in Asia could be reestablished — with Communist Russia's acquiescence and cooperation.[27]

Now, obviously, this citizen assignment involves "unlearning" much that has been systematically brainwashed into and absorbed by us in several decades of cold war indoctrination. That *indoctrination* has come to us from our highest official sources, our mass media, our family and personal conversation, and from our academic and professional classrooms, textbooks, and journals.[28]

Obviously also, our official cold war operators and indoc-

The Warfare State (New York: Macmillan, 1962); John M. Swomley, *The Military Establishment* (Boston: Beacon, 1964); and Tristram Coffin, *The Passion of the Hawks: Militarism in America* (New York: Macmillan, 1964) — Penguin paperback title is *The Armed Society*.

[26] See Kenneth Ingram, *History of the Cold War* (New York: Philosophical Library, 1955); D. F. Fleming, *The Cold War and Its Origins, 1917–1960* (Garden City: Doubleday, 1961) I; and Fred Warner Neal, *U.S. Foreign Policy and the Soviet Union* (Santa Barbara: Center for the Study of Democratic Institutions, 1961).

[27] See Neal D. Houghton, "Historical Bases for Prediction in International Relations: Some Implications for American Foreign Policy," *Western Political Quarterly*, XVII (December, 1964), 632–58; and Gar Alperovitz, *Atomic Diplomacy: Hiroshima and Potsdam* (New York: Simon & Schuster, 1965).

[28] See Neal D. Houghton, "The Challenge to Political Scientists in Recent American Foreign Policy: Scholarship or Indoctrination?" *American Political Science Review*, LII (September, 1958). The tonnage of official, mass media, and professorial cold war indoctrinating reading matter is so tremendous as not to require documentation here. Just write to either the Department of State or the U.S. Government Printing Office, Washington, D.C., for information on any aspect of contemporary foreign policy. Examine any available public school textbooks on "Problems of Democracy" or related social science courses. Examine several unselected college-level textbooks on "International Relations" or "American Foreign Policy."

trinators are not going to be easily affected merely by increasing passive citizen enlightenment.

IV

Emergence of a Washington Power Psychosis with the Collapse of the World of the 1890s

Since the leadership of the so-called "free world" in this cold war era has been assumed by United States officialdom — with popular approval — we and the world may be entitled to examine some pertinent national proclivities. One has been a sort of evil-sin-devil complex with respect to foreign and international goings-on, called by one student "The Paranoid Style in American Politics."[29] Two closely related characteristics are an inordinate fear of those foreign goings-on — fear, in fact, to live in the normal course of world history — and recurring periods of "McCarthyism." All these proclivities showed up very early in our national history, in the course of the French Revolution and the Napoleonic Wars. All have recurrently persisted and, in recent decades, have run wild. In the 1790s and the early 1800s the Founding Fathers assumed — and passed on to later generations — the pleasurable proclivity for identifying the righteous protagonists in successive European wars and revolutions. That has allowed each such development in Europe to become a potential "crisis" for United States political and intellectual leadership. More recently, that potentiality has been extended to Asia and Africa; so that almost inevitably any major disturbing occurrence on any continent or any island — no matter how normal or predictable — has become, for stateside leadership a "surprise" and a "crisis," a probable "threat" to our "security" and to our "very survival as a free people."

As even General Douglas MacArthur (by vocation, certainly no noted "dove") has said:

Our government has kept us in a perpetual state of fear — kept us in a continuous stampede of patriotic fervor

---

[29] Richard Hofstadter, *The Paranoid Style in American Politics* (New York: Knopf, 1965).

— with the cry of national emergency. Always there has
been some terrible evil at home or some monstrous foreign power that was going to gobble us up . . . yet, in
retrospect, these disasters seem never to have been quite
real.[30]

Another prideful myth is that the States are populated by a
unique "peace-loving" folk, who have gone reluctantly into
their war-making, only to fulfill their Manifest Destiny or to
"save" something great and noble.[31] That myth has survived
and persisted, as we have found our repeated war-making
ventures against a succession of foreign "menaces" in the
twentieth century to be increasingly frustrating — as each
vanquished "menace" has been succeeded by a still more
fearsome one. Always, up pops another devil!

Closely connected with this complex of national characteristics is a bent (apparently untempered by a public sense of
humor) for moralizing and angelizing our "side," while demonizing and castigating the other side in those successive
crusades. We have enjoyed Presidential and Cabinet-rank
Secretarial *sermonizing* toward other governments and their
policies. The late Professor Spykman of Yale put it this way:

The heritage of seventeenth-century Puritanism is responsible for one of the characteristic features of our
[American] approach to international relations. Because
of its concern with ethical values, it has conditioned the
nation to a predominantly moral orientation. It makes
our people feel called upon to express moral judgments
about the foreign policies of others and demand that our
presidents transform the White House into an interna-

---

[30] See Fred J. Cook, "Juggernaut: The Warfare State," *The Nation*
(Special Issue), October 28, 1961, p. 299.

[31] See A. K. Weinberg, *Manifest Destiny* (Baltimore: Johns Hopkins
University Press, 1935); Frederick Merk, *Manifest Destiny and Mission
in American History* (New York: Knopf, 1963); and Robert E. Osgood,
Ideals and Self-Interest in America's Foreign Relations (Chicago: University of Chicago Press, 1953, and Toronto: University of Toronto Press,
1964).

tional pulpit from which mankind can be scolded for the evil of his ways.[32]

So, it has come easily to recent Presidential and State Department pulpiteers to declaim, pleasingly, that the United States is in some special way the protector of the world's "freedom" — a most essential component of which is freedom *of enterprise* — as proclaimed by President Truman[33] and reiterated by his successors.

Finally, and very significantly, it may be pointed out here that our leadership in the decades since World War II has increasingly proclaimed a sense of *world destiny*. For example, in the summer of 1960, the Secretary of Labor, with State Department approval, solemnly announced that:

Strict adherence to our ideals requires us to face the challenge of re-shaping the world in the image of human dignity, political freedom, and authority by consent, not decree. We are beginning to see as the destiny of our people . . . the duty and clear purpose to accept that challenge.[34]

About the same time, Harvard's Dr. James B. Conant demanded an "invulnerable system" of "retaliatory power" so overwhelming that even after:

Surviving a thermonuclear barrage, [we] would be able to deliver thermonuclear weapons to such an extent and in such a way that at least three-fourths of the industrial complexes of the Soviet Union would be utterly destroyed.[35]

In a comprehensive official State Department "Report to the Citizen," in 1963, the Department's Policy-Planning Council expressed the confident conviction that "the future can be

---

[32] Nicholas J. Spykman, *America's Strategy in World Politics* (New York: Harcourt, Brace, 1942), p. 216.

[33] See D. F. Fleming, *op. cit.,* pp. 436–37.

[34] State Department, *Foreign Policy Briefs,* June 24, 1960.

[35] See *Department of State 1963: A Report to the Citizen, op. cit.*

shaped. . . . The larger purpose of such [State Department] planning is to shape history in our favor."[36]

In the summer of 1964, President Johnson boasted:

> United States military strength now exceeds the combined military might of all nations in history, stronger than any adversary or combination of adversaries . . . against such force the combined destructive power of every battle ever fought by man is like a firecracker thrown against the sun.

And by February 12, 1965, Mr. Johnson was proclaiming publicly:

> History and our own achievements have thrust upon us the principal responsibility for protection of freedom on earth. . . . No other people in no other time has had so great an opportunity to work and risk for the freedom of all mankind.

In fact, even as early as August of 1962, President Kennedy had predicted dramatically:

> For the next ten or twenty years, the burdens will be placed completely upon our country for the preservation of freedom. We stand in the center . . . it all depends upon the keystone, which is the United States.[37]

---

[36] See *The New York Times,* June 4, 1964.

[37] *Ibid.,* August 29, 1962. And as early as the spring of 1961, Mr. Kennedy, provoked by what he considered "bullying" by Mr. Khrushchev in a meeting in Vienna, for just having failed to make good on the recent U.S.-sponsored Bay of Pigs invasion of Cuba, made a decision to make U.S. power "credible" to Khrushchev by increasing the military budget by $6,000,000,000, by sending the Rainbow Division to Germany and by sending 12,000 men to Vietnam — against the advice of at least two of his advisers, one of whom said, "No, don't go down that track," and the other of whom advised that, "If you go that way, it may take 300,000 men." All this came in course of a conversation with James Reston, columnist and Associate Editor of *The New York Times,* as revealed by Reston in a National Education Television interview of January 16, 1966. See also, Edward Weintal and Charles Bartlett, *Facing the Brink* (New York: Scribner's, 1967).

It may not be impertinent, I submit, to observe that certainly not since *Mein Kampf* and perhaps not ever has the political leadership of any other Western nation talked so much, and so ambitiously, of its duty and its power to direct the destiny of the world as have the highest leaders in the United States, beginning seriously in the 1940s.[38] Hitler's horrendous threats and tragic operations are widely considered to have been, to some degree at least, the work of an irresponsible psychopath.[39] Japan's far less ambitious "co-prosperity" operations in the 1930s provided the London-Washington base for the Asian part of World War II, partly as a desperate and futile effort to save the collapsing remnants of Western colonial imperialism in Asia. And contemporary Russian and Chinese developments have generated semi-hysterical cold war reactions and responses in the United States.

Rapidly, these power- and wealth-based Washington responses are taking shape as the intent to reinstate the white man's world of the 1890s, as it looked (unrealistically) to its nineteenth-century builders and its twentieth-century inheritors.

That dream world of the 1890s and early 1900s looked indeed promising to Western white capitalistic profit-seekers. Europe seemed (not too) comfortably in balance-of-power control by Britain, France, and Russia. Asia had been "opened" to Western economic exploitation by European warmaking on the Asian mainland, including the British "Opium War" on China in 1839 and later follow-up operations, and

---

[38] For a comprehensive compilation of pertinent comparably ambitious declamations by highest leadership in the Rome-Berlin-Tokyo Axis of the 1930s and 1940s, see Frederick L. Schuman, "U.S. Policy: 1965 (Quotable Notables)," *Minority of One*, August 19, 1965. And, for a related compilation of pertinent statements about President Johnson's conceptualities of his leadership role by friendly observers, associates, and newspapermen during the year 1965, see M. S. Arnoni, "How Rational Is LBJ?" *ibid.* See also James Reston, "President Johnson's Dreams," *The New York Times*, February 26, 1966.

[39] For a short treatment of Hitler, "as a political genius," for whom "no single human virtue redeems his infamous acts and disastrous policy," without impugning his sanity, see Hugh Trevor-Roper, *Hitler's Place in History*, University Lecture Series, No. 5 (Saskatoon: University of Saskatchewan, 1965).

British-encouraged American Pacific insular occupations in the late 1890s.[40] Africa had literally been parceled out among European governments and corporate economic operators. And Latin America, by less spectacular processes, seemed to have been put on ice, under the "protection" of the "Monroe Doctrine," hopefully available for future American and European economic exploitation of its resources and markets.

Perhaps it was not to be expected that the Western shapers and expectant beneficiaries of that unrealistic world should discern its ephemeral nature. But a few decades of major war among the white "free enterprise" lords of its creation — and emergence of explosive human forces from the vast mass-poverty areas — have brought the whole structure tumbling down upon the confused heads of two generations of people.[41]

Perhaps nowhere else has the confusion been greater than in the United States, whose talents and energies had so little to do with the building of the overseas parts of that world. And, ironically, it is that stronghold of confusion and inexperience that now offers its "leadership" in the rebuilding of that never-never world of the 1890s, in the vastness of Asia. We are to accomplish this by a ruthless application of unlimited military power and some sort of overseas "war on poverty" in peripheral spots of what Walter Lippmann has alertly called "artificial and ramshackle debris of old [European] empires," into which Washington got as "an accidental and unplanned consequence of the second world war."[42]

---

[40] British wooing of the youthful American giant, after 1895, reversed a century of mutually enjoyable feuding. It might be helpful to have American possessions in the Asian area of vast British involvement, and possibly also American support for the British balance-of-power stance in Europe, if and when it might be challenged by the rising power of Germany. See Charles S. Campbell, Jr., *Anglo-American Understanding, 1898–1903* (Baltimore: Johns Hopkins University Press, 1957); and P. A. Varg, *Open Door Diplomat: The Life of W. W. Rockhill* (Urbana: University of Illinois Press, 1952).

[41] See Barbara W. Tuchman, *The Proud Tower: A Portrait of the World Before the War, 1890–1914* (New York: Macmillan, 1965); and Edmund Stillman and William Pfaff, *The Politics of Hysteria* (New York: Harper & Row, 1963).

[42] See "The Pledge of Honolulu," *Department of State Bulletin*, February 28, 1966; *The Promise of the New Asia: United States Policy in*

The Asian world that is dead cannot be recreated in this great convulsive period — no matter how bloodily the "free world" leadership may try.

V

Some Basic History-Impelling Factors and Forces

This great convulsive transition period, in which we have been living for many decades, and in which we must live for the predictable future, is both revolutionary and uniquely world-wide. Europe and the Mediterranean Basin, with whose history we are likely to be most familiar, have experienced some well-known periods of regional upheaval including: (1) the rise of the Roman Empire; (2) its decline and fall; (3) the 1,000-year unpreplanned development of modern nation-states from the wreckage of the Roman Empire; and (4) the parallel development, in the nineteenth century, of modern industrialism and constitutional government in the West. But we are now in the *first global* convulsive period in recorded history. The great human and technological forces at work in this multi-revolutionary period are producing (as such periods have produced in the Mediterranean Basin) vast, *basic and permanent change on every continent.*

For any who may well be allergic to expressions of "historicism" or "determinism," may I offer assurance that I shall not propound any such academic sacrilege.[43] I shall not even propound the notion that "history repeats itself." My purpose is simply to insist that much that is indispensably useful can be learned only from the experiences of mankind. And to say

the *Far East as Stated by President Johnson on His Pacific Journey,* Department of State Publication 8166, Far Eastern Series 152, November, 1966. For sale by Supt. of Documents (Washington, D.C.: U.S. Government Printing Office). Price $1; and "Johnson Sees Asia at Turning Point," *The New York Times,* October 18, 1966.

[43] But, see Glen Tinder, "The Necessity of Historicism," *American Political Science Review,* LV (September, 1961), 560–65; C. Vann Woodward, "The Age of Reinterpretation," *American Historical Review,* LXVI (October, 1960), 1–19; and Crane Brinton, *The Anatomy of Revolution* (New York: Norton, 1938).

that much of what is to be learned about regional convulsions which I have listed could and should enable our leadership — and our followership — to make indispensable adjustments to this global one. For it is in this area that both we and our leadership are so terribly, and so dangerously, confused. We can learn that in such periods old orders, old attitudes, old ways of operating are challenged. New attitudes and new orders are born and go "on the make," in competition with — and in defiance of — the traditional order. Old public policies and old orders are permanently changed, and are to some extent displaced, by new and virulent systems — all without too much regard for traditional "values," "principles," and old rules of the game.

We can learn that the only practicable way out of such a period of great social convulsion has been *to get on through it.*

Characteristically, such periods are marked by much disturbance, disquietude, some kinds of revolution, some social "progress," much tragic disappointment — and great social costs. Always, satisfied adherents to, and beneficiaries of, old orders and old rules of the game resist the disturbing changes and seek to preserve or restore status quo.

Rarely, if ever, does the intellectual and political leadership of such resistance movements seem to recognize the nature of the period. Always that recognition has had to come later, with benefit of hindsight and time-enforced acceptance of the consummated and futilely resisted change.

What a pity that the recognition could not have come contemporaneously — so that enlightened accommodation might have been made! For example, the irrepressible rise of the first modern nation-states in Europe was consummated in the fifteenth and sixteenth centuries, in spite of 1,000 years of costly but futile efforts to rebuild "world empire" on the old basic Roman pattern. And modern constitutional government developed, in spite of all-out military resistance efforts by the combined monarchies of nineteenth-century Europe.[44] May I remind you that the *fearsome ism* to the satisfied leadership of the old order in early nineteenth-century Europe was *constitu-*

---

[44] See W. A. Phillips, *Confederation of Europe* (London: Longmans Green, 1920).

tionalism. Quite as fearsome as *Communism* — and "Black Power" — have been for some men in places of leadership in the twentieth century.

As Toynbee advised in the mid-1950s:

> To see what we ought not to do, we should take warning from the repressive policy that was followed by Metternich and his respectable European associates in the first half of the nineteenth century. In 1848, an eruption blew Metternich sky high . . . and his fellow westerners of a later generation ought to take to heart the fate that Metternich brought on himself.[45]

This contemporary multi-revolutionary world is being impelled by a number of basic — and apparently irrepressible — human and technological forces. Some of them are identifiable. (1) An unprecedentedly escalating population on all continents promises to reach some 7 billion within thirty or thirty-five years — perhaps 15 billion before 2025 A.D. (as compared with approximately 3.3 billion in the mid-1960s), in spite of all contemplated birth control efforts.[46] (2) More than two-thirds of the current 3.3 billion are existing in extreme poverty and distress, including one-fifth of our own pridefully "affluent" North American societies on both sides of our border.[47] (3) There is an increasing determination among the

---

[45] Arnold J. Toynbee, "The Revolution We Are Living Through," *The New York Times Magazine,* July 25, 1954. See also Toynbee's *America and the World Revolution* (New York and London: Oxford University Press, 1962).

[46] For classic and still useful treatment, see Harrison S. Brown, *The Challenge of Man's Future* (New York: Viking Press, 1954); Robert C. Cook, *Human Fertility* (New York: Sloane, 1951). For a thoroughly unorthodox job, see also Josue De Castro, *Geography of Hunger* (Boston: Little, Brown, 1952). For recent Department of State-sponsored attention, see "Humanity's Greatest Challenge: The Population Explosion," *Department of State Newsletter,* December, 1966: "Losing Battle to Feed the Hungry," *ibid.,* January, 1967; and "Contraceptive Research and the Population Crisis," *ibid.,* February, 1967. Others to follow.

[47] See Michael Harrington, *The Other America: Poverty in the United States* (New York: Macmillan, 1963); and Gabriel Kolko, *Wealth and Power in the United States* (New York: Praeger, 1962).

leaders in the vast mass-poverty areas of the world to seek economic betterment for their areas. (4) There is the closely related determination of that leadership to be rid of white race and foreign political and economic domination.[48] And (5) there are the recent and prospectively spectacular scientific and technological developments, potentially available to all social orders, old and new, to serve — or destroy — people.[49]

These vast history-making forces are, I submit, the basic *keys* to any constructive contemplation of a tolerable future for mankind.[50] It is to these great forces that the United States is challenged to *adjust* and to *accommodate*.

Professor Kenneth Boulding warned in 1966 that, "If the human race is to survive, it will have to change its ways of thinking more in the next twenty-five years than in the last 25,000."

Yet unfortunately, many responsibly placed intellectuals and politicos seem content to refer glibly and apparently uncomprehendingly to this complex of history-impelling forces in *clichés*. Among these *clichés* are "population explosion," "revolution of rising expectations," "rising tide of color," "scientific revolution," "triple revolution."

Ordinarily, these phrases are used introductorily or interjected into the user's discourse to describe a disturbing — but far from simple — situation to which he offers some oversimple "solution." The "pill" or the "coil," or the "loop" — or even economic "modernization" and "industrialization" — may be confidently proposed as the *answer* to the "population

---

[48] See Frantz Fanon, *Studies in a Dying Colonialism* (New York: Monthly Review Press, 1965), originally published in France by François Maspero in 1959 as *L'An Cinq de la Révolution Algérienne*: and *The Wretched of the Earth* (New York: Grove Press and Toronto: Saunders of Toronto, Ltd., 1963).

[49] See Eugene Rabinowitch, *The Dawn of a New Age: Reflections on Science and Human Affairs* (Chicago and London: University of Chicago Press and Toronto: University of Toronto Press, 1963).

[50] For any who may possibly find this emphasis upon nonhero and nonvillain personality forces bothersome, see Robert L. Heilbroner, *The Future as History* (New York: Harper & Row, 1960); and Edward H. Carr, *What Is History?* (New York: Knopf, 1962).

explosion." So the audience, or the reader, is supposed to go home and/or to bed feeling assured that the "population explosion" — and, presumably the vast social challenges associated with it — are safely under control.

The speech, or the article, may well be a cold war discourse as well, in which the discourser uses the clichés to frighten or to rally his public toward acceptance and support of a going or prospective cold war operation, purportedly in harmony with his clichéd situation. For example, the so-called "Alliance for Progress" has been sold to our people, beginning in 1960, as an enormous gadget designed to keep Latin America with its terrifying "population explosion," its associated mass poverty — and its "revolution of rising expectations" — from embracing "Communism."[51]

The great challenges *to* mankind — and to our power-drunk, and relatively affluent segment of it — are the challenges *of* mankind, which have been partially listed here. Those challenges cannot be helpfully oversimplified. Even my partial listing is necessarily an oversimplification of them.

These basic challenges arise from the all-too-many billions of people, now and prospectively on the earth. Yet our government did not even get around to setting up an "Interagency Committee on Population Matters" till the spring of 1967. We were and are too fully occupied with the "evils" and "menaces" of *Communism.*[52]

VI

Communism, Wherefore Art Thou?

Noticeably, *Communism* has not been listed here as one of the history-impelling forces — because it is *not a primary force* in this great complex. Communism is a *normal product* of these primary forces. Only *secondarily* is Communism an activating force.

---

[51] For an alert and in-depth Latin American view see Alonso Aguilar, *Latin America and the Alliance for Progress* (New York: Monthly Review Press, 1963).

[52] See "Interagency Committee Created to Handle Population Matters," *Department of State Newsletter*, April, 1967.

That is not, however, to say that evolving Communism is socially unimportant. Already, it is viably operative, as a great new, raw, and evolving social order — in fact, a whole set of national and regional social orders — spanning the great Eurasian land mass, from the Elbe to the Pacific. These existing and prospective new socialistic orders have varied — and changing — *programs* designed to deal with the vast problems of humanity, posed by the great primary impelling forces of this area. These evolving programs may be expected to appeal widely to alert native leadership of the vast areas which have never been served — even moderately badly — by any other social order.[53] And the relative permanence of the new evolving orders is as predictable as any major social phenomenon has ever been. They will have to be *lived with* — and *adjusted to* — if the masses of mankind are to be allowed to develop and utilize viable social systems, on their own impulsion.[54]

Yet, since 1917[55] (and increasingly frantically, since the mid-1940s), stateside social and political leadership has been behaving as though Communism were the *major* — and intolerably evil — impulsion for this era of irrepressibly rapid social change. For example, President Kennedy, in a 1960 campaign speech, declared dramatically, "The enemy is the ruthless, tireless communist system now infiltrating the world's less prosperous area . . . the real issue is world freedom or world slavery, world peace or world war."[56]

Declaredly and observably, this dogma — embracing a psychotic fear of revolutionary and evolving "Communism" and "Communist aggression" — has been, and remains the principal basis for Washington's cold war operations. But observably and rationally, it has never made sense. It is no more an

---

[53] See Morris H. Rubin, "Dynamite on Our Doorstep," *The Progressive* (Special Issue), June, 1961. See also, Arnold J. Toynbee, "Supersam," *Ramparts,* December, 1965.

[54] See Karl Jaspers, *The Future of Mankind* (Chicago: University of Chicago Press, 1963).

[55] See N. D. Houghton, "Policy of the United States and Other Nations with Respect to Recognition of the Russian Soviet Government, 1917–1929," *International Conciliation,* No. 247 (February, 1929).

[56] *The New York Times,* November 5, 1960.

adequate basis for twentieth- and twenty-first-century American foreign policy than was fear of revolutionary *constitutionalism* an adequate basis for the policies of monarchical Western Europe in the nineteenth century.[57]

Actually, the convenient "Communism" label, carrying a connotation of incarnate evil, has facilitated Washington's increasingly drastic efforts to prevent or destroy all unwelcome basic social revolutions, everywhere on earth.[58]

Yet, it is of the very essence of this great convulsive period that alert and impatient leadership of the current and prospective billions of increasingly poor and distressed peoples of Asia, Africa, and Latin America are actively or potentially engaged in revolution against harsh and long-standing social and economic domination by native upper classes and white European and/or United States "imperialists." The traditional old order of things is just no longer acceptable in those vast areas — where three-fourths of the possible seven billion people of the earth will live by or before the year 2000 A.D.[59]

---

[57] See Phillips, *op. cit.;* Toynbee, *op. cit.;* Walter Lippmann, *The Communist World and Ours* (New York: Little, Brown, 1958); and George F. Kennan, *On Dealing with the Communist World* (New York: Harper & Row, 1964).

[58] See Juan J. Arevalo, *Anti-Communism in Latin America* (New York: Lyle Stuart, 1963); and Sidney Lens, *The Futile Crusade* (Chicago: Quadrangle Books, 1964).

[59] See Carlos Fuentes, "The Argument of Latin America: Words for the North Americans," *Monthly Review,* January, 1963; Andre Gunder Frank, *Capitalism and Underdevelopment in Latin America* (New York: Monthly Review Press, 1967); and "The Latin American Revolution: A New Phase," (ed.) *Monthly Review,* February, 1967, 1–23. See also, Ronald Steel, "One Millionaire and Twenty Beggars — Why Violent Revolutions Probably Are Inevitable in Latin America," *Harper's,* CCXXXIV (May, 1967), 81–87.

Introduction
Colonialism and the United States

ARNOLD J. TOYNBEE

One of the wonders of the world today is the frustration of the United States in Vietnam. The armed forces of the United States is the mightiest military machine that there has ever been so far. This machine is serviced by the wealthiest and best-equipped economy that the world has yet known; all the resources of American science and technology have been applied to the arming of the American military machine with ingeniously inhuman weapons, and, though the Administration at Washington has so far refrained from using the atomic weapon in Vietnam, it is using there its whole inventory of "conventional" weapons — an inventory that now includes napalm and anti-personnel bombs. Yet North Vietnam and the Vietcong resistance movement in the South have, so far, successfully withstood the huge deployment of American military might. Since the Tet offensive, the Americans' opponents have undone all that the Americans had achieved in the South in the way of "pacification"; they have thrown the American forces in Vietnam on the defensive; their latest feat has been to shake the stability of the dollar. How have the Vietnamese achieved this? And what has been their motive for standing up to America at the cost of such fearful sacrifices? No country has ever been devastated more ruthlessly than Vietnam — especially the South — is being devastated by the Americans in this war.

The nature of the battlefields has, of course, told in the

Vietnamese resistance's favor. Jungle and irrigated paddy fields are unfavorable terrain for highly mechanized forces of the American kind, and, now that the Vietnamese have carried the war into the built-up areas in the cities, the only alternative for the Americans to hand-to-hand fighting from street to street and from house to house is to use their planes and artillery at long range to lay Vietnam's cities flat. Moreover, the inequality in equipment has now been appreciably reduced. In 1940, Churchill said to the Americans: "Give us the tools, and we will do the job." The Vietnamese have said the same to the Russians and to the Chinese; and these backers of theirs have been responsive. They have equipped the Vietnamese with up-to-date small arms, rockets, and even tanks. Here are two factors that partially account for the amazing success of the Vietnamese resistance; but there is a third factor which is the decisive one. The Americans' Vietnamese opponents are willing to give their lives. They are not deterred by suffering sacrificial casualties that the American troops and their South Vietnamese auxiliaries could not be asked to endure. This readiness to die in large numbers is by far the biggest factor in the Vietnamese resistance movement's success. The greatness of the sacrifice is evidence of the strength of the motive for making it. What is the motive by which the Vietnamese resistance movement is inspired?

The motive is, I believe, a determination to rid their country, once and for all, of Western domination. Vietnam has been under Western domination now for a century. First it was the French; and the French had no sooner been pushed out than the Americans stepped in. The resentment at being dominated by successive hordes of Westerners is cumulative. For the Vietnamese resistance movement the issue is a simple one. As they see themselves, they are "freedom-fighters," giving their lives to liberate their country.

Of course, the Americans see them as something quite different. They see their Vietnamese opponents as the advance guard of "monolithic world Communism" on the warpath. Which of these two incompatible pictures is the true one? I myself believe that the American picture is a mirage. It is obvious that there is no such thing as "monolithic world Communism." The Communist part of the world, like the capitalist part, is a house divided against itself. Communist China has carried her feud with Communist Russia to greater lengths than capitalist France has carried her feud with capitalist America. The Americans have, I believe, mistaken the identity of the opponent whom they have challenged. The force with which they have joined battle is not their imaginary "world Communism"; it is Vietnamese patriotism; and the Americans' failure to recognize this explains why they have so greatly underestimated the strength of the resistance that they were going to provoke.

Just one more turn of the screw, just one higher rung on the ladder of escalation, and the enemy will give in. This calculation might have been justified by results if the North Vietnamese and the Vietcong had been fighting — as the Americans are fighting — to make the world safe for some ideology. The reason why the American calculation has been proved mistaken, again and again, is surely because their opponents are fighting for something that comes much nearer home to the ordinary man than either Communism or Democracy. To fight to expel a foreign intruder who is dominating one's country by force of arms is a cause that anybody can understand, and that most people will fight for. Americans understood it and fought for it during the Revolutionary War, though, in that war, the foreigners were the Americans' British "kith and kin." The issue is more obvious in Vietnam today, for here the foreign intruders are aliens in race and in civilization.

When the Americans intervened in Vietnam, they saw themselves as democratic crusaders, fighting "the free world's" battle against a Communist equivalent of a Medieval Muslim aggressive "holy war" for imposing the wrong religion on the whole human race. But this is not how America's war in Vietnam is seen by most other people. Most of us see it, not as a Medieval crusade, but as a modern colonial war of the kind that was waged by European powers for more than four centuries, beginning with the Spanish conquest of Mexico and Peru and ending with France's abandonment of her attempt to continue to hold Algeria down by force of arms. In the

days of European colonialism — days that are now past —
Americans used to denounce it, and this on the whole with
justice. Now that the Europeans have relinquished their colonial empires, partly under duress but also partly of their own
free will, the United States has started to try to build up a
colonial empire of her own in eastern Asia.

Most Americans will reject this charge indignantly. They
believe that they are waging war in Asia not to subjugate
Asian peoples but to liberate them. They point self-righteously
to their Asian "allies." Yet the classical first move in the
building up of the now defunct European colonial empires
was to act in the name of puppet "native" governments that
were not representative of their peoples and that could not have
stood for a day without the support of their foreign patrons'
and manipulators' bayonets. When the British conquered Ben-
gal, they ruled it, to begin with, in the name of the powerless
Mogul emperor at Delhi; when the French conquered Morocco, they claimed that they were altruistically re-establishing
the Sultan of Morocco's authority. Citizens of ex-colonial-
power European countries who know something about their
own countries' colonial records find present-day American
activities in Asia familiar. They recognize here an attempt to
repeat what their own countries did in the eighteenth and
nineteenth centuries. At the same time, European observers
are sceptical about America's prospects of success.

The European ex-colonial powers' experience in our lifetime
has taught Europeans that times have changed. In the first
chapter of the story of European colonialism, vast Amerindi-
an, Asian, and African territories and populations were conquered with ease by tiny European armies that won sensational
victories at small cost. In our day this European colonial story
has ended in sensational European defeats — for instance, at
Dien Bien Phu, in Algeria, in Cyprus, at Aden. Every European ex-colonial people now recognizes that it has been well
advised to cut its colonial losses, however humiliating the process may have been in the cases in which the colonial power
put up a fight to resist being thrown out. Europeans marvel
that the Americans, with the spectacle of the collapse of European colonialism before their eyes, should have rushed in

where Europeans now fear, with excellent reason, to tread. As between the European powers and their former colonial dominions, the reversal of fortunes within our lifetime has been dramatic. In 1914, on the eve of the outbreak of the first world war, almost the whole of the world outside Europe was under European control in some form and some degree. The colors on the pre-1914 political map of the world, which show the territories that were then under direct European rule, do not reveal the full extent of European colonialism at that date. European economic and financial power ramified far more widely than European colonial administrators, garrisons, or even gunboats. The United States itself was Europe's debtor. Latin America was an economic dependency of Europe (the Monroe Doctrine could not veto that). Russia, Turkey, Iran, and China were semi-colonial countries. In Africa, the only genuinely independent country was Ethiopia. (Liberia was virtually an American protectorate.) In Asia the only genuinely independent countries were Japan, Thailand, and Afghanistan. This pre-war European world empire was imposing. Yet within our lifetime it has melted away like snow under a heat ray.

What has been the cause of this dramatic liquidation of European colonialism? Not the two world wars. The liquidation of colonialism was no doubt speeded up by the cumulative effect of the world wars in weakening the European powers. In particular, Japan's sweeping conquests of European colonial territories during the months following the Japanese attack on Pearl Harbor demonstrated to all Asians and Africans, once and for all, that the Europeans' invincibility was obsolete. (Incidentally, Japan showed that the United States was not invincible either. The fall of Corregidor made history as irreversibly as the fall of Singapore.) However, it is now clear in retrospect that the European colonial empires would have been liquidated by the end of the present century, even if the two world wars had never been waged.

Colonialism is intrinsically self-liquidating because it stimulates its victims to master the use of the weapons by which they have been subjugated, and then to fight their foreign conquerors with those weapons that the conquerors themselves had invented. The colonial powers' two most potent weapons were their nationalism and their technology, and they conquered their empires with ease because, at that time, the Amerindians and Africans and Asians were politically passive and technologically backward. But it was only a matter of time for the subject peoples to become as dynamically nationalistic as their European rulers and to become proficient enough in Western technology to be able to challenge the West in this field too.

However, the main reason that colonialism is bound to liquidate itself is that it is unnatural for any people to be ruled by foreigners. The longer the foreign rule lasts, the greater the subjects' resentment grows. This mounting resentment is the motive that has stimulated the European ex-colonial powers' former subjects to learn how to use the instruments of European power and to employ these instruments for liberating themselves. "European" means "Western" and "Western" includes "American." America has now challenged the force, conjured up by Europeans, to which the European powers have found themselves compelled to give way. America has embarked on colonialism at the moment when colonialism has been proved to be no longer practicable.

Thus, in Vietnam today, America has taken on a far more formidable opponent than she had supposed. She is being opposed in Vietnam, not by "world Communism," but by the determination of the great non-Western majority of mankind to shake off Western domination at whatever the cost. This determination has behind it the momentum of generations of mounting resentment against Western rule, and this determination is shared with the Vietnamese people by all other peoples that have experienced Western domination in some form. The Vietnamese are fighting their own battle. They are doing the job with tools that Russia and China supply. We cannot yet foresee what the military outcome of the war in Vietnam is going to be, but we can see already that the Vietnamese resistance movement has made history; and this piece of history could not be undone even if Vietnam were to be wiped out. (The history that Japan made in 1941 has not been undone by Japan's capitulation in 1945.)

In Vietnam the United States has challenged a spiritual force — the force of cumulative worldwide anti-colonialism — which it is beyond even the United States' strength to overcome by military force. This is surely a situation that calls for moral courage in Americans — the courage to make "an agonizing reappraisal" of American policy in Vietnam; the courage to admit that America may have made a big mistake; and the courage to change the policy, if second thoughts were to convince Americans that this policy is the wrong one. There is still just time, but the sands are running out.

Struggle
Against History:
U.S. FOREIGN POLICY
IN AN AGE
OF REVOLUTION

Rise of an American World Power Complex

WILLIAM APPLEMAN WILLIAMS

I

Empire is as American as apple pie.

Or as American as the ever westward moving frontier.

Or as American as helping other people, who believe the way Americans do, to continue living the way they want to live.

Or as American as saving the world from the devil.

Or as American as the veils that Americans have woven to obscure the harsh reality of their imperial record. One of those is the myth of an original happy valley of innocence and isolationism. Another is the fantasy that world power was somehow, by someone, forced upon the United States at the end of the nineteenth century against its will. And the third is the legend that Americans have used their vast power with unique restraint and only in behalf of self-determination, freedom, and prosperity.

Those shrouds have made it possible for Americans to cohabit with their conscience despite their many transgressions of their avowed faith. The sophistry has been necessary not to mask evil intentions but to bridge the chasm between noble pretenses (and high expectations) and the results. The American empire has been created and maintained by men who have known precisely what they were doing and have considered it necessary for their own welfare and desirable (if not likewise necessary) for the welfare of others.

Americans have always wanted empire, but they have also

1

always believed that they discovered the secret of transforming benevolent despotism into philanthropic democracy. For Americans, "imperialism" has always been a dirty word used by those who failed to understand that they were expanding the area of freedom. But the logic of their alchemy contained contradictions, and produced less than perfect results, that could not always be ignored or discounted as minor costs of magnificent successes. Given their honest belief in the morality and beneficence of what they considered necessary, those confrontations led them to seek the rationalizations they needed in order to continue doing what they considered moral and necessary.

The process began soon after colonization, for Americans opened their imperial history with the transoceanic colonization of black chattel-slaves. And, far from wanting to have outsiders force such status upon them in the 1890s, Americans made the United States something of a world power between 1763 and 1783 as they initiated and won their war for independence from Great Britain. They consolidated and strengthened that position during the next generation through an undeclared war with France and a second conflict with England.

They next claimed and conquered a continent, in the process destroying the Indian society and culture that occupied the area. At the end of the nineteenth century, in one of the grand transitions of imperial history, the United States then shifted from continental empire to the imperium of overseas economic control, political influence, and military predominance greater than any other imperium in world history.

That shift, and the ensuing expansion, are usually treated as phenomena largely unrelated to the nation's earlier foreign policy. And there is some justification for that approach, as well as a satisfactory explanation of its development and acceptance. It has facilitated, for example, the kind of sharp focus in research and analysis that produces extensively detailed and footnoted reconstructions and coherent interpretations.

But it also has significant if not grave weaknesses. The most important of these is that treating the twentieth century as a self-contained unit produces a basic misconception about the dynamics of American expansion. The transition from continental to overseas expansion, from agrarian to industrial imperialism, was not effected by making a break with the past. It evolved, instead, through the adaptation of an existing nineteenth-century outlook to new conditions. And, contrary to much that has been written, the majority of the American people was actively engaged in the intellectual and emotional, and the political and economic, processes of that adjustment.

These considerations do much to clarify important aspects of modern American foreign policy. They go far to explain the deep, sustained support for America's expansion despite the periodic eruption of vigorous arguments about specific policy choices. The disagreements have been tactical rather than strategic. And if that is understood, more attention can be focused on the way in which the empire has been institutionalized.

Both of those factors have to be confronted and dealt with if a new and nonimperial strategy is to be evolved and substituted for the existing outlook and approach. It is not only that the majority, as well as the elite, has to be induced to accept a new conceptual framework, it is that many of the reformers themselves think they are offering strategic alternatives when they are in truth proposing nothing more than tactical changes. For they, too, look at the world in the traditional American way.

II

The key to understanding the American empire is found in comprehending how the economically natural or easy or desirable came to be considered the economically necessary, and how the ideas and ideals of "freedom" and "democracy" came to be integrated with the categorical imperative empire. The history of the American empire is the history of the famous frontier thesis: that hallowed but false syllogism by which Americans have traditionally asserted that their prosperity, freedom, and security — and that of other peoples — is the inexorable product of the expansion of the United States.

The theory and the practice of the frontier thesis have always been at the core of the American experience. It first appeared as a central part of an outlook — a *Weltanschauung* — generally known as British mercantilism. Based on the premise that the world was a finite and fearsome place, mercantilism called for centralized organization and control, and for militant nationalistic expansion. The mercantilist considered the metropolis superior to the colonies, and viewed expansion as the best method of providing markets, raw materials, security, and prestige for the center of the imperial system. But he also acknowledged a mutuality of interest between the metropolis and the colonies; and, ideally, the mercantilist empire was to be an aristocratic community in which those with power and wealth accepted and discharged the *noblesse oblige* inherent in the concept of a conservative and corporate Christian order.

The development of the American colonies was perhaps the greatest achievement of British mercantilism. Their revolutions against the Crown were mercantilist colonial revolts against a mercantilist metropolis that was extending and integrating its power by dominating the marketplace it had created. During the Revolutionary War, and through the period of transition that followed, the central problem for stateside leadership involved overcoming the great difficulties inherent in sustained cooperation among thirteen newly independent and sovereign mercantilist states. That crisis was finally resolved by the knowing, determined action of an aristocratic elite committed to creating a functioning mercantilist country out of the thirteen states. The Founding Fathers met the challenge by forging a sophisticated, supple, and enduring mercantilist instrument of government in the Constitution of 1787.

And the rationalizing philosophical argument that played the primary role in winning the acceptance of the Constitution was provided by James Madison's equation linking expansion and democracy in a positive causal relationship. It Americanized the key expansionist axiom of mercantilism and produced the first mature statement of the frontier thesis in American history. Madison offered it as policy for his own time, however, rather than as an historical explanation of what had happened. And it was accepted and acted upon between 1787 and 1828 by the citizens who voted as well as by the elite who governed.

That mercantilist outlook led directly to the development and institutionalization of a colonial policy whereby the metropolis ruled the territories. The metropolis not only dominated the vast economic development of the back country, but also exercised controlling political authority over that area and set the terms (and the timing) of its admission, state by state, to membership in the national system ruled by the metropolis.

Within the same framework, Americans also launched a sustained drive to win and hold a preponderant position in world shipping and overseas markets. Simultaneously, they opened a militant and determined campaign to acquire territory. The Louisiana Purchase did not change American history; it merely accelerated the established pattern of development. And the War of 1812, a classic mercantilist conflict for economic independence, trade, and land, represented the convergence of those themes of American expansion.

The Monroe Doctrine was the culminating product of that outlook. A manifesto of commercial as well as territorial expansion, it was a grandiose option on hemispheric empire. And, in the greatest moment of American mercantilism, John Quincy Adams confronted the inner paradox of that *Weltanschauung* even as he expressed it in all its imperial splendor. Recognizing that expansion in the name of freedom and prosperity would ultimately subvert those goals and ideals, he cautioned his countrymen to rest content with predominance in half the world. Go not abroad in search of monsters to destroy, he warned, else America lose the reality of its achievement and the promise of its vision. Even wars in the name of expanding freedom, he admonished, would curtail and ultimately destroy that freedom.

III

As it had been in England, however, so was it in America. Mercantilism begot laissez faire, and with it an era of wild, individualistic, and competitive economic expansion, and righteously reforming imperialism. Along with his emphasis on the magic powers of competition, Adam Smith laid equal stress on the necessity of market expansion as a dynamic factor in preserving liberty and prosperity. It was, indeed, the Not-So-Hidden-Power behind the Hidden Hand. For without the continued expansion of the marketplace, competition would sooner rather than later recreate the centralized power of mercantilism. By definition, as well as by ambition and opportunity, the world became the potential American frontier. Laissez faire was the seminal fountain of one-worldism, and Americans erupted in a wave of entrepreneurial activity that crashed into every shore around the globe.

At the same time, the leaders of the American metropolis turned to expansion as the means of resolving the competitive tensions between the constituent groups of the empire. Smith understood that the functioning of the laissez-faire marketplace perpetuated the mercantilist division of the economy into town and country sectors, and pointed out very clearly that the metropolis enjoyed a structural advantage over the colonial sector. The expansionist solution to the resulting conflicts, so bluntly stated and used by President James K. Polk and others, was the political dynamism and strategy inherent in laissez faire.

The town-country conflict generated no insurmountable problems as long as expansion provided benefits for both sectors. After the acquisition of Texas, California, and Oregon, however, the struggle for empire, and hence the conflict between the metropolis and the country, became increasingly internalized. The expansion of the marketplace involved the trans-Mississippi back country that had been acquired, and the tension between the city and the country ultimately erupted into a Civil War.

The abolitionist movement, which insisted upon the necessity of the universality of laissez-faire freedoms, did exert a force making for war. But the determining factor was the power of the expansionist thrust in all American thought. That, rather than any general crusade to free the black man, was what made the war unpreventable or, in the words of

William E. Seward, himself a vigorous expansionist, what made the war an "irrepressible conflict."

Seward made a last effort to use expansion as an instrument for transforming a civil war into a national war for a greater empire that would underwrite a final compromise. His proposal was spurned by Abraham Lincoln, but Seward's vision of America as the mightiest empire of the world, an irresistible force for freedom and prosperity, nevertheless proved correct.

Seward was an early prophet of the United States evolving from *a* world power into *the* world power as it became the most powerful industrial metropolis on the globe. And his projection seemed to be accurate history, as well as perceptive extrapolation, when the United States, directed by an industrial elite, dramatically renewed its expansionist thrust through the war against Spain and the adoption of the Open Door Policy at the end of the century.

IV

As it happened, however, the agricultural majority played the central part, between 1860 and 1901, in the evolution and acceptance of an imperial outlook that combined the necessity of market expansion with the desirability and obligation — and even the necessity — of also expanding American freedoms overseas. The basis of the crucial agrarian influence was the large and sustained volume of agricultural exports. Those exports were responsible for the famous turning of the trade balance in 1876–1877, and they carried the balance-of-payments load of the United States through the last part of the nineteenth century just as they had prior to the Civil War. Having mastered the lesson of exports during the war-induced depression of 1861–1862, the agrarians agitated vigorously during the postwar downturn for direct trade with Europe, for reciprocity treaties to win new markets, and for related expansionist policies.

Their constantly increasing production, coupled with the severe depression that began in 1873, intensified those efforts. They were temporarily saved by the bonanza market created by the collapse of European agriculture between 1876 and

1883. The resulting boom brought prosperity and further growth to the agricultural sector, and pulled the entire economy out of the massive depression. The farmers and related processors became even more conscious of their central role in the functioning of the system, and more determined to sustain the expansion of their markets.

But the metropolitan leaders of the country were not responsive. Bankers, manufacturers, and urban politicians candidly admitted that agricultural exports had been crucial in ending the crisis, and that they were equally important during prosperity. But they were more interested in transferring the lesson about exports to their own sector of the economy than in helping the agriculturalists.

The resulting agrarian anger was intensified when foreign opposition decreased the overseas market for agricultural surpluses, and as agriculture entered a serious decline. Agriculture rather than industry alerted Europe and the rest of the world to the power and the dangerous challenge of the American economy. The result was an intensified anti-Americanism, and the appearance of restrictions designed to thwart the American giant. Farmers demanded vigorous measures to keep those markets, and militant efforts to open and enlarge alternate markets in Latin America and Asia.

The metropolis responded very slowly. The agrarian reaction took two principal forms: an intensification of their assertive economic nationalism, which came rapidly to be directed against the American metropolis as part of the world industrial metropolis that was hurting them so badly; and a restatement of the frontier thesis linking American freedom and prosperity with expansion. They simply, but forcibly and effectively, substituted overseas economic expansion for territorial expansion as the dynamic element in sustaining American welfare.

As a result, they increased their agitation for traditional measures of economic expansion and advanced new programs of their own. Their most important proposals called for the remonetization of silver and a subtreasury system of storing commodity crops. The agrarians saw silver as the weapon that would destroy Britain's control of the world commodity market, and also enable Americans to displace the British in the markets of Latin America and Asia. Those who brought silver bullion to Washington would carry away food from the West, cotton from the South, and even manufactured goods from the East. And if the remonetization of silver lowered the price level, the loss would be more than recovered through greater sales in a vastly expanded market.

The subtreasury plan was specifically designed to dominate the international commodity market. By controlling and manipulating the major available supplies of wheat, corn, cotton, and tobacco, the American producer could enforce a high price level, and then use that power to win other concessions in the markets of the world. As with the silver argument, the subtreasury proposal manifested a vast confidence in the overwhelming power of the American economy. American strength, the agrarians argued, could win the vital battle for markets without recourse to colonial wars and colonial empire. That certainty, based on the logic of marketplace capitalism, became an article of faith and a cornerstone of policy for the agricultural majority.

The agrarians became increasingly angry with metropolitan leaders who refused to use America's vast power to enlarge the free marketplace for all men. Far from turning to a vigorous foreign policy only after being defeated in the election of 1896, the agriculturalists demanded nationalistic overseas economic expansion throughout the post-Civil War period. Their agitation became particularly intense in 1888 and 1889.

Led by William Jennings Bryan, one bloc of the agrarians turned the Democratic Party into a vehicle for the nationalistic free-silver argument for the expansion of the free marketplace and the related extension of freedom. The Republicans, under the perceptive leadership of James G. Blaine, fought back with a program of vigorous nationalistic expansion keyed to reciprocity treaties designed to win markets for the farmers, and for the metropolitan interests that were increasingly accepting and acting on the export experience and argument of the agrarians.

Blaine's strategy proved effective. His reciprocity treaty with Spain rapidly tied the agrarian economy of the politically crucial upper Midwest to a vastly expanded market in Cuba. Then, as the deepening depression of the 1890s increased the importance of exports, the Democrats cooperated by abrogating all his reciprocity treaties. As a man of considerable intelligence as well as great political sensitivity, William McKinley dropped his emphasis on protection and seized reciprocity and market expansion as the issues with which to reunite the metropolis and a crucial segment of the agricultural sector. Blaine's expansionist epoxy required time, and the heat generated by the Democratic blunder and the depression, but it restored the Republican coalition and elected McKinley in 1896.

McKinley wanted to settle the Cuban crisis, which had been triggered by the abrogation of the reciprocity treaty, without war, and then embark upon a vigorous program of overseas economic expansion. That proved impossible. The President was confronted at home by the sustained agrarian pressure to extend the free marketplace to Cuba, thus simultaneously restoring agricultural prosperity, expanding freedom for the Cubans, and striking a blow against all European colonial empires. And abroad he faced Spanish and Cuban opposition to any peaceful compromise.

Sensing the ultimate necessity of military intervention in order to prevent the agrarians from taking control of policy, McKinley began at least as early as September, 1897 to discuss American control of the Philippines as a base for market expansion in Asia. In the end, a majority of the agrarians accepted the need for that action. The Philippines were deemed temporarily necessary as an instrument of American strength in the campaign to establish the principle and the practice of an open-world marketplace in which the economic power of the United States would become predominant and thereby enlarge the freedom of all men.

V

The agrarian belief in the necessity of overseas economic expansion, and faith in the overweening power of the American economy, both of which were accepted by the metropolitan leadership of the country between 1890 and 1898, were the assumptions upon which the strategy of the Open Door Policy was based. And the agrarian logic of freedom and prosperity for all through the expansion of American economic power around the world was the rationalizing logic of those famous diplomatic notes of 1899 and 1900.

The Open Door Policy was designed to establish and maintain open access and fair competition in the markets of the world by placing the power and influence of the United States publicly and formally on the line in support of the principles of self-determination and equal opportunity. It was a classic statement of the central axioms of laissez-faire capitalism applied to foreign policy.

The history of the American empire that has been created through the strategy of the Open Door Policy has three principal themes: first, the development and administration of the empire; second, the challenges raised against the empire; and third, the contemporary crisis of the empire and the fitful beginnings of a debate about its viability, and the fumbling search for alternatives.

The extension of American power throughout the world after the war against Spain proceeded in a manner that often misled contemporary and later observers. The explanation of this lies in the steady, quiet, and routine manner in which American economic power was deployed to penetrate world markets and obtain control of raw material supplies. Individual entrepreneurs and corporations, driven by their own requirements and operating within the strategy of the Open Door Policy, won an increasing share of the world market without parading their profits in public.

Much of that expansion went largely unnoticed, therefore, until the situations of strength it had created produced problems or crises that required political decisions. The resulting discussions thus concerned expansion that had already occurred, rather than the issue of whether or not to undertake such expansion. The interests of the political economy (and hence of the nation) were already involved, and the psychology of the situation was always weighted against withdrawal.

Perhaps the classic illustration of this pattern is provided by Theodore Roosevelt's updating of the Monroe Doctrine, in response to such a crisis, from an option on empire in the Western Hemisphere to a positive assertion of America's general right and obligation to intervene in order to avoid losing what it had already gained, and to create conditions for winning more. There was nothing in Roosevelt's so-called corollary to the Monroe Doctrine, either literally or logically, that confined its application to Latin America. Nor, of course, was it so limited. And the succeeding doctrines of twentieth-century American foreign policy have all involved a similar extension of American power.

The major arguments about foreign policy concerned questions of imperial tactics rather than the alternative of adopting a nonimperial strategy. After the enunciation of the Open Door Policy, for example, two main issues had to be resolved. One involved the best way to guarantee the principles of the policy, and the structural framework for its operation. The choice was between cooperating with Japan, with Russia, or with China, and the decision called for working with and through Japan, in order to control its actions, and at the same time helping China unilaterally. The United States used force and the threat of force to support that tactic during the Boxer Rebellion, during the Russo-Japanese War when Japan intervened in Siberia, and at the Washington Disarmament Conference. And it ultimately went to war when Japan's actions threatened to destroy the Open Door Policy.

The related question involved the most effective way of deploying American economic power. One choice was to operate within an international syndicate in the belief that the United States could thereby enjoy the benefits of a greater capital fund while at the same time controlling key decisions through the size of its own investment. The alternative, favored by Woodrow Wilson, called for unilateral action except in cases where American domination of a syndicate was assured. American leaders followed that tactical approach through the rest of the century.

That decision raised in unavoidable form the primary question of how, and from what source, to obtain the capital required for major overseas expansion. Even the largest corporations needed assistance for some of their undertakings, and the requirements for entering new areas and consolidating the political economy of a region already penetrated were far beyond their resources.

Presidents Theodore Roosevelt and William Howard Taft met that problem by backing security issues with statements approving and supporting such expansion. That action facilitated the sale of the paper to the public. As he came to understand the situation, and as he established the principle of unilateral American action, Wilson accepted and reinforced that policy and practice.

Assistance from present and future taxpayers became far less indirect, and more overtly monetary, during World War I and the decade of the 1920s. Congress chartered corporations to finance exports and to enlarge the merchant marine, for example, and the executive department cooperated intimately and actively in expanding American loans and investments. And, as had been the case before the war, the armed forces continued to be used during peacetime to defend and advance the Open Door Policy. That action was also paid for by the citizen.

The depression completed the process. The key institution was the Export-Import Bank, originally chartered to finance exports to Russia and provide assistance for American operations in Cuba. Its activities were then extended to include underwriting the foreign business of the American trading system created by the reciprocity treaties negotiated by the first administration of Franklin Delano Roosevelt.

The last step was taken during Roosevelt's second term, in 1939, when the Export-Import Bank began to make developmental loans. From the outset, they were designed to preserve and expand existing American operations, to enlarge the market for American products, and to acquire control over raw materials. Subsequent operations were merely refinements and projections of an established procedure. At the same time it was extending the income tax into the lower levels of American society, the New Deal was thus integrating the taxpayer into the basic financial operations of the American empire.

The most intense and embittered debate over the tactics of the American empire came in the fight over the League of Nations. That dispute concerned the most effective way to continue and guarantee American expansion, furthering the extension of freedom as well as extending the economic outreach of the United States. Wilson had taken America into World War I both to defend and to advance the Open Door Policy, and his proposed League was designed to apply and institutionalize that policy in a way that would enable the United States to consolidate its economic and political predominance for an indefinite period.

Despite his deep desire to extend American freedoms as well as the American economic system, Wilson either ignored or overrode the powerful logic of John Quincy Adams. For Wilson was arguing, in essence, that the United States could secure the markets of the world and at the same time reform the world without losing its soul. The coalition that defeated him was composed of intelligent and responsible men who insisted that the project was practically impossible and a grave distortion of the traditional American commitment to freedom and self-determination. They maintained that the League would subvert both the freedom and the expansion of the United States, and that it would define America as the enemy of freedom and the primary target of all the forces throughout the world that were working for change.

On balance, Wilson's opponents had the best argument even though the United States did not avoid the fate they feared. Collective security was a tactic for preserving the foundations of the imperial status quo, and it did not offer enough meaningful opportunities, or encouragement, for the creative development of the forces for change that had been generated in response to three centuries of imperial expansion by European powers and the United States. Neither did it offer any real promise of being able to channel serious disputes between competing imperial metropolises into peaceful rivalries.

For that matter, Wilson was no more willing to see Latin America break free of the limits established by the United States than were Britain and France ready to abandon their imperial prerogatives. The freedom that the agrarian majority had wanted extended to Cuba so that it could develop its own potentialities as part of the American marketplace had within a generation been transformed into the liberty to define and practice freedom as approved by the United States — or face the antagonism and the power of the United States.

VI

Though it was inherent in the dynamism of America's imperial expansion, this progressive restriction of self-determination and liberty in the name of freedom was accelerated and intensified by the rising opposition to the empire. One challenge was the secular, theoretical attack on the premises and the logic of the argument that the marketplace expansion of the United States produced prosperity and freedom for all. Another was the moral assault upon the validity of the American definition of freedom; and, if that were granted, upon America's moral right to impose that definition upon the rest of the world. The other principal challenges involved the overt opposition to American expansion by rival industrial powers, and by the poor, nonindustrialized societies whose development was controlled or limited by the United States.

Different countries raised each of those challenges. The Chinese, for example, offered a conception of creative human life that clashed sharply with the image of the good society presented by the American theory and practice of marketplace capitalism. Beginning in 1910, the Mexicans challenged the theory of capitalism with an alternative of communal economic life derived from their own Indian culture. Cubans and Filipinos raised direct resistance to American power even as it was being established in their countries, and other poor nations in the colonial sector did likewise as they felt the heavy hand of the American metropolis.

As for the industrial rivals, Germany and Japan were only the most determined and ultimately willing to resort to force. The long and bitter conflict between America and England, for example, generated by Washington's determination to penetrate and destroy Britain's imperial preference system, is a major but neglected part of the history of the American empire. The only phase even partially recorded involves the climax of the battle, which began with the preliminary negotiations for lend lease in 1941, and culminated in the defeat of Lord Keynes at Bretton Woods in 1944.

The nature of these challenges to America's imperial expansion should make it clear why the problem of Russia has been at the center of American foreign policy since the adoption of the Open Door Policy. In the beginning, between 1899 and 1917, the Russians were viewed as industrial rivals for control of the northeastern Asian marketplace. Then the Bolshevik Revolution symbolized and materialized the theoretical and moral critique of America's marketplace capitalism and its imperial expansion. And the Soviet Union, in the course of its development, has moved through the entire spectrum of opposition manifested by poor and backward countries, and by mature industrial competitors.

American leaders immediately recognized the significance of the Bolshevik Revolution, and understood the moral and practical dilemma that it created for the United States. After their attempt to help overthrow the Revolution ended in failure, during World War I and immediately thereafter, their response took the form of complementary campaigns to isolate the Soviet Union while at the same time extending and strengthening the American imperium.

Despite the rhetoric and appearances to the contrary, confidence — not fear — was the major theme of American foreign policy after 1917, just as it had been the feeling that had infused the developing American expansionist sentiment during the late nineteenth century and characterized the strategy of the Open Door notes. The paradox in American imperialism remained intact: the urgent sense of necessity about expansion matched by a certainty that it could be accomplished with a concurrent extension of freedom.

Both the necessity and the confidence emerged unscathed, moreover, from the trials of World War II. That was not surprising: on the one hand, only the war ended the depression of the 1930s; and, on the other hand, the Open Door Policy and the related concepts of "freedom" had been successfully defended against a grave challenge to their legitimacy and existence. The element of fear has been seriously misconceived and vastly overestimated in most accounts of postwar American diplomacy. The fear of another depression did exist, and exerted a very strong influence on policy decisions. But there was very little fear of the Soviet Union. Pre-atomic planning for the postwar era was predicated upon the overwhelming power of the American economy — and the grave weaknesses of the Soviet Union. And confidence to the point of arrogance was President Harry S. Truman's response upon learning that the United States had perfected a nuclear weapon. That weapon was used, moreover, in the belief that it would consolidate the Open Door Policy in Europe as well as in Asia.

America's postwar programs and policies were based on the confidence that the economic power of the United States, deployed in keeping with its traditional ideas and practices of open door expansion, would simultaneously generate recovery in Europe and development in the colonial areas of the world. That would block further uprisings in the idiom of the Bolshevik Revolution and at the same time sustain the isolation of the Soviet Union. And it was a sense of urgency born of the need to correct initially mistaken estimates of the aid required, not the rumblings of a deep fear, that motivated the intensification and enlargement of those programs after 1947.

It is very difficult, because there are so many, to choose one document to symbolize that extraordinary confidence. But certainly one of the most striking was George Frost Kennan's famous 1947 "X" article, an official policy paper based on the proposition that the United States had enough power to continue the containment of the Soviet Union until that policy produced fundamental changes making that society acceptable by American standards. Whatever Kennan's personal attitude, his argument seemed to exude full confidence in the power of the United States to impose its will and say upon the postwar world, as a projection of the same conviction held by agrarian democrats in the latter part of the nineteenth century. And they would have supported his effort to reform the Russians, even as they fought the metropolitan elitism of that era.

VII

Despite the crises, stalemates, and even defeats that the United States has experienced since 1947, that misplaced confidence in the power and righteousness of the American empire has not yet been shaken to its foundations. China became the enemy to be contained as the Russians transcended containment and continued the development of their own traditions and approaches. Cuba wrenched itself free of the American empire only to be cruelly punished with the economic power that had failed to produce its welfare and freedom. And the Marines continued to be deployed as the advance agents of social welfare and representative government.

Karl Marx once said that all significant events occur a second time as farce, and American leaders seem determined to prove him correct. Consider the Bay of Pigs invasion as the repeat performance of Theodore Roosevelt's charge up San Juan Hill. Or the use in the Dominican Republic of 25,000 troops to suppress a long-repressed outburst of popular outrage against the era of United States rule that had been established by an admiral and a handful of bankers and bureaucrats. But there was — and is — as yet no sign of the kind of mature confidence that would enable Americans to laugh at such absurdities. And be done with the men who were responsible for them.

Perhaps the strongest reason for hope has been provided by the Soviet Union's containment of the nuclear power of the United States. Along with the gross transgressions of American ideals by America's imperial leaders, that clear revelation that the frontier thesis can produce catastrophe has stirred doubts in the minds of some Americans. Some members of the metropolitan elite, and even more citizens of the lower orders, have come to question the practicality, the morality, and the cost of the traditional outlook and the empire it has produced.

But the primary response has been to use the power to

realize the ideas and the ideals by imposing upon the rest of the world the forms that those ideas and ideals produced when they were being more honored in practice. It is a tragic example of the process of reification whereby the abstraction becomes reality and human beings are reduced to things to be manipulated in the service and the verification of the abstraction.

John Quincy Adams must writhe in his grave as he observes how very near the United States has come to proving him correct. We have achieved the imperial success inherent in the frontier thesis and the Open Door Policy and we have paid almost the full price of that triumph. The freedoms that were to be expanded are now seriously curtailed and circumscribed, even literally threatened, by the American empire and the policies designed for its preservation.

It is small wonder that some young Americans emigrate to the land of LSD. It is no wonder at all that many of them contract out of the American empire in the hope of finding a fulcrum for destroying the empire and creating an opportunity to replace it with a democratic American community. They have seen the truth that all we have to lose is our frontier thesis, which has in the end served only to carry us further from the ideals it was supposed to realize. The real frontier is in ourselves, and in our relationships with other human beings. What we need is an Open Door Policy for creating that empire of true community.

The Cold War In Europe: 1945-1967

FRED WARNER NEAL

This paper deals chiefly with the question of the American fears of Soviet military aggression, which is basic to much of U.S. foreign policy following World War II. And that fear also underlies the broader fears of Communism that are the basis of American views of the world. It is a fear which was — and I am convinced still is — held by large segments of officialdom and the general public. I have not attempted here to analyze in any scientific details its fundamental causes but have treated mainly its manifestations and the evidence on which they are based.

Tensions and misunderstanding between Russia and the West, with their roots in history, geography, and religion, long pre-dated the Bolshevik Revolution. The Revolution itself angered the Western Allies in World War I by upsetting their war aims and military calculations. It frightened them because they saw the Bolsheviks' call for world revolution as a threat to their social structures. There followed the invasion effort by the West, joined by Japan, which tended to bear out Lenin's thesis of "inevitable capitalist hostility." The Versailles powers then created a *cordon sanitaire,* in the words of Clemenceau, "to isolate the West from the germs of Bolshevism in the East." The inter-war period was characterized more by mutual fear and hostility than cooperation, culminating in what the USSR saw as a Western betrayal at Munich and what the West saw as a Soviet betrayal in the Nazi-Soviet

Pact. In the United States, the latter, plus the Winter War against Finland, gave rise to strong anti-Soviet feelings which, even earlier, were never far beneath the surface.

The World War II military alliance of the Soviet Union, the United States, and Great Britain was thus one of convenience only, abnormal and always uneasy. When the Red Army, in the course of defeating the Nazis, occupied Eastern Europe, Western pre-war fears were revived. And so differences with the Soviet Union over post-war reorganization of the world arose, the specter of Communism — in the form of a Soviet military advance to the English Channel — did, as Marx once said, haunt Europe, and the United States as well. In the United States, now assuming the role of military protector of the West, the specter soon became an obsession. Today, afer 20 years, it is easier to state it than to explain how it came about.

There is no doubt that economic forces, the nature of American society, etc., have played a role in producing an American view of the world in which fear of "Communist aggression" has been the central aspect. But it is, in my opinion, far too simplistic to assume that they have been determinative. And whereas one may analyze deep, underlying, and fundamental trends in a society, it is unlikely that one can alter them. One advantage, it seems to me, of dealing with the issues of specific United States fears is that so many of them can be proved groundless; and if this can be done, then there is at least a chance that a healthier attitude for public consideration of our foreign policy can be brought about. Even if the fears were artificially engendered — and I do not think so — and if what we do is not really based on them (as I think it is), at least they are used to justify what we do. It is with these fears, then, that I think we should start.

There is a strong tendency for foreign policies — foreign policies of all states — to be irrational. A corollary of this principle is that the more irrational a foreign policy, the more vigorously it is pursued. If in this regard United States foreign policy since World War II is exceptional, it is only that its irrationality is greater than the usual run and that because of the extent of American power we can pursue it more vigorously. And, one should add, that given the nature of the modern world, it is therefore more dangerous.

The key factor in American policy since the war is the obsession that we have faced the constant and pressing danger of Soviet military aggression. At times, this has taken on the aspects of national paranoia. It arose primarily out of events in Europe and the United States interpretation of them, but it is the kingbolt of American *Weltpolitik* and of the crusade against Communism, cold and hot.

There is now beginning to be some limited recognition that the danger of Soviet military aggression never existed, that the fear so deeply imbedded in a whole generation of Americans was based on a fantasy. But the whole history of an era has been colored by this fear and it has assumed a psychological significance so great in the American mind that one wonders if it can ever be overcome. It has become an unquestioned basis for all of our foreign policy.

This is, of course, not the first time a nation has succumbed to irrational fears. To cite only one other notorious case, the British fear that Czarist Russia was out to conquer India — a fear that dominated much of British policy during the nineteenth century — was almost wholly without foundation in fact. There simply was no evidence to support it, yet the hardheaded British, masters of the seas and the dominant nation of the time, really believed it.

In our case, we have become entrapped in an almost unbreakable vicious circle of reasoning about our fear of Soviet military aggression. The fact that Soviet military aggression has not occurred is now cited as proof of the validity of what we did to prevent it, and containment policies that will not work in Asia are based on the presumed success of containment policies that did not work in Europe.

The best analogy I can think of is a story Neal Houghton told once about a man in a midwestern bar who kept smashing glasses after every martini. When asked why, he said: "It keeps the rhinoceri away." "Rhinoceri!" snorted the bartender. "Why, there isn't a rhinoceros within 10,000 miles of here." "You see," said the man, "it works."

How Americans came to their obsession that the Soviets

were plotting physical, military aggression may seem really to be a problem for a psychiatrist. What is involved is not only an obsession based on fantasy but also a rejection of the real world. There are two aspects to the unreality. On the one hand we have been so obsessed with what the Soviets might do that it has colored all our acts. And at the same time, on the other hand, we have been unable to accept the reality of the Soviet Union and as a result have often acted in ways to promote the very things of which we were afraid. Not only Soviet hostility and intransigence — which obviously existed — but even Soviet acts clearly defensive in nature were seen as evidence of aggression. There are unrealistic and rationalizing prophecies on both sides, of course, and it may be that if the Soviet Communists had acted, and reacted, in different ways, the outcome might have been different. But this is not a very useful approach to the problem, which concerns primarily what it was *Washington* thought posed a danger to them.

The "evidence" usually advanced to bulwark the fear of Soviet military aggression concerns Communist ideology, the Soviet domination of Eastern Europe, postwar developments in Greece and Turkey and the conflict over Germany. Let us look briefly at each of them. To defend our policies we have developed in all of these areas a set of apocrypha which distorts fact to the point of falsehood, and sometimes beyond.

The general Washington view of Soviet Marxist theory has it that there is a Soviet ideological imperative to wage military war against capitalist states, to intervene militarily in underdeveloped areas and to work for world domination. The facts are that Marxist-Leninist theory sees capitalism being destroyed as a result of its own internal contradictions, country by country, taken advantage of by local revolutionaries. One of the contradictions concerns war. Up until Khrushchev, the theory proclaimed that wars were inevitable. Assuming as unquestionable the hostility of *capitalist states*, the theory did indeed foresee military conflict between the Soviet Union and its capitalist adversaries. But the war seen as inevitable by *Marxist-Leninist theory* was war between or among capitalist states or wars launched by capitalist states against socialist states.

The theory also foresees "wars of national liberation," and, moreover, it calls for support for them. In the military milieu of World War I, the Revolution, and the capitalist intervention in Russia, Lenin *did* see the future primarily in *terms* of military conflict, with the Revolution in Russia, once successful, giving military assistance to revolutionaries elsewhere. But in the basic ideology there is nowhere a call for military aggression by socialist states or for military intervention to aid foreign revolutionary movements. Indeed, Lenin set forth the tactical theory of objective conditions for revolution, which held that revolution could not be imported and could occur successfully only when the internal decay of a capitalist society was so advanced that the social fabric could be easily rent by domestic hands.

The Comintern, it is true, was created to aid and coordinate revolutionary activities, in short to aid Communists everywhere to do their best to bring about the objective conditions for revolution. But from the beginning the Comintern was tied exclusively to the Soviet Union, first as a result of trying to stem the capitalist invasion, and as a "general staff for world revolution" — which was what Lenin called it — it was not successful. Once Lenin saw that the earlier reports of the demise of capitalism were exaggerated, he called a halt to revolutionary activity, launched the NEP and concluded that capitalism, although certain to fall in the end, was in a period of some relatively long-run stability. This began the long period of the Soviet defensive that lasted more or less down to 1952.

Under Stalin, with his theory of the ebb and flow of the revolutionary tide, this took on such isolationist tones that Moscow and its minions actually spent more time trying to restrain Communist revolutionary activity than to promote it. This was, of course, not because Stalin did not want to see Communism spread but because, adhering to his and Lenin's tactical theories, he was convinced that left-wing revolutionary activity could not then succeed. The task of the Communists was to secure a sound base, help the Soviet Union where they could and to wait. And if they would not do this — as with the Polish Communists before the war, for example — it was held better not to have a Communist Party at all rather than to have one that would risk everything by improper orientation and action.

Now this meant a sort of de facto coexistence, in the sense that the Soviet Union would try to avoid military conflict with the capitalist world if at all possible. It was to be a strictly temporary coexistence — war was still seen as inevitable and almost certain to involve the Soviet Union when it came. The USSR and its foreign minions would continue to denounce capitalism and the capitalists in harsh terms and make revolutionary propaganda where they could. But no matter how much hostility for capitalism was implicit in all this ideology, there was nothing calling for initiation of military action by Moscow. To make up for this lack, there has arisen a body of wholly false quotations attributed to Lenin, Stalin and others, in which they carefully explained that all Russians were waiting for was for the West to let down its guard.[1] Many honest and otherwise perspicacious people have been taken in by this, but it in no way alters the facts about what the ideological pronouncements actually say and do not say.

Having determined to their satisfaction that Soviet ideology called for military aggression, the United States then proceeded to see evidence of it in what happened in Eastern Europe. There is no question that the Soviet Union long had its sights on extending its influence to Eastern Europe. In part, this was the natural attitude of a great power toward a core interest of geographic proximity. In part, it reflected Soviet reaction to

---

[1] For example, Governor Rockefeller's researchers gave this one, attributed to Lenin, for use in his 1960 campaign: "Our immutable aim, after all, is world conquest. . . ." Another bit of apocrypha has Dimitry Manuilsky, onetime head of the Comintern, saying that Soviet talk of peace is merely a trick to lull the capitalist nations and that "as soon as their guard is down, we shall smash them with our clenched fist." This one is circulated, *inter alia,* in Anthony Bouscaren's *A Guide to Anti-Communist Action* (Chicago: Regnery, 1958). Some of these false quotations were exposed by Abraham Brumberg, editor of the State Department's publication *Problems of Communism* in *The New Republic,* August 29, 1960, pp. 15–16. Another gambit, not infrequently used, is to quote the Soviet leaders out of context. See my *U.S. Foreign Policy and the Soviet Union* (Santa Barbara: Center for the Study of Democratic Institutions, 1961), p. 10.

the *cordon sanitaire* and Munich, under which hostile great powers extended their influence into this area. With the break-up of the pre-World War I empires, Eastern Europe represented something of a power vacuum. The traditional Russian influence there was excluded by the *cordon sanitaire,* and the Bolsheviks were too weak to do anything about it. It was doubtless the experience of the interwar period, in which Soviet influence was so unnaturally contained, that made it difficult for the United States and Britain to recognize that this was an abnormal situation in international politics and unlikely to continue long.

At this point, it is necessary to distinguish between the reality of the World War II agreements between the Soviet Union and the Anglo-American allies and the pseudohistory about them which is prevalent in the United States. This pseudohistory has it that Soviet diplomacy succeeded beyond all expectations by hoodwinking the Western powers; that the United States appeased the Soviets by "giving" them Eastern Europe; and that Moscow then violated the agreements by destroying democracy in that area.

It is important, in considering the reality, to see that as far as postwar goals are concerned, Moscow was singularly unsuccessful in its wartime diplomacy. The major political goals sought by Stalin at Teheran, Yalta, and Potsdam were: first, Western agreement to Soviet hegemony in Eastern Europe; second, United States assistance in rebuilding the USSR after the war; and third, a revision of the Montreux Convention giving Moscow some say in controlling the Dardanelles. Despite apparent agreement to these Soviet demands on the part of Roosevelt, Churchill, and even Truman, in the end the Soviets achieved none of them.

Specifically regarding Eastern Europe, two points are significant. First, the wartime agreements did little if any more than recognize the military realities. Just as the United States and Great Britain defeated the Nazis in the West and were in military possession of Western Europe, so the Soviet Union defeated the Germans in the East and were in military possession of Eastern Europe — the only difference being that Soviet power was well on the way to being ensconced in the

East before the Nazis were subdued in the West. There was no alternative to recognizing this in the wartime agreements, and it was so recognized at the time. Moreover, there never had been a United States interest in Eastern Europe, which was clearly of the most vital concern to the USSR. The basically unwarranted idea that Yalta, for example, "gave" something to the Russians at the expense of the United States interests and ideals developed only later out of the anti-Communist vagaries of Washington's domestic politics.

Certainly, Moscow interpreted the wartime agreements as signifying Western acceptance of Soviet hegemony in Eastern Europe, and they probably were justified. It must be remembered that Yalta in effect underwrote the results of the Second Moscow Conference of 1944, where Churchill took the initiative in proposing to Stalin a division of spheres of influence which clearly acknowledged the dominant Soviet position in all of Eastern Europe except for Yugoslavia and Greece. And it was only after this position was reversed, by the challenge to Soviet policies in Bulgaria in the Anglo-American note of September, 1946, that one can distinguish beginnings of a clear Soviet "cold war attitude."

The wartime agreements were ambiguous about their references to political democracy. It is perhaps true that the naive Americans did not realize that the Soviets would utilize their dominant position in Eastern Europe to install the local Communists in power. It is hardly true, however, that the Soviets "destroyed" democracy in Eastern Europe. Democracy in its Western political sense had not flourished in this area — if one excludes Czechoslovakia — and less propitious conditions for it to be instituted, given the revolution-ridden chaos left by the Nazis, could hardly be imagined. You cannot destroy what doesn't exist, any more than you can give up something you don't have. In any event, the point is that first Soviet military domination and then local Communist domination came to Eastern Europe as a normal consequence of military occupation at the close of World War II.

A special word should be said about the case of Czechoslovakia. Those who purport to see what happened in Eastern Europe as evidence of Soviet military aggression invariably cite Czechoslovakia as their most conclusive point. Ironically, it was in Czechoslovakia that the Soviet Union had the least to do with the coming of Communism. Not only were there no Soviet troops in Czechoslovakia at the time of the Communist coup d'état, but all Soviet military units withdrew from Czechoslovakia in 1945 after having allowed parliamentary democracy to be reinstituted there. The Communist take-over in Czechoslovakia may have had Soviet approval or even connivance, but it was done by the Czechoslovaks themselves and no one else. Yet four Secretaries of State have solemnly told the American people that the coup d'état in Czechoslovakia is one reason why we must be on our guard militarily.

The role of Soviet actions in Eastern Europe, although highly important, can be exaggerated in explaining United States fears of the USSR. Quite independently of this, even under Roosevelt, there were always powerful segments of Washington officialdom whose fear of and opposition to the Soviet Union were so great that it dominated their view of the world. However, President Roosevelt was monumentally sound in his recognition that in the postwar world there was either going to be some form of United States-Soviet cooperation or there was going to be dangerous instability. Roosevelt's emphasis on the importance of good relations with Moscow was always perturbing to many in his administration, and almost immediately after his death the views of this group became dominant. Its main spokesman was Secretary of Defense Forrestal, in whose ultimate tragedy paranoia and deathly intense fear of the Soviet Union played a large part.

In George F. Kennan, the anti-Soviet group found an earnest but somewhat ambiguous philosopher, and in Harry Truman they found a willing tool. Indeed, Truman, who brought to the Presidency a sort of average man, American Legion view of the world, mixed with Southern Baptist morality and New Deal liberalism, soon led the charge himself. As for Kennan, it is quite true that his reasoning was more sophisticated and was not predicated on the assumption that the Soviet Union was plotting military aggression. But, certainly, it was also quite confusing. Mr. Kennan has long since made it clear that he was not talking about military containment. As one rereads his "The Sources of Soviet Conduct"[2] today, it appears to be a restrained statement. But failing to identify just what aspects of Soviet conduct it was necessary to contain, and failing specifically to abjure military connotations, Kennan's persuasively written ideas seemed to advocates of the hard-line policy to be not only a justification of what they had done but also a justification of what they wanted to do. This was especially true of Kennan's thesis that the United States should adopt "a policy of firm containment designed to confront the Russians with unalterable counterforce at every point where they show signs of encroaching upon the interests of a peaceful and stable world."

Taken literally — as it was — this seemed to mean that Soviet influence had to be contained, by force, wholly within Soviet borders while United States influence was to spread throughout the world to make sure the Soviets were contained. If the Soviet Union, as a nation-state, had any vital interests at all outside its borders, this point was ignored in the containment doctrine, as was the fact that challenges to such vital Soviet interests — as the doctrine required — were certain to produce strong reactions and even counterchallenges. Unfortunately, Kennan's repeated subsequent disclaimers[3] have never been able to overcome the impact of the interpretation placed on his words in 1947.

So earnestly did Americans believe in the containment doctrine, with its fear of Soviet aggression on the one hand and its refusal to accept the reality of the USSR on the other hand, that we were unable to conceive of any of our own actions as other than *defensive*. Yet it requires only the slightest trace of objectivity to realize that Moscow could only see as *aggressive threats* our war games along Soviet borders, missile emplacements on Soviet frontiers, air probes into the Soviet interior, and naval exercises in the Baltic and the Black Sea. Washington's unreality in this respect reached its height during the

---

[2] *Foreign Affairs,* July, 1947.

[3] In various writings, from "Overdue Changes in Our Foreign Policy," *Harper's,* August, 1956, pp. 27–33 to *Memoirs 1925–1950* (Boston: Little, Brown and Company, 1967), Chap. 15.

U-2 affair of 1960, when our position almost seemed to deny that the Soviet Union had a vital interest in its own territorial integrity. The wonder is that the chickens coming home to roost — in the form of Soviet missiles in Cuba — did not come sooner.

In the days when the containment doctrine was formulated, few if any doubted that revolutions meant Communist revolutions and that Communist revolutions were Soviet-inspired and dominated and a part of some overall master plan engineered by Moscow. Interestingly enough, after the Soviet-Yugoslav dispute demonstrated that this was not necessarily the case, the idea actually grew stronger. When the Korean War broke out, Washington nervously anticipated a Soviet military offensive in Europe. And our now long-discredited China policy was based on the idea that, in the words of Dean Rusk, "the Chinese Communists were simply agents of the Soviet Union."

No sooner had the Kennan thesis been set forth than the British appealed for help in combating revolution in Greece. Although Kennan himself opposed the idea, his doctrine seemed to most policy-makers to demand United States military intervention. That it was to be intervention to save Greece from Soviet domination few doubted for a moment. The result was the Truman Doctrine. Its impact was great immediately, but its long-range significance was to be even greater. There were two major premises to the Truman Doctrine. First, revolutions in which Communists played a part were instigated by the Soviet Union as a means of extending its own power and as a step toward world domination. Second, since this threatened the United States, it was necessary for us to intervene militarily against such revolutions. It was not too long before this was escalated into justification for military intervention against *any* revolutions we might not like. The Truman Doctrine has had many manifestations, has had many names, and has been implemented in many places. The line from Greece to Vietnam goes through Korea, Lebanon, Laos, Cuba, and the Dominican Republic, but it is clear and direct.

Now the facts of the Greek Revolution were almost the opposite of what was assumed in Washington. Far from having started the Greek Revolution and supporting it, Stalin — as a pursuit of his essentially defensive, isolationist policy — was opposed to it — not, of course, because he did not want Communism to triumph in Greece if it could do so without jeopardizing the USSR's position, but because he didn't think it could do so at that point. There is every evidence that Stalin lived up to the agreement Churchill made with him in 1944 that Great Britain was to have dominant influence in Greece. In Greece, as in Yugoslavia, and in lesser degree other places, opposition to the Germans was carried on by a coalition of nationalist and revolutionary forces, and once the Nazis were defeated the two groups turned on each other for entirely Greek reasons which had nothing to do with the Soviet Union.

That the Greek Communists played a leading role among the Greek guerrillas is clear, and they had, at one point, a small Soviet military mission with them. But if the Soviet Union played any political role there at all during the war, it was to urge restraint and nonrevolutionary activity on their Greek comrades. The political-military organization of the Greek guerrillas was undertaken by the Yugoslav Communists, led by Svetozar Vukmanovic. An ebullient Montenegrin activist, Vukmanovic was for pushing the revolution and the guerrilla war at the same time. The Soviet advisers demurred. Following the Churchill-Stalin agreement on spheres of influence, the Soviet advisers were withdrawn, and from that point until the fall of 1946 — after the Anglo-American attack on Soviet policies in Bulgaria — no word of encouragement or support for the Greek Revolution came from Moscow. There was a short period, from the fall of 1946 until the spring of 1947, when the Soviet propaganda organs did back the Greek Revolution, but even then, as far as is known, there was no Soviet military aid and there certainly were not any Russians. Military aid to the Greek guerrillas, coming primarily from Yugoslavia with lesser amounts from Albania and some from Bulgaria, was an important factor in the revolution. A good deal of it was, in fact, arms of Soviet manufacture. There is no evidence, however, that it was sent from the USSR for that purpose, and, according to Vukmanovic, it was all either surplus Soviet equipment left by the Red army or equipment which had been supplied by Moscow to the Yugoslav army.

Never having favored the Greek Revolution in the first place, by 1947 Stalin actively opposed it. On one occasion he sent word to Greece to that effect, and at least twice he scolded the Yugoslavs for continuing to aid the Greek guerrillas. The second time was after the United States intervention had been mounted. The first time he warned the Yugoslavs against aiding the Greek Revolution, however, was before strong United States military involvement was certain. Doubtless this reflected both his belief that Communist revolutions without the Red army could not succeed, as well as his well-founded fears that the Greek Communists were very much under Titoist influence. As effective as General Van Vliet's forces may have been, there can be little doubt that Stalin's actions against Yugoslavia — first expulsion from the Cominform and then imposition of an economic blockade — were as much if not more responsible for the failure of the Greek Revolution.

All this remained unspoken by Washington policy-makers and the haste with which the Truman Doctrine was readied precluded any subsequent public comments. Even today, twenty years later, it is an implicit article of Washington cold war faith that our military intervention "saved" Greece from Soviet domination. Over and over again, our intervention in Greece is cited as argument for United States military action elsewhere. This "Greek syndrome" is the other side of the coin to the "Munich syndrome," which holds that since British and French appeasement of the Nazis encouraged Hitler, we must always stand up to the Soviets.

The situation in Turkey was somewhat different. Foiled in its efforts to gain allied support for obtaining a say in control of the Dardanelles, Moscow raised the question directly with Ankara and simultaneously made ominous demands against the long-disputed Turkish border provinces of Kars and Ardahan. There was little likelihood that Moscow would have risked war with Turkey, and even less likelihood that the Turks would have given in otherwise, but United States aid to Turkey — which later led to United States bases right on the Soviet border — undoubtedly encouraged Ankara to be firm. The case of Turkey, where Soviet demands were direct, contrasts with that of Greece where the USSR was not involved at all. Oddly enough, it is the latter rather than the former that is usually cited to justify our attitudes toward the Soviet Union, possibly because in Greece we could claim we "won" a shooting war against the Communists.[4]

Perhaps American post-war policy was at its best in the initial economic-aid program for Western Europe. With its social structure as well as its productive capacity badly rent by the war, Western Europe did not feel secure from internal Communist subversion without outside assistance and felt helpless alongside Soviet military power. The American answer was the Marshall Plan, which played an important part in hastening Western European recovery. Although certainly generosity was involved, the Marshall Plan was hardly the saintlike, selfless undertaking we sometimes represent it as having been. Not only did it help dispose of United States surpluses and encourage exports generally but it also laid the groundwork for the later United States economic expansion into Europe. Over and above this, however, the Marshall Plan was also seen by its initiators as a ploy against the Soviet Union. It is doubtful if there was ever serious consideration of the possibility that Moscow would accept the offer to include the Communist states in the Marshall Plan. Moreover, the plan was seen from the beginning partly in military terms. European recovery was a necessary prelude to European rearmament and participation in the defense against the Soviet Union.

Plans for NATO were advanced before the first dollar of Marshall Plan funds trickled into Europe, and with plans for NATO went consideration of the rearmament of Germany. It was primarily the civilian decision-makers — Truman, Acheson, Forrestal — who were responsible for this development. They were convinced that the major problems were more military than political because the main danger was the threat of Soviet military aggression. Consciously or unconsciously, this led them from an early date to adopt what might be called "the Locarno psychology." The essential idea here is that it is necessary to have a strong and friendly Germany in order to have adequate defenses against the Soviet Union.

---

[4] Those who considered it a victory for "democracy" may have been somewhat disillusioned by the military coup d'état in Greece in 1967.

The trend was accentuated by the fact that military men — e.g., Marshall and Bedell Smith — played such an important role in the foreign policy-making machinery. And directly in regard to Germany, military men of another type, with a special background in investment banking — Clay, Draper, *et al.* — influenced Washington policy.

Early postwar American policy on Germany was confused. At the very time that the Potsdam Agreement proclaimed that occupied Germany would be governed on the principle of five "ds" — demilitarization, denazification, deindustrialization, decentralization and democratization — the Washington government was swinging toward a policy which precluded their implementation. The five "ds" would have meant a weak Germany, whereas Forrestal and his cohorts felt there should be a strong one, and the "ds" could have been put into effect only on the basis of Washington-Moscow cooperation, which Washington, if it wanted this at all, wanted only on terms that in fact made it impossible. This situation was further complicated because, in regard to the important issue of reparations, the Yalta and Potsdam agreements were in conflict with each other. It is difficult if not impossible to say who was responsible for the series of steps that led to the breakdown of four-power occupation of Germany, and it is now of little importance in any event. While it is clear that all sides were at fault, the fact is that the first decisive step was taken by the West, led by the United States, with the merger of the Western zones and the establishment of a separate West German state. There the Western actions amounted to recognition of the fact that the wartime agreements on Germany were already a dead letter. The Berlin blockade initiated by the Soviets in response to our extralegal currency reform in Berlin was also in recognition of this. On this basis, United States-Soviet cooperation might still have been possible. The United States, however, then proceeded to insist that in other areas, particularly in regard to Berlin, the wartime agreements were still valid and intact.

Although the decision to establish a separate German state was influenced by a number of factors, it cannot be considered apart from the need that was early felt in Washington to erect strong military barriers against the Soviet Union. Consider the chronology: As early as 1946, Secretary of State Byrnes hinted at a fusion of the United States and British zones of occupation for economic purposes. Almost as soon as Bizonia was formed, the London Conference in the spring of 1948 decided to create a West German government. The same period saw the initiation of the Marshall Plan, under whose largess West Germany was one of the principal beneficiaries. In late 1949 NATO was formed, and in September, 1950, the NATO Council decided that West Germany should be permitted to contribute to an integrated force. It was not long before the West German army was the main bulwark of NATO.

The American decision to rearm West Germany — as indeed our whole postwar policy toward Germany — is an example of the Locarno psychology. Even Mr. Dulles was not oblivious to the dangers of an armed Germany. But the important thing was to create military strength to guard against Soviet military aggression. The whole policy has turned out to be a trap, from which thus far the United States has been unable to extricate itself. Nowhere is this more apparent than in the problem of Berlin.

Establishment of the West German state resulted in the establishment of the East German state. If one state is valid, so is the other. Our initiative in this matter could be justified legally only if the wartime agreements were considered a dead letter. But if they were a dead letter, then there was no legal basis for United States military presence in West Berlin — an enclave wholly inside the East German state — unless one accepted, as an indefinite matter, the so-called "rights" of conquest or of "belligerent occupation." But we deny the legality of the East German state and justify our continuing in Berlin on the grounds that it is authorized by the wartime agreements, plus rights of occupation.

The legal side of the question is the less significant part of the trap, however. Our nonrecognition of East Germany and of the Oder-Neisse frontier, along with our continued presence in West Berlin, constitute an assault against the status quo and thus contribute to instability and tension in Central Europe. Whether we could ever have reached an agreement with the Soviet Union may never be known. But, between 1955 and 1959, there were several occasions when an agreement with the Soviet Union might possibly have been achieved. How great the possibilities were we don't know because we never tried to find out. As George Kennan put it, we would never know whether the Soviets would go through an open door or not until we stopped trying to push them through a closed one. We never did, in large part because we were always fearful of West German reactions — and we were afraid they might pull out of NATO.

The Alice in Wonderland quality of all this is apparent when it is realized that NATO plans were based on the virtual certainty not of a conventional but of a thermonuclear war in which conventionally armed troops would play a very small part. Since NATO, even with the Germans, was never a match for Communist strength in the East, and since, by definition, Soviet military aggression was restrained only by counterforce, it was explained that the Red hordes were held at bay by the American thermonuclear umbrella.

It took a long time for somebody with sufficient importance to be heard to ask, "If that is so — why all the fuss about NATO in the first place?"

But this is not all. This virtual dependency on West Germany which our present policy entails — because we consider West Germany so vital to NATO — has led us into policies which now seem likely to destroy NATO. West Germany, not content with having the most powerful continental forces in terms of conventional weapons, has shown an understandable penchant for acquiring nuclear weapons. To forestall this, we came up with MLF. And MLF launched a chain of events which led to de facto French withdrawal from NATO and thus removed its geopolitical underpinning.

For the same reasons we are unable to make any meaningful moves toward disarmament or arms limitation. Possibly the most promising small step in that direction would be a nuclear arms freeze in Central Europe, as proposed by the Poles. We are stopped from espousing this idea, again because of West German opposition.

Under Khrushchev, Moscow moved to put the concept of coexistence on a more permanent and meaningful basis. This implied a détente between Moscow and Washington, and a détente almost certainly requires some settlement of the German question. It was Washington's policy which encouraged the West Germans under Adenauer to adopt attitudes that are both intransigent and unrealistic. But it is precisely these attitudes that now prevent Washington from moving toward any real settlement of the German question and thus from achieving a détente with the USSR. It may even be that now the United States would like to achieve such a détente, which, if so, would mean that earlier fear of Soviet military aggression, which has been the basis of our whole policy in Europe, no longer exists. To cap the climax of this absurd illogic, Germany itself may be moving away from positions which we have felt it necessary to appease.

Immobility and rigidity may not be the most serious consequence of this twenty years of unrealism, but they are bad enough.

Total collapse of Washington's European policy is now a likelihood. This whole policy was based on Washington's cold war concepts, and almost no one really believes in them anymore, possibly not even the Germans. It is questionable, however, whether our present policy-makers, inured in the solipsism that enables them to ignore that which they fear the most, will in fact be able to readjust. The trouble, from the standpoint of Washington policy, is not only that the Western European nations are reevaluating their cold war positions; it is also that from a strategic point of view the whole containment thesis made any sense only if one assumed continued, clear United States military superiority over the Soviet Union. This, of course, was what Washington did assume and, when proved wrong, at the time of the Soviet *sputniki*, the reaction ranged from fear to frenzy. According to American cold war ideology, Soviet military aggression had been restrained only by our superior military strength. Now that it wasn't so superior any more, the Soviets should have attacked, and, truth to tell, Washington was hard pressed to say why they didn't. The Soviet successes were explained in terms of various United

States weaknesses, ranging from bad teaching of arithmetic to lack of enough physical training, but never in terms of the simple truth that the Soviet Union was basically strong and that its new prowess was very much a natural — not to say inevitable — development.

The Soviet *sputniki* were clear handwriting on the wall for the containment policy. At the Nineteenth Party Congress in 1952, Stalin had discovered nationalism as a revolutionary force and had brought to an end the long defensive, isolationist period of Soviet policy. Following through on this at the Twentieth Congress in 1956, Khrushchev revised the traditional theory on the inevitability of war. He put coexistence on a firmer basis, but at the same time firmly pledged Soviet military assistance to socialist governments once they were established. As Cuba was to demonstrate, the day when the United States could act with impunity anywhere in the world was over.

In Vietnam we have thus far escaped nuclear war, but the specter of it is ever present and has to be considered in every decision to escalate. In terms of Europe, as de Gaulle was soon to point out, the United States deterrent was not only not credible anymore but it was dangerous as well. In the absence of disarmament, this meant for France either an independent nuclear capacity or breaking with American policy and seeking direct rapprochement with the Soviet Union. De Gaulle has done both. His first approaches to the problem were undertaken in a friendly and cooperative spirit, but Washington — feeling like the king must have felt when attention was called to the fact he didn't have any clothes on — was at first unable to take him seriously and then unable to take him rationally. Secretary Rusk, apparently utterly unable to comprehend the situation, made matters worse by asserting that the U.S. involvement in Vietnam involved NATO too. If one didn't know it were so, it simply would be unbelievable that he made this assertion at a conference called to strengthen NATO.

It could well be that if the United States extricates itself from Vietnam, there would be an opportunity to adjust to the new situation in Europe, seek a rapprochement with the Soviet

Union, settle the German question and progress toward disarmament. But without a reevaluation first of the bases of the containment doctrine, this is unlikely to occur. If Washington is really willing to reconsider its approach to the Soviet Union, it may be more because of a hope to aggravate the Soviet-Chinese split than anything else. Accustomed, now, to having a devil — a Communist devil, and with the whole society increasingly geared to it — Washington appears, to some extent, now to be shifting devils in the middle of the stream. If the United States is, in fact, starting out on the whole course over again in regard to China, it will be an illustration of Marx's idea that history repeats itself as farce. Only it will be a highly dangerous farce, with the likelihood of other Vietnams on the way, ultimately turning into tragedy.

Bibliographical Note

In this paper, I have drawn copiously from my own works — *inter alia, U.S. Foreign Policy and the Soviet Union*, Center for the Study of Democratic Institutions, 1961; *Titoism in Action*, University of California Press, 1958; *Yugoslavia and the New Communism*, Twentieth Century Fund, 1962; *War and Peace and Germany*, W. W. Norton, 1962; and "Coexistence: Practical Problems and International Politics," *Co-Existence*, January, 1966 — all of which are fully documented with detailed footnotes. Some of the material of Soviet and Yugoslav relations with the Greek revolutionaries comes from my own as yet unpublished researches on the question. These consist largely of private conversations with Yugoslav and Greek participants in the revolution.

For the section dealing with theory, see also Stalin, *Marx-Engels-Marxism* and *Leninism*; Lenin, *Imperialism, the Highest Stage of Capitalism, State and Revolution*, and *Two Steps Backwards, One Step Forward*; "Theses of the Sixth World Congress of the Communist International," *International Press Correspondence*, No. 84, November 28, 1928; *Fundamentals of Marxism-Leninism*, 2nd revised edition, Foreign Languages

Publishing House, Moscow, 1963; and Carew Hunt, *Communist Theory and Practice*.

Additional material on the Greek situation may be found in the books on Greece by William MacNeill; the report of the UN Commission of investigation headed by Mark Ethridge; Robert Lee Wolff, *The Balkans of Our Time*; Vladimir Dedijer, *Tito;* Jovan Skorovic, *Stalin je kao Imperialist*, Jugostampa, 1950; Veljko Vlahovic, *Marksism i Savetski Savez*, Jugoslevenska Kniga, 1953; *Borba*, various issues between March and June, 1947; and *For a Lasting Peace, for a Peoples Democracy* (The Cominform Journal), various issues between March and June, 1948.

In addition I have drawn on various United States and English books dealing with U.S. policies during and immediately after the war, including works on Forrestal, Acheson and Stimson, and on the unpublished papers of Harold Smith, Roosevelt's Budget Director.

The Military-Industrial
Alliance

JOHN M. SWOMLEY, JR.

A high-ranking army officer said in 1948, according to a newspaper columnist, "We had our sights on the next war long before we got to Tokyo."

"War with Russia?"

"Who else? Not with Russia because Russia is Russia, but because she is the potential enemy. It happens to be the army's business to work out our defenses against the rest of the world. Russia happens to be the only power for the time being, at least, that could take us on."[1]

It is the military economic and political planning for this eventuality that provided the context for the cold war.

The military planning presupposed a large army, a large defense industry and overseas allies. Coincidentally, financial and industrial interests were thinking in the same terms. James Forrestal, who had been the president of the investment banking firm of Dillon Read and Company before entering the Roosevelt administration, organized the National Security Industrial Association, a group of industrial firms with major military contracts, in order to insure that "American business will remain close to the services." Charles E. Wilson, President of General Motors, had already suggested the cold war pattern in an address to the Army Ordnance Association when he proposed a military-industrial alliance which would be the

---

[1] Jennings Perry, *PM*, May 19, 1948.

creature of "a continuing program and not . . . of an emergency."[2]

It was in 1944 also that the army and business leaders began the drive to secure a permanent peacetime conscription program, thus insuring a large postwar army. A Citizens Committee for Universal Military Training of Young Men was organized on Wall Street by persons prominent in financial circles. In addition, the Chamber of Commerce of the United States and other business interests supported the army's campaign.[3] When this campaign failed to convince Congress, the army began in 1947 to talk of war danger from Russia.

In the meantime, it had become apparent to political and financial circles in the United States that Great Britain was no longer powerful enough to maintain her empire and order at other key points throughout the world. Most of Eastern Europe had passed under the control of the Soviet Union and capitalism seemed to be threatened in Western Europe. The wartime destruction in Western Europe coupled with the trend toward neutralism and socialist or coalition governments, required economic reconstruction as the base for overseas alliances. Military and business leaders, while continuing their conscription campaign, turned their attention to promoting the plan, formally announced by General George Marshall, for the reconstruction of Western Europe.[4]

When Congress seemed reluctant to adopt either program, Defense Secretary James Forrestal and Army Secretary Kenneth Royall told Congress in January, 1948 that if the Marshall Plan were not adopted it would be forced to spend an equal or greater amount on military preparedness. In desperation the army handed President Truman a false intelligence report which "pictured the Soviet army as on the move" when "actually the Soviets were redistributing their troops to spring training stations."[5] President Truman called a joint emergency session of both Houses of Congress on March 17, 1948, to ask

---

[2] John M. Swomley, *The Military Establishment* (Boston: Beacon Press, 1964), pp. 100–1.

[3] *Ibid*, Chap. ii.

[4] *Ibid.*, Chap. v.

[5] *Chicago Tribune*, June 19, 1948.

the immediate adoption of the Marshall Plan and the Selective Service Act. After the adoption of these two measures the way was open for the military to push the formation of a Western European military alliance as the forerunner of NATO.

Military Support of Industry

After the initial collaboration between the military and business to develop the structure of postwar military policy there was continuing cooperation to enlarge military appropriations. One illustration of this was the boost given to the idea of large appropriations for air power by the President's Air Policy Commission, and by the Congressional Aviation Policy Board. In each Commission, aircraft industrial executives, through their testimony or participation as advisers, had a prominent role. It is not surprising that the President's Commission came to the conclusion that the air force should be increased "at once." The Commission report stated: "A strong aircraft industry is an essential in the nation's air power."[6] In similar fashion, the Congressional Aviation Policy Board indicated that "maintenance of a healthy and expandable aircraft industry is required for national security." The report added that, "Procurement policies of the Government will determine the financial condition and survival of most companies engaged in making aircraft."[7]

This demonstrates that one of the major by-products of the cold war is the creation and support of key industries by military expenditures. *Business Week* pointed out in 1959 that "Defense work has been the making of a score of small and obscure companies. . . . Military contracts may not make giants of small companies, but they can bring them growth in great leaps and bounds."[8]

The military assists existent or nonexistent firms to enter the weapons industry by a device known as facilities contracts.

---

[6] *Survival in the Air Age* (Washington, D.C.: U.S. Government Printing Office, 1948), p. 45.

[7] Report No. 949, 80th Congress, 2nd Session, p. 34.

[8] *Ibid.*, October 10, 1959, p. 90.

For years it has provided part or all of the capital investment for certain industries to move into production. It put some $233 million into missile plants and $32 million into aircraft plants from February, 1956 to February, 1958.[9]

In 1954 the air force made it possible for two moderately paid aerospace scientists, Drs. Simon Ramo and Dean Wooldridge to build from scratch the Thompson-Ramo-Wooldridge Corporation, one of the nation's largest industrial combines. In less than four years the two scientists had become multimillionaires. Their firm was among the top fifty defense contractors, moving ahead of numerous old and established corporations.[10]

The aerospace industry, as such, is entirely the creature of the cold war and government contracts.

The aircraft industry was built up in the postwar period of Russian war scares. Then came sputnik and the missile race. More recently, the first space flights of the Russians plus an imminent economic recession in the States led President Kennedy in May, 1961 to announce the space race to the moon.[11] In 1966 the aerospace industry listed record sales of $23.8 billion. In the course of its government nurture the industry had gradually picked up some nonaerospace business but in 1966 75% of the total business was still with the government.[12]

The impact of military contracts on industry may be seen from an analysis of the business of Western Electric Inc. Total (including commercial) sales jumped from $985 million in 1951 to $2,640.8 million in 1968. Total profits rose from $142.9 million in 1951 to $258.4 million in 1960. During those years government business was much smaller than commercial business. In 1960, for example, total sales to government were $724.3 million in contrast to $1,916.5 million commercial sales. The ten-year average shows, however, that Western Electric made a profit of 28.3 cents on every dollar

---

[9] *Ibid.*, p. 84.
[10] H. L. Nieburg, *In the Name of Science* (Chicago: Quadrangle Books, 1966), Chap. xi.
[11] *Ibid.*, p. 51.
[12] *The New York Times*, January 9, 1967.

invested of government business, in contrast to 22.2 cents on the dollar for the amount invested in commercial business.[13]

Moreover, since Western Electric's commercial sales are almost entirely to the American Telephone and Telegraph Company of which it is a subsidiary, its rate of profit is higher than if it were in competitive selling. The higher military profit is therefore significant.

Some industries with defense business, of course, make a very small percent of their sales to the military and yet enough to make a difference in their total earnings. Burlington Industries in the textile field had government business in 1966 of just under 5% of a total sales volume of $1.3 billion.[14]

Military Support of Education

A second area where the military makes a major economic impact is in educational institutions. Dr. Vannevar Bush, wartime Director of the Office of Scientific Research and Development, said in December, 1951, that "Many universities are carrying the bulk of their research and the salaries of their graduate faculties on Government funds."[15] Among the nonprofit institutions with whom the Pentagon has almost a billion dollars in research contracts are the nation's leading universities. The Massachusetts Institute of Technology ranked first with $70,284,000 in fiscal year 1963. Johns Hopkins University was second with $65,483,000. Some eighty other educational institutions had contracts ranging from $312,000 to $22,052,000.[16]

One result of the military-space financing of research and development in universities is the "danger that engineering education programs have become ill-balanced in favor of training graduates for advanced degree work that will lead them into the space race."[17]

---

[13] "Senate Committee on Government Operations, Pyramiding of Profits and Costs in the Missile Procurement Program," Part II, 1962, pp. 423–24.

[14] *The New York Times,* January 9, 1967.

[15] *Ibid.,* December 15, 1951.

[16] *Aviation Week and Space Technology,* January 20, 1964, p. 101.

[17] John R. Dixon, "Engineering, Affluence and Poverty," *Bulletin of the Atomic Scientists,* April, 1966, p. 33.

An estimated eight out of every ten new graduates in the field of science and engineering will go into nongrowth or military and space research and development.[18] This means that defense-oriented research is draining off money and men from both pure research and from research and development for civilian industry.

Military Impact on Regional Income

A third way in which the cold war military budgets affect the economy is evident in regional employment and income. The assignment of the Manned Spacecraft Center to Houston is a case in point. At Clear Lake near Houston the population jumped from 6,520 in 1960 to about 30,000 in 1965. Family income averages $9,500 in the vicinity of the space center in contrast to $6,040 for the entire metropolitan area. The land value increased four times on the average and in the immediate vicinity of the center about seven times its 1960 value. Bank deposits in June, 1965 reached $25 million from a 1961 peak of less than $5 million. Because of the space center, Humble Oil and Refining Company has started a 7,250-acre industrial park at Bayport.

The government has put $173 million into buildings and equipment and the center's annual budget is about $90 million. The space center employs some 4,500 scientists, engineers, and other space-age personnel. Aerospace contractors in the vicinity employ approximately 3,000.

The Houston metropolitan area has also gained substantially though it is impossible to credit all of the gains to the space center. The population increased about 230,000, employment about 70,000, retail sales a half-billion dollars and bank deposits $600 million between January 1, 1962 and June 30, 1965.[19]

Hawaii's economy is also partially dependent on military spending. A Bank of Hawaii economist estimated the 1966 defense spending at $510 million which exceeded the com-

---

[18] Nieburg, *op. cit.*, p. 79.
[19] *Business Week*, September 11, 1965, p. 90.

bined total of the tourist industry, $300 million, and the sugar industry, $190 million.[20]

A study of national defense expenditures in New Mexico reveals that over half the state's revenue is derived from military activities.[21] In certain other areas such as the Tacoma-Seattle area and New London-Groton-Norwich area, in Connecticut, military activity is the most important single source of employment.[22]

The Washington State Employment Security Department in July, 1965 released a study of *The Dyna-Soar Contract Cancellation*. The study was based on questionnaires sent to more than 5,000 employees who had been dismissed by the Boeing Company between December, 1963 and March, 1964 as a result of a manned space vehicle program cancellation. Over 70% of those canvassed returned their questionnaires. Seventy-eight percent of the men and 41% of the women had found new jobs by August, 1964 but most of them had to take a cut in salary. Of those employed 33% of the men and 11% of the women had to move to other areas to find work. The men who found other jobs did so only after an average of 14.3 weeks unemployment or about 32,000 cumulative weeks of lost income.

The report stated:

A number of workers told of years of long tenure abruptly ending, with a new start or a new and different job necessary. Many indicated great losses on sales of their homes in the Seattle area to move to other areas for work. Depletion of savings, long periods of unemployment, foregone education because of loss of work, loss of equity in assets purchased on credit — these are all some of the personal hardships which do not show up in the body of the report but should be kept in mind.[23]

[20] *The New York Times,* January 9, 1967.

[21] *Adjustments to Reduced National Defense Expenditures in New Mexico,* Kirschner Associates, December, 1965, Albuquerque, New Mexico.

[22] *Community Readjustment to Reduced Defense Spending,* National Planning Association, December, 1965, Washington, D.C.

[23] For summary of these and other similar studies see review by Betty Goetz Lall, *Bulletin of Atomic Scientists,* September, 1966, p. 42.

The military impact upon the economy must be seen also in terms of military payroll which has in normal cold war years included about a million civilians in the Defense Department, about 40 to 50,000 in related activities such as the Atomic Energy Commission, Selectice Service and the National Aeronautics and Space Administration, and 2½ million in the armed forces. Every state of the Union profits directly from this payroll which in 1959 was well over $11 billion in the United States. That payroll according to a government report was more than double the payrolls of the automobile industry.[24] In addition, soldiers and sailors overseas returned money to relatives throughout the country and about $1.4 billion in 1959 also went into the economy via military construction projects.[25]

One by-product of this military money is congressional competition to secure contracts or bases for their districts. Congressmen rarely question and almost never vote against military budgets. In 1958, Chairman Vinson of the House Armed Services Committee said to the House in the course of presenting a military construction bill which amounted to about a billion dollars: "My friends, there is something in this bill for every member." Representative J. L. Whitten (D. Miss.) in reminding the House of this on May 3, 1960, added: "And sure enough, when you read the requests for military construction they had them listed by states so you could see every member had a monetary interest in passage."

Such statements, of course, may distort the military contribution to local economies. Ten states in the year ending June 30, 1965 received 66% of all the prime military contracts. One of these, California, received 22.1%. When military payroll and construction are considered, it is chiefly southern and southwestern states that benefit. There are probably only about 300 to 400 out of the more than 3,000 counties in the United States where the local economy is enhanced in a major way by military bases or armaments firms. In

---

[24] U.S. Congress Joint Economic Subcommittee on Defense Procurement and Supply, Background Material on Economic Aspects of Military Procurement and Supply, February 16, 1960, p. 23.

[25] *Ibid.*, p. 25.

most of the rest of the country purchasing power is reduced by the withdrawal of money for taxes to pay for the inflated military budgets of the cold war era.

Investments Overseas

The fourth and most important economic aspect of the cold war is the overseas growth of American industry. American industry has tended to invest in those countries where the presence of American troops has brought some assurance of security and stability.

About 500 American manufacturers are doing business in Taiwan where the United States has about 50,000 troops. The First National City Bank of New York and the Bank of America have established branches there. In 1966 the Taiwan government approved foreign investment projects of $35 million for fifty-two factories.[26]

In Korea where the United States maintains a force of 50,000 men, twenty-five American companies with investments of $41 million have been doing business. In 1966 representatives of more than 100 American companies visited Seoul to look into investment possibilities.[27]

In Japan, where the United States has a garrison of 40,000, direct private investments as of the end of 1965 totaled $676 million, according to the Department of Commerce.[28] Actual investments are probably double or triple this amount since the Department of Commerce uses book value rather than market value for direct investment overseas of American industries.[29]

By far the largest direct investments of American capital overseas have been in Western Europe where NATO has been operating and 300,000 American troops are stationed. Aside from the political stability of Western Europe the economic boom has encouraged American financial and industrial circles

---

[26] *The New York Times,* January 20, 1967.
[27] *Ibid.*
[28] *Overseas Business Reports,* October, 1966 (OBR 66–70).
[29] *Fortune,* October, 1956, p. 93.

to invest there. That boom has been stimulated by a number of factors including the Common Market.

Business Week in 1959 described the military-economic base for the boom:

> . . . the economic cards still are stacked somewhat in favor of Western Europe and Japan. A good part of the gold and dollars being accumulated today in these areas comes from U.S. military expenditures — troop pay and local procurement for U.S. forces stationed in Western Europe and Japan. . . . For U.S. investors abroad, whether they have put money into European stocks or into production facilities in Western Europe or Japan, the new business boom abroad provides a pleasant prospect. In fact, it probably will lead to still further investment in these areas, both direct and portfolio.[30]

American capital moved into Europe so rapidly after 1950 that by the summer of 1965 direct investments there had reached a total of more than $12 billion, according to *Fortune,* "a 360% increase in only ten years time." In the five-year period, 1960–1965, American investment in West Germany went up about 165% to $2 billion. In France it increased 130% to $1.5 billion; in Italy 150% to $800 million; in the Netherlands 115% to $525 million; in Belgium and Luxembourg it almost doubled in going up to $430 million.[31]

Direct private stateside investment in United Kingdom commerce and industry was estimated at $5.2 billion in 1965, up $600 million from 1964.[32]

Over the years a major portion of the income produced from such overseas investments has returned to the United States. According to the National Industrial Conference Board, "Repatriated dividends and interest, together with royalties and management fees, amounted to 76.1% of the income earned in all industries in 1965."[33] The total earned income from all such direct investments overseas in all indus-

[30] *Ibid.,* October 17, 1959, pp. 28–30.
[31] *Ibid.,* August, 1965, p. 126.
[32] James Reston, *Kansas City Times,* December 2, 1966.
[33] *Roadmaps of Industry,* No. 1558, November 15, 1966.

tries was $6.4 billion in 1965. The value of direct investment abroad amounted to 60.8% of the total private foreign investment in 1965.[34]

The cold war provides the political and military rationale for maintaining troops overseas. It also is the basis for the huge taxation of civilians which is transferred to the military and in turn to large corporations doing business with the military. It is not surprising then to note that business leaders as well as the military are interested in keeping the cold war going.

At the executive level of government, business leaders are highly influential. The various industrial suppliers of the Pentagon are organized into such groups as the Army Ordnance Association and the Navy League. An overall group of corporate executives and board chairmen function in a Business Council. A *New York Times* dispatch from Hot Springs, Virginia, where the Council met in 1966, stated: "Most of the Council members have had extended personal dealings with Johnson and they feel he respects and understands them. . . . The Council's role as consultant to the government has expanded enormously since Johnson has been President and is continuing to expand."[35]

Typical of business influence upon Congress is the testimony in 1960 of business leaders before the Senate Government Operations Subcommittee. Thomas J. Watson, Jr., head of the International Business Machines Corporation, told the committee, "We are in a critical contest with the Soviet Union. Therefore we must be willing to accept any 'sacrifices' necessary to win." Watson asked that public discussion of defense matters be limited, with debate on controversial subjects remaining behind closed doors. He added, "I do not agree with people who suggest that we must not push our economy to any point necessary in competing with the Soviet. . . ."[36]

Previously the same committee heard two Republican bankers champion the need for greater "sacrifices" to deal with the Russians. They were Robert A. Lovett, former Secretary of

[34] *Ibid.*
[35] *Kansas City Times,* October 24, 1966.
[36] *The New York Times,* February 26, 1960.

Defense and Robert C. Sprague, a former Presidential adviser on security.[37]

Watson's International Business Machines system operates in eighty-seven countries and has nineteen foreign manufacturing plants. It was seventh in the top 100 prime contractors for NASA in fiscal year 1965 with $128,312,000 in contracts.[38] In fiscal year 1963 before the Vietnam buildup it was fifty-seventh in the list of top military prime contractors with a total of $9,999,000.[39]

It is not just the indirect influence of business executives that determines government policy but the direct participation of these executives in policy-making positions. Over the years financial and industrial leaders such as James Forrestal, Nelson Rockefeller, Averell Harriman, John Foster Dulles, Robert A. Lovett, Charles E. Wilson, Robert McNamara and numerous others have held the important decision-making posts in the executive branch.

In addition, such semiofficial foreign policy projects as Crusade for Freedom and its affiliate, Radio Free Europe, which operates the largest radio stations in Europe, are big business enterprises. Every one of its ten directors is a major Wall Street figure.[40]

In the United States also there is extensive cooperation between the military and the nation's publicity media so as to keep alive the myths and realities of the cold war.[41]

One further economic factor, though this does not exhaust the list, is the direct government sale of arms and munitions abroad. The United States has increased its arms sales abroad from about $330 million in 1961 to $1.5 billion in 1965.[42] In the past five years foreign countries have bought about $7 billion worth of arms.[43]

The Pentagon itself, under the leadership of a Deputy As-

37 *Ibid.*

38 *Missiles and Rockets,* December 20, 1965, p. 20.

39 *Aviation Week and Space Technology,* January 13, 1964, p. 83.

40 Victor Perlo, *The Empire of High Finance* (New York: International Publishers, 1957), p. 305.

41 Swomley, *op. cit.,* Chap. x.

42 *New Republic,* June 5, 1965.

43 *Business Week,* December 3, 1966, p. 67.

sistant Secretary of Defense, Henry J. Kuss, Jr., is doing the selling on behalf of private arms firms. To promote these sales the Pentagon maintains a special program in Western Europe at a cost of about $500,000 a year.[44]

Kuss and his twenty-two aides arrange financing if it is needed through private banks, the Export-Import Bank or a special credit program provided by the Pentagon. About $3 billion in credit has been arranged for the $10.5 billion in sales and commitments already achieved. Kuss justifies this on the ground that cash receipts from this sales program will come close to offsetting the dollar drain from defense spending abroad. He also says that this program has provided 1.4 million man-years of employment in 40,000 firms in all of the fifty states. Out of a total of $10.5 billion in sales and commitments the private arms industry "will reap a profit of well over $1 billion."[45]

The cold war is the context for these arms sales since Kuss also insists that if the U.S. didn't provide arms to a number of these countries we would leave a vacuum into which Russia or China could move.[46]

Kuss indicated in 1965 that defense industries in the U.S. could look to a potential yearly market of $5.4 billion in military exports by 1967. By 1971, he added, the minimum market should be $10 billion and the potential market $15 billion a year.[47]

It is obvious that the boosting of sales of arms required the use or creation of armed "enemies" as incentives. In selling arms to Israel, for example, a market is created in Jordan. John Galbraith, former ambassador to India, told the Senate Foreign Relations Committee on April 24, 1966, that "the arms we supplied . . . caused the war between India and Pakistan. . . . If we had not supplied arms, Pakistan would not have sought a military solution to the Kashmir problem."[48]

---

[44] *The New York Times*, May 24, 1965.
[45] *Business Week*, December 3, 1966, pp. 66–70.
[46] *Ibid.*
[47] *The New York Times*, May 24, 1965.
[48] *Ibid.*, April 26, 1966. See also "Uncle Sam's Increased Activity as 'Merchant of Death' — How We Foment Arms Races and Encourage Militarization Abroad," *I. F. Stone's Weekly*, February 6, 1967.

The policy of arms sales has also produced other repercussions such as resentment in British, French, and German industrial and nationalist circles. The electoral gains by a neo-Nazi party in Germany, according to Paul Leucke, West Germany's Minister of the Interior, were in part caused by that party's attack on Washington's insistence on military purchases to offset the cost of maintaining American troops on German soil. These demands led party leaders to compare them with the high reparation costs after World War I.

"Chancellor Ludwig Erhard's failure to get any substantial relief from this commitment," said *Business Week*, December 3, 1966, "and his plan to raise German taxes to help pay for it helped bring about the recent collapse of his ruling coalition."[49]

The unrest in Germany over the more than $675 million worth of arms that Germany is required to purchase annually has existed for several years. Representative Paul Findley (R. Ill.) made public a series of army reports and other data which showed that the Pentagon had agreed to buy a 20-mm. cannon from German firms in November, 1964, even though it failed tests and did not work. This data, said Findley, revealed that the sole reason for the purchase was to ease German unrest over the large quantities of American weapons that Germany had to purchase.[50]

Conclusions

During the early years of the cold war, military spending maintained a relatively stable rate of about 10% of the Gross National Product. In 1964 it began to drop — relatively — until now it is just under 8%. During the six-year boom from 1961 through 1966, corporate after-tax profits rose about 64%. This achievement, said *The New York Times* of January 9, 1967, "was also accomplished in a mainly civilian rather than war-dominated economy to which the nation appears to be shifting." It can also be said that the economies of some states,

---

[49] *Kansas City Times*, November 8, 1956.
[50] *Kansas City Star*, December 11, 1966.

Oregon, for example, where there is relatively little military spending, are in healthier shape than those of some heavily militarized states such as Washington. In other words, it is possible to make a case for a profitable civilian economy. Any such effort, however accurate, misses the point.

Although it seems clear that the United States could, with careful planning, have a healthier economy in a partially or totally disarmed world than it now has, there are other economic factors that militate against a change in military spending policies and against an ending of the cold war. The first of these is the fact of Communism. Any area of the world to which American capitalists are denied access — or where they consider investment to be unsafe — is seen as capable of expansion and hence a threat. It may be feasible to have a partial détente with the Soviet Union but this is in part because responsibility for the cold war momentum can be shifted to China.

A second economic reason for continuing the cold war is the tremendous volume of profits and the employment of personnel by the arms industry. The weapons industry, said *Business Week* as early as 1959,

> is bigger than any other industry. It runs to $14½ billion a year if you count only major military hardware contracts. . . . It climbs to $25 billion a year when you add research and development, operation and maintenance of such vast systems as DEW line, and construction of air fields and missile launching bases. It hits around $41 billion a year when you include everything else on which the Defense Department spends money. By way of a yardstick: the international oil business, the world's largest single industry, pumps up around $10 billion worth of petroleum a year.[51]

Moreover, it is not always easy to diversify or reduce industry dependence on the military. One important analysis of twelve case studies made by the Denver Research Institute revealed that all of the twelve, six of them large aerospace indus-

---

[51] October 10, 1959, p. 71.

tries, had tried to diversify. ". . . all have had some failures. Of twenty-three internal developments attempted nine were profitable but only after three to seven or more years of trial."[52] It is also evident from this and other studies that the Defense Department is not encouraging efforts to diversify.[53]

A third economic reason for the continuance of the military-industrial complex and the cold war is its virtual invulnerability to political control. So long as congressmen in any sizable numbers believe, as they do, that opposition to the cold war and military spending will result either in reprisals from the Pentagon and economic injury to their district or in a failure to secure new spending, there will be no real effort to change the system. In addition to this, there is a sense in which major corporations have gone international to such a degree that their commercial activity is multinational or global, rendering national regulation difficult if not obsolete. This is especially true when arms industries receive the combined support of the Pentagon and its allied counterparts in other countries. A study prepared by the staff of the Senate Foreign Relations Committee contends that the international arms sales program has become a "vested interest" of the Pentagon and the armaments industry, not subject to political control by the administration or Congress.[54]

Finally and obviously, the cold war and military spending give the major American corporations access to the public treasury as no other device would do. A real or alleged move by Russia or China can be very profitable to American business. *The New York Times* of December 25, 1966, reported that "American capitalists are extremely intrigued" by the Nike X project which is our response to a Russian antiballistic missile system. This project, said *The New York Times*, prom-

---

[52] *Defense Industry Diversification* (January, 1966) reviewed by Betty Goetz Lall, *Bulletin of Atomic Scientists,* September, 1966, p. 43.

[53] *Ibid.*

[54] See John W. Finney, "Senate Study Questions U.S. Arms Sales Abroad," *The New York Times,* January 30, 1967. See also *Arms Sales and Foreign Policy,* Staff Study for the Committee on Foreign Relations, United States Senate (Washington, D. C., U.S. Government Printing Office, January 25, 1967).

ises "tremendous profits" for about 3,000 companies that would be directly involved.

About 500 corporations own about two-thirds of all economically productive nonagricultural assets. They employ the bulk of the working population and exercise tremendous influence in the political and economic life of the nation. All of the top prime military contractors are in this group. Many of them such as General Electric, General Motors, IBM, Western Electric, Ford are not primarily in the defense business but are among the top contractors. In fiscal year 1962 such nonmilitary firms as General Tire and Rubber had 34% of its total sales in military business, Sperry Rand 38%, Radio Corporation of America 19%, American Machine and Foundry 52%.

All of the big firms in the aerospace and arms industry subcontract to other large corporations and to a whole network of smaller firms. It is possible, therefore, to say as did one economist, Sumner Rosen, that defense industry "supports and reinforces the predominant role of giant corporations in our economic and political life." Speaking of the military-industrial complex, he added,

> It is integral to the structure of the system quite as much as the level of spending which it absorbs is an integral part of the total spending stream. It helps to shape and to reinforce all the characteristic features of modern economic life. It is big, concentrated, and affluent, and we depend on it. Its reduction or elimination would shake the industrial structure to its roots.[55]

This means that the nation's private corporations are given each year an enormous government subsidy. That subsidy makes possible high salaries for executives in the arms industry, large profits for business in general and corporate power which is felt in governments around the world. In short, big government and big business are intertwined in such a way that the taxpayer is induced to support both because of the

---

[55] Sumner M. Rosen, "The New Orthodoxy on Disarmament Economics," *The Correspondent,* Winter, 1965.

alleged danger to the nation. The military is the necessary partner of industry for the distribution of public funds.

An important by-product of this alliance is the steady demand that military spending must have priority and that tax savings are to be made by reducing nondefense spending. In turn, this means that public works, antipoverty campaigns, and welfare spending are to be minimized with consequent maintenance of large pockets of poverty, unemployment and depressed wages. Tax cuts are made for the purpose, not of alleviating poverty, but of stimulating private capital expansion.

Theoretically, demand for production could be stimulated through the elimination of poverty and large public works products but these have generally been unprofitable, government-consummated projects which smack of socialism. The cold war, on the other hand, has kept profits high, kept organized labor as well as the poor united against the external "enemy," and kept the entire nation willing to subsidize from taxes the profit and salary requirements of the military-industrial complex.

The cold war and the military-industrial complex have created and sustained each other. Their impact on the domestic scene is overwhelming but on the international scene they perpetuate the arms race and heighten international tensions.[56]

---

[56] See John Kenneth Galbraith, "The Cold War and the Corporations," *The Progressive,* July, 1967.

Cold-War-Mindedness and the Mass Media

D. W. SMYTHE AND H. H. WILSON

Is the central issue in the world today the "perpetual conflict" between the ideologies of capitalism and Communism? Whether the answer is yes or no depends on whether it is given by the power structure of the country with about 5% of the world's population but the demonstrated capacity to destroy all life on this planet, or by the peoples of the rest of the world. For the latter the answer is a clear negative.

Today, as in all of man's history, the central issue for the bulk of the world's population is the essential means of survival (safety of life, enough to eat, shelter, medical care when needed) and the prospect of their children's children developing into the human maturity which would be marked by self-respect and respect for the human animal. Modern science and technology offer the possibility of meeting this central issue.[1]

---

[1] Lee A. DuBridge, president of the California Institute of Technology, has said:

"From a purely technical standpoint, we now know enough to: Produce enough food to feed every hungry mouth on earth — and to do this even though the population should double or treble.

Make fresh water out of sea water, and thus irrigate all the earth's arid regions.

Produce enough energy from uranium to light and heat our homes and offices, electrify our railroads, and run all our factories and mills.

Build houses, buildings, and indeed whole cities, which are essentially weatherproof. . . ."

But, Dr. DuBridge points out, "A host of techniques capable of solving mankind's problems and easing his burdens cannot be used because we

The agenda for the bulk of the world's population is therefore headed by the problems of so organizing social relations and so using science, technology and social resources as to meet this elemental objective.

Cold-war-mindedness outside the United States, to the extent that it has existed at all, has been largely subordinated to regional, national and local problems. And these problems stem from historical processes which long predate the cold war. The cold war began with the rivalries and suspicions of the United States and the USSR during World War I. Superficially, it may have seemed to have subsided somewhat, in the course of the abnormal World War II relationships. But those relationships were only temporary. As one British student of the matter stated, as early as 1955: "That the Western distrust of Russian integrity and condemnation of the Soviet system never abated during the war years can be confirmed by many incidents which came during the war," with a number of which he deals, explaining that, "Once the war was at an end, the deep underlying estrangement was about to be revealed more blatantly."[2]

In fact, the reopening of the cold war did not wait until "the war was at an end." Certainly, by the early part of 1943, and intermittently thereafter, evidences of it were readable in our own newspapers.[3] Washington and London wartime as-

---

do not know how to bring adequate resources of money, labor and materials, and most of all, management to bear on the problems — or bring them to bear in such a way that the results achieved would, in a monetary sense, justify the costs." [Quoted in A. T. Waterman, "Science in the Service of Man," *Bulletin of the Atomic Scientists,* XVIII (May, 1962).]

[2] Kenneth Ingram, *History of the Cold War* (New York: Philosophical Library, 1955), Chap. i.

[3] See, for example, a February 8, 1943, *Pravda* announcement in *The New York Times* of February 12, 1943, that Russia meant to claim as Russian territory the Baltic states of Latvia, Lithuania, and Estonia. That announcement was "interpreted in Washington to apply also to parts of Poland and to Moldavia, Karelia and Bukovina," *ibid.,* February 27, 1943. So it was also during the last two years of the war. From Europe and Washington came news reports indicating the buildup of mutual animosities. See, typically, *The New York Times,* October 14, November 15 and 19, 1943, January 11, 18 and 27, February 13, July

sumptions that Moscow would cooperate in restoring the essentials of prewar — and pre-1917 — Europe and Asia were thus revealed simply not to have been realistic. They were not in accord with Russian historical ambitions and they certainly were not in accord with Communist Russian ambitions.

Washington and London persisted in pursuit of their own unrealistic goals — and the cold war was revived. And what appeared to be a spectacular reversal of Washington wartime policy toward the Soviet Union occurred within days of Franklin Roosevelt's death. It was actually the declared policy of the dominant advisers around Harry S. Truman from the time when he became President. Winston Churchill formally declared the opening of the cold war at Fulton, Missouri, in 1946 with Truman's blessing, but Truman's prior meeting with Soviet Foreign Minister Molotov on April 23, 1945, in Washington, had launched the new "get tough" policy that was to characterize United States policy for twenty years.[4] Within the much narrower limits of its material and manpower resources, the Soviet Union under Stalin reciprocated. Stalin consolidated Soviet influence in the Soviet sphere in Eastern Europe. But he and his successors reacted conservatively or not at all to the United States military encirclement of the USSR with bases in Italy, Greece, the Near East, Pakistan, and elsewhere. Looking back from the vantage point of 1967, it seems clear that the most significant development which exposed the fallacies in the bipolarized cold war concept was the Sino-Soviet split. Since 1960, the fact of a polycentric world power struc-

24, August 4, November 19, December 18 and 19, 1944. See also Demaree Bess, "What Does Russia Want?" *The Saturday Evening Post,* March 20, 1943.

[4] The occasion for the Washington meeting between Truman and Molotov was a courtesy call by Molotov upon the President, on Molotov's way to the San Francisco Conference. It appears that, insofar as identification of influential personalities may be important, perhaps Fleet Admiral William D. Leahy, Chairman of the Joint Chiefs of Staff, Chief of Staff to the President, and top-ranking man among the whole group of army, navy, and air officials, may have been in closest contact with the President of all Mr. Truman's advisers. See Frank Gervasi, "Watchdog in the White House," *Colliers,* October 9, 1955, p. 77; cited by D. F. Fleming in his *The Cold War and Its Origins* (Garden City: Doubleday, 1961), pp. 265–68.

ture in reality has given the lie to the facile and unreal doctrine of a cold war based on the assumed worldwide conflict of a monolithic Communist conspiracy and the equally monolithic forces of freedom and democracy.

In Europe, the cold war provided a double arch under which Europe was regenerated from the devastation of World War II. In the Soviet sphere of influence, the East Germans, the Czechs, and other Eastern Europeans proceeded to the joint tasks of rebuilding their material plant and developing institutional patterns more or less compatible with their aspirations to socialist models. And there was a partial integration of their economies with the Soviet Union. In Western Europe, lavish flows of United States funds and materials speeded "recovery" and penetrated deeply into the fabric of institutional organization and control. Under this double arch, old institutional forces gave rise to new autonomous tendencies. The resurgent power structures of the Western European countries produced the Common Market, the European Economic Community, and the French-activated atrophy of NATO. The shield of United States military force and cold war ideology in Western Europe was thus irretrievably shattered. In its stead, the regional and national concerns of Western European countries largely displaced cold war policies. Concurrently, comparable forces in Eastern Europe have produced diversity in national policies vis-à-vis the Soviet Union and the West which visibly negates the myth of a monolithic Communist bloc. Yugoslavia now differs no more from the other East European countries than they differ amongst themselves in their policy orientations. And tendencies toward rapprochement appear constantly between Soviet bloc states (especially Rumania) and West Germany, between the Soviet Union and the Vatican, between the Soviet Union and France, between the Soviet Union and Britain. In its lead editorial on the visit of Mr. Kosygin to Mr. Wilson in mid-February, 1967, *The New York Times* concluded:

> Kosygin and Wilson provided additional proof, if any were needed, that the era of ideological war is ending in Europe, and that the national interests — not propa-

ganda shibboleths — are the chief impellers of statements and the nations they rule.

Outside of Europe the regional and national forces unleashed by the impact of the technology of World Wars I and II on colonial systems and the remnants of feudalism were affected but not controlled by the cold war. China underwent its revolution partly before and partly outside the cold war. The Indochinese fighting — first against the Japanese, then the French and now the United States — clearly was the result of the breakdown of the nineteenth-century colonial policy. The fate of Indonesia is typical of the Asiatic situation. The Indonesian revolution, like that of Indochina, grew out of the crisis of colonialism following two world wars. The United States intervention there in recent years, as with Vietnam and China, is a subsequent development. From Algeria to Ghana, the political upheavals in Africa have arisen from forces indigenous to the area. Guatemala, Cuba, Brazil, and the Dominican Republic provide Latin American examples of similar historical processes which started to work themselves out in local terms and then incurred pressures from the United States.

This is not to say that cold war considerations were absent from revolutionary developments outside of Europe. It is simply that cold war considerations were not central to those developments. The peoples of those countries did not perceive those developments in cold war terms. And the rhetoric of those struggles was cast in local terms which were independent of the simplistic view of the world which the United States ideological formula prescribes.

If one were to analyze systematically the rhetoric with which issues involving national identity and national interest are treated, outside the United States since 1945, the salient themes would involve such items as economic recovery from war damage, relations with neighboring nations, relations with ex-"mother" countries, national destiny, and technical assistance from advanced nations. This is not to say that United States cold war rhetoric has been entirely absent. It has perhaps been most evident in West Germany, South Korea, Formosa, and South Vietnam. But the amount of such cold war rhetoric outside the United States has been roughly proportionate to the amount of United States influence, and, in the case of Eastern Europe, Soviet influence. Moreover, even where such cold war rhetoric has been imported, its form and content do not exhibit the consistency and intensity which it has had in the United States. The reason seems obvious: that the nations of the world have conducted their national affairs in terms of a rhetoric which reflects directly their perceived national interests.

President Lyndon B. Johnson, speaking to United States troops in Korea on November 1, 1966, said:

> There are 3 billion people in the world and we only have 200 million of them. We are outnumbered 15 to 1. If might did make right they would sweep over the United States and take what we have. We have what they want.[5]

As an expression of cold war policy this no doubt accurately states the United States point of view. But besides monstrous hubris, it betrays a vast ignorance of the way the peoples of the world see their chief problems.

Mass media policy outside of the United States corresponds to the style of dealing with international and national affairs which we have been describing. In the superpowers (USA, USSR, and China) and in nations under their control such as Formosa, Thailand, South Vietnam, Albania, and to a diminishing degree in the Eastern European nations neighboring on the Soviet Union, the information effectively available to the public from the mass media has been managed in the interest of the respective superpowers. To a lesser degree, but in an ideologically similar fashion, press controls in Spain, Portugal, Greece, Asia Minor, Latin America, African and some Southeast Asian countries have restricted the effective availability of information concerning international affairs. In the Scandinavian countries, the Netherlands, France, Germany, Italy, Switzerland, Ireland, the United Kingdom and

---

[5] *The New York Times*, November 2, 1966, p. 16.

Commonwealth countries, however, the information available to the public from the mass media provides a diversity sufficient to reflect the real problems which confront the peoples of the world. This is not to say that perfect freedom of information exists in this group of countries; merely that the myth of a bipolarized, rigidly structured world conflict is not the prime preconception which screens the information available to the public in those countries. And so in order to find out what has been happening in Vietnam since 1960, Americans have had to read French or English newspapers or magazines. Since 1949, a golden curtain has denied to the American audiences information about what was happening in China which did not pass through the China lobby filter. Similarly, information has been denied American audiences concerning Cuba which did not conform to the hard cold war line adopted by the United States toward that country in 1960. While all of this has been going on, the mass media of the relatively free-information countries have informed their populations substantially more fully about events in Vietnam, China, and Cuba as well as in the rest of the world.

In the United States the American mass media have consistently perpetrated the image of a monolithic Communist bloc, indoctrinated a disease theory of Communism, and accepted all the explicit and implicit assumptions of the web of cold war ideology.

To sustain popular support for cold war policies it has been necessary to construct a dream world of popular myths. Seven of these myths are: (1) We are good; they are bad. Thus William Shannon, a liberal columnist, writes: "The fundamental reason why our bases are justified and Russian bases are not justified is that we stand for what is good in the world and the Russians stand for what is evil."[6] (2) Communism is an international monolithic conspiracy. (3) Our foreign relations problems are caused by Communists and therefore counterrevolution anywhere in the world is good and will be supported by the United States. (4) The only appropriate response to foreign problems is military; we must be tough for

---

[6] Margaret Halsey, *The Pseudo-Ethic* (New York: Simon & Schuster, 1963).

force is the only thing Communists respect. "General Mark
Clark (Ret.) says the United States should resort to quick
retaliatory strikes against Communist North Vietnam and
'slaughter the hell out of them for a long time'. . . . Clark told
the 25th anniversary dinner of the Veterans of the 7th Regi-
ment: 'You can't do business with the Commies except by
force, and with no appeasement whatsoever.' "[7] (5) Foreign
policy is too complex for citizens to understand, and therefore
decisions are to be made by the President and his military
advisers; we must trust our leaders. At the same time the myth
is proclaimed that "we" are a pluralistic society, free to think,
act, participate since for us the individual is sacred, while
"they" are monolithic, told what to think and for them only
the system is sacred. (6) Technology, know-how and winning
are the all-important values and our high moral ends justify
our means. (7) We are the defenders of the "free world" and
we will take any risks to preserve our system. So, President
Johnson proclaims that, "History and our own achievements
have thrust upon us the principal responsibility for protection
of freedom on earth. . . . No other people in no other time
has had so great an opportunity to work and risk all for the
freedom of all mankind."[8]

In presenting a critical analysis of the mass media it is
essential to make explicit the underlying premise. This is that
freedom of expression and communication is essential to a
free society, to the survival and development of political
democracy. In the United States this was recognized in the
extraordinary guarantee provided in the First Amendment.
The importance of this principle has been further recognized
by the various subsidies provided for the dissemination of
information: cheaper mailing rates for newspapers, books and
magazines, and granting broadcasting licenses for the use of
public property. A second complementary premise is that this
freedom carries with it certain responsibilities and requirements. The purpose of mass communications in a democratic
society is (*should* be, *must* be, if democratic participation is
to mean anything) *education*; its function is a teaching func-

[7] *New York Post,* February 11, 1965.
[8] *The New York Times,* February 12, 1965.

tion.[9] Without the recognition and the practice of this function, "mass publicity in a mass society caters to mass amnesia." The obligation of the mass media, therefore, is "to remain disengaged from the apparatus, to criticize its aims and claims, to keep ethical questions in clear view, to let the citizenry know what is happening to them as they lean more and more on muscle and less and less on mind; and above all, to stay out of the cheering section."[10] In addition, to facilitate citizen participation, the mass media should serve as stimulator of the "civilization of the dialogue" — Robert Hutchins' definition of democracy.

How did a system designed for free expression of opinion come to accept a cold war propaganda rhetoric so out of touch with the real world? The answer is to be found in the nature of the politico-economic forces which have shaped the present United States system, from its very inception. The private business system, enjoying substantial autonomy from the political state and employing the possessive individualistic ethic from the 1790s has never abdicated it. In the 1890s, as Gabriel Kolko has demonstrated, conservatism vanquished the populist forces which threatened that autonomy.[11] The trade association movement and peak organizations representing private business had developed the organization and policy with which to hold the power which would keep business safely autonomous by the 1920s, as Robert A. Brady demonstrated in *Business as a System of Power.* In World Wars I and II, private business took advantage of the nation's dependence on it for the production of war goods even further to penetrate and control the national political apparatus and in the latter war largely escaped from the setbacks suffered in the depression years from the inroads of governmental activity in the interest of the poorest third of the population. By 1945, American capitalism was again secure and knew it.

[9] For an excellent statement of this responsibility, see W. H. Ferry, "Masscomm as Guru," in W. H. Ferry and Harry S. Ashmore, *Mass Communications,* An Occasional Paper, Center for the Study of Democratic Institutions.

[10] *Ibid.,* pp. 15–16.

[11] Gabriel Kolko, *The Triumph of Conservatism* (New York: Free Press, 1963).

Henry Luce expressed this confidence when he then looked forward to "The American Century" on the world scene.

An increasingly powerful role in the American capitalist system came to be played by that group of profit-seeking institutions specialized to the mass production of communications. The newspaper and magazine press, adopting the technology of high-speed printing in the 1890s, increasingly became big business, the rising price tag to enter which created more and more monopoly conditions. The trend toward fewer newspapers was continuous after about 1920 and the proportion of stateside communities with competitive newspapers shrank until today it is minuscule. The technology of motion pictures mechanized theatrical entertainment from the 1890s on and established the economic organizations which would mass-produce the value-forming entertainment later to be used for production of TV entertainment. Radio broadcasting found its role as an entertainment and marketing agent supported entirely by advertising and became a significant part of the national power structure by World War II. Television's structure and role grew naturally out of the technologies of radio and the motion picture industry and television's structure performed the additional function of integrating the control of big business within the communications field and beyond it. The controlling elements in the TV-radio-film industry today are found also to be among the twenty largest contractors with the Pentagon. The electronics industry which produced TV and radio was simultaneously developing the technological basis for automation and computer-processing of information of all kinds. The consequent integrative influence of the corporations which control this technology (e.g., IBM, ATT and a few others) served to knit together functionally the mass media and the large corporations which provide the bulk of the consumer goods and advertising revenue which supports the mass media.

Increasingly, it appears that the intelligence agencies (e.g., CIA) may guide the whole network of institutional control. Following the disclosure by *Ramparts* of CIA financial support of the National Student Association:

> The White House endorsed . . . a report saying that the Central Intelligence Agency had acted in accordance with Government regulations in its secret penetration of educational, labor and church groups. . . .
>
> Mr. Katzenbach, chairman of a special three-man committee assigned by Mr. Johnson to investigate the controversy surrounding the agency's funding of private institutions, praised the "many farsighted and courageous Americans" who had quietly cooperated with the Agency "in terms of challenge and danger to the United States and the free world." . . .
>
> The Central Intelligence Agency and the Security Council were reported to have been proud of the United States' first major postwar secret operation abroad, a well-financed program that helped defeat the Communists in the 1948 election in Italy.[12]

Is this an admission that in addition to providing financial support for "educational, labor and church groups," the CIA has penetrated business organizations in the mass media and elsewhere (where financial support from outside would not be necessary) thanks to *quiet* cooperation with the agency? Time may tell, but the question deserves an answer.

The principal *function* of the commercially supported mass media in the United States is to market the output of the consumer goods industries and to train the population for loyalty to the American economic-political system. The principal *product* of the advertiser-supported mass media in the United States is the audience, which is planned by skilled engineers, produced, and measured (by ratings).[13] The in-

---

[12] *The New York Times,* February 24, 1967.

[13] President Robert D. Stuart, Jr., of Quaker Oats Co., ". . . stated that while a show failure is certainly a painful headache for the network, it has even more serious consequences for the advertiser. Quaker Oats had budgeted 'O.K. Crackerby' on the basis of attaining a 30% audience share — reaching an average of 10,000,000 with a cost per thousand of $3.80. It ended up with a 24% share, barely an 8-million home audience, and a $5.04 cost per thousand — 33% less efficient than planned. Stuart compared this type of programming to 'wildcatting' for oil, without the oil companies' tax advantages and depletion allowances." *Variety,* April 20, 1966.

tended function of the news, the information, the entertainment in the advertiser-supported mass media is thus to provide the "free lunch," or the "loss leader" which draws the public into the measured, marketed audience. Speaking of news policy on TV, Edwin Newman of the National Broadcasting Company not long ago said:

> The general level of TV behavior in news reflected the American society [and] it was not reasonable to expect an organization that is financed by advertisers to pioneer in fields that may offend people. TV covers what flows naturally from the organizational system in which we live.[14]

The principal answer to the question, how a system designed for free expression of opinion has come to accept a cold war rhetoric so out of tune with reality, thus is that the system permitted the functions of *informing* citizens on issues

---

A standard set of specifications given by major national advertisers to writers of TV and radio dramas: "In general, the moral code of the characters in our dramas will be more or less synonymous with the moral code of the bulk of the American middle class, as it is commonly understood. There will be no material that may give offense either directly or by inference to any organized minority group, lodge, or other organizations, institutions, residents of any state or section of the country, or a commercial organization of any sort. This will be taken to include political organizations; fraternal organizations; college and school groups; labor groups, industrial, business, and professional organizations; religious orders; civic clubs, memorial and patriotic societies, philanthropic and reform societies (Anti-Tobacco League, for example); athletic organizations; women's groups, etc., which are in good standing. . . . There will be no material for or against sharply drawn national or regional controversial issues. . . . Where it seems fitting, the characters should reflect recognition and acceptance of the world situation in their thoughts and actions, although in dealing with war, our writers should minimize the 'horror' aspects. . . . Men in uniform shall not be cast as heavy villains or portrayed as engaging in any criminal activity. There will be no material on any of our programs which could in any way further the concept of business as cold, ruthless and lacking all sentiment or spiritual motivation." Quoted from "Madison Avenue's Program Taboos," *Variety,* October 26, 1960.

[14] Quoted by Jack Gould in his column, *The New York Times,* February 19, 1965.

of their times and of *entertaining* them to be taken over by institutions whose chief concern is their own self-perpetuation. The role of the family, the school, the church, and social organization, the political party as of 1967 has been eroded, distorted and perverted, while commercial vendors of popular culture substantially take their place as molders of character and vehicles for decision-making. In all of this, individual responsibility or virtue is irrelevant; the responsibility rests with institutions. But institutional responsibility is so fragmented and then integrated that the whole system is one of loosely organized irresponsibility for the consequences it produces.

In a large sense it is always true that the communications agencies, by the selection and priority given to content, set the effective agenda for members of societies. In the United States in the past half century the mass media have become not only the agenda-setters but they canalize the information concerning the agenda they set so that predetermined policies emerge from the political process.

The dream world of communism-as-a-disease rhetoric to which we referred to earlier has its domestic counterpart.[15] And the domestic and foreign portions neatly complement each other.

Granted that the mass media set the effective agenda for the public's attention, then what is *not put on the agenda* for discussion may be as significant as or even more significant than what is included in it.

Even before TV had assumed its present size and power, Paul Lazarsfeld and Robert Merton in 1948 said on this score:

> To the extent that the media of mass communication have had an influence upon their audiences, it has stemmed not only from what is said, but more significantly from what is not said. For these media not only

---

[15] Here the principal themes are (1) Look out for number one; let the other fellow take care of himself. (2) Public government is inherently bad and politics are dirty; private business is clean and efficient; public taxation is malevolent, private taxation benevolent; that government is best which governs least. (3) Private property approaches the sacred; public planning which would interfere with it is inherently bad.

continue to affirm the *status quo* but, in the same measure, they fail to raise essential questions about the structure of society. Hence by leading toward conformism and by providing little basis for a critical appraisal of society, the commercially sponsored mass media indirectly but effectively restrain the cogent development of a genuinely critical outlook.

This is not to ignore the occasionally critical journal article or radio program. But these exceptions are so few that they are lost in the overwhelming flood of conformist materials. . . . Minor tokens of "progressive" views are of slight importance since they are included only by the grace of the sponsors and only on the condition that they be sufficiently acceptable as not to alienate any appreciable part of the audience. Economic pressure makes for conformism by omission of sensitive issues.[16]

In today's world what we don't know *can* hurt us. But in addition to setting our agenda, the mass media, through the way in which they report or portray the problems, be it in news and commentary or in drama and documentary, educate us to support or oppose particular solutions for these problems. In practice "the medium mediates between us and raw reality, and the mediation more and more replaces reality for us."[17]

The failure of the media is documented in the United States by their almost total ignoring of crucial issues confronting American society, and the failure to communicate the urgency for positive action: the implications for our institutions of permanent preparation for war, the ramifications of the industrial-military complex; the paralyzing effect of the anti-Communist phobia. There has been little basic discussion of the

---

[16] Paul F. Lazarsfeld and R. K. Merton, "Mass Communication, Popular Taste and Organized Social Action," 1948, in W. Schramm (ed.), *Mass Communications* (Urbana: University of Illinois Press, 1949), pp. 459, 470–71.

[17] Randall Jarrell, "A Sad Heart at the Supermarket," in Norman Jacobs (ed.), *Culture for the Millions?* (Boston: Beacon Press, 1964), p. 105.

long-range implications of the United States declared intention to police the "free world." The media have not learned to deal with catastrophe before it happens. They have failed to present an agenda relevant to the deepest needs and concerns of our society.

Instead of helping to create an informed citizenry whose opinions are consulted by their leaders, it is more realistic to suggest that the media *manufacture* public opinion and then send out the pollsters to measure it. Some sort of sanction called "public opinion" is needed to validate administration proposals. What is the meaning of "public opinion" in this context? Public opinion as registered by the polls is not what we mean: for it is remote from the decision-making process. Actually the product of the press itself is taken as a substitute for meaningful public opinion. Crises are manufactured by managing the news, by using news as a weapon, by utilizing propaganda techniques with the cooperation of the mass media. The government uses information manipulation to give the people the illusion of participating in policy formulation.

Over and above the institutional inertia which manages the news, the very volume of information results in confusion and acceptance of the notion that issues are too complex for citizens to understand — hence we must rely on "experts." In addition, the volume of government and industry handouts creates a problem for the media and contributes to the standardization of content and the mobilization of response. "The press, once conceived as a check on arbitrary power, thus becomes one of its instruments. . . ."[18]

It is no longer possible to believe in freedom of access to the marketplace of ideas. Legally this may be true, but in practice few have the millions of dollars required to start a newspaper or to buy a radio or television station. As Lionel Gelber has said, "In an oligopoly of opinion . . . it is harder and harder for an individual view, without organized backing, to get itself heard. . . . The private individual is not techno-

---

[18] Christopher Lasch, "A Profusion of Information," *The Nation,* April 4, 1966, p. 398.

logically equipped to argue back."[19] Further, our social climate does not encourage the discussion of alternative policies or challenge to those in authority. There is general hostility to the conception of controversy as creative. The result is, as Judge Learned Hand noted, "we have deliberately systematized the production of epidemics in ideas."

News — especially foreign coverage — has become increasingly unimportant. Most daily newspapers have no foreign correspondents, but rely on the wire services or on lifting from *The New York Times*, a fact which led A. J. Liebling to comment that "the country's supply of foreign news . . . depends largely on how best a number of drygoods merchants in New York think they can sell underwear."[20] None of the five news agencies covers all countries of the world with competent reporters. Four are commercial organizations, engaged in producing, distributing and marketing a product — news. Conflicts of interest abound in the commercial wire services: in many countries the wire service both sells incoming news and buys outgoing news, and the price of doing the former is tailoring the latter to the country's propaganda policy. All services reflect the political and business systems of their home countries.

As commercial instruments designed to deliver a salable audience and serve as spokesman for the corporate system, the media in the States have also largely surrendered their obligation to be independent critics of government, notably in foreign policy matters. They have become almost an arm of the state. The techniques which are employed to sell goods and services are often applied to selling ideas, official interpretations and policy decisions. Erich Fromm defines the art of brainwashing as "suggestive-hypnoid techniques which produce thoughts and feelings in people without making them aware that 'their' thoughts are not their own."[21] There is a growing tendency to use and justify official deceit as an in-

---

[19] Lionel Gelber, *The American Anarchy* (New York: Schuman, 1953), pp. 142, 192.

[20] A. J. Liebling, *The Press* (New York: Ballantine Books, 1964), p. 9.

[21] *Liberation,* October, 1961, p. 11.

strument of national policy. In polite terms this is referred to as government management of news and it is noteworthy that it is most strongly advocated by the Department of Defense and the State Department.[22] There is nothing new in the attempt to manage news, though perhaps the amount of official distortion is a recent development. What does seem to be new is the general acceptance of the tactic without significant public protest, and the too common acquiescence of the media.

There seems to be a deliberate policy of cultivating ignorance. One aspect of this is the result of the media's conception of the reader, listener, or viewer as "a person stupider than the editor, whom the editor both fears and patronizes."[23] This attitude is expressed in the standard argument that the mass media cannot successfully, i.e., profitably, hold a higher standard than their publics. The cultivation of ignorance is further abetted by government or editorial policy. For example, much of the ignorance about China in the United States today stems from the fact that American reporters have been denied passports to travel there.[24] A more subtle encouragement to ignorance comes from distortion due to preconceived notions; the causes of this are harder to determine: pressures of established ideology, of received wisdom, a desire to make facts conform to a predetermined editorial policy, perhaps just plain poor reporting. Harrison Salisbury said the "shock value" of his despatches reporting civilian bombing casualties in North Vietnam would have been lessened had the American press not ignored articles by respected French correspondents. "It would be fair to fault the American press for not picking up those reports."[25] Because of the concept of news, even those papers whose editorial policies oppose the

---

[22] Theodore Draper, "The Dominican Crisis: A Case Study in American Policy," *Commentary,* December, 1965, and the remarks of Clifton Daniel about events preceding the Bay of Pigs, *The New York Times,* June 2, 1966.

[23] Mary McCarthy, "The Menace to Free Journalism in America," *The Listener,* May 14, 1953.

[24] Felix Greene, *A. Curtain of Ignorance* (Garden City: Doubleday, 1964).

[25] *The New York Times,* February 1, 1967.

Vietnam war and who have reported the reality of our tactics, perpetuate official government distortions in the bulk of their coverage.

With a few notable exceptions, most American institutions — schools, churches, universities — have accepted uncritically the fundamental assumptions of the cold war. Scholars who should have been independent critics, or at least independent observers, remained silent, or actively enlisted in the Establishment and joined the chorus, often providing elaborate justifications for official policy.

An unreasoned, unexamined acceptance of the cold war mythology was abetted by the doctrine of anti-Communism. Prominent public figures, publicists, erstwhile left-wing intellectuals, professional liberals, and many academicians discussed Communism as though it were a contagious disease. Rather than analyzing Communism as a political movement, a viable means of organizing a society, they talked of it as "total evil" and a "satanic" worldwide conspiracy.

Following the declaration of the cold war abroad, the anti-Communist crusade at home was sanctified by the Truman Loyalty Order of March 21, 1947. One is reminded of Senator Vandenburg's advice to President Truman to "scare hell out of the country" if he wanted to get money for his doctrine. Though allegedly adopted as a political tactic to head off more extreme action by the Republicans, the Executive Order provided justification for an ideological-screening program, extended to private employment as well as public.

The essence and essential motivation of the Washington cold war abroad is counterrevolutionary. Not fear of Communist expansion, but determination to prevent social revolution unacceptable to American interests anywhere in the world. At home the anti-Communist crusade served to stifle criticism and divert attention from the costs of our foreign interventions. In effect, the Loyalty Order removed all the restraints on the loyalty-security bureaucracy. What had been the aberration of a handful of antilibertarian congressmen and police agents now seemed to receive official approval — "the reality of the Communist menace became established by law . . . the American people concluded that there must be a

Communist menace because the government had set up a drastic program to deal with it."[26]

The anti-Communist phobia in the United States serves the same function as racism and anti-Semitism did in Nazi Germany. It serves to short-circuit rational, intellectual discussion of issues, policies, philosophical differences. In practice it has become paralyzing because "Communist" is used so loosely as to be all but meaningless. To those addicted to "anti-Communism," as distinct from non-Communism, facts, logic, reason have no impact. No reasoned analysis is effective in alleviating the terror the phobia produces. In its McCarthyite form, the phobia "managed, for a time, to make politics in America seem almost entirely a matter of idiotic chatter about 'loyalty risks' and 'security risks.' "[27]

We are fond of saying that the Russians and Chinese are prisoners of an unrealistic ideology. But we are prisoners of an ideology which is rigid and blind to the reality of what is happening in the world. Our leaders and our mass media generally lump together in undiscriminating denunciations all the different political forms which call themselves socialist or Communist. This reflects a bias which can only blind our public to the situation in the world. The "disease theory," Communism as contagious, leads to a shotgun attack on individuals and organizations advocating, or even discussing, ideas that challenge orthodox authority.

> We have transformed our politics into a faith, our way
> of life into a world crusade of absolute good against
> Satan's utter evil. Between such extremes there can be
> no dialogue, no agreement, and no peace until Satan is
> annihilated and communism vanishes from the face of
> the earth. In every area of his life we confront modern
> man with a choice of our absolute over Satan's. If he
> declines the choice, we isolate or bribe him until he
> acquiesces. If he chooses Satan's absolute, we will kill

[26] Benjamin Ginzberg, *Rededication to Freedom* (New York: Simon & Schuster, 1959), p. 123.

[27] Richard Rovere, *Senator Joe McCarthy* (New York: Harcourt, Brace, 1959), p. 17.

him on the spot, or, if that be found inopportune, add his name to the lengthening list of those to be ministered unto at Armageddon. The first commandment of the new secular religion is to hate; its last commandment is to kill. We have heard them repeated so often in schools, churches, government, and press that no one dreams any longer of challenging the concept that brought them forth. By rote we have learned the faith and now by rote we believe it.[28]

James Reston's recent *Artillery of the Press: Its Influence on American Foreign Policy* may be somewhat more remarkable for its gems of realistic wisdom than for its ambiguities and naive assertions. He opens realistically with:

My theme is that the rising power of the United States in world affairs, and particularly of the American President, requires, not a more compliant press, but a relentless barrage of facts and criticism, as noisy but also as accurate as artillery fire. This means a less provincial, even a less nationalistic, press, because our job in this age, as I see it, is not to serve as cheerleaders for our side in the present world struggle but to help the largest possible number of people to see the realities of the changing and convulsive world in which American policy must operate.

And in his final chapter, he deplores the fact that:

In the press, the networks, politics, the church, the schools and universities, and in commerce, the pressures today are running in favor of the [brainwashed] conformist majority that offers the popular and easy answers to our problems. . . .

---

[28] Dalton Trumbo, "Honor Bright and All That Jazz," in David Boroff (ed.), *The State of the Nation* (Englewood Cliffs: Prentice-Hall, 1966), pp. 114–15.

Dynamics of Cold War Psychology

JEROME D. FRANK, M.D.

For discussion purposes, our world-control policies can be divided into peaceful and military. The peaceful policies consist primarily of trying to buy political allegiance through economic aid of various sorts; the military ones have now come to focus primarily on the Vietnam war.

Certain aspects of our foreign aid programs may have blinded us to the fact that they may be increasing suffering instead of reducing it. The standard of living in many of the developing nations has been decreasing both relatively and absolutely, not only as a result of the economic disruption caused by political turmoil but by the growing discrepancy between prices of the raw materials they sell and the manufactured goods they buy. Futhermore, the administration of the aid programs is often *increasing* the gap between the rich and the poor in the recipient countries rather than raising the general standard of living. This occurs because the moral code in these countries places the welfare of one's family and friends ahead of that of the nation as a whole. As a result, the strongest impulse of anyone who gets into a position to do so is to increase his own and his kin's affluence. The net effect is to increase what the sociologists have called relative deprivation. Deprivation in itself is not a source of bitterness or violence. It has led to resignation. What is unendurable is the gap between what one has and what one thinks one is entitled to — that is, the gap between reality and expectation. In the traditional social systems of the undeveloped countries, it was taken for granted that some people would be rich and others poor, and the poor passively accepted their lot. The Recent political and social upheavals in these lands have upset this system, while the ideologies of both democracy and Communism preach the equality of man. The effect has been to create a surge of expectation in the poorer classes which cannot possibly be met. Dominantly and ultimately the resulting fury may be expected to be directed toward the traditional ruling affluent upper classes. But much of it is now aimed at the affluent nations, from whom the poor of the developing countries have quite urealistic expectations. As Dr. Brock Chisholm has pointed out, in past famines in India people starved to death without a murmur because this was fate. Now, they believe that the United States could save their lives by shipping wheat if it would, so their starvation becomes evidence of our indifference to their plight, and they may hate us for it.

The so-called shrinkage of the world through mass communication and transportation has heightened the sense of deprivation of the deprived groups. "A generation or two ago the Colombian peasant was considerably more content with his lot in life. But the cheap transistor radio has changed that. Today, the native of even the most remote Andean village is aware that a different way of life is available to some, if not yet to him. The result has been a new feeling of frustration and resentment."[1]

The way we give aid too often also creates resentment in the dominant groups of the societies receiving it, because it is so obviously an instrument of control. We demand concessions in return and try to tell them how and where to spend the money, insofar as money may be involved. It is humiliating enough to have to receive a handout without being told how one must spend or use it.

All too often, then, foreign aid programs, however well-meaning they may be, create resentment instead of gratitude. Since most Americans see only the charitable purposes of foreign aid, this response is incomprehensible to them. The

---

[1] P. Sukman, "South America's Shattered Showcase," *Fortune,* LXXII (November, 1965), 202.

counterresponse is to feel resentment toward the recipients for their ingratitude, and this, in turn, may blind us to some extent to the actual state of affairs.

Shifting now to the *military* aspect of our world-control policies, one psychological dynamism that obscures our vision of the effects of our policies is what has been called the strain to consistency. This simply means that individuals and groups must always justify their behavior. If they find themselves committed to a series of actions that violate their principles, they must either change their principles or reinterpret their actions to fit the principles. The latter is more common. Thus we have to tell ourselves that we are fighting for "freedom" and "democracy" throughout the world. This blinds us to the fact that we are supporting many governments which do not represent the aspirations or desires of their peoples. We justify our Vietnam adventure in part on the grounds that the smaller nations of the world are relying on us to protect them from Communism. What we really mean is that the *client govern-ments* of these nations are relying on us. As long as the governing group is anti-Communist, we assume that it speaks for the nation as a whole, although in many cases it repre-sents only a small governing clique.

This brings me to a final obstacle to our perception of the true nature of many of the revolutionary struggles going on throughout the world. This is that they are couched by both sides in ideological terms rather than simply in terms of the aspirations of deprived people for a better way of life and a greater sense of self-determination. This is a matter to which I shall return at some length presently.

Insofar as our world-control policies involve war, they have obviously dehumanizing effects. War does have a brutalizing effect, especially with respect to attitudes toward the "enemy." Rome killed every citizen of Carthage and ploughed the land with salt. Tamerlane erected mountains of human heads. To come to our own country, one need only recall our brutal treatment of the Indians in the eighteenth and nineteenth cen-turies. We killed some 600,000 and herded the rest on to what was considered relatively worthless land. In the twentieth century we have witnessed the ruthless bombings of Coventry

and Dresden, the firebomb raids on Japanese cities and, finally, Nagasaki and Hiroshima.

Our Vietnam war-making may actually be — in principle —
no more dehumanizing than war-making has traditionally
been. But never before in modern history has so powerful a
country rained such overwhelming murder and destruction
upon the people of so small a country.

In any case, the dehumanizing effects, at home, of our
efforts to achieve world control by war-making seem less
important than the increasing menace to the survival of our
civilization which this policy creates. With each successive
year, as weapons technology improves and genocidal weapons
spread, it becomes increasingly possible for a weak, small nation to destroy a much stronger and larger one. Sooner or
later, one of the weak nations, made desperate by the efforts
of a stronger one to subdue it, will do just this; and the United
States is the most likely victim. It is worth remembering that
even forty missiles in Cuba might have been enough to disrupt
our society.

Since the underlying purpose of this conference, if not the
directly expressed one, is to foster a change in attitude toward
the foreign policy of the United States, perhaps the best contribution I can make to the discussion is to review some of
the psychological aspects of national images that foster conflict and war. Psychological forces, to be sure, comprise only
a small part of the causes of war but — to the extent that
they are relevant — the better they are understood, the better
the chance of averting their catastrophic effects.

The aim of war is always to achieve victory over the "enemy" and is always conceived as protection or promotion of
"national interest." Many national interests are tangible, such
as control of territory, human labor, natural resources or
wealth, and it is usually assumed that these are what war is
about. But intertwined with these are interests determined by
the particular view or image of itself and its place in the
world that a nation holds, and these are the concern of psychologists. Mussolini conquered Ethiopia long after colonies
had become economic liabilities, because he envisaged Italy
as a great nation and all great nations had colonial empires.

The issues at stake in the Vietnamese war are heavily colored by psychological considerations. The desperate intensity of the struggle arises from the fact that both sides see themselves as fighting to defend certain abstract concepts. The primary one is "freedom," but this has quite different meanings for the Americans and the National Liberation Front. The latter are fighting to free their land from a foreign, white, neoimperialistic invader; the former, allegedly, to enable the Vietnamese to be free to choose their own form of government without foreign (North Vietnamese) interference. For many on each side, "freedom" is a component of a more comprehensive ideology, which they perceive as dangerously threatened by the ideology of the opponent. Thus, an American opinion survey in 1966 found that 76% of the respondents agreed that the United States actions in Vietnam were part of our worldwide commitment to stop Communism.

In addition, the United States, at least, is motivated by a determination to show the world that it is strong and steadfast and keeps its "commitments." It perceives this as essential to the maintenance of its national prestige, even though the government to which the original commitment was made has long since vanished, and that commitment bears only the faintest resemblance to the one Washington claims we are fighting to uphold.

From the psychological standpoint, then, the hope of learning to reconcile clashes of national world views without violence depends on understanding: (1) the contents of these views that lead to conflict, (2) why nations cling so tenaciously to them, and (3) the process by which they are maintained and changed.

Strictly speaking, of course, *nations* cannot have world views since they have no sense organs or mind. The term "national world view" is a convenient way of indicating the common features of the world views of most of the citizens of a nation and especially those who make and execute its policies.

An important aspect of the world view of every nation is its image of itself. This has at least three characteristics that contribute to war.

The first is national sovereignty. Each nation believes it has a right to pursue its "vital interests" regardless of the effect on the "vital interests" of other nations. Today, no nation can be secure at the expense of the security of other nations. Yet such is the power of this group standard that nations cannot be persuaded to relinquish aspects of their sovereignty which, in fact, they no longer possess.

A second troublesome component of national images is strength. With small nations, strength finds expression as a sense of unity of purpose and firmness of will in the face of a menacing world. With great nations, strength is additionally equated wth military power, probably because they have been formed through wars, and must have won more than they lost or they would not be extant today. Every national image is formed by memory of shared events, as preserved by history, and "war is the one experience which is dramatic, obviously important, and shared by everybody."

A corollary of a nation's self-image as sovereign and strong is the inevitability of "enemies." Before turning to the third attribute of the national image, ideology, let me digress a few moments to consider the image of the enemy. This seems to develop the same features no matter what the actual characteristics of the groups involved. Since these features contribute heavily to the outbreak and escalation of war, they require brief comment.

To forestall possible misunderstanding, let me stress at the start that enemies are usually not figments of the imagination. They are often real and very dangerous to one another and often possess the malevolent characteristics attributed to them. In any given case, certain aspects of the image may correspond more closely to the reality than others, but the degree of distortion is hard to determine. The chief danger of the *enemy image* is that it makes false perceptions as resistant to changes as if they were true ones. Only by becoming highly self-conscious about the enemy image can one hope to dispel its false aspects, and to this extent reduce the likelihood of war.

Reciprocal distortions of each other by enemies lead to what has been termed the mirror image of the enemy. A well-documented example is afforded by studies of mass media and elite publications in the Soviet Union and the United States. For example, each nation's media portray the other as aggressive and treacherous. Each society sees the national goal of the other as domination or expansion and its military doctrine as including a preemptive or preventive strike. Neither accepts the view that the goal of the other's operational code is self-preservation. Each sees its own motives for offering foreign aid as altruistic, but the other nation's as in the service of its expansion.

The mirror image of the enemy has also been documented by many firsthand observations. Some years ago, a scientist reported, after long, informal conversation with his Russian colleagues:

> The Westerner regards the Russians as controlled, for the most part without their knowledge, by an oligarchy of rapacious and malevolent men who seek constantly to foment world revolution. The Russian is equally convinced that the United States is being victimized by a small group of profit-mad "monopolists" who pull the strings that control government, press, and radio and who try to instigate wars in order to sell munitions.

Once the enemy image is formed, it strongly resists modification. There are several sources for this, of which perhaps the most significant is the so-called double standard of evaluation. The same behavior is viewed as in the service of good motives if performed by "our side" and as bad if performed by an "enemy." A psychologist tells of showing some American fifth- and sixth-graders photographs of Russian roads lined with young trees. When asked why the Russians had trees along the road, they answered: "So that people won't be able to see what is going on beyond the road," or "It's to make work for the prisoners." When asked why some American roads have trees planted along the side, the children said: "for shade" or "to keep the dust down."

The actual difficulties of communicating with an enemy, and the distortions and misinterpretations of information that does get through, result in a progressive hardening of the image. To the extent that fantasy fills the gaps left by insufficient information, the enemy image becomes colored by hopes and fears, and either type of distortion can make matters worse. The enemy arouses fears to the extent that his capabilities and intentions are unknown. Under such circumstances, it is easy to give way to what has been termed "possibilistic thinking," characteristic of the paranoid person. He views other persons' intentions in the light of the worst that could possibly happen instead of what the probabilities are. He may conclude, for example, that his psychiatrist is a secret member of the Communist Party or the FBI, assigned to get him into trouble. This is indeed possible, but not exactly probable. The mythical missile gap with which Americans frightened themselves in 1957 seems to have been based on similar thinking. By basing estimates of Russian intercontinental missile production on their largest possible capacity and the assumption of their worst possible intentions, instead of considering the probabilities, United States planners overestimated their production by about *thirty times.*

To the extent that fantasies about an enemy are colored by hope, they may foster underestimation of his actual power. Military overconfidence is usually characteristic of both sides before a war breaks out, and this was true of the Vietnam war. Remember Secretary McNamara's prediction that United States troops could leave Vietnam by the end of 1965. The belief of the National Liberation Front and the North Vietnamese that they could push us into the sea was equally unrealistic. This mutual underestimation of the "enemy" is based on wishful thinking, supported by the image of one's own nation as strong and united and the image of the enemy as irresolute and internally divided.

If the issues over which nations find themselves at odds include differences in their basic ideologies, wars between them tend to be especially bitter and prolonged.

Every nation has a more or less explicit ideology — that is, a belief system — that gives meaning to the lives of its citizens and includes an explicit or implicit program of action. An individual human life is a tiny, momentary flash of experience squeezed between two oblivions in a universe that appears indifferent to human existence. At least it gives no sign of caring that is convincing to everyone. The full recognition of one's utter insignificance is intolerable, so everyone has some way of shielding himself from the awful truth. Most persons accomplish this by identifying themselves with some enduring, and larger, group and, beyond this, by viewing their lives as in the service of some abstraction that is more or less permanent — like freedom, democracy, Communism, human welfare, or a religious creed. ". . . conceptual order to which we submit ourselves . . . is the bark that holds us above the sea of chaos in which we would otherwise drown. This is why people give their allegiance so passionately, so unreservedly, and so irrevocably to the grand doctrinal systems that invite their adherence."

Just as an ideology is essential to an individual's psychological well-being, so a shared ideology is a powerful cement holding a group together. Other things being equal, a nation's capacity to survive depends on its morale. This depends largely on its sense of shared purpose and destiny and the conviction that its way of life will ultimately prevail. When the citizens of a nation lose faith in its ideology, it eventually disintegrates. Hence ideologies of groups strongly resist change.

For true believers, the mere existence of another group professing a different ideology is threatening because it suggests that their own may be wrong. An atheistic society that survives and prospers is, by this very fact, a threat to a theistic one, and vice versa. The mutual sense of threat is sharply increased if each of the rival ideologies requires its adherents to convert or destroy believers in the other, as has been true in the past of Islam and Christianity and, more recently, capitalism and Communism. When the ideologies are incompatible, holders of each demand that the others surrender their beliefs. As Harvey Wheeler put it, "This is precisely the sort of change that most terrifies men and leaves them rootless."

For many persons, loss of their ideology, by depriving their lives of meaning, would be a kind of psychological death, harder to contemplate than biological death. Thus, wars initiated wholly or in part by ideological conflicts often terminate only when the adherents of one belief system are exterminated. More commonly, they have ended in mutual exhaustion after tremendous carnage, with the survivors still clinging to their respective beliefs. In such wars, combatants on each side are convinced that they will never yield, no matter how much suffering they have to endure. At the same time, each believes it can punish the other into submission. This belief should have died in Rome with the Christian martyrs. Its persistence in the face of all the evidence is one of the unsolved mysteries of human behavior.

Whereas, in the past, ideological wars often ended with mutual exhaustion, today they are more likely to end in mutual total destruction. The world can no longer afford holy wars.

Unfortunately, all the efforts of the United States to assert world control are couched in ideological terms — that is, the containment of Communism. This makes today's wars especially dangerous.

I should now like to turn to a brief consideration of some of the psychological features of war that press toward escalation. These all spring from the direct efforts to inflict pain and death on the adversary — efforts that sharply heighten the mutual enemy images and increase mutual hatred. These forces free man from the inhibition, apparently shared by all other vertebrates, against massive slaughter of his own kind.

Perhaps the most powerful inciter of hatred against an enemy is the injury and pain he inflicts, especially on civilians. War frees the behavior of soldiers from the customary moral restraints of peacetime living, so that rape and pillage have been features of all wars. In modern wars, killing of civilians has become increasingly prominent and has taken the additional form of mass destruction by shells or bombs. The ratio of Vietnamese civilians to soldiers killed by American weapons, for example, is said to be about ten to one. It is assumed that slaughter of civilians will weaken the morale of the enemy by terrorizing the population and by upsetting the soldiers through harming their families. In addition, especially in guerrilla wars, many of the fighters are not uniformed, so combatants cannot be distinguished from the noncombatants. The killing of civilians by enemy soldiers is still not generally accepted as legitimate by the side whose civilians are victimized, so it arouses stronger feelings than the killing of their soldiers, which is in accord with the rules of war. Furthermore, although only a minority of the population may be actually endangered, the rest identifies vicariously with them and shares the thirst for revenge. Thus, attacks against civilians by soldiers of each side confirm the other's view of them as bestial and justifies their own similar conduct.

The double standard of morality comes into play not only with respect to who is killed but how it is done. Conventions grow up according to which some methods of killing are legitimate and others are regarded as atrocities. This distinction appears to be unrelated to the suffering the different methods cause.

Often a method of killing is regarded as atrocious by one side but not by the other. Americans are outraged by disemboweling and beheading when performed by the Vietcong, and Communists refer to napalm and crop poisoning as "the most cruel and barbaric means of annihilating people."

Each side uses psychological defenses to hide its own atrocious acts from awareness or to justify them. Barbarisms of the enemy are attributed to their bestiality. Those of our side, if they are recognized as blameworthy at all, are viewed as regrettable necessities, or as justified by the atrocities of the enemy. For example, in the first world war, the German General Von Hausen justified rounding up and shooting civilian hostages on the grounds that the Belgian government "approved perfidious street fighting contrary to international law."

By playing up enemy atrocities, each side not only justifies its own cruelties and dehumanizes the enemy, but further inflames the blood lust of its own citizens. This can reach such a pitch that a respected United States senator could advocate "desolating" North Vietnam in reprisal for the threatened trial and execution of a few American fliers.

In short, the ferocity of war is both made possible and enhanced by the denial of humanity to the enemy. He becomes a statistic, an abstraction and a beast. The perception of the enemy as subhuman reinforces the conviction that, like an animal, he is impervious to reason and will respond only to punishment. This discourages search for means of peacefully resolving the conflict.

Escalation is fostered not only by the dehumanization of the enemy but by increasing psychological commitment on both sides. As military and civilian casualties mount and more and more resources are committed to the struggle, continuing the fight becomes a means of justifying past sacrifices. This behavior is somewhat like that of a gambler who keeps raising his bets to recoup his past losses. Only if the goal for which the sacrifices were made was really worthwhile would they be justified, and the way to prove that the goal is worthwhile is to redouble the efforts to gain it. The gambler is usually motivated in part by the need to show that his judgment or his faith in his skill — or his luck — that led him to incur his original losses is after all correct. That is, the purpose of the effort now becomes to protect his self-image, and achieving the goal becomes a means to this end.

In war the same process may lead to a shift in motivation. Proving one's courage and determination by continuing to fight becomes an end in itself, more important than gaining the object that the fight is about. A tragic example was the struggle for Verdun in the First World War, which continued after its "strategic significance . . . had long since passed out of sight; yet the battle had somehow achieved a demonic existence of its own, far beyond the control of generals of either nation. Honor had become involved to an extent which made disengagement impossible."

In view of the degree of commitment, the size of the stakes, and the heightened emotional tension, it is not surprising that combatants become increasingly wedded to their respective courses of action, and that filtering and reinterpretation of information to support these courses reaches monumental proportions.

Military leaders show extraordinary ability to reject information that would necessitate a change of their plans. Turning again to World War I, which is far enough in the past to be safely studied, nothing could convince Marshal Joffre in the first days of the war that the Germans were following the Schlieffen Plan and making their main thrust through Belgium, since to believe this would require that the French General Staff abandon their "Plan 17" which called for leaving two-thirds of the Belgian frontier undefended. On the third day of the war, "All day [Intelligence] collected information, interrogated prisoners, deciphered documents, and passed on its reports to [Operations]. All day [Operations] read the reports . . . and refused to believe them if they pointed to conclusions that would require the French to modify their plan of offensive." As late as the ninth day, when Germans were beginning to cross into Belgium, French headquarters felt "confirmed in the impression that the principal German maneuver would not take place in Belgium." One cannot help wondering what went on in General MacArthur's headquarters during the Korean War that enabled him to remain firm in the conviction that the Chinese would not cross the Yalu if he pushed through North Korea.

These considerations may help explain why it is hard for psychologists to place much faith in the capacity of modern nations to keep war limited. Each step up the ladder intensifies the forces toward further intensification of the conflict. As Homer put it some three thousand years ago in describing Strife, the War-god's sister: "Once she begins, she cannot stop. At first she seems a little thing, but before long, though her feet are still on the ground, she has struck high heaven with her head."

As I see it, any ground for hope — if there be any — must rest shakily on the fact that, in the past, human beings have sometimes managed to take action in time to avert disaster; although often they have waited until the last moment. The alcoholics' therapists talk about an alcoholic having to hit bottom before he joins "Alcoholics Anonymous." They add that some alcoholics are fortunate enough to be able to see bottom before they hit it. Many hit it without being saved. I am afraid that nations will have to move to the very brink of catastrophe before they seriously consider abandoning reliance on superior violence. Possibly, enough national leaders will be able to see bottom before they hit it and take this step in time to avert catastrophe. In the meanwhile, the efforts of groups and conferences like this one increase the chance for this happy outcome. Although we do not see too much tangible evidence of the results of our work, undoubtedly the considerations we are expressing are reaching the ears of national leaders, and perhaps are seeping into their minds.

May we hope that at the moment of showdown — or sooner — these ideas will come to the surface and exert enough effect to tip the balance in favor of survival?

The Moral Climate of the United States

GEORGE B. VETTER

The Declaration of Independence of the United States expresses a concern for "a decent respect for the opinion of Mankind, [for] liberty and social justice." It is relevant to explore the basis in fact for our attitude relating to these words.

We have traveled an interesting road from the "Witch Trials" at Salem to the McCarthy hearings of the early 1950s and to the continued perversions of the House Committee on Un-American Activities; we have covered a distance measured only by time from a war of continental imperialism against the American Indian (and the resultant slaughtering of some 600,000 of them), to the present United States war in Southeast Asia. The Monroe Doctrine-Platt Amendment rallying point for countless interventions in Central America in the 1800s and early 1900s offers us a comfortable comparison with the "Good Neighbor Policy" — and the subsequent invasions of Guatemala (1954), Cuba (1961), the Dominican Republic (1965) and elsewhere.

The United States is now engaged in armed intervention in at least ten nations of the world. It is using the most sophisticated techniques of anti*population* warfare in history. Napalm, phosphorus, biological and chemical warfare, antipersonnel fragmentation bombs and "Puff, the Magic Dragon" are a few examples of the means by which we pursue our indiscriminate policy of applied terror tactics. And all of this in the name of

"freedom, democracy, and anti-Communism." The attitude of
the American people today toward these revelations differs
only in slight degree from that of our eighteenth-century an-
cestors. The picture of the colonial patriarch watching, with
ill-concealed relish, the reaction of an Indian couple as they
are forced to witness their two children slowly tortured to
death can be compared to twentieth-century viewing of United
States aircraft dropping napalm on civilian populations in
Southeast Asia, or in Latin America, or in Africa. The difference is to be found only in the distance and the detachment.
To that extent, we have made progress. We can now "watch"
our atrocities on television in comfort and anonymity. We
have become sophisticated. We are even privileged enough to
be able to read an article by Dr. Clifford F. Rassweiler entitled "What's So Terrible About Germ Warfare?" (in a
January, 1965, issue of *The Saturday Evening Post*). Dr.
Rassweiler, who is a vice president of Johns Manville Corporation and adviser to several government agencies, including
the Pentagon, suggested that the use of chemical warfare really isn't so bad either.

Peace reigns in C. Wright Mills's trinity of power and the
public, as always, is content to go along. A recent Harris Poll
(May 16, 1967) showed that 72% of the people were in
favor of U.S. military presence in Vietnam, 59% called for
further escalation of the war, and 45% favored a "total military victory." Dissent and demonstrations notwithstanding,
we are left with a basic necessity to "support our boys." (See
Newsweek, July 10, 1967.)

Further, to quote William S. White in his column of April
14, 1967:

> The best news about Vietnam is coming not from the
> battlefronts, though the situation there is progressively
> improving, but rather from within the American political
> community. The policy of determined United States mili-
> tary resistance to the Communist invasion of South Viet-
> nam has now reached a point of bipartisan support so
> massive as all but to guarantee that the 1968 Presidential

campaign will be free of divisive in-fighting on that policy here at home.

Our popular information media are again able to maintain a predictable and controlled public opinion and the mass of people is induced to go along with the dominant mythology. There is, however, an illusion of freedom in communications, in that a few heretics are left around unthrottled. These dissidents remain, for the most part, lone voices, influencing few, and help give substance to this illusion of freedom. But the daily grist of the propaganda mills drowns all opposition and in the end does an even better job of opinion control because of the openly allowed opposition.

The continuing burden of this propaganda campaign has been a combination of fear and Satanism. To move people to action, an endless litany of fear of both Communism as an evil, and of the nations embracing it as aggressive, militant enemies, has been stressed by all possible media of communication. The pious are constantly reminded that Communism is Godless, the petite bourgeoisie that its means of living will be destroyed, the farmers that their land will be collectivized, the teachers are told that they will have to teach dialectic materialism, and all are told that the midnight knock on the door will be inevitable. These horrors are to be brought on a wave of force and violence, of which the Communists have a monopoly.

This American bent for "moralizing and angelizing their 'side,' while demonizing the other side," provides us with a not so surprising relationship vis-à-vis Washington leadership. As stated by the late Professor Spykman of Yale:

> The heritage of seventeenth-century Puritanism is responsible for one of the characteristic features of our [American] approach to international relations. Because of its concern with ethical values, it has conditioned the nation to a predominantly moral orientation. It makes our people feel called upon to express moral judgments about the foreign policies of others and demand that our presidents transform the White House into an inter-

national pulpit from which mankind can be scolded for the evil of his ways.[1]

With this *Weltpolitik* as a base, we are able to sustain a multitude of contradictions:

a. We are told that a Communistic economy is by definition so inefficient that it is unable to produce even the bare necessities of life for its citizenry — but that we now have to spend $20 to $60 billion a year to prevent this menace from conquering the world.
b. North Vietnam is depicted as a puppet of Red China in spite of a millenium or more of warfare between these states, and also in spite of an absence of any report indicating the presence of Chinese soldiers on Vietnamese soil — but South Vietnam is NOT our puppet, in spite of our continued support of a variety of coups designed to maintain United States control of the government in Saigon, and also in spite of the fact that we presently have some half-million of our best-equipped soldiers on Vietnamese soil [and elsewhere in Southeast Asia] and untold masses of matériel, to protect the Saigon regime from its Vietnamese opposition.
c. The guided missiles we have installed in Turkey are clearly no menace to the Soviet Union and give her no cause to intervene — but a Soviet rocket in Cuba is an entirely different situation.
d. Our Monroe Doctrine clearly permits us to exercise sovereignty over two continents — but Chinese concern over events directly on her borders is concrete evidence of her aggressive nature and character.
e. We swear by the principle of freedom of the seas — but when it suits us, we interdict shipments to any country whose government happens not to suit us.

This phenomenon is further exemplified by what has come to be called the "Credibility Gap." As stated by J. Russell Wiggins, Editor of the Washington *Post*: "Our government

---

[1] N. J. Spykman, *America's Strategy in World Politics* (New York: Harcourt, Brace, 1942), p. 216.

repeatedly resorts to lies in crises, where lies seem to serve its interests best. It will one day be unable to employ the truth effectively when truth would serve its interests best. The government that too readily rationalizes its right to lie in crisis will never lack for either lies or crises." It is on this level where the people's right to know is precariously balanced with the "people's right not to know," where diplomacy and political maneuver reinforce our "end justifying the means" Machiavellian system of government.

In 1960, the government of Dwight D. Eisenhower lied about the U-2 plane shot down over Russia. In 1961, the government of John F. Kennedy lied about the Bay of Pigs invasion. In 1964, the government of Lyndon B. Johnson lied to us about the Tonkin Gulf attack, and again in 1965, regarding the truth about the happenings in the Dominican Republic. These are but a few examples where morality and necessity clash, always at the expense of morality.

In August, 1966, the Prime Minister of Singapore, Lee Kuan Yew, claimed a CIA agent had offered him a $3.3 million bribe five years before — and the State Department promptly denied the charge. Kuan Yew then produced an earlier letter from Secretary of State Dean Rusk in which Mr. Rusk had apologized for the incident — and the State Department admitted that the charge was accurate. Then and now, the State Department insists the denial was a result of a bureaucratic error; that the man issuing the denial hadn't known the facts.

In the spring of 1965, the government announced that U.S. forces were landing in the Dominican Republic to protect "thousands" of Americans and others imperiled by the uprising there. Later, as the U.S. force grew greatly, there was another official reason given for the intervention — to prevent a Communist take-over. Describing the dangers, President Johnson told a news conference on July 17 that "some 1,500 innocent people were murdered and shot and lying in the streets. . . ." and that "there are some 53 Communists presently in control of the rebel forces." (Perhaps reminiscent of the days of the late junior senator from Wisconsin.) Later information proved that the body count was 6, not 1,500, and the "Communist count" was three, not fifty-three.

In October, 1963, Defense Secretary Robert McNamara said that we were winning the war in Vietnam and predicted that the bulk of American military forces would be out of the area by the end of 1965. Late in 1965, the Secretary said that neither additional U.S. combat troops nor more money would be needed in Vietnam and "we have *stopped* [emphasis supplied] losing the war." We now have in excess of 500,000 ground troops in Vietnam, with no comment as to who is winning the war. Perhaps it would not be improper to remind ourselves at this time of Assistant Secretary Arthur Sylvester's statement from the Pentagon, in which he asserted the "government's right to lie in emergencies."

Reports of war casualties in Vietnam offer us another indication of our government's thinking along these lines. One might ask how the government can call our losses "light" when a whole company has been wiped out? The government's answer is that "this is an accurate appraisal of the situation when an entire battalion was involved *somewhere in the area.*" (Emphasis supplied.)

As it is with all nations, American history abounds, not only in examples of official secrecy, but also in contradictions between government postures and government acts. During the Texas revolution against Mexico the United States government pretended to be neutral, but wasn't. In 1952 the Eisenhower administration came in with much talk of "massive retaliation" and the "unleashing" of Chiang Kai-shek, and delivered neither. In 1961, according to Arthur Schlesinger, Jr., President Kennedy told UN Ambassador Adlai Stevenson *"you have the hardest thing in the world to sell, it really doesn't make any sense, the idea that Taiwan represents China* — but if we lose this fight, if Red China comes into the UN during our first year in town, your first year and mine, they'll run us both out...."* (Emphasis supplied.) In the campaign of 1964, Lyndon Johnson appeared as the apostle of restraint in Vietnam and Barry Goldwater a champion of escalation — and the war was escalated a year later under President Johnson.

The list is endless, the actors change, but the production remains the same. At this stage it behooves us to ask ourselves where our responsibilities lie. Our position stems from the resolute belief that, as a society, we are justified in using all means available to us to achieve a just and worthwhile end. Of course, we always reserve the right to insert definitions of "just" and "worthwhile." This was stated rather succinctly by Professor Henry Steele Commager in the *Saturday Review*, July 10, 1965, "A Historian Looks at Our Political Morality":

> The arguments that were invoked to justify religious wars and religious persecution in past centuries are invoked now to justify sleepless hostility to Communism — even preventive war,

and that

> for years now we have heard, and not from extremists alone, that the struggle between democracy and Communism is the struggle between Light and Darkness, Good and Evil, and that the moral distinction is an absolute one.

It is just this "evil-sin-devil complex" that provides us with the rationale for our public posture and until we are able to strike at the roots of our Puritan heritage, we must content ourselves with a continuing procession of the examples cited above. And these examples are, of course, merely the symptoms of the disease and not the disease itself. As long as we are willing to accept these conditions then we shouldn't be surprised at the resultant moral decay that surrounds us. Official pronouncements of today have a ring vaguely reminiscent of those of another regime under similar circumstances:

> I have offered the enemy my hand again and again. It was the very essence of my program to come to an understanding with them. We have never demanded anything from them and we have never insisted on anything. I repeatedly offered my hand, but always in vain. Even after the war had begun there were possibilities for an

agreement . . . I demanded nothing. Still all was in vain.
. . . We have been drawn into this war against our will.
No man can offer his hand more often than I have.[2]
(The speaker is Adolf Hitler.)

There can be no doubt that the legacy of the cold war years has left a direct imprint on the American scene. Extremism (which, of course, ". . . in defense of freedom is no vice") is a permanent part of the landscape. Free travel, free assembly and free speech are not "rights." We must be protected from ourselves! A member of the Indiana State Textbook Committee attempted to ban any reference to the story of *Robin Hood* in the state school system since ". . . there is now a Communist directive in education to stress the story of *Robin Hood* . . . because he robbed the rich and gave to the poor. That's the Communist line."[3] The works of José Clemente Orozco were banned at the University of California at Los Angeles because of the artist's "leftist leanings"; the American Legion decried the Girl Scouts as being a subversive organization; former Texas Governor Allan Shivers called for the death penalty for membership in the Communist Party;[4] and a statue of Tom Paine was not allowed in the town square of Providence, Rhode Island because he was "too controversial a figure."

There are other, more familiar, indices of an alienated society. As stated in a bulletin of the Department of Health, Education and Welfare:

> . . . juvenile court cases per 1,000 children in the 10 to 17 year age group have almost tripled in the past two decades . . . there are more than five million alcoholics in the Nation today. . . .[5]

Increased crime and divorce rates are indicative of our

---

[2] The quotation is from a speech made by Hitler to the German people shortly before the Battle of Stalingrad.

[3] *The New York Times,* November 14, 1953.

[4] *Ibid.,* February 12, 1954.

[5] *Converging Social Trends: Emerging Social Problems,* U.S. Department of Health, Education and Welfare, Publication Number 6, 1964.

basic lack of stability. The increase in the rate of violent crimes is most spectacular. We complacently accept large-scale price fixing and other examples of "big business" swindles as being routine. Misappropriation of funds in public office and favoritism in the awarding of government contracts do not evoke public protest (the Apollo and TFX contracts still have not been explained). And the trend continues. A recent National Crime Commission report stated, in part:

> White-collar crime pervades American society causing enormous harm. The cost of such white-collar crimes as tax and stock fraud, embezzlement, price-fixing, food and drug and antitrust violations runs into billions of dollars. . . . Aside from its dollar cost, white-collar crime damages the nation's social and economic institutions and affects [and reflects] the moral climate of our society . . . tending to erode the moral base of the law and gives other kinds of offenders an opportunity to rationalize their crimes.[6]

Headlines of "big business" and government involvement in what has come to be thought of as "legalized crime" are all too frequent. We are only momentarily indignant, if at all, over widespread corruption in the handling of government contracts and regulatory control of industry. Examples of recent news items, such as the following, are "normal" occurrences:

LOCAL EDITOR BATTLES OIL SHALE GIVEAWAY TO MAJOR
OIL COMPANIES

---

[6] *Los Angeles Times,* June 25, 1967. Partial estimates of the costs of white-collar crime were listed as follows: "Between $25 billion and $40 billion of taxable income is not reported to the federal government annually. . . . Americans spend nearly half a billion dollars a year on 'worthless or extravagantly misrepresented' drugs and therapeutic devices. . . . Losses from fraudulent and deceptive practices in the home repair and improvement field amount to between $500 million and $1 billion annually. . . . Fraud in the automobile and repair field is in the $100 million annual range."

TFX CONTRACT CALLED POLITICAL SCANDAL

EL PASO NATURAL GAS TRIES FOR BIGGEST PIPE LINE MONOPOLY GRAB IN HISTORY

MAJOR U.S. ELECTRONICS FIRMS CHARGED IN GIGANTIC PRICE FIXING

FLORIDA POWER AND LIGHT ACCUSED OF OVERCHARGING PUBLIC BY MILLIONS OF DOLLARS

BOBBY BAKER TIED IN WITH APOLLO SCANDAL. CONTRACT WITH NORTH AMERICAN AVIATION INVESTIGATED

COLONIAL PIPE LINE COMPANY INVOLVED IN CONSPIRACY AND BRIBERY. ANTI-TRUST LAWS VIOLATED

$3.5 BILLION GOUGE LAID TO OIL PRICE-FIXING CARTEL INCLUDES LARGEST U.S. OIL COMPANIES

MEAT-PACKING INDUSTRY CHARGED WITH WIDESPREAD USE OF DISEASE-CAUSING MATERIAL AND FAULTY LABELING

And with it all, we still refuse to reexamine our basic societal structure in an attempt to understand the source of our dehumanization. A vital insight was offered by the late British historian, R. H. Tawney:

[The revolt] has its source, not merely in material miseries, but in resentment against an economic system which dehumanizes existence by treating the mass of mankind, not as responsible partners in the co-operative enterprise of subduing nature to the service of mankind, but as instruments to be manipulated for the pecuniary advantage of a minority of property owners, who themselves, in proportion as their aims are achieved, are too often degraded by the attainment of them.[7]

A materialistic society depends upon man's baser motives for its continuation. Since the acquisition of material "things" becomes a standard measurement of achievement and desirability, man himself thus tends to look upon his being as something secondary — he begins the process of alienation. There evolves a dissociation between that which man produces and acquires, and the one doing the producing. We find ourselves but a cog in this vast, private profit production apparatus, and with it all we wonder why we feel frustrated. And the time is fast approaching when even that luxury may be conditioned out of us. Today, we do not question; tomorrow, there may be no need to question. Our distorted sense of priorities has left us empty — dehumanized.

A pertinent example of our sense of priorities as an outgrowth of the system is our attitude toward solving the pressing technological problems facing the world today. The *problem* was most graphically presented in the Sylvia Porter column in the *New York Post* of March 8, 1967, in part:

1. The world's population now stands at 3.35 billion, more than double the figure of 1900, and at the present rate will reach 7 billion by the year 2000. This is only 33 years, or one generation away.
2. Half of today's world population has been born since the end of W.W. II. Each year 65 million people are added to the world total, an average of 180,000 a day.
3. Of the children now being born, 85% are born in the underdeveloped countries of Asia, Africa and Latin America.
4. The population of Latin America is now tripling every 35 years.
5. The population of Pakistan is predicted to triple (from 100 million to 300 million) by the year 2000.

[7] R. H. Tawney, *The Radical Tradition,* Rita Hinden (ed.) (London: Allen & Unwin, 1964), p. 139.

"Within a decade," says Pakistan's presiding Ayub Khan, "human beings will eat human beings in Pakistan."

6. India is adding 1 million new people *each month* and at the current rate her population will reach 1 billion by the year 2000 — only 33 years away.

7. World population is now growing at the rate of 2% per year — but the world's food supply is growing at a rate of only 1% per year.

8. 70% of the world's children under six years of age already suffer from malnutrition.

9. Starvation is now [directly] *killing* an estimated 12,000 people *each day* — more than 4 million each year.

10. Two-thirds of the world's population lives in areas where per-capita income is $160 per year or less.

11. Of the adults in Asia, Africa and Latin America, 750 million have never been to school. World illiteracy has grown by more than 200 million since *1960*.

The *answer* to these pressing problems of mankind, with which we are all too familiar, was supplied by Dr. L. T. Radir, president of Sperry Rand's Univac Division:

> From a purely technical standpoint, we know enough to produce food for every hungry mouth . . . We know how to build virtually indestructible autos, washing machines, houses and other devices that will last a hundred years or more. We know how to build entire cities which are essentially weather-proof. Why do we not do these things? *Today, it is not economically feasible.*[8] (Emphasis supplied.)

When human needs are in conflict with the economics of production, the former is always sacrificed to the latter. And this is the basis of the real war all mankind is engaged in. Yet we are still able to ignore the major issues and to bring home

---

[8] *Automation: The Potential for Prosperity,* a Sperry-Rand Corporation publication, Winter, 1964.

to the public the necessity for rigidly supporting the admittedly nationalistic, narrow idea of United States vital interest in a cold war against the needs and demands of some 70% of the people of the world, i.e., the underdeveloped countries of the world.

Admittedly, in wars of all kinds a level of uncritical "my country, right or wrong" type of patriotism tends to develop. But in our continuing crusade against the irrepressible demands of the vast majority of mankind to devise a means of securing the basic necessities of life, we have reached a level of "social blindness" unprecedented in history. And we are the first casualty. We are faced with an all-pervasive alienation which threatens our very being, a dissociation so aptly phrased by Richard Elman in *The Commonweal* (June 26, 1965):

> Must it always be so — never quite coherent, perceived hermetically, a rushing about the ears, without obvious sequences, a garble of sounds, confusing us, leaving us directionless, without any moral center, quite mortal, solitary, quite without any point of reference aside from our dissociated selves?

The contradiction is not to be found solely in our current posture, for it follows a centuries-old tradition of elitist, economic expediency. If we are to understand today's "social blindness," we must learn to understand the functional historical development of our society and of our nation.[9] Then, and only then, can we attempt to build a society based on the true foundations of humane consideration and equality of man. When we realize that the contradictions lie in our hollow shibboleths and fine-sounding rhetoric, then we can begin to develop a "decent respect for the opinion of Mankind, [for] liberty and social justice."

---

[9] See Neal D. Houghton, "Social Structure and Foreign Policy of the United States," *Year Book of World Affairs, 1961, XV* (London: London Institute of World Affairs, University of London), 93–134; "Historical Bases for Prediction in International Relations," *Western Political Quarterly,* XVII (December, 1964) 632–58; and "The Cold War and Social Blindness," an address in the *Plain Talk Series,* University of Saskatchewan, February 21, 1966.

The Revolution of Rising Expectations: Rhetoric and Reality[1]

ROBERT L. HEILBRONER

Is the United States fundamentally opposed to economic development? The question is outrageous. Did we not coin the phrase, "the revolution of rising expectations"? Have we not supported the cause of development more generously than any nation on earth, spent our intellectual energy on the problems of development, offered our expertise freely to the backward nations of the world? How can it possibly be suggested that the United States might be opposed to economic development?

The answer is that we are not at all opposed to what we conceive economic development to be. The process depicted by the "revolution of rising expectations" is a deeply attractive one. It conjures up the image of a peasant in some primitive land, leaning on his crude plow and looking to the horizon, where he sees dimly, but for the *first time* (and that is what is so revolutionary about it), the vision of a better life. From this electrifying vision comes the necessary catalysis to change an old and stagnant way of life. The pace of work quickens. Innovations, formerly feared and resisted, are now eagerly accepted. The obstacles are admittedly very great — whence the need for foreign assistance — but under the impetus of new hopes the economic mechanism begins to turn faster, to

[1] This article was originally published under the title 'Counterrevolutionary America," in *Commentary* Magazine, April, 1967. Copyright, ©, 1967, by Robert Heilbroner.

gain traction against the environment. Slowly, but surely, the Great Ascent begins.

There is much that is admirable about this well-intentioned popular view of "the revolution of rising expectations." Unfortunately, there is more that is delusive about it. For the buoyant appeal of its rhetoric conceals or passes over in silence by far the larger part of the spectrum in realities of the development process. One of these is the certainty that the revolutionary aspect of development will not be limited to the realm of ideas, but will vent its fury on institutions, social classes, and innocent men and women. Another is the great likelihood that the ideas needed to guide the revolution will not only be affirmative and reasonable, but also destructive and fanatic. A third is the realization that revolutionary efforts cannot be made, and certainly cannot be sustained, by voluntary effort alone, but require an iron hand, both in the spheres of economic direction and political control. And the fourth and most difficult to face is the probability that the political force most likely to succeed in carrying through the gigantic historical transformation of developments is some form of extreme National Collectivism or Communism.

In a word, what our rhetoric fails to bring to our attention is the likelihood that development will require policies and programs repugnant to our "way of life," that it will bring to the fore governments hostile to our international objectives, and that its regnant ideology will bitterly oppose capitalism as a system of world economic power. If that is the case, we would have to think twice before denying that the United States was fundamentally opposed to economic development.

But is it the case? Must development lead in directions that go counter to the present American political philosophy? Let me try to indicate, albeit much too briefly and summarily, the reasons that lead me to answer that question as I do.

I begin with the cardinal point, often noted but still insufficiently appreciated, that the process called "economic development" is not primarily economic at all. We think of development as a campaign of production to be fought with budgets and monetary policies and measured with indices of output and income. But the development process is much wider and deeper than can be indicated by such statistics. To be sure, in the end what is hoped for is a tremendous rise in output. But this will not come to pass until a series of tasks, at once cruder and more delicate, simpler and infinitely more difficult, has been commenced and carried along a certain distance.

In most of the new nations of Africa, these tasks consist in establishing the very underpinnings of nationhood itself — in determining national borders, establishing national languages, arousing a basic national (as distinguished from tribal) self-consciousness. Before these steps have been taken, the African states will remain no more than names insecurely affixed to the map, not social entities capable of undertaking an enormous collective venture in economic change. In Asia, nationhood is generally much further advanced than in Africa, but here the main impediment to development is the miasma of apathy and fatalism, superstition and distrust that vitiates every attempt to improve hopelessly inefficient modes of work and patterns of resource use: while India starves, a quarter of the world's cow population devours Indian crops, exempt either from effective employment or slaughter because of sacred taboos. In still other areas, mainly Latin America, the principal handicap to development is not an absence of national identity or the presence of suffocating cultures (although the latter certainly plays its part), but the cramping and crippling inhibitions of obsolete social institutions and reactionary social classes. Where landholding rather than industrial activity is still the basis for social and economic power, and where land is held essentially in fiefdoms rather than as productive real estate, it is not surprising that so much of society retains a medieval cast.

Thus, development is much more than a matter of encouraging economic growth within a given social structure. It is rather the *modernization* of that structure, a process of ideational, social, economic, and political change that requires the remaking of society in its most intimate as well as its most public attributes.[2] When we speak of the revolutionary nature

---

[2] See C. E. Black, *The Dynamics of Modernization*.

of economic development, it is this kind of deeply penetrative change that we mean — change that reorganizes "normal" ways of thought, established patterns of family life, and structures of village authority as well as class and caste privilege.

What is so egregiously lacking in the great majority of the societies that are now attempting to make the Great Ascent is precisely this pervasive modernization. The trouble with India and Pakistan, with Brazil and Ecuador, with the Philippines and Ethiopia, is not merely that economic growth lags, or proceeds at some pitiable pace. This is only a symptom of deeper-lying ills. The trouble is that the social physiology of these nations remains so depressingly unchanged despite the flurry of economic planning on top. The all-encompassing ignorance and poverty of the rural regions, the unbridgeable gulf between the peasant and the urban elites, the resistive conservatism of the village elders, the unyielding traditionalism of family life — all these remain obdurately, maddeningly, disastrously unchanged. In the cities, a few modern buildings, sometimes brilliantly executed, give a deceptive patina of modernity, but once one journeys into the immense countryside, the terrible stasis overwhelms all.

To this vast landscape of apathy and ignorance one must now make an exception of the very greatest importance. It is the fact that a very few nations, all of them Communist, have succeeded in reaching into the lives and stirring the minds of precisely that body of the peasantry which constitutes the insuperable problem elsewhere. In our concentration on the politics, the betrayals, the successes and failures of the Russian, Chinese, and Cuban revolutions, we forget that their central motivation has been just such a war *à l'outrance* against the archenemy of backwardness — not alone the backwardness of outmoded social superstructures but even more critically that of private inertia and traditionalism.

That the present is irreversibly and unqualifiedly freed from the dead hand of the past is, I think, beyond argument in the case of Russia. By this I do not only mean that Russia has made enormous economic strides. I refer rather to the gradual emancipation of its people from the "idiocy of rural life," their gradual entrance upon the stage of contemporary existence. This is not to hide in the smallest degree the continuing backwardness of the Russian countryside where now almost 50% — *and formerly perhaps 80%* — of the population lives. But even at its worst I do not think that life could now be described in the despairing terms that run through the Russian literature of our grandfathers' time. Here is Chekhov:

> During the summer and the winter there had been hours and days when it seemed as if these people [the peasants] lived worse than cattle, and it was terrible to be with them. They were coarse, dishonest, dirty, and drunken; they did not live at peace with one another but quarreled continually, because they feared, suspected, and despised one another. . . . Crushing labor that made the whole body ache at night, cruel winters, scanty crops, overcrowding, and no help, and nowhere to look for help.

It is less certain that the vise of the past has been loosened in China or Cuba. It may well be that Cuba has suffered a considerable economic decline, in part due to absurd planning, in part to our refusal to buy her main crop. The economic record of China is nearly as inscrutable as its political turmoil, and we may not know for many years whether the Chinese peasant is today better or worse off than before the revolution. Yet what strikes me as significant in both countries is something else. In Cuba it is the educational effort that, according to *The New York Times*, has constituted a major effort of the Castro regime. In China it is the unmistakable evidence — and here I lean not alone on the sympathetic account of Edgar Snow but on the most horrified descriptions of the rampages of the Red Guards — that the younger generation is no longer fettered by the traditional view of things. The very fact that the Red Guards now revile their elders, an unthinkable defiance of age-old Chinese customs, is testimony of how deeply change has penetrated into the texture of Chinese life.

It is this herculean effort to reach and rally the great anonymous mass of the population that is *the* great accomplishment of Communism — even though it is an accomplishment that is still only partially accomplished. For if the areas of the world afflicted with the self-perpetuating disease of backwardness are ever to rid themselves of its debilitating effects, I think it is likely to be not merely because antiquated social structures have been dismantled (although this is an essential precondition), but because some shock treatment like that of Communism has been administered to them.

By way of contrast to this all-out effort, however short it may have fallen of its goal, we must place the timidity of the effort to bring modernization to the peoples of the non-Communist world. Here again I do not merely speak of lagging rates of growth. I refer to the fact that illiteracy in the non-Communist countries of Asia and Central America is increasing (by some 200 million in the last decade) because it has been "impossible" to mount an educational effort that will keep pace with population growth. I refer to the absence of substantial land reform in Latin America, despite how many years of promises. I refer to the indifference or incompetence or corruption of governing elites: the incredible sheiks with their oildoms; the vague, well-meaning leaders of India unable to break the caste system, kill the cows, control the birthrate, reach the villages, house or employ the labor rotting on the streets; the cynical governments of South America, not one of which, according to Lleras Camargo, former president of Colombia, has ever prosecuted a single politician or industrialist for evasion of taxes. And not least, I refer to the fact that every movement that arises to correct these conditions is instantly identified as "Communist" and put down with every means at hand, while the United States clucks or nods approval.

To be sure, even in the most petrified societies, the modernization process is at work. If there were time, the solvent acids of the twentieth century would work their way on the ideas and institutions of the most inert or resistant countries. But what lacks in the twentieth century is time. The multitudes of the underdeveloped world have only in the past two decades been summoned to their reveille. The one thing that is certain about the revolution of rising expectations is that it is only in its inception, and that its pressures for justice and action will steadily mount as the voice of the twentieth century penetrates to villages and slums where it is still almost inaudible. It is not surprising that Princeton historian C. E. Black, surveying this labile world, estimates that we must anticipate "ten to fifteen revolutions a year for the foreseeable future in the less developed societies."

In itself, this prospect of mounting political restiveness enjoins the speediest possible time schedule for development. But this political urgency is many times compounded by that of the population problem. Like an immense river in flood, the number of human beings rises each year to wash away the levees of the preceding year's labors and to pose future requirements of monstrous proportions. To provide shelter for the three billion human beings who will arrive on earth in the next forty years will require as many dwellings as have been constructed since recorded history began. To feed them will take double the world's present output of food. To cope with the mass exodus from the overcrowded countryside will necessitate cities of grotesque size — Calcutta, now a cesspool of three to five millions, threatens us by the year 2000 with a prospective population of from thirty to sixty millions.

These horrific figures spell one importunate message: haste. That is the *mene mene, tekel upharsin* written on the walls of government planning offices around the world. Even if the miracle of the loop is realized — the new contraceptive device that promises the first real breakthrough in population control — we must set ourselves for at least another generation of rampant increase.

But how to achieve haste? How to convince the silent and disbelieving men, how to break through the disgruntled glances of women in black shawls, how to overcome the overt hostility of landlords, the opposition of the Church, the petty bickerings of military cliques, the black-marketeering of commercial dealers? I suspect there is only one way. The conditions of backwardness must be attacked with the passion, the ruthlessness, and the messianic fury of a jehad, a Holy War. Only a campaign of an intensity and single-mindedness that must approach the ludicrous and the unbearable offers the chance to ride roughshod over the resistance of the rich and the poor alike and to open the way for the forcible implantation of those modern attitudes and techniques without which there will be no escape from the misery of underdevelopment.

I need hardly add that the cost of this modernization process has been and will be horrendous. If Communism is the great modernizer, it is certainly not a benign agent of change. Stalin may well have exceeded Hitler as a mass executioner. Free inquiry in China has been supplanted by dogma and catechism; even in Russia nothing like freedom of criticism or of personal expression is allowed. Furthermore, the economic cost of industrialization in both countries has been at least as severe as that imposed by primitive capitalism.

Yet one must count the gains as well as the losses. Hundreds of millions who would have been confined to the narrow cells of changeless lives have been liberated from prisons they did not even know existed. Class structures that elevated the flighty or irresponsible have been supplanted by others that have promoted the ambitious and the dedicated. Economic systems that gave rise to luxury and poverty have given way to systems that provide a rough distributional justice. Above all, the prospect of a new future has been opened. It is this that lifts the current ordeal in China above the level of pure horror. The number of human beings in that country who have perished over the past centuries from hunger or neglect is beyond computation. The present revolution may add its dreadful increment to this number. But it also holds out the hope that China may finally have been galvanized into social, political, and economic attitudes that for the first time make its modernization a possibility.

Two questions must be answered when we dare to risk so favorable a verdict on Communism as a modernizing agency. The first is whether the result is worth the cost, whether the possible — by no means assured — escape from underdevelopment is worth the lives that will be squandered to achieve it.

I do not know how one measures the moral price of historical victories or how one can ever decide that a diffuse gain is worth a sharp and particular loss. I only know that the way in which we ordinarily keep the books of history is wrong. No one is now toting up the balance of the wretches who starve in India, or the peasants of northeastern Brazil who live in the swamps on crabs, or the undernourished and permanently stunted children of Hong Kong or Honduras. Their sufferings go unrecorded, and are not present to counterbalance the scales when the furies of revolution strike down their victims. Barrington Moore has made a nice calculation that bears on this problem. Taking as the weight in one pan the 35,000 to 40,000 persons who lost their lives — mainly for no fault of theirs — as a result of the Terror during the French Revolution, he asks what would have been the death rate from preventable starvation and injustice under the *ancien régime* to balance the scales. "Offhand," he writes, "it seems unlikely that this would be very much below the proportion of .0010 which [the] figure of 40,000 yields when set against an estimated population of 24 million."[3]

Is it unjust to charge the *ancien régime* in Russia with ten million preventable deaths? I think it not unreasonable. To charge the authorities in pre-revolutionary China with equally vast and preventable degradations? Theodore White, writing in 1946, had this to say: ". . . some scholars think that China is perhaps the only country in the world where the people eat less, live more bitterly, and are clothed worse than they were five hundred years ago."[4]

I do not recommend such a calculus of corpses — indeed, I am aware of the license it gives to the unscrupulous — but I raise it to show the one-sidedness of our protestations against the brutality and violence of revolutions. In this regard, it is chastening to recall the multitudes who have been killed or mutilated by the Church which is now the first to protest against the excesses of Communism.

But there is an even more terrible second question to be asked. It is clear beyond doubt, however awkward it may be for our moralizing propensities, that historians excuse horror that succeeds; and that we write our comfortable books of moral philosophy, seated atop a mound of victims — slaves, serfs, laboring men and women, heretics, dissenters — who were crushed in the course of preparing the way for our tri-

[3] *Social Origins of Dictatorship and Democracy*, p. 104.
[4] *Thunder Out of China*, p. 32

umphal entry into existence. But at least we are here to vindi-
cate the carnage. What if we were not? What if the revolutions
grind flesh and blood and produce nothing, if the end of the
convulsion is not exhilaration but exhaustion, not triumph but
defeat?

Before this possibility — which has been realized more than
once in history — one stands mute. Mute, but not paralyzed.
For there is the necessity of calculating what is likely to happen in the absence of the revolution whose prospective excesses hold us back. Here one must weigh what has been done
to remedy underdevelopment — and what has not been done
—— in the past twenty years; how much time there remains
before the population flood enforces its own ultimate solution;
what is the likelihood of bringing modernization without the
frenzied assault that Communism seems most capable of
mounting. As I make this mental calculation I arrive at an
answer which is even more painful than that of revolution. I
see the alternative as the continuation, without substantial relief — and indeed with a substantial chance of deterioration
— of the misery and meanness of life as it is now lived in the
sinkhole of the world's backward regions.

I have put the case for the necessity of revolution as
strongly as possible, but I must now widen the options beyond
the stark alternatives I have posed. To begin with, there are
areas of the world where the immediate tasks are so far-reaching that little more can be expected for some decades than
the primary missions of national identification and unification.
Most of the new African states fall into this category. These
states may suffer capitalist, Communist, Fascist, or other kinds
of regimes during the remainder of this century, but whatever
the nominal ideology in the saddle, the job at hand will be
that of military and political nation-making.

There is another group of nations, less easy to identify, but
much more important in the scale of events, where my analysis
also does not apply. These are countries where the pressures
of population growth seem sufficiently mild, or the existing
political and social framework sufficiently adaptable, to allow
for the hope of considerable progress without resort to violence. Greece, Turkey, Chile, Argentina, Mexico may be rep-

resentatives of nations in this precarious but enviable situation. Some of them, incidentally, have already had revolutions of modernizing intent — fortunately for them in a day when the United States was not so frightened or so powerful as to be able to repress them.

In other words, the great arena of desperation to which the revolutionizing impetus of Communism seems most applicable is primarily the crowded land masses and archipelagoes of Southeast Asia and the impoverished areas of Central and South America. But even here, there is the possibility that the task of modernization may be undertaken by non-Communist elites. There is always the example of indigenous, independent leaders who rise up out of nowhere to overturn the established framework and to galvanize the masses — a Gandhi, a Marti, a pre-1958 Castro. Or there is that fertile ground for the breeding of national leaders — the army, as witness Ataturk or Nasser, among many.[5]

Thus there is certainly no inherent necessity that the revolutions of modernization be led by Communists. But it is well to bear two thoughts in mind when we consider the likely course of non-Communist revolutionary sweeps. The first is the nature of the mobilizing appeal of any successful revolutionary elite. Is it the austere banner of saving and investment that waves over the heads of the shouting marchers in Jakarta and Bombay, Cairo and Havana? It most certainly is not. The banner of economic development is that of nationalism, with its promise of personal immortality and collective majesty. It seems beyond question that a feverish nationalism will charge the atmosphere of any nation, Communist or not, that tries to make the Great Ascent — and as a result we must expect the symptoms of nationalism along with the disease: exaggerated

---

[5] What are the chances for modernizing revolutions of the Right, such as those of the Meiji Restoration or of Germany under Bismarck? I think they are small. The changes to be wrought in the areas of greatest backwardness are much more socially subversive than those of the nineteenth century, and the timespan allotted to the revolutionists is much smaller. Bourgeois revolutions are not apt to go far enough, particularly in changing property ownership. Still, one could imagine such revolutions with armed support and no doubt Fascistic ideologies. I doubt that they would be any less of a threat than revolutions of the Left.

xenophobia, a thin-skinned national sensitivity, a search for enemies as well as a glorification of the state.

These symptoms, which we have already seen in every quarter of the globe, make it impossible to expect easy and amicable relations between the developing states and the colossi of the developed world. No conceivable response on the part of America or Europe or, for that matter, Russia, will be able to play up to the vanities or salve the irritations of the emerging nations, much less satisfy their demands for help. Thus, we must anticipate an anti-American, or anti-Western, possibly even anti-white animus from any nation in the throes of modernization, even if it is not parroting Communist dogma.

Then there is a second caution as to the prospects for non-Communist revolutions. This is the question of what ideas and policies will guide their revolutionary efforts. Revolutions, especially if their whole orientation is to the future, require philosophy equally as much as force. It is here, of course, that Communism finds its special strength. The vocabulary in which it speaks — a vocabulary of class domination, of domestic and international exploitation — is rich in meaning to the backward nations. The view of history it espouses provides the support of historical inevitability to the fallible efforts of struggling leaders. Not least, the very dogmatic certitude and ritualistic repetition that stick in the craw of the Western observer offer the psychological assurances on which an unquestioning faith can be maintained.

If a non-Communist elite is to persevere in tasks that will prove Sisyphean in difficulty, it will also have to offer a philosophical interpretation of its role as convincing and elevating, and a diagnosis of social and economic requirements as sharp and simplistic, as that of Communism. Further, its will to succeed at whatever cost must be as firm as that of the Marxists. It is not impossible that such a philosophy can be developed, more or less independent of formal Marxian conceptions. It is likely, however, to resemble the creed of Communism far more than that of the West. Political liberty, economic freedom, and constitutional law may be the great achievements and the great issues of the most advanced nations, but to the least developed lands they are only dim abstractions, or worse, rationalizations behind which the great powers play their imperialist tricks or protect the privileges of their monied classes.

Thus, even if for many reasons we should prefer the advent of non-Communist modernizing elites, we must realize that they too will present the United States with programs and policies antipathetic to much that America "believes in" and hostile to America as a world power. The leadership needed to mount a jehad against backwardness — and it is my main premise that only a Holy War will begin modernization in our time — will be forced to expound a philosophy that approves authoritarian and collectivist measures at home and that utilizes as the target for its national resentment abroad the towering villains of the world, of which the United States is now Number One.

All this confronts American policy-makers and public opinion with a dilemma of a totally unforeseen kind. On the one hand we are eager to assist in the rescue of the great majority of mankind from conditions that we recognize as dreadful and ultimately dangerous. On the other hand, we seem to be committed, especially in the underdeveloped areas, to a policy of defeating Communism wherever it is within our military capacity to do so, and of repressing movements that might become Communist if they were allowed to follow their internal dynamics. Thus, we have on the one side the record of Point Four, the Peace Corps, and foreign aid generally; and on the other, Guatemala, Cuba, the Dominican Republic, and now Vietnam.

That these two policies might be in any way mutually incompatible, that economic development might contain revolutionary implications infinitely more far-reaching than those we have so blandly endorsed in the name of rising expectations, that Communism or a radical national collectivism might be the only vehicles for modernization in many key areas of the world — these are dilemmas we have never faced. Now I suggest that we do face them, and that we begin to examine in a serious way ideas that have hitherto been considered blasphemous, if not near-traitorous.

Suppose that most of Southeast Asia and much of Latin

America were to go Communist, or to become controlled by revolutionary governments that espoused collectivist ideologies and vented extreme anti-American sentiments. Would this constitute a mortal threat to the United States?

I think it fair to claim that the purely *military* danger posed by such an eventuality would be slight. Given the present and prospective capabilities of the backward world, the addition of hundreds of millions of citizens to the potential armies of Communism would mean nothing when there was no way of deploying them against us. The prospect of an invasion by Communist hordes — the specter that frightened Europe after World War II with some (although retrospectively, not too much) realism — would be no more than a phantasm when applied to Asia or South America or Africa.

More important, the nuclear or conventional military power of Communism would not be materially increased by the armaments capacities of these areas for many years. By way of indication, the total consumption of energy of all kinds (in terms of coal equivalent) for Afghanistan, Bolivia, Brazil, Burma, Ceylon, Colombia, Costa Rica, the Dominican Republic, Ecuador, El Salvador, Ethiopia, Guatemala, Haiti, Honduras, India, Indonesia, Iran, Iraq, Korea, Lebanon, Nicaragua, Pakistan, Paraguay, Peru, the Philippines, U.A.R., Uruguay, and Venezuela is less than annually consumed by West Germany alone. The total steel output of these countries is one-tenth of U.S. annual production. Thus, even the total Communization of the backward world would not effectively alter the present balance of military strength in the world.

However small the military threat, it is undeniably true that a Communist or radical collectivist engulfment of these countries would cost us the loss of billions of dollars of capital invested there. Of our roughly $50 billions in overseas investment, some $10 billions are in mining, oil, utility, and manufacturing facilities in Latin America, some $4 billions in Asia including the Near East, and about $2 billions in Africa. To lose these assets would deal a heavy blow to a number of large corporations, particularly in oil, and would cost the nation as a whole the loss of some $3 to $4 billions a year in earnings from those areas.

A Marxist might conclude that the economic interests of a capitalist nation would find such a prospective loss insupportable, and that it would be "forced" to go to war. I do not think this is a warranted assumption, although it is undoubtedly a risk. Against a Gross National Product that is approaching three-fourths of a trillion dollars and with total corporate assets over $1.3 trillions, the loss of even the whole $16 billions in the vulnerable areas should be manageable economically. Whether such a take-over could be resisted politically — that is, whether the red flag of Communism could be successfully waved by the corporate interests — is another question. (I do not myself believe that the corporate elite is particularly war-minded — not nearly so much as the military or the congressional — or that corporate seizures would be a suitable issue for purposes of drumming up interventionist sentiment.)

By these remarks I do not wish airily to dismiss the dangers of a Communist avalanche in the backward nations. There would be dangers, not least those of an American hysteria. Rather, I want only to assert that the threats of a military or economic kind would not be insuperable, as they might well be if Europe were to succumb to a hostile regime.

But is that not the very point?, it will be asked. Would not a Communist success in a few backward nations lead to successes in others, and thus by degrees engulf the entire world, until the United States and perhaps Europe were fortresses besieged on a hostile planet?

I think the answer to this fear is twofold. First, as many besides myself have argued, it is now clear that Communism, far from constituting a single unified movement with a common aim and dovetailing interests, is a movement in which similarities of economic and political structure and ideology are more than outweighed by divergencies of national interest and character. Two bloody wars have demonstrated that in the case of capitalism, structural similarities between nations do not prevent mortal combat. As with capitalism, so with Communism. Russian Communists have already been engaged in skirmishes with Polish and Hungarian Communists, have nearly come to blows with Yugoslavia, and now stand poised at the threshold of open fighting with China. Only in the mind of the *Daily News* (and perhaps still in the State Department) does it seem possible, in the face of this spectacle, to refer to the unified machinations of "international Communism" or the "Sino-Soviet bloc."

The realities, I believe, point in a very different direction. A world in which Communist governments were engaged in the enormous task of trying to modernize the worst areas of Asia, Latin America, and Africa would be a world in which sharp differences of national interest were certain to arise within these continental areas. The outlook would be for frictions and conflicts to develop among Communist nations with equal frequency as they developed between those nations and their non-Communist neighbors. A long period of jockeying for power and command over resources, rather than anything like a unified sharing of power and resources, seems unavoidable in the developing continents. This would not preclude a continuous barrage of anti-American propaganda, but it would certainly impede a movement to exert a coordinated Communist influence over these areas.

Second, it seems essential to distinguish among the causes of dangerous national and international behavior those that can be traced to the tenets of Communism and those that must be located elsewhere. "Do not talk to me about Communism and capitalism," said a Hungarian economist with whom I had lunch this winter. "Talk to me about rich nations and poor ones."

I think it *is* wealth and poverty, and not Communism or capitalism, that establishes much of the tone and tension of international relations. For that reason I would expect Communism in the backward nations (or national collectivism, if that emerges in the place of Communism) to be strident, belligerent, and insecure. If these regimes fail — as they may — their rhetoric may become hysterical and their behavior uncontrolled, although of small consequence. But if they succeed, which I believe they can, many of these traits should recede. Russia, Yugoslavia, or Poland are simply not to be compared, either by way of internal pronouncement or external behavior, with China, or, on a smaller scale, Cuba.

Modernization brings, among other things, a waning of the stereotypes, commandments, and flagellations so characteristic of (and so necessary to) a nation engaged in the effort to alter itself from top to bottom. The idiom of ceaseless revolution becomes less relevant — even faintly embarrassing — to a nation that begins to be pleased with itself. Then, too, it seems reasonable to suppose that the vituperative quality of Communist invective would show some signs of abating were the United States to modify its own dogmatic attitude and to forgo its own wearisome clichés about the nature of Communism.

I doubt there are many who will find these arguments wholly reassuring. They are not. It would be folly to imagine that the next generation or two, when Communism or national collectivism in the underdeveloped areas passes through its jehad stage, will be a time of international safety. But as always in these matters, it is only by a comparison with the alternatives that one can choose the preferable course. The prospect that I have offered as a plausible scenario of the future must be placed against that which results from a pursuit of our present course. And here I see two dangers of even greater magnitude: (1) the prospect of many more Vietnams, as radical movements assert themselves in other areas of the world; and (2) a continuation of the present inability of the most impoverished areas to modernize, with the prospect of an eventual human catastrophe on an unimaginable scale.

Nevertheless, there *is* a threat in the specter of a Communist or near-Communist supremacy in the underdeveloped world. It is that the rise of Communism would signal the end of capitalism as the dominant world order, and would force the acknowledgment that America no longer constituted the model on which the future of world civilization would be mainly based. In this way, as I have written before, the existence of Communism frightens American capitalism as the rise of Protestantism frightened the Catholic Church, or the French Revolution the English aristocracy.

It is, I think, the fear of losing our place in the sun, of finding ourselves at bay, that motivates a great deal of the anti-Communism on which so much of American foreign policy seems to be founded. In this regard I note that the nations of Europe, most of them profoundly more conservative than America in their social and economic dispositions, have made their peace with Communism far more intelligently and easily than we, and I conclude that this is in no small part due to their admission that they are no longer the leaders of the world.

The great question in our own nation is whether we can accept a similar scaling-down of our position in history. This would entail many profound changes in outlook and policy. It would mean the recognition that Communism, which may indeed represent a retrogressive movement in the West, where it should continue to be resisted with full energies, may nonetheless represent a progressive movement in the backward areas, where its advent may be the only chance these areas have of escaping misery. Collaterally, it means the recognition that "our side" has neither the political will, nor the ideological wish, nor the stomach for directing those changes that the backward world must make if it is ever to cease being backward. It would undoubtedly entail a more isolationist policy for the United States vis-à-vis the developing continents, and a greater willingness to permit revolutions there to work their way without our interference. It would mean in our daily political life the admission that the ideological battle of capitalism and Communism had passed its point of usefulness or relevance, and that religious diatribe must give way to the pragmatic dialogue of the age of science and technology.

I do not know how to estimate the chances of effecting such deep-seated changes in the American outlook. It may be that the pull of vested interests, the inertia of bureaucracy, plus a certain lurking fundamentalism that regards Communism as an evil which admits of no discussion — the anti-Christ — will maintain America on its present course, with consequences that I find frightening to contemplate. But I believe that our attitudes are not hopelessly frozen. I detect, both above and below, signs that our present view of Communism is no longer wholly tenable and that it must be replaced with a new assessment if we are to remain maneuverable in action and cogent in discourse.

Two actions may help speed along this long-overdue modernization of our own thought. The first is a continuation of the gradual thawing and convergence of American and Russian views and interests — a rapprochement that is proceeding slowly and hesitantly, but with a discernible momentum. Here the initiative must come from Russia as well as from ourselves.

The other action is for us alone to take. It is the public airing of the consequences of our blind anti-Communism for the underdeveloped world. It must be said aloud that our present policy prefers the absence of development to the chance for Communism — which is to say, that we prefer hunger and want and the existing inadequate assaults against the causes of hunger and want to any regime that declares its hostility to capitalism. There are strong American currents of humanitarianism that can be directed as a counterforce to this profoundly antihumanitarian view. But for this counterforce to become mobilized it will be necessary to put fearlessly the outrageous question with which I began: Is the United States fundamentally opposed to economic development?

Contrasts in Economic Development: China and India

JOAN ROBINSON

Professor Heilbroner points out that the anti-Communist policy of the United States may be fundamentally opposed to economic development. Let us consider in more detail how this comes about.

The success of economic development cannot be measured by the rate of growth of statistical Gross National Product. The aim of development in the less developed countries is first and foremost to overcome poverty and to establish national self-respect — to throw off the aura of colonial inferiority and to claim to be taken seriously on the world scene.

The basic requirements for economic development may be listed as follows, not in order of importance but in a circle in which each element requires and contributes to the rest.

(1) The whole people must be involved in production and organized so that all can contribute to the economy and all share in the benefit.

(2) There must be a sufficient agricultural output to provide a surplus for industrial development (and, unfortunately, for defense) without starving the agricultural labor force.

(3) There must be general education, not only in the sense of abolishing illiteracy and setting up schools, colleges and research institutes, but also in the sense of emancipation from superstition and cultivation of a rational approach to practical problems.

125

(4) Industrial development — that is to say the application of power to production — is the necessary condition for raising output per head, and therefore consumption per head, above the level possible by mere muscle.

These requirements of development can be illustrated by reference to the experience of India and China in the last sixteen years.

The Whole People

It is sometimes said that an appeal of the ideals of freedom and human dignity makes no sense to hungry men. This is the patronizing view of the well fed. Until the other day it was commonplace for a Chinese peasant to be reduced to selling his daughter to pay the rent, and his wife could be raped by the landlord even without payment. The appeal of the revolution was not only to feed the hungry but to establish the right of every individual to freedom and self-respect. At the same time the revolution makes great demands. There is no virtue in merely receiving benefits. The people are shown how to work to help themselves.

In India under the British administration the rights of the individual were in some ways better preserved than in China, but old customs were far more oppressive. In Chinese history there was always a tradition that "a man's a man for a' that." This was totally lacking in India. And overall was the humiliation of living under foreign rule that was resented for its virtues even more than for its vices. Some progress has been made since independence in combating old customs and establishing social equality, but it has not gone very far. Indeed, the contrast between India and China today is distressing. In China everyone has a job, an income, a place in society; beggary and prostitution have been eliminated. There is a standard of civic morality that surpasses Sweden and there is very little crime. In India, it is common still to see families living in the street, and the sidewalks have been appropriated by toughs who exact a rent for the space. Horrible beggars, whose sores are cultivated because they are a source of income, are passed by in the streets by nice, liberal, good-hearted people, who could not preserve their sanity if they allowed themselves to see the misery around them.

Michal Kalecki has observed that a new social and economic system has come into being in the ex-colonial world, of which India, Egypt, and perhaps Mexico are the leading examples. In this system, for the first time in history, the petite bourgeoisie — rich peasants, small businessmen, traders, minor professionals — are the leading class. The government, under slogans of planning, provides its infrastructure for them and regulates the economy in a manner which permits them to flourish.

This class in India grows and prospers. They carry on an uneasy struggle with the big capitalists and Western educated intellectuals above them and the miserable people below them.

Once this formula has been established it is very hard to move forward to a thoroughgoing revolution. In China the policy of the Communists was to organize the poor peasants and landless laborers, unite with the middle peasants and isolate the rich peasants and landlords — to exalt the humble and meek and send the rich away empty. In India in every village there is an established hierarchy which cannot be unseated. The new parties which have come up in the last general election to challenge Congress are representatives of the petite bourgeoisie, with an obscurantist ideology and an economic philosophy of devil take the hindmost. In China, once the revolution was firmly established, rich peasants, landlords and capitalists, who were willing to work for their country, were allowed to find a place. The greater part of those who, from religion or education, most disliked Marxism, shared in the satisfaction of restored national pride which the liberation established.

Some observers like to believe that the present Cultural Revolution means a breakdown of national unity in China. To me it seems rather a sign of remarkable self-confidence.

China is by no means an egalitarian economy. Starting from such a low level, equality is not practicable, but the Chinese economy is set up in a way which leads toward some degree of equality, while the Indian economy leads away from it.

The Agricultural Surplus

The first act of the new government established in China in 1949 was to spread the land reform, already carried out in the old liberated areas, to the whole country (with the exception of national minority regions, which were left to go at their own pace).

The distribution of land was carried out village by village, so that the amount available for the landless and poor peasants of a particular village depended upon how much could be taken from the landlords of that village. The landlords, once dispossessed, became landless and received a share in the distribution. The result was to create a mass of middle peasants, with holdings of an average of one and a half acres per head.

One reason why collectivization met with so much less resistance in China than in the Western Communist countries was that all could see that there was no future for individual enrichment with holdings of this size. By a gradual process, the peasants were brought into cooperative organizations; the present system of communes, as they were modified through experience after the Great Leap, is now considered to be a satisfactory framework within which development can go on for a long time. They have made possible a rise in technique and great progress in land conservation, irrigation, electrification of the countryside, and they have established a kind of grass-roots democracy that exists nowhere else in the world.

After the Great Leap in 1958, agriculture suffered a severe setback. Chinese spokesmen say that it was to some extent due to "mistakes in our work." These mistakes were partly technical — using overall slogans such as deep ploughing and close planting irrespective of the variation of conditions in different regions, and partly political — pushing the peasants faster toward collectivization and egalitarianism than they were ready to go. The main cause of the setback, however, was disastrous weather conditions. Near famine threatened, but the country was nursed through it. Probably some elderly people died sooner than they would have died in good times, but there was no starvation. Grain was imported to help feed the cities without having to squeeze the peasants too hard. The imports were paid for on commercial terms.

Since then development has been proceeding, with some ups and downs, till it was possible to announce that the harvest of 1967 was the largest ever known in Chinese history. It is true, of course, that the population is also the greatest in Chinese history, but for the time being food supplies are keeping ahead. The contrast with the situation in India today needs no elaboration.

Education

Professor Mahalanobis (founder of the Indian Statistical Institute) propounds the thesis that the essential difference between the developed and the underdeveloped economies is that in the West the scientific revolution is taken for granted and in two hundred and fifty years has soaked into the mentality of the people. For China, with long traditions of superior culture and contempt for the outer barbarians, it was disturbing to have to admit the necessity of learning from the West. The great cult of the "Thought of Mao Tse-tung" is a method of bringing the scientific attitude into a Chinese form. Western observers smile when a team leader in a commune tells them, "By applying the thought of Chairman Mao, we grow bigger cabbages." But it is not at all silly. Mao teaches them to serve the people — that is, to work together and help each other instead of fragmenting their efforts in jealous individualism; to respect the facts, not to operate with preconceived superstitious notions; to carry out experiments and observe their results; to learn from errors and follow up successes. Applying these methods can be expected to produce bigger cabbages.

Education in this general sense lies in a very thin layer on the surface of Indian life. The difference cannot be attributed mainly to the character of socialist education. The Chinese always had the great advantage over the Indians for economic life in that their tradition was basically rationalist. They never took religion so seriously. There is no doubt, however, that political reaction takes advantage of superstition in India in a manner that is opposing the kind of education that Mahalanobis convincingly argues to be the sine qua non of modern development.

Formal education, also, is an important element in development in all socialist countries. To give formal education to a population of peasants is a formidable task. In principle there is universal primary education in China; in some backward areas, no doubt, it is at a very primitive level. Not more than 6% of the age group in the countryside can go on to secondary education, which however is universal in the cities. Perhaps 1 or 2% of the age group proceed to higher education. The absolute numbers concerned, of course, are very great. Many new universities and institutes of every sort have been established and a corps of doctors, scientists, technicians of all kinds, has been built up, while the arts, music and theater are not neglected.

In India also there is a drive for education, but illiteracy is still prevalent and higher education has not been geared in to development so that there is a notorious unemployment of intellectuals at home while a few (often the most brilliant) find a use for their gifts abroad.

Both countries have formidable difficulties in mass education. India because of the multiplicity of languages and alphabets and China because of the lack of an alphabet. To become even moderately literate in Chinese characters is a hard task. Experiments in simplification and in alphabetization are being undertaken but they meet with great difficulties.

Industry

Chinese industrialization proceeds in the principle of "walking on two legs." At one extreme the most modern, sophisticated and highly automated installations are set up (at first under Soviet influence, nowadays mainly of Chinese design, with some Western and Japanese importations). At the other extreme, manpower is still used at the lowest possible level. The great dams and embankments of the river-control schemes were built by armies of men almost literally with their bare hands. It is still a common sight on the roads leading into towns to see carts pulled by humans carrying produce to be marketed. Handicraft cooperatives set to work with the simplest tools, and gradually mechanize themselves step by step. The overall strategy of development, pioneered by the USSR, requires at the first stage heavy investment in industries, to lay a base for industrialization.

Professor K. N. Raj of Delhi University has surveyed Indian and Chinese experience in this sector. He comes to the conclusion that the success of China is to be attributed to a different strategy in planning investment — a greater concentration in what he called the "machine tool sector," that is, investment in the production of investment goods.

He quotes from the first five-year plan (1953–1957):

The machine-building industry is the key to the technological transformation of our national economy. During the course of our First Five-Year Plan, we must develop our machine-building industry on the basis of the growth of our iron and steel and nonferrous metals industries. . . . A heavy responsibility rests on our existing machine-building factories during the period of the First Five-Year Plan. We will ourselves manufacture from 30 to 50% of the equipment needed for 156 projects which are being designed with the help of the Soviet Union; at the same time the machine-building industry is faced with many demands from various branches of the national economy. It is therefore necessary, on the basis of a higher technical level, to fully utilize and expand the productive capacity of existing machine-building works, and to increase their production of new types of products. In this period, we must rely on our original enterprises as well as new and reconstructed enterprises that come into production to produce equipment for iron smelting and steel-making, equipment for small and medium hydroelectric and thermal power industry; accessories and complete sets of equipment for the coal, nonferrous metals, and cement industries; drilling machines together with accessories for the oil industry; various metal-cutting machine-tools; rolling stock and vessels needed for transport; and complete sets of equipment for textile, printing and dyeing, sugar-making, paper-making and food industries.

And, as an example of the way in which this policy was carried through, he quotes from a survey by Harold Munthe-Kaas:

> Before then the industry had mainly confined itself to producing fairly simple medium-size equipment, providing parts to keep the old machinery running and complementing newly imported machinery. . . . Starting with the Second Five-Year Plan, greater emphasis was put on the independent designing and production of complete sets of machinery and special tools, and advances are said to have been made in all sectors of the machine-building industry.[1]

In India, on the other hand, following a market-oriented strategy, the major part of investment (apart from transport) has been in equipment for light industry. India still depends to a large extent upon imports of machinery and equipment. The great advantage of carrying out development after a socialist revolution is that the economy is not burdened with providing for a relatively luxurious standard of life for the middle class. (In China a small number of "patriotic capitalists" are allowed large incomes, but the general fashion of life is extremely simple.)

The dependence upon imported equipment leads to dependence upon foreign know-how and the perpetuation of a colonial inferiority complex in regard to the Western world.

Raj comments:

> The continued dependence of India on imports of machinery and equipment on a large scale has no doubt meant that it has often been able to install better-quality products manufactured in the more advanced countries

---

[1] "China's Mechanical Heart," *Far Eastern Economic Review,* May 27, 1965.

and therefore often embodying more recent improvements in technology. However, as will be evident from the following observation made by a Western visitor who inspected comparable industries in both countries, India has had to pay a price for this in terms of development of technical expertise and skill within the country: "It was instructive to compare two new chemical fertilizer plants, one in Nangal [Punjab] and the other at Wuching [Shanghai]. . . . Wuching cost $25 million, makes 100,000 tons a year, employs 2,400 people for an average $30 a month — and is completely Chinese in design, construction and operation. Nangal cost $65 million, produces 375,000 tons a year, employs 3,500 people for a similar average wage — and sixty foreign technicians supervised the installation of the latest British, French, German and Italian machinery. Wuching is home-spun, almost amateurish, but with a lived-in look; Nangal is elegant and efficient but the Indian staff look almost out of place, scared to touch their sophisticated surroundings."[2]

The inability to manufacture machinery within the country has not been of course the only factor responsible for the dependence on imports. Some of the other factors at work, and the consequences, will be evident from the following comments of the member in charge of industry in the India Planning Commission:

For one thing, there is an omnipresent, though unspoken, inferiority complex in the field of industrial production. Goods and machines will sell only if they have a foreign brand or patent name. Even industrialists

who loudly and bitterly complain of the market resistance to their indigenous products, strain every nerve to obtain foreign brands when they procure equipment for themselves. . . . Foreign collaboration, apart from roy-

---

[2] S. G. Barve, *Problems of Industrial Growth in India,* Planning Commission, Government of India, May, 1966, pp. 10–12.

alties, and the stultification of indigenous capability, invariably brings in its train a bias for the import of foreign machinery. The foreign collaborator is interested even more in exporting his machinery than in exporting the know-how. . . . Our current troubles have arisen out of the fact that the new industries set up with imported equipment and know-how and dependent upon imports of components and raw materials have not been able collectively to develop an export potential adequate to foreign loans and royalties.[3]

The United States and Development

It is obvious enough that the United States crusade against Communism is a campaign against development. By means of it the American people have been led to acquiesce in the maintenance of a huge war machine and its use by threat or actual force to try to suppress every popular movement that aims to overthrow ancient or modern tyranny and begin to find a way to overcome poverty and establish national self-respect.

In those countries whose governments have been prepared to accept American support, "aid" is given in a form which may do more to inhibit development than to promote it.

A great deal of anti-aid was given to India by arming Pakistan. The absurd assumption was made (or at least proclaimed) that the arms of Pakistan were a defense against the USSR. Indians knew very well, however, against whom the arms would be used and had to waste a great part of their own resources in arming in reply. The dispute with China also was kept alive at great loss and with no advantage. Chinese are sitting today on the frontier lines which they originally offered to settle with India. Allowing themselves to be embroiled in the American crusade has certainly not helped to establish Indian self-respect.

The use of propaganda and the economic leverage given by loans and grants to promote the private sector in India at the

[3] *Ibid.*

expense of the public has, as Raj shows, done a great deal to deflect investment into the most profitable, as opposed to the most useful, channels. The puritanism of China helps to preserve the investable surplus from being frittered away and the cult of simplicity prevents envy and chagrin from exacerbating poverty, while in India the ideals of Gandhi are being supplanted by the ideals of Madison Avenue.

Even the use of PL 480 to supply wheat has not been an unquestionable benefit to Indian development. Rather it helped fend off the necessity of getting agricultural development and family planning under way in good time. The Indian economy, having become dependent upon it, is now threatened with its cessation.

China is showing the world how much devotion, hard work and hard thinking are necessary to get a nation onto the path of development. India is showing the world what happens when the devotion, work and thought are insufficient. America seems to be bent on terrorizing any people who starts to find a way into the path, to head them off it.

Underdevelopment and U.S. Foreign Policy

N. B. MILLER

Much has been written in recent years about the plight of the underdeveloped countries of the so-called "Third World." In the United States the approaches to this problem range from the conservative — "Let *them* do it on their own, the way we did" — to the liberal, which offers such programs as the Alliance for Progress, common markets, etc. These approaches always have at least two assumptions in common: (1) underdevelopment is an isolated phenomenon in each area, to be eliminated by treating the symptoms (hunger, disease, unemployment, etc.) rather than the cause; and (2) regardless of methodology, development must not interfere with the security and expansion of U.S. investments and markets.

We therefore have an Alliance for Progress which is supposedly designed to promote economic, cultural, and technological development for the people of Latin America. But at the same time and within the same foreign policy, the U.S. continues to provide the land-owners and their military partners with an unceasing supply of weapons, financial assistance, and, if all else fails, U.S. Marines. The paradox is only superficial. It is no accident that, during the short life of the Alliance, successful right-wing military takeovers have occurred in Argentina, Brazil, Honduras, Guatemala, Ecuador, Salvador, and the Dominican Republic.

A study of U.S. foreign policy, past and present, reveals

continuous and consistent efforts to incorporate (by both liberal and conservative means) the now underdeveloped countries into a single mercantile and industrial capitalist system. The economic surplus (raw materials, cheap labor, etc.) of the underdeveloped countries has been and continues to be appropriated for the benefit of the capitalist structure, i.e., the United States.[1] The flow of capital *away* from the subordinate areas of the world *to* the dominant unit perpetuates underdevelopment. It is thus to capitalism that we must look, and not to the population growth, apathy, or traditionalism of the inhabitants of these areas to explain the structure of underdevelopment. As Andre Gunder Frank states:

> This is equally true of Africa, Asia, and Latin America, which are distinguished by the remarkable uniformity of their structure of underdevelopment rather than by differences of nationhood, fatalism and institution. . . . In all of these, power has come to rest primarily in the control of their commerce and that control has been and still is substantially exercised by and on behalf of the interests of the bourgeoisie in the capitalist metropolis and its junior partners in the therefore underdeveloped countries.[2]

U.S. Foreign Aid Programs

We can begin to see how U.S. foreign aid and technical assistance fit into and support the structure of underdevelopment by examining some of the relevant programs. Perhaps the clearest statement of the purpose of these programs comes from Congress in Public Law 165 (October 10, 1951, 82nd Congress, first session) and in an amendment to the Mutual Security Act of 1951 promoting "military, economic and technical

---

[1] Paul Baran, *The Political Economy of Growth* (New York: Monthly Review Press, 1957).

[2] Andre Gunder Frank, "The Development of Underdevelopment," *Monthly Review*, Vol. 18, No. 4, September, 1966. See also "Sociology of Development and Underdevelopment of Sociology," *Catalyst*, No. 3, June, 1967, and *Capitalism and Underdevelopment in Latin America* (New York: Monthly Review Press, 1967).

assistance to friendly foreign countries to strengthen the mutual security and defenses of the free world, to develop their resources in the interest of [this] security . . . and the national interest of the United States." Further clarification appears in a report from the Senate Committee on Foreign Relations (*Technical Assistance and Related Programs,* 1956, p. 4) which states:

> Technical assistance is not something to be done, as a government enterprise, for its own sake or for the sake of others. The United States government is not a charitable institution, nor is it an appropriate outlet for the charitable spirit of the American people . . . [Technical assistance] is one of a number of means available to the United States to carry out its foreign policy and to promote its national interests abroad.

The Export-Import Bank was established in 1934 to promote the sale of U.S. products abroad by making financing available to foreign buyers. In effect, it uses government resources to extend the American banking system. Its loans are usually set up to serve whatever section of the American economy is particularly in need of sales outlets. The Bank scrupulously adheres to a policy of non-competition with private capital and its interest rates are indicative of this policy.

Since the Bank is a government agency, its loans must conform to U.S. foreign and economic policy. All loans must be reviewed by the National Advisory Council on International Monetary and Financial Problems, and the President of the United States is empowered to dismiss the directors of the Bank at any time.

The Bank's primary considerations in granting loans are the following: (1) the borrower must be able to repay in dollars; (2) private entities are preferred to foreign governments as borrowers for projects of a commercial nature; (3) eligibility depends on our existing foreign policy (with the result that large geographical areas are eliminated from consideration and preferential treatment is extended to others); (4) U.S. Embassy influence affects determination of eligibility; (5) The

Office of Defense Mobilization assigns priorities for loans; (6) loans are generally made only to finance purchases of materials and equipment produced in the U.S.; and (7) U.S. vessels must be used to transport products whose export is fostered by Bank loans.

The Export-Import Bank thus serves primarily the interests of the exporter and private U.S. investment sources and insures maximum profit advantages for U.S. producers. It also serves as an extension of U.S. foreign policy aims in the cold war competition. A January, 1967 Senate Foreign Relations Committee study notes that "the active interest of [the Export-Import Bank] in financing of military export sales (arms sales) since 1963 . . . for the Department of Defense . . . has primarily been directed at the lesser-developed countries (which can least afford it)." Thus this so-called development bank is a major factor in developing arms races.

The Agriculture Trade Development and Assistance Act of 1954 (Public Law 480) is often cited as an example of mutually beneficial foreign-trade programs providing development assistance to the foreign country. In fact, the word "development" in the title of the act refers to the development of new markets for U.S. agricultural products (House Report No. 432, 1957). That this act is not intended to produce foreign development was clearly stated, at its inception, by Secretary of State Dulles. The then Assistant Secretary of Agriculture further assured Congress that "the administration of this entire program is directed toward protecting and expanding our dollar market abroad." Another function of the act is the purchase of domestic surplus commodities which are then substituted for some of the dollars normally available to foreign countries under the mutual security acts. In other words, the United States uses this so-called development program to divert dollars to surplus commodities agencies at home, the commodities then being used for mutual security objectives abroad. These objectives, as brought out in Department of State Bulletin 476, 1958, include housing and base-construction for U.S. military personnel, production of propaganda in the language of the foreign country, and the support of local military forces. Thus development abroad is subordinated to development at home, and development generally is subordinated to security and foreign policy objectives.

The Development Loan Fund was established under the Mutual Security Act of 1957 to operate under the International Cooperation Administration (ICA). The status of the Fund was changed by the Mutual Security Act of 1958 to that of a government corporation and it functions as another government bank. At that time, Congress declared the purpose of the fund to be "to strengthen friendly foreign countries by encouraging the development of their economies through a competitive free-enterprise system. . . ." The same "sound loan" policies we find in other agencies are followed by the Fund and the rates of interest are comparatively high. Loan agreements, though permitting repayment in local currencies, are dollar dominated and contain "maintenance of value" conditions. The Fund is also prohibited from competing with private capital and the other main governmental agencies. Although the Fund has no "tied loan" policy requiring that proceeds of loans be spent for U.S. goods and services, its other requirements make "tied loans" unnecessary. An amendment to the 1958 Mutual Security Act states that the Fund must give consideration to the "possible adverse effects upon the economy of the U.S. with special reference to areas of substantial labor surplus." In other words, "protect American markets." The cold war aspects of the Fund's operation were clearly stated by John Foster Dulles before a House subcommittee in 1957: "I believe this fund . . . should be operated primarily as an instrument of foreign policy," and by the then Secretary of Treasury Anderson as quoted in *The New York Times* (March 19, 1958, p. 3): "Development needs must be exploited for political purposes in the national interest."

The Alliance for Progress in Latin America is another U.S. aid program serving U.S. economic interests. A brief analysis of some stipulations of the Alliance charter indicates its purpose.

Under Section 1.04a, resources of the Fund shall not be used for the purchase of agricultural land (thus preventing land reform). Under Section 2.01c, loan requests shall be granted only for projects in which the applicant bears an appropriate share of the cost. (Since ability to repay is the main consideration for eligibility [according to Section 5.02, below], loans are granted only to highly solvent corporations and do not serve the purpose of social reform.)

Under Section 4.05, no part of the Fund shall be used for purchase of goods or services originating in any nonmember country and (Section 4.06) funds shall be used for the purchase of goods and services from the United States or from the country receiving assistance. (In effect, the vast majority of goods and services are purchased from the U.S. Thus the country receiving aid may not purchase goods wherever they are cheapest — and they are usually cheaper outside the U.S. — and the dollars rarely leave the U.S.)

Under Section 4.07, repayment must be either in dollars or equivalent in value to the dollar-denominated amount due. (Thus the already serious dollar drain in Latin America is increased and dollar dependency is heightened.)

Section 5.02 defines the role of the Inter-American Development Bank, the administrator of the Fund, which is to manage the Fund as it manages "its own affairs." This means that: (1) ability to repay is the primary factor; (2) interest is charged at normal bank rates; (3) all loans are controlled by the U.S., which controls the Bank. (Since a two-thirds vote is required for approval of a loan, the U.S., with 40% of the votes, can veto any loan.)

Under Section 6.02, the United States can terminate the Fund at any time with thirty days' notice and (Section 6.03) any assets remaining shall be returned to the United States and outstanding loans inure to the credit of the United States.

Perhaps Washington is less than candid when it talks about development in the underdeveloped countries. If its purpose is to improve the lives of the people in these countries its effectiveness is open to question. An example of "progress in development" is present-day Guatemala, a major recipient of U.S. aid, in which:

75% of the people exist on what the United Nations has termed "below starvation level."
80% of the people are illiterate.
80% of the people do not have drinking-water facilities.

84% of the people do not have toilet facilities.
65% of the population exists completely outside the money economy.
22% of the population dies before reaching 5 years of age.

Eugene Black, for many years the president of the World Bank and now President Johnson's advisor on Asian development problems and Administrator of the one-billion-dollar U.S. Asian Development Program, offers a more realistic analysis:

> Our foreign aid programs constitute a distinct benefit to American business. The three major benefits are: (1) foreign aid provides a substantial and immediate market for U.S. goods and services; (2) foreign aid stimulates the development of new overseas markets for U.S. companies; (3) foreign aid orients national economies toward a free enterprise system in which U.S. firms can prosper.[3]

The "success" of these programs is readily demonstrated. For example, in Latin America, for the period 1950–1965, the flow of direct investment from the United States totaled $3.8 billion. Income on this investment transferred *to* the United States *from* Latin America was $11.3 billion for the same period — representing a *net loss* to Latin America of $7.5 billion. At the same time, the value of U.S. corporate investments in Latin America increased from $4.5 billion to $10.3 billion.

Turning to Southeast Asia, are we then to believe that the Mekong River development project represents the dove wing of the administration and escalation of the war the hawk wing? The answer to this question is given by the Vice President in charge of Far Eastern Operations of the Chase Manhattan Bank (speaking in 1966 after the Vietnam war had been escalated to include bombing of the North):

> In the past, foreign investors have been somewhat wary of the overall political prospects for the [Southeast Asian] region. I must say, though, that the U.S. actions

---

[3] *Columbia Journal of World Business*, Vol. 1, Fall, 1965, p. 23.

in Vietnam this year — which have demonstrated that the U.S. will continue to give effective protection to free nations and investments of the region — have considerably reassured both Asian and Western investors.

Thus the dove position, favoring development aid to the underdeveloped countries, and the hawk position, opposing popular nationalist revolutionary activity in these countries, are not contradictory after all. Any doubt of the connection between them should have been obviated in the summer of 1953. At that time the Eisenhower administration placed the Point Four Program (originated by President Truman in the late 1940s and generally considered the model for current programs) under control of the newly established Foreign Operations Administration. Development spending was thus placed under the same roof with military and economic aid. Further clarification appears in the Mutual Security Act of 1956, in which Congress declared that the U.S. technical assistance policy should be continued "as long as such [Communist] danger to the peace of the world and to the security of the United States persists." This act clearly made the Communist threat (the threat to U.S. investments and markets) a basic criterion of eligibility for U.S. aid.

In short, nations are permitted to "develop" only under U.S. auspices. Those nations that attempt to free themselves from this yoke and take a "nationalist route" to development are perceived as posing a threat to the U.S. economy. Witness U.S. military intervention in Guatemala, the Dominican Republic, Iran, the Congo, Vietnam, Indonesia, Laos — to name but a few. The perception is indeed quite accurate. The growing concentration of monopoly corporations in the United States depends more and more on foreign economic and political control to maintain — and expand — the benefits made possible by the existing system. By 1957 three hundred U.S. corporations owned 88% of U.S. investment abroad and, of these, 45 firms owned 57%.[4] Since then the degree of concen-

---

[4] This and the following data are all from Harry Magdoff, "Economic Aspects of U.S. Imperialism," *Monthly Review,* Vol. 18, No. 6, November, 1966.

tration has certainly increased. More importantly, in 1964 domestic sales of all moveable goods were $280 billion; foreign sales by U.S. corporations amounted to $168 billion, of which $88 billion were by wholly or substantially owned foreign subsidiaries of U.S. corporations.

The sum of exports and federal purchases for military expenditures amounts to between 20% and 50% of the total sales in all U.S. manufacturing industries (except farm machinery, in which the percentage is lower, and aircraft and ordnance industries, in which it is higher). Moreover, the share of total output devoted to military and foreign buyers is steadily increasing. During the last ten years, while domestic sales of U.S. manufacturing industries have increased 50%, the foreign sales of U.S. owned factories have increased 110%. And the concentration of profits is still higher than that of sales.

Development and Underdevelopment: Two Sides of the Same Coin

The increase in U.S. control of (and dependency on) foreign markets must, of course, be related to the direction of economic change in these market areas. One index of this change is per capita production and consumption. A report from the United Nations Food and Agriculture Organization, *The State of Food and Agriculture 1964* (Rome, 1965) reveals that since World War II the combined per capita food production for Asia (excluding China), Africa, and Latin America has fallen 3%. In the formerly underdeveloped countries of Eastern Europe and the Soviet Union, over the same period, it has risen 45%.[5]

From the average yearly per capita production of the prewar years 1934–1938, per capita food production in the world as a whole (excluding China) has risen 12%. The increase has been greatest in the developed capitalist countries. In Africa,

---

[5] This and following data are from the United Nations Food and Agriculture Organization report cited above. The analysis is based on Andre Gunder Frank, *op. cit.*, as well as (to date) unpublished material by Professor Frank.

for example, the increase has been barely 3%. At the same time, in Asia (excluding China) per capita food production has decreased 3% and in Latin America 7%. Agricultural production per capita has dropped 10% in Latin America.

The world supply of animal proteins, which are of such importance for the physical development of human beings, especially the young, has increased by 15%. The production of animal protein in relation to all classes of protein has increased by 12% throughout the world, but in Latin America it has decreased by 18%.

In the prewar years the countries with a high per capita level of protein consumption were Europe, North America, Oceanea, and (in Latin America) Uruguay and Argentina. Their per capita consumption has since risen from 85 grams to 90 grams. In the rest of the world (excluding China) protein consumption declined from 62 grams daily then to 52 grams now.

This black picture of declining food production in the underdeveloped countries, and above all in Latin America, is aggravated by various factors which combine to spell out mass hunger.

While in the developed countries maximum production has been reached in the most recent years, the contrary has been the case in the underdeveloped countries. Here, and again especially in Latin America, the post-war production peak was reached years ago, and in the last few years per capita food production has declined constantly and increasingly. In Africa the production peak was 6% over the prewar level, but this was in 1960–1961. Since then it has fallen by 3%. In Asia (excluding China) the post-war production peak (also occurring in 1960–1961) was no higher than the prewar level. Since then, per capita food production has fallen to 3% below the prewar level. In Latin America the high point was 1% over the prewar level — in 1958–1959. Thereafter per capita food production decreased, reaching a level 7% below prewar figures by 1963–1964.

In other words, during the last five years, or during the first half of the decade called, by the United Nations, "The Decade of Development," and during which the American nations have formed an Alliance for Progress, the situation has improved significantly — in the developed countries. In the underdeveloped countries it has become worse than ever.

In Mexico, for example, according to the Bank of Mexico, 52% of the Federal District (Mexico City) does not eat meat.[6] In 1960 24% of the Mexican people did not consume any sources of animal proteins, such as meat, fish, and eggs. 36% of the people living in the rural areas did not have access to these products.[7].

The London *Times* of November 15, 1965, succinctly states the problem for India: "The approaching [food] troubles are not just incidental; it is not a matter of ill fortune (as proclaimed by the government of India). By all signs India has entered a period of food scarcity which will be prolonged for as long as it takes to revolutionize agricultural production — which would require in turn profound changes in social and political attitudes."

Another country noted for its agricultural failures is Cuba. As Professor Frank observes:

There is no doubt that sugar production, which in 1959 was 6 million tons and in 1961 was 6.8 million, decreased to 3.8 million in 1963. It is no less certain that the sugar harvest in 1965 again passed 6 million tons. On the other hand, as the United Nations Economic Commission for Latin America (UN-ECLA) pointed out "agricultural production for internal consumption [in Cuba] has increased at an annual rate of 5.8% which, when corrected to take into account population growth, indicates an annual per capita growth rate of 3.8% between 1957–1963. Furthermore, this constitutes the most dynamic agricultural sector, both for its average rate of expansion and for the rapid recovery which it made after the overall decline of 1961." The figures indicate a total increase of agricultural produce, excluding sugar cane and other industrial products . . . of 25% between 1958 and 1963.

[6] Banco Nacional de Mexico, *Examen de la situacion económica de Mexico,* March, 1965.

[7] Gonzales Casanova, Pablo, *La democracia en Mexico* (Mexico: Era, 1965), pp. 210–11.

For all of Latin America during these same last few years UN-ECLA reports an increase of agricultural production for internal consumption of 21% and a population growth higher than in Cuba. In addition, taking into account the relative equality of income distribution in Cuba, and its growing inequality in the rest of Latin America throughout these years, we find to what extent agriculture has "failed" in revolutionary socialist Cuba and "progressed" in Alliance for Progress Latin America.[8]

Thus it is not "rising expectations" but declining consumption that makes genuine economic development a real and urgent necessity for the underdeveloped nations of the world. And it is clear in Guatemala, the Dominican Republic, Iran, the Congo, Indonesia, Laos, and, of course, Vietnam, that any attempt to transform the structure of underdevelopment into one of development necessarily meets armed resistance by the leadership of the United States, liberal and/or conservative. This necessity inheres in the structure of the capitalist system. In short, the United States is engaged in the Vietnamization of Asia, Africa, and Latin America, with all its inevitable consequences and implications.

It is impossible not only in the economic and political colonies but also in the metropolis of the United States itself to reverse this process by a simple change in attitude and ideology. It can be reversed only by a change in class structure. And such a change involves mobilization of the masses of the people, as they are now mobilized in Vietnam — and as President Johnson feared they threatened to become mobilized in Santo Domingo, Watts, Detroit, and elsewhere. The importance of this change lies not in its potential effect on the balance of military strength in the world but in the impact of such popular movement, at home and abroad, on the political balance of the capitalist system.

---

[8] Andre Gunder Frank, *op. cit.*

The Impact of the Cuban Revolution

RAMÓN EDUARDO RUIZ

I

Senator J. William Fulbright's recent book on American foreign policy, *The Arrogance of Power*, explores what the Senator believes is the erroneous "tendency of great nations" (i.e., the United States) "to equate power with virtue and major responsibilities with a universal mission."[1] Latin Americans will applaud his observation. Yet paradoxically their response will be ambivalent. The Cubans and nationalistic Latin American rebels who are struggling to transform their societies will even differ with Fulbright.

For Fulbright's interpretation, despite its strong criticism of America's claim to virtue, accepts a widely held United States conviction that Americans are somehow responsible for events in Latin America. Fulbright still believes that Americans should intervene to modify those events. That belief in American duty is shared in the United States by two antagonistic schools of thought. Fulbright calls the first school, Lincoln's tradition of "democratic humanism." This group wants American policy to intervene to encourage popular change in Latin America. The antithetical position, the "intolerant puritanism" of Theodore Roosevelt and his school, insists on "big-stick" diplomacy to keep out anti-American rulers, to squash Communists, and to preserve the status quo.[2]

---

[1] J. William Fulbright, *The Arrogance of Power* (New York: Random House, 1966), p. 9.
[2] *Ibid.*, p. 250.

On the surface the two interpretations are diametrically opposed; yet both spring from a similar view of the American role in world affairs: that of an omnipotent United States which should oversee the course of Latin American development.

It is, of course, true that historically the United States has wielded what could be called the "command factor," the will and ability to intervene directly or indirectly to alter temporarily the political course of a Latin American republic. Employing overwhelming economic and military superiority, the United States has dictated decisions — and will no doubt do so again in the future. Examples of American intervention are self-evident to any beginning student of inter-American affairs. In Cuba, the Platt Amendment, the military occupation of the island, the refusal to recognize Ramón Grau San Martín, and the episode of the Bay of Pigs demonstrate conclusively the American faculty for intervention. American diplomacy hindered the course of the Mexican Revolution, limited the scope of the Constitution of 1917, and compelled President Alvaro Obregón in 1923 to betray Mexican legislation based on popular demands for effective national sovereignty. In Guatemala in 1954 State Department-backed rebels toppled a constitutionally elected reform government. And in 1965, we intervened directly, and militarily, in the Dominican Republic.

However, in the opinion of some observers, the American proclivity to make so-called "command decisions" will be increasingly limited in the future. For American opinion and objectives, whether of the big-stick or the do-good schools, are subject to a noncontrollable factor in foreign affairs — the internal dynamics inherent in the history and in the societies of the Latin American republics themselves. After more than four centuries of development, spanning at least three hundred years of Spanish colonial tutelage and a century and a half of political independence, the Latin American republics have evolved historical processes beyond the power of great nations to modify. To reshape that reality would require herculean efforts, including permanent occupation by American armed forces and aid programs that the American taxpayer would be unwilling to bear.

The American predilection for directing or controlling development in Latin America is subject to another historical pattern. The *active* component of that pattern has been United States economic and political programs for the Western Hemisphere that date from the early nineteenth century. The Monroe Doctrine, Pan-Americanism, the Roosevelt Corollaries, and Woodrow Wilson's moral diplomacy are some of these. The *passive* component of the American relationship to its Western Hemisphere neighbors has been shaped by the obvious military, economic, and political superiority of the United States.

The United States reaps an uncertain harvest from both. As the "Colossus of the North," the United States helps to create a peculiar chain of thought and reaction throughout Latin America. Most Latin Americans, whether they profit or lose from their ties to the United States, resent their own "colonial status." Given the opportunity, nearly all of them would modify drastically their situation vis-à-vis the United States. To a majority of them a larger degree of independence from the United States represents freedom, personal dignity, and national sovereignty. Previous Washington policy has generated predictable responses and opinions in Latin America, which severely curtail the freedom of present-day American diplomats to improve the image of the United States. Only a radical transformation of American foreign policy, for example, would satisfy Latin American intellectuals. Meanwhile, North American statesmen find it extremely difficult, if not impossible, to make a revolutionary change in United States-Latin American policy. State Department policy-makers are heirs to a historical record of almost constant hostility and opposition on the part of the United States toward revolution in Latin America. Washington is as much the captive of history as are the Latin Americans.

Thus, American diplomatic alternatives are circumscribed. The character of United States power and diplomacy, plus the American public's acceptance of them as God-given blessings for the entire world, has generated a historical response in Latin America that American statesmen are now virtually powerless to circumvent. That, of course, does not deny the need to rectify past mistakes or the necessity of marching in step with national aspirations in Latin America. But the need to accept the historical reality rather than the hope of modifying the future sharply must underlie any transformation in American opinion and policy.

The Cuban Revolution, its origin and its durability in the face of nearly seven years of implacable United States hostility, which includes a naval blockade of the island since 1962, illustrates this problem. Though unique in salient ways, Cuba shares common historical and social traits and values with her sister Spanish American republics. Similar economic and political maladies afflict them, ills that threaten to undermine a status quo still favored by United States politicians and businessmen despite the lesson of Cuba.

II

Recent Cuban history is a paradox. Until 1958 the island was simply another Caribbean republic, the "sugar plantation" of the world. Yet that monocultural economy, the target of bitter and persistent criticism, had produced one of the highest standards of living in Latin America. Between the United States, North American "paradise," and the purgatory of Haiti, the poorest of the Caribbean republics, the Cubans were more children of Jehovah than of Mephistopheles. But, in a most perplexing manner, and to the surprise of the experts, it was Cuba and not its more poverty-burdened neighbors that had a social revolution.

No one can with absolute certainty explain why a radical upheaval engulfed the island in 1959. Whatever answer is proposed, however, cannot minimize the role of the historical background that precipitated the explosion. The key to the understanding of the revolution lies in the island's history. The shape and course of the revolution were controlled primarily by local circumstances, which were the products of a special society. Foreign factors helped to transform the revolution, but that transformation would have been impossible if the historical character of Cuban society had not encouraged and permitted it.

Cuban aspirations for reform in 1959 had been shaped by the repudiation of a Cuban society that had relied on the United States. In the minds of the rebels, local ills originated in Cuba's close ties to the United States. Castro's integrity as a leader, and that of the revolution he symbolized, depended on the extent to which he remained free of former commitments. The marked anti-American tone of Cuban thought, and the manner in which the youth of the island viewed the United States, suggests that Castro and his insurgents probably arrived at decisions independently of Washington's diplomacy.

For men of Castro's stamp had erected a model for the future that almost certainly prompted verdicts antagonistic to American interests. A clash was inevitable unless American leaders tolerated the new policy to an unusual degree. Washington cannot be acquitted of its share of the blame for the rupture of relations in 1961. The Eisenhower administration, with its stress on the role of private foreign investment in Latin America, would hardly have offered the aid Castro could accept and remain loyal to his beliefs. However, it is a mistake to fasten the entire responsibility on Washington for the conflict between the two countries.

The international scene, in which two colossi, the USSR and the United States, were competing for world supremacy, proved a decisive factor. This global rivalry permitted Castro to brush aside American objections to his program by turning to the Soviet Union. History gave him alternatives denied to previous rulers of Cuba. Castro could seek a novel solution to the island's difficulties. He undoubtedly realized that he could use the new international situation to enact the socio-economic blueprints long envisaged by nationalistic and youthful reformers and long delayed. In this endeavor, he desired the cooperation of the Soviet Union and the Cuban Communist Party. Both offered him the opportunity to consolidate the workers behind his regime. The secret of Castro's startling departure from previous Cuban diplomacy, therefore, lies not merely in the nature of Washington's policies, but in the nature of Cuban society.

Nor is the revolution's subsequent conversion to Communism divorced from the historical setting. True, when Cuba embraced Marxism in 1961, that ideological shift marked a departure from former patterns. But, the revolution which preceded this epoch-making decision had roots in local history. There was a continuity between the upheaval of 1959 and the frustrated revolution of 1933, and both reflected the mood of the independence struggle of 1895. The new Marxism had roots not only in the Cuban Communist Party, the most successful in Spanish America, but also in the island's labor movement, which Marxists of varying hues had built and dominated until the late 1940s.

Castro did not have to hide his supposedly Communist background. He could have become a convert after he won power; there was precedent to follow. The history of the island was colored with the case histories of the Mellas, Roig de Leuchsenrings, Baliños, and Martínez Villenas who later turned Communist. Castro walked in their footsteps. Further, as the island's pre-1958 history illustrates, the Cubans had never put much emphasis on the ability to keep political secrets. If young Castro was a Communist before his victorious entry into Havana, that story was the best-kept secret in a land notorious for rumors and gossip.

Americans were baffled by what transpired. Few had taken the time or the trouble to study Cuba. Recent events were generally interpreted with a superficial knowledge of the island's history and society. Nearly all studies had focused on Cuba's relations with the United States, and primarily on problems that had originated in the island's reliance on a United States-dominated sugar industry. The psychological impact of this pattern on Cuban thought and aspirations, and on the Cuban character were slighted. Political, social, and economic events, from 1898 to 1959, often connected with American policy, had foreseeable if not predictable consequences. A distinct pattern of reaction to these characteristics of Cuban society had developed among the generations of the young and hopeful. Each generation had tasted the bitter fruit of defeat and frustration; all had seen their dreams thwarted. The generation of independence had to accept limited sovereignty; that of the twenties lost its revolution in 1934. The youth of the fifties lived in a society of bankrupt politicians whom Fulgencio Batista had manipulated, while the economic barons had made their peace with him.

The triumph of the revolution in 1959 climaxed a long historical struggle, Fidel Castro has said. The victory capped the dream of people who began to fight in the nineteenth century.[3] That statement cannot be challenged. From the day in 1953 that Castro and his militants attacked Moncada, down to 1959, they copied a pattern of action nearly a hundred years old. Their tactics and programs were neither new nor original. Only national Communism was an innovation, and that, too, was not entirely alien. The guerrilla warfare adopted in 1956, writes Armando Hart, one of Castro's intimates, had a blueprint to follow that dated back to the nineteenth century.[4] The architects were the mulatto warrior Antonio Maceo and the men of 1895, who, inspired and led by José Martí, initiated the final battle for independence.

The enigmatic story has another side. Economically, the Cubans had been helped by the United States. Cuba ranked among the most advanced countries in the Spanish-speaking world. In the minds of Cubans satisfied with the status quo, their country had, in the words of W. W. Rostow, reached the "takeoff" stage.[5] According to statistics of the *Banco Nacional de Cuba* for 1956, per capita income was 336 pesos (the peso was on a par with the dollar) — the second highest in Latin America. The national sugar industry was a mechanized operation, resting on one of the three highly developed railway networks in Latin America and up-to-date highways and ports. On the basis of population, the island was the most heavily capitalized in Hispanic America.[6] Cuba

[3] *Obra Revolucionaria,* September 6, 1960, p. 18.

[4] *Ibid.,* November 10, 1962, p. 22.

[5] José M. Illán, *Cuba; Facts and Figures of an Economy in Ruins,* Miami, Fla., 1964, p. 10. Editorial ATP.

[6] U.S. Department of Commerce, *Investment in Cuba,* Washington, D.C., 1956, p. 4.

was second in gold reserves and foreign trade per capita. Only Mexico, Brazil, and Chile outranked Cuba in the value of industrial production. One of every five Cuban workers was a skilled worker. Over two-thirds of the population could read and write, a figure surpassed only by the "European" nations on the South American continent. Cuba ranked third in the number of physicians. The island had the greatest number of television stations and receiving sets in Latin America. Only North Americans attended movies more frequently than Cubans.[7] The island, observed Arthur M. Schlesinger, Jr., was the perfect test for the Eisenhower administration's thesis that "unhampered private investment was Latin America's road to salvation."[8] But the foreign tutelage had a contradictory effect on the Cuban mind, fostering a spirit of frustration and rage, especially among the young, over the island's inability to travel alone along the road to nationhood.[9] That same frustration fed an intense feeling of nationalism, which underlay the three revolutionary episodes of 1895, 1933, and 1959. For the Cubans had transformed their nationalism into a veritable cult of resentment.

That cult was the logical aftermath of an identification with the United States. For more than a hundred years of colonial life the Cubans were the offspring of a Spain in a state of decline, which was compelled on more than one occasion to reject brash American bids for Cuba. The Cuban republic had to accept a Platt Amendment that circumscribed the island's freedom of action.[10] The winning of independence, and later its defense, required, more than anything, a militant nationalism.

In addition, it has been demonstrated that some measure of economic progress in Cuba had not brought a sufficient degree

---

[7] Luis V. Manrara, *Cuba Disproves the Myth That Poverty Is the Cause of Communism* (Miami: The Truth About Cuba Committee, 1963), p. 7.

[8] Arthur M. Schlesinger, Jr., *A Thousand Days. John F. Kennedy in the White House* (Boston: Houghton-Mifflin, 1965), p. 215.

[9] Fernando Ortiz, *Cuban Counterpoint: Tobacco and Sugar* (New York: Knopf, 1947), p. 70.

[10] Felix Lizaso, *Panorama de la cultural Cubana* (Mexico: Fondo de Cultura Económica, 1949), p. 104.

of social justice for all. Schlesinger concedes that there were "shocking disparities in the distribution of wealth, especially between city and countryside and between white and Negro."[11] And a growing equality in the distribution of income was not to be expected. A fraction of the population enjoyed a monthly per capita income of 540 pesos; the majority of rural families had only seven pesos.[12] The rising cost of living, as the table demonstrates,[13] had sharply reduced real income. Cuba's per capita income was only 336 pesos in 1956 in comparison with Mississippi's $829, the lowest in the United States. The Cubans compared themselves with the United States, and not with the rest of Latin Amerca.

Year	Per Capita Income at Current Prices	Per Capita Income at 1945 Prices
1945	228	228.0
1951	344	134.7
1952	354	159.5
1953	301	161.8
1954	304	107.1
1955	312	112.4
1956	336	120.9

In these statistical contradictions lies an indispensable insight into the character of the Cuban Revolution and the path it subsequently adopted. Economic progress had encouraged the growth of a relatively sizable middle sector, which had both profited and suffered from the peculiar nature of the national picture. Expectedly, the middle sector had only a fringe role to play in the island's economic life. A favored coterie of wealthy Cubans and foreigners had a tight grip on the sugar economy. In an economic sense, the middle sector was the most frustrated. It was comparatively well off, but not sufficiently to satisfy the appetite for more.

The members of the Cuban middle sector could not aspire to the top positions in the social or business structure. A local

---

[11] Schlesinger, *op. cit.*, p. 216.
[12] Ramiro Andrade, *Cuba, el vecino socialista*, Bogotá, 1961, p. 157.
[13] *Ibid.*, p. 155.

landed clique had filled the ranks of the Cuban "four hundred," while the nation had given foreigners the favorite's place in their economies.

Denied the lion's share of the economy, the Cuban middle sector turned to political activity. Since 1940 politicians of the middle sector had more or less controlled the political apparatus. The *Auténticos,* the party of Ramón Grau San Martín and Carlos Prío Socarrás, had won the national elections of 1944 and 1948. Individual members of the middle sector had held political posts at the local, state, and national levels since the twenties. The frustrated revolution of 1933 was essentially the contribution of the middle sector, despite the tardy collaboration of Batista and his sergeant allies.

Unfortunately for Cuba, the middle-sector politician had not offered able class or national leadership. More frequently than not, he had coveted public office for personal profit. Both the middle sector and the nation suffered. Ultimately, the politician had formed a distinct and separate class in society. He was castigated by society for his disregard of the public good. In 1958 the professional politician had scant prestige among the people of Cuba.

The Cuban experience casts doubts on the validity of the popular theory held by some political scientists who envisage the salvation of Latin America in terms of middle-sector rule. For in Cuba the middle sector had power, but that stratum of society had totally discredited itself and, in the eyes of lower-class Cubans, the system of representative government. The lower classes saw themselves no better off with the professional politicians than in the days of the former insurgents and sugar barons of the era from independence to 1940.

One explanation lies in the nature of the middle sector. No cohesive, well-knit middle class existed. Draper errs when he ascribes a "middle-class way of life" to "middle-class" Cuban families. Nor, as he claims, had Cuba "already had its bourgeois revolution."[14] That nebulous stratum between the upper and lower echelons of Cuban society was made up not of one

---

[14] Theodore Draper, *Castro's Revolution* (New York: Praeger, 1962), p. 52.

but of several sectors.[15] Neither separately nor as a whole did the parts have a consciousness of class.[16] Each sector had its own needs. No consensus or unanimity of opinion held them together. All aspired to join hands with the more affluent. The hard times of the fifties had pinched them more than other segments of the population. In an ironical sense, the middle sectors had been compelled to assume the role of a permanent middle class, which they were unwilling to do. That they should voice the strongest protest, and provide that protest with leadership, was inevitable.

But that does not demonstrate that the revolution was middle class. Castro's speech at the Moncada trial eventually received public support from the middle sectors, but for many varied and conflicting reasons, each of the middle sectors saw its own special formula in Castro's indictment. Later, the various sectors were to disagree vociferously with Castro and among themselves. To allege that the revolution was monolithically "middle class," therefore, and that Castro betrayed it when he adopted nonmiddle-class goals, as Draper believes, is to stray from the complexity of the truth.[17] The revolution had neither a self-conscious middle class at its helm nor well-defined middle-class objectives. The revolution had the backing and leadership of middle sectors which had no common program. Ultimately, Castro and his coterie, the spokesmen for the most frustrated of the lot, the youth of the island, imposed their program on the others. The Communists eventually joined the Fidelistas.

Still, the revolution had little leadership outside of the nebulous and divided middle sectors. The one conspicuous example was Castro, himself, the son of a planter. Labor, for instance, stood outside of the revolution. In the past history of the island, only the upheaval of 1933 had drawn the worker into its vortex. In the general strike of that year, the worker

---

[15] Lowry Nelson, *Rural Cuba* (Minneapolis: University of Minnesota Press, 1950), p. 139.

[16] Juan F. Carvajal, "Observaciones sobre la clase media en Cuba," Theo R. Crevenna (ed.), *Materiales para el estudio de la clase media en la América Latina,* Washington, D.C., 1950, p. 34.

[17] Carvajal, *op. cit.,* p. 20.

had advanced beyond the protest advocated by his leaders. Labor radicals had organized "rural soviets" in the sugar mills.[18] In 1933, however, jobless and hungry men had been driven to take extreme measures. No such situation existed in 1958. Not once did organized labor heed Castro's call for a general strike. In the earlier struggle against Gerardo Machado, the Communists had fomented work stoppages; until the summer of 1958 they opposed Castro. Blas Roca, one of the Communist stalwarts, called Castro and his circle "petty bourgeoisie."[19]

Nor did peasants furnish the leadership and program of the revolution. That the *guajiros* later supplied the rebels with food, as Ernesto Guevara says, is true.[20] Yet, since Castro's tiny band never numbered more than 300 guerrillas, only a fraction of the rural population participated directly in the armed conflict. Not until the guerrillas had virtually triumphed late in 1958 did the people of the countryside join the vocal supporters of the revolution. Castro's agrarian promises ultimately awakened a rural discontent that had remained dormant through nearly all of the anti-Batista protest. Yet, there was sufficient dissatisfaction in the ranks of rural labor to provide Castro with the backing he later sorely needed. In summary, rural labor had had enough progress to keep it somewhat neutral in times of political stress, but not enough to prevent the worker from supporting a victorious revolutionary movement that promised to alleviate old grievances.

The revolution traveled with astonishing speed and alacrity. One answer lies in the nature of the island's society (as well as in Castro's extraordinarily able political leadership). No insuperable barriers were in the path of the revolution. Cuban society was weak. It was a dependent society, the child of American tutelage as much as of Spanish rule. It was split

---

[18] Commission on Cuban Affairs, *Problems of the New Cuba* (New York: Foreign Policy Association, Inc., 1935), p. 183.

[19] *World Marxist Review,* August, 1959.

[20] Ernesto Guevara, *Guerrilla Warfare* (New York: Praeger, 1961), p. 35.

by economic, social, and ethnic divisions.[21] No homogeneous middle-class or national bourgeoisie existed.[22] The welfare of the sugar barons and the middle sectors relied on the United States. The two groups had no clearly defined or class interest to defend. Both were international in character, more reliant on foreign interests than on local factors. In a political sense, Cuba had reached the end of an era; parties and politicians were bankrupt. The structure of society simply crumbled. The guerrilla phase of the revolution lasted a short two years; fighting was sporadic and limited in territorial scope. Castro's militants alone did not vanquish Batista. The *caudillo* fell also because he lost the support of the politically aware segments of the population. Without the inherent weakness of Cuban society, and Batista's mistakes, Castro's band could not have triumphed.

The absence of ideology in the Fidelista camp, in a similar manner, reflected the prerevolutionary picture. Cuba had no concise national ideology or set of universal beliefs. Of the political groupings, the Communists alone had an ideology and a unity. Therefore, confronted with the need for political allies and given his analysis of Cuban history and ills (an interpretation shared widely by the young), Castro turned to the Communists. The Communist Party offered him the ideology, discipline, and organization he desperately needed to rally the population behind him. No other institution was available to provide them.

Further, the Cuban people had lost faith in themselves and in their leadership. Cuba was in a state of moral chaos. "It is difficult to meet," Luis Aguilar perceptively recognized, "a more skeptical and distrustful people than ours."[23] Nor had economic stagnation or dishonesty in government alone produced this moral turpitude. The crisis went deeper. To Aguilar it stemmed from a profound debasement of national ideals, which should have sustained the politician as well as the

---

[21] Robin Blackburn, "Prologue to the Cuban Revolution," *New Left Review,* London, October, 1963, p. 54.

[22] Carvajal, *op. cit.,* p. 36.

[23] *Pasado y Ambiente en el Proceso Cubano,* Havana, 1957, p. 74.

worker, the landlord and teacher, the soldier and the student. "The absence of higher motives, of common beliefs, which unite and identify people as members of one and the same collectivity, and which discipline and group them together in a common endeavor, had produced the crisis."[24] No group was more aware of this perversion of values than the Cuban youth.

Mexico's experience with revolution, in which the United States was a determining factor, had an important effect on the course of post-1959 Cuban events. The leaders of Cuba saw the Mexican Revolution as a historical failure and as a bad example to follow. Mexico, declared the prominent Cuban Communist, Blas Roca, had enjoyed a national liberating revolution; the Cardenista upheaval of the thirties had influenced the framers of the Cuban constitution of 1940. But despite all this, the Mexican Revolution had stayed within a capitalistic framework, and had fallen into the hands of the North Americans and their allies. The revolution had perished in the process.

In Mexico, as of 1965, just 400 private corporations controlled 77% of all invested capital in the country. Of these, 185 corporations control 55% of invested capital. These 185 corporations are either *wholly United States owned or are controlled by United States investment*. (The rest of the "400" includes 38 corporations owned by the Mexican government — representing 25% of the capital, and 127 private Mexican corporations — representing 20%) Thus United States business interests control 55% of all capital invested in the pace-setting corporations, 42% of all corporations (55% of 77%) and 32% of all money invested in Mexico whatsoever. In addition, since 43% of all deposits are in United States-owned banks, the United States, in effect, controls 43% of all money loaned in the country.[25] If the Cuban Revolution were to survive, said Roca, the revolution had to avoid the pitfalls into which the Mexicans had wandered. The revolution had to sever the old relationship of Cuba with the United States,

---

[24] *Ibid.*, p. 54.
[25] John Gerassi, *The Great Fear* (New York: Macmillan, 1963).

which dictated the pattern of local society, and which the frustrated Mexican Revolution had left intact.[26]

III

Cuba's successful flight from United States orbit provides a lesson that should be heeded by thoughtful Americans. Though the United States sphere of influence in the Western Hemisphere still remains largely intact, that sphere is neither free of the winds of revolution nor isolated from the currents of world conflict. The past, in which Latin Americans had almost no contact with the people of other continents (outside of an export trade with Britain and one or two other European nations friendly to the United States), has disappeared. Latin America has joined the modern world of international rivalry and ideological conflict.

Cuba's recent experience demonstrates two truths: (1) a successful social revolution can be carried out in Latin America against the wishes of the United States; (2) escape from United States domination is possible. On the surface Cuba is an outcast in the Western Hemisphere, and may be so in reality. But that is not the crux of the problem; what matters is that Cuba has apparently altered a historical pattern — a goal of reformers in the Western Hemisphere. Whether friends or foes of the United States, a majority of Latin Americans desire a much larger measure of independence from their northern neighbor.

As the Cuban experience demonstrates, the power of the United States to direct political and economic change is not inexhaustible. A new international situation has upset the traditional picture. Forces inherent in Latin American societies, over which the United States has only peripheral sway, are at work. Social change in Latin America is on the horizon. Only time will determine the appearance of that change.

[26] Blas Roca, *Los fundamentos del socialismo en Cuba,* Havana, 1962, p. 109.

The United States and Revolution in Latin America

JOHN GERASSI

Much is being written in the United States these days about Pax Americana and American hegemony in the underdeveloped world. Even calm, rational, conscientious academicians are publicly lamenting these increasingly bellicose policies from Vietnam to the Dominican Republic. Suddenly, intellectuals are discovering such words as "imperialism" and "expansionism." Some are asking: Why? Who's to blame? What can be done to stop all this?

The questions reflect a liberal point of view that there is a qualitative difference between United States imperialistic policies of today and yesterday; whereas in reality, the basic difference between United States imperialism today and United States imperialism a century ago is that it is more far-reaching and more consciously conceived today. But United States foreign policy has always been assertive, always expansionist, always basically imperialist from the 1790s.

From the 1790s to the mid-1800s, our imperialism was dominantly *continental* imperialism. For a century, there was sufficient land area, and other resources, within relatively easy reach of escalating numbers of home-seekers and economic entrepreneurs, merely by "going west." There was no urgent need to pursue them in far places.

The "underdeveloped" people of that century, who occupied our vast continental area, were of course Indians, of whom we killed some 600,000 — and dehabitated nearly all the others

— in the process of "subduing a continent," and "rounding out our national boundaries." And that century saw all of Florida acquired under duress, and more than half — the better half — of Mexico annexed by processes involving war-making.

It has been pertinently observed that, "By far the most basic of all basic factors influencing the foreign policy of the United States has been economic,"[1] both continentally and in far places. Our private corporate economic operators in shipping, trading, and whaling pursuits began in the early decades of our national history. Our government, from its very beginning and increasingly, provided congressional and diplomatic support for their operations from the West Indies to the Orient.[2] For example, after Britain made war upon China to compel the admission of opium into China, in 1839 — the "Opium War" — our government managed to get the same trading privileges for our private shipping and trading operators in Chinese ports (except for opium) which British war-making had exacted for British shipping and trading concerns. Then, when in the late 1850s, more British and French war-making forced the helpless Chinese government to open more ports to foreign traders, our government accepted for our private operators the same privileges.

Only in the late 1890s, however, did our imperialistic doings begin to head toward potentially spectacular proportions in far places.

Imperialism has always operated in three specific, recognizable and analyzable stages: (1) to control the sources of raw material for the benefit of the imperializing country; (2) to control the markets in the imperialized country for the benefit of the imperializing country's producers; and (3) to control the imperialized country's internal development and

---

[1] See W. A. Williams, *The Tragedy of American Foreign Policy* (New York: World, 1962). Also Neal D. Houghton, "Social Structure and Foreign Policy of the United States," *The Year Book of World Affairs, 1961,* XV (London: London Institute of World Affairs, University of London).

[2] See Benjamin H. Williams, *Economic Foreign Policy of the United States* (New York: McGraw-Hill, 1929).

economic structure so as to guarantee continuing expansion of stages (1) and (2).

That has been our way of operating in Latin America. It was more than coincidence that in 1823, when our government proclaimed the Monroe Doctrine — the first of a series of imperialistic Presidential "doctrines" — one-fifth of all foreign trade from the United States was with Latin American countries. That famous "doctrine" was no mere generous gesture of concern for Latin American "independence" from the European "system," in the 1820s or in the twentieth century.[3]

Looking backward, with the perspective of historical hindsight, that pronouncement said, in effect, that Europeans must stay out of Latin America because it is to become essentially a United States empire. As Salvador de Madariaga has said:

> I only know two things about the Monroe Doctrine: one is that no American I have met knows what it is; the other is that no American I have met will consent to its being tampered with. That being so, I conclude that the Monroe Doctrine is not doctrine but a dogma, for such are the two features by which you can tell a dogma. But when I look closer into it, I find that it is not one dogma, but two, to wit: the dogma of the infallibility of the American President and the dogma of the immaculate conception of American foreign policy.[4]

And, with its later unilateral Presidential corollaries and interpretations, it served frankly as a vehicle to carry forward a vast expansion of "Yankee imperialism" in the early decades of this century, particularly in the Central American and Caribbean area.

From 1907 to the mid-1930s, flagrant and spectacular United States military and financial interventions virtually took over economic and political control of a large part of

---

[3] See Dexter Perkins, *Hands Off: A History of the Monroe Doctrine* (New York: Little, Brown, 1941). See also Luis Quintanilla, *A Latin American Speaks* (New York: Macmillan, 1943).

[4] Salvador de Madariaga, *Latin America Between the Eagle and the Bear* (New York: Praeger, 1962).

that area. Our military forces never left that area during those two decades.[5] As the much-decorated Major General Smedley D. Butler has said:

> I helped make Mexico, and especially Tampico, safe for American oil interests. I helped make Haiti and Cuba a decent place for the National City Bank to collect revenue. I helped pacify Nicaragua for the international banking house of Brown Brothers. I brought light to the Dominican Republic for American sugar interests. I helped make Honduras "right" for American fruit companies. . . .[6]

Against such interventions, some local patriots fought back. For example, in Haiti, where United States Marines landed in 1915 and stayed until 1934, 2,000 rebels called Cacos had to be killed before the United States "pacified" the island. And there were other rebellions everywhere. In Nicaragua, one such rebel had to be tricked to be eliminated. Augusto Cesar Sandino fought American marines from 1926 until 1934 without being defeated, though the marines razed to the ground various towns in Nicaragua and, by accident, some in Honduras to boot. In 1934 when he was offered "negotiations," he came to the United States Embassy to confer with Ambassador Arthur Bliss Lane, and was assassinated.

In time, however, accumulated Latin resistance had some effect. Ultimately, it impelled Washington to accept the so-called "Organization of American States," which was supposed to "multilateralize" the Monroe Doctrine. But that development has, in the final analysis, only helped to reinforce a basic policy of United States control.

---

[5] See Williams, *op. cit.,* especially Chaps. 9–12; Juan José Arévalo, *The Shark and the Sardines* (New York: Lyle Stuart, 1961); see also a series of studies published by the World Peace Foundation, including: Isaac J. Co., *Nicaragua and The United States,* 1927; Arthur C. Millspaugh, *Haiti under American Control,* 1931; and Dana G. Munro, *The United States and The Caribbean Area,* 1934.

[6] Maj. Gen. S. D. Butler, in *Common Sense,* November 19, 1933, quoted in C. Wright Mills, *Listen Yankee* (New York: Ballantine Books, 1960).

On March 4, 1933, the United States officially "changed" its policy. Beginning with his inauguration address, Franklin D. Roosevelt, launching his "Good Neighbor" policy, told the world that American imperialism in Latin America was at an end and that from now on the United States would be a good neighbor. He voted in favor of a nonintervention pledge at the 1933 Montevideo Inter-American Conference, promised Latin American countries tariff reductions and exchange trade agreements, and a year later abrogated the Platt Amendment. His top diplomat, Sumner Welles, even said, in 1935, "It is my belief that American capital invested abroad must, in fact as well as in theory, be subordinated to the authority of the people of the country where it is located."

But, in fact, only the form of United States interventionism changed. Roosevelt was the most intelligent imperialist the United States has had in modern times. As a liberal, he knew the value of rhetoric. As a capitalist, he knew that he who dominates the economy of an area dominates the politics. As long as United States interventionism for economic gain had to be defended by United States Marines, rebellions and revolutions would always be inevitable. When a country is occupied by marines, the enemy is clearly identifiable. He wears the marine uniform. But if there are no marines, if the oppressors are the local militia, police, or military forces, if these forces' loyalty to Washington interests can be guaranteed by their economic ties to United States commercial interests, it will be difficult, even impossible, for local patriots to finger the enemy That, Mr. Roosevelt understood. Thus, he launched a brilliant series of policies meant to tie Latin American countries to the United States.

In 1938, he set up the Interdepartmental Committee of Cooperation with American Republics, which was, in effect, the precursor of today's technical aid program of the Organization of American States (OAS). (The OAS itself had grown out of the Pan American Union which had been set up by Secretary of State James G. Blaine as "an ideal economic complement to the United States.")[7]

---
[7] Lloyd Mecham, *A Survey of United States–Latin American Relations* (Boston: Houghton Mifflin, 1965).

President Roosevelt's Interdepartmental Committee assured Latin America's dependency on the United States for technical progress. During the war, the United States Department of Agriculture sent Latin America soil conservation research teams which helped increase Latin America's dependency on one-crop economies. In 1940, President Roosevelt said that the United States government and United States private business should invest heavily in Latin America in order "to develop sources of raw materials needed in the United States." On September 26, 1940, he increased the limitations of the Export-Import Bank, which is an arm of the United States Treasury, from $100 million to $700 million, and by Pearl Harbor Day most Latin American countries had received "development loans" from which they have yet to disengage themselves. Latin America's economic dependency was further secured during the war through the United States Lend Lease program which poured $262,762,000 worth of United States equipment into eighteen Latin American nations (the two excluded were Panama, which was virtually a United States dependency, and Argentina which was rebellious at the time).

Roosevelt's policies were so successful that his successors — liberals all, whether Republican or Democrat — continued and strengthened them. By 1950, 70% of Latin America's sources of raw materials and 50% of its Gross National Product were controlled from the United States. Theoretically at least, there was no more need for military intervention.

As early as 1884, official United States government commercial missions were introduced throughout Latin America for the purpose of promoting the effective influence of United States business operators. As the head of one such mission reported, after some years of work, the purpose was successfully carried out: "Our countrymen easily lead in nearly every major town. In every republic will be found businessmen with wide circles of influence. Moreover, resident merchants offer the best means to introduce and increase the use of our goods." (Nothing, of course, has changed in this respect. Notice, for example, a report in *Newsweek* magazine of April 19, 1965: "American diplomats can be expected to intensify their help to United States businessmen overseas. Directives now awaiting Dean Rusk's signature will remind United States embassies that their efficiency will be rated not only by diplomatic and political prowess but by how well they foster American commercial interests abroad. Moreover, prominent businessmen will be recruited as inspectors of the foreign service.")

Latin American reformers did not realize to what extent the economic stranglehold by the United States insured pro-United States-business governments. They kept thinking that if they could only present their case to their people they could alter the pattern of life and indeed the structure itself. Because the United States advocated, in rhetoric at least, free speech and free institutions, they hoped that it would help them come to power. What they failed to realize was that in any underdeveloped country the vast majority of the population is either illiterate and therefore cannot vote or else lives in addressless slums and therefore still cannot vote. What's more, there is no surplus of funds available from the poor. Thus, to create a party and be materially strong enough to wage a campaign with radio and newspaper announcements for the sake of the poor is impossible. The poor cannot finance such a campaign. That is why Washington has often tried to convince its puppets to allow freedom of the press and freedom of elections; after all, the rich will always be the only ones capable of owning newspapers and financing elections.

Now and then, of course, a reformist president has been elected in Latin America. But, if he then tried to carry out his reforms, he was always overthrown. This is what happened in Guatemala where Juan José Arévalo and then Jacobo Arbenz were elected on reform platforms. Before Arévalo's inauguration in 1945, Guatemala was one of the most backward countries in Latin America. The rights of labor, whether in factories or in fields, including United Fruit Company plantations, had never been recognized; unions, civil liberties, freedom of speech and press had been outlawed. Foreign interests had been sacred and monopolistic, and their tax concessions beyond all considerations of fairness. Counting each foreign corporation as a person, 98% of Guatemala's cultivated land was owned by exactly 142 people (out of a total population of 3 million). Only 10% of the population attended school. Arévalo and Arbenz tried to change these conditions. As long as they pressed for educational reforms, no one grumbled too much. Free speech and press were established, then unions were recognized and legalized, and finally, on June 17, 1952, Arbenz proclaimed Decree 900, a substantial land reform program, which called for the expropriation and redistribution of uncultivated lands above a basic average. But Decree 900 specifically exempted all intensively cultivated lands, which amounted to only 5% of over-1,000-hectare farms then under cultivation. The decree ordered all absentee-owned property to be redistributed but offered compensation in twenty-year bonds at 3% interest, assessed according to declared tax value.

Stateside agronomists applauded Decree 900. On page 179 of *Latin American Issues* published by the Twentieth Century Fund, one can read: "For all the furore it produced, Decree 900, which had its roots in the constitution of 1945, is a remarkably mild and fairly sound piece of legislation." But, since much of Guatemalan plantation land, including 400,000 acres not under cultivation, belonged to the United Fruit Company, the United States became concerned. When Arbenz gave out that fallow land to 180,000 peasants, the United States condemned his regime as "Communist," convened an OAS conference in Caracas to make that condemnation official and found a right-wing Colonel named Carlos Castillo Armas, a graduate of the Command and General Staff School at Fort Leavenworth, Kansas, to do its dirty work. From the States, he was fed arms and dollars to set up a rebel force in Honduras and Nicaragua and helped to overthrow Arbenz. No matter how good a neighbor the United States wanted to appear, it was observably willing to dump such neighborliness and resort to old-fashioned military intervention when the commercial interests of its corporations were threatened. And the basic conditions in Guatemala today approximate those of pre-1945 — another example of the "*development* of underdevelopment."

Since then, of course, the United States has intervened again, on occasion, most visibly in the Dominican Republic in

1965 and in Cuba from 1961. Today, there can no longer be more than two positions in Latin America. As a result of the Dominican intervention, in which 23,000 American troops were used to put down a nationalist rebellion of 4,000 armed men, the United States has made it clear that it will never allow any Latin government to break its rigid economic control.

And what is that control? Today, 85% of the sources of raw material are controlled by operators from the United States. One United States company (United Fruit) controls over 50% of the foreign earnings, therefore of the whole economic structure, of six Latin American countries. In Venezuela, Standard Oil Company of New Jersey (Rockefeller), through its subsidiary the Creole Oil Corporation, controls all the bases of the industrialization processes. Venezuela may be potentially the second richest country in the world. Its $500,000,000-plus net annual revenue from oil could guarantee every family an annual income of almost $3,000. Instead, 40% of its population lives outside the money economy; 22% are unemployed, and the country must use over $100 million a year of its revenue to import foodstuffs, whereas the country has enough land, under a proper agrarian reform, to be an exporter of food.

Chile, with enough minerals to develop a modern industrial economy, flounders in inflation (21% in 1966) while, despite all the talk of "Revolution in Freedom," there is only freedom for at most one-fifth[8] of the population and revolution for no one. So far, about the best that Frei has been able to do is to launch sewing classes in the slums. The right accuses him of demagogy, the left of paternalism; both are correct while, as the *Christian Science Monitor* (September 19, 1966) says, "Many of the poor are apathetic, saying that they are just being used, as they have in the past."

The continent as a whole must use from 30 to 40% of its foreign earnings to pay to the industrialized world — mostly the United States — interest and service charges, *not the principal*, on loans. Recently, spokesmen for the Alliance for

---

[8] Federico G. Gil, *The Political Systems of Chile* (Boston: Houghton Mifflin, 1966). See also his "Chile: 'Revolution in Liberty,'" in *Current History*, LI, No. 303 (November, 1966).

Progress have said that it is helping Latin America to indus-
trialize on a social progress basis.[9] Now, more than six years
old, it has witnessed some peculiar developments: right-wing
coups in Argentina, Brazil, Honduras, Guatemala, Ecuador,
the Dominican Republic and Salvador. In exchange, United
States businessmen have remitted to the United States $5 bil-
lion of profits while investing less than $2 billion. And the
Alliance itself, which is supposed to lend money for strictly
social progress projects, has kept 86% of its outlay to credits
for products from the United States, credits which are guaranteed by Latin American governments and are repayable in
dollars.

But then, under President Johnson, the Alliance no longer
maintains its social pretenses, as the President himself made
clear in November, 1966 when he told American GIs at Camp
Stanley, Korea (and as recorded and broadcast by Pacifica
radio stations), "Don't forget, there are only 200 million of
us in a world of three billion. They want what we've got and
we're not going to give it to them."

Interventionist and imperialist policies of the United States
in Latin America are now successfully in the third stage. Not
only do United States operators largely control Latin America's sources of raw material, not only does the United States
largely control its Latin markets for United States manufactured goods, but it also heavily controls the internal money
economy.

Karl Marx had once warned that the first revolutionary
wave in an imperialized country will come about as the result
of frustration by the national bourgeoisie, which will have
reached a development stage where it will have accumulated
enough capital to want to become competitive to the imperializing corporations. This has not been allowed to happen in
Latin America.

As United States corporations became acutely plagued by
surplus goods, they realized that they must expand their

---

[9] Jorge Graciarena, "Desarrollo y Política," *Argentina, Sociedad de
Mases,* Torcuato S. Di Tella, Gino Germani and Jorge Graciarena (eds.),
1965. Also, Henri Edme, "Révolution en Amerique Latine?," *Les Temps
Modernes,* XXI, No. 240 (May, 1966).

markets in underdeveloped countries. To do so, however, they would have to help develop a national bourgeoisie which could purchase these goods. This "national" bourgeoisie, as with all such classes in colonialized countries, had to be created by the service industries, yet somehow limited so that it did not become economically independent. The solution was simple. United States corporations, having set up assembly plants in São Paulo or Buenos Aires, which they called Brazilian or Argentinian corporations, decided actually to help create the subsidiary industries — with local money — themselves. Take General Motors, for example. First, it brought down its cars in various pieces called parts (thus eliminating import duties). Then it assembled them in São Paulo and called them Brazil-made. Next, it shopped around for local entrepreneurs to launch the subsidiary industries — seat covers, spark plugs, etc. Normally, the landed oligarchy and entrepreneurs in the area would do its own investing in those subsidiary industries, and having successfully amassed large amounts of capital, would band together to create their own car industry. It was this step that had to be avoided. Thus General Motors first offered these local entrepreneurs contracts by which it helped to finance the servicing industries. Then it brought the entrepreneurs' capital into huge holding corporations which, in turn, it rigidly controlled. The holding corporations became very successful, making the entrepreneurs happy, and everyone forgot about a local, competitive car industry, making General Motors happy.

This procedure is best employed by International Basic Economy Corporation (IBEC),[10] Rockefeller's mammoth investing corporation in Latin America. IBEC claims to be locally owned by Latin Americans since it does not hold a con-

---

[10] IBEC, which claims (in each country) to be a "small, locally owned organization" is, in fact, a gigantic investment concern which *completely* controls its interests. An indication of the "smallness" of IBEC can be gained by noting the wide area of its investments. The home office is 30 Rockefeller Plaza, New York City, with operations in: Argentina, Brazil, Canada, Chili, Colombia, El Salvador, France, Germany, Great Britain, India, Ireland, Italy, Japan, Mexico, the Netherlands, Pakistan, Peru, Rhodesia, Spain, Sweden, Switzerland, Thailand, Uruguay, Venezuela and Zambia.

trolling interest. But the 25 to 45% held by Rockefeller (it varies from Colombia to Venezuela to Peru) is not offset by the thousands of individual Latin investors who, in order to set policy, would all have to agree among themselves and then vote in a block. When one corporation owns 45%, while sizable numbers of individual investors split the other 55%, the corporation sets policy — in the United States as well as abroad. Besides, IBEC is so successful that the local entrepreneurs "think American" even before IBEC does. In any case, the result of these holding corporations is that the national bourgeoisie in Latin America has been eliminated. It is really a United States bourgeoisie.

IBEC and other holding corporations use their combined local-stateside capital to invest in all sorts of profitable ventures, from supermarkets to assembly plants. Naturally, these new corporations are set up where they can bring the most return. IBEC is *not* going to build a supermarket in the Venezuelan province of Falcon, where the population lives outside the money economy altogether and hence could not buy goods at the supermarket anyway. Nor would IBEC build a supermarket in Falcon because there are no roads leading there. Thus, the creation of IBEC subsidiaries in no way helps to develop the infrastructure of the host country. What's more, since such holding corporations have their tentacles in every major segment of the economy, they control the money market as well. (Which is why United States corporations backed — indeed pushed — the formation of a Latin American "common market" at the 1967 Punta del Este Conference. Such a common market would eliminate duties on United States goods assembled in Latin America and being exported from one Latin American country to another.) Hence no new United States investment needs to be brought down even for the 45% of the holding corporations.

New United States investment in Latin America today is a paper investment. But a new corporation set up with local funds may only drain the local capital reserves. And the result may be an industry benefiting, dominantly, those sectors of the economy which purchase surplus products from the United States.

But, it needs to be emphatically stated that the ruling and upper economic classes in Latin America have never avidly invested their local earnings in locally organized industrial corporations. Notoriously, in considerable numbers, they have invested more freely in the relatively "safe" parts of the world — Europe and the United States — and have kept sizable fortunes in the banks of those areas.

And, having seen the local Latin American economic and political elites so behave, becoming increasingly tied up with stateside corporations — official Washington now rarely needs to intervene with marines to guarantee friendly governments. The local military, bought by the United States national interests, guarantees friendly regimes — with the approval of the local press, the local legal political parties, the local cultural centers, all of which the local money controls. And the local money is now tightly linked to United States interests.

Latin American reformers have finally realized all this. They now know that the only way to break that structure is to *break* it — which means basic social revolution. Hence there are few *reformers* in Latin America anymore. They have become either *pro-Americans*, whatever they call themselves, who will do America's bidding, or they are *revolutionaries*.

Liberal historians, social scientists and politicians in the United States insist that there is still a third way: a nonviolent revolution which will be basically prodemocracy, i.e., pro-American. They tell us that such a revolutionary process has already started and that it will inevitably lead to equality between the United States and its Latin neighbors. Liberal politicians here also like to tell their people that they should be on the side of that process, help it along, give it periodic boosts. In May, 1966, Robert Kennedy put it this way in a Senate speech: "A revolution is coming — a revolution which will be peaceful if we are wise enough; compassionate if we care enough; successful if we are fortunate enough — but a revolution which is coming whether we will it or not. We can affect its character, we cannot alter its inevitability."

What Kennedy may seem not to understand, however, is that if the revolution is peaceful and compassionate, if Americans *can* affect its character, then it will be no revolution at all. There have been plenty of such misbred revolutions already.

For example, in Uruguay, at the beginning of this century, a great man carried out Latin America's first apparently basic social revolution, and he was very peaceful, very compassionate, and very successful. José Batlle y Ordoñez gave his people the eight-hour day, a day of rest for every five of work, mandatory severance pay, minimum wages, unemployment compensation, old-age pensions, paid vacations. He legalized divorce, abolished capital punishment, set up a state mortgage bank. He made education free through university, levied taxes on capital, real estate, profits, horse racing and luxury sales (but not on income, which would curtail incentive, he thought). He nationalized public utilities, insurance, alcohol, oil, cement, meat-packing, fish-processing, and the principal banks. He outlawed arbitrary arrest, searches and seizures, separated the state from the Church, which was forbidden to own property. He made it possible for peons to come to the city and get good jobs if they didn't like working for the landed oligarchy. All of this he did before the Russian Revolution — without one murder, without one phony election.

But what happened? A thriving middle class became more and more used to government subsidy. When the price of meat and wool fell on the world market, the subsidies began to evaporate. The middle class was discontented. Used to government support, it demanded more. The government was forced to put more and more workers, mostly white collar, on its payroll. The whole structure became a hand-me-down because the people had never participated in Batlle's great revolution. Nobody had fought for it. It had come on a silver platter, and now that the platter was being chipped away, those who had most profited from the so-called revolution became unhappy. There was no personal involvement, therefore no personal responsibility.

Today, in Uruguay, more than one-third of the working force is employed by the government — but does not share in the decision-making apparatus. And the government, of course, is bankrupt. It needs help, and so it begs. And the United States, as usual, is very generous. It is rescuing Uruguay —

but Uruguay is paying for it. It has too much of a national-istic tradition to be as servile as the banana republics, but on matters crucial to the United States, Uruguay now toes the line. It either abstains or votes yes whenever Washington wants the Organization of American States to justify or ra-tionalize United States aggression. And, of course, free enter-prise is once again primary.

The oligarchy still owns the land, still heavily hoards and invests its fat earnings in Europe and the United States. There are fewer poor people in Uruguay than elsewhere in Latin America, but those who *are* poor *stay* poor. The middle class, self-centered and self-serving, takes pride in being *vivo*, shrewd and sharp at being able to swindle the government and one another. Uruguay is politically one of the freest countries in the world and Montevideo is one of the most pleasant places to live, but only if one has money, only if one has abandoned all hope of achieving national pride — or of a truly equitable society.

In 1910, while Uruguay's peaceful revolution was still un-folding, Mexico unleashed its own — neither peacefully nor compassionately. For the next seven years, blood was shed throughout the land, and the Indian peasants took an active part in the upheaval. But Mexico's revolution was not truly a people's revolution, insofar as it was basically controlled by the bourgeoisie. Francisco I. Madero, who led the first revo-lutionary wave, was certainly honest, but he was also a wealthy landowner who never felt the burning thirst for change that Mexican peasants fought for. He did understand it somewhat and possibly for that reason was assassinated, with alleged complicity of the United States Ambassador, Henry Lane Wilson.[11] But he was incapable of englobing into his program the unverbalized but nonetheless real plans that such peasant leaders as Pancho Villa and Emiliano Zapata embodied in their violent reaction to the long torment suffered by their people.

Andre Gunder Frank has written that the bourgeoisie and the peasants, "faced a common enemy, the feudal order and

---

[11] Jesús Silva Herzog, *Breve historia de la revolución Mexicana* (Mex-ico: Fondo de Cultura Economica, 1960).

its supporting pillars of Church, army, and foreign [United States] capital. But their goals differed — freedom from domestic and foreign bonds and loosening of the economic structure for the bourgeoisie; land for the peasants. Although Zapata continued to press the interests of the peasants until his murder in 1919, the real leadership of the revolution was never out of the hands of the bourgeoisie, except insofar as it was challenged by the Huerta reaction and United States intervention. The weakening of the traditional feudal order was of course in the interest of the emerging bourgeoisie as well as of the peasants. Education became secularized, Church and state more widely separated. But accession to power by the peasantry was never really in the cards."[12]

Thus kept out of power, the peasants never genuinely benefited from their revolution. They did receive land periodically, but it was rarely fertile or irrigated, and the *ejidos*, communal lands, soon became the poorest sections of Mexico. The bourgeois-revolutionary elite grew into Mexico's new oligarchy, and while some of its members did have darker skins than the old Spanish colonialists, the peasants were never integrated into the new Institutional Party power structure.[13]

Today, not only do they rarely vote (in the 1958 Presidential elections, for example, only 23% of the population voted officially, and that only after frauds upped the count),[14] but they barely profit from the social laws instituted by the revolution. As Vincett Padgett, who is no revolutionary, has written: "To the marginal Mexican, the law and the courts are of little use. The formal institutions are not expected to provide

[12] Andre Gunder Frank, "Mexico: the Janus Faces of Twentieth Century Bourgeois Revolution," *Monthly Review*, XIV, No. 7 (November, 1962.) For a comprehensive treatment of the Mexican Revolution and the part played by private and official United States influences, see Daniel James, *Mexico and the Americans* (New York: Praeger, 1963), especially Chaps. 6–16.

[13] See Anita Brenner and George R. Leighton, *The Wind That Swept Mexico: History of the Mexican Revolution, 1910–1942* (New York: Harper & Row, 1943). See also Martin C. Needler, "The Political Development of Mexico," *American Political Science Review* (June, 1961), pp. 308–12.

[14] See Phillip B. Taylor, Jr., "The Mexican Elections of 1958: Affirmation of Authoritarianism," *ibid.*, XIII (September, 1960), 722–44.

justice. There is only acceptance and supplication. In the most unusual of circumstances there is for the marginal man the resort to violence, but the most significant point is that there exists no middle ground."[15]

In Mexico today, peasants still die of starvation. Illiteracy is about 50%, and 46% of school-age children do not attend schools at all. Most of the cotton is controlled by one state-side outlet, Anderson-Clayton, and 55% of Mexican banks' capital is dominated from the United States. Yet Mexico's Revolution was both anti-American and violent. What went wrong?

What went wrong is that the revolution failed to sustain its impulses. It is not enough to win militarily. A revolutionary must continue to fight long after he defeats the enemy. He must keep his people armed, as a constant check against himself and as a form of forcing the people's participation in his revolutionary government. Yet he must also be careful not to guide this popular participation into a traditional form of party or state democracy, lest the intramural conflicts devour the revolution itself, as they did in Bolivia.[16] He must make the transition from a generalized concept of anti-Americanism and "reform" to a series of particular manifestations — that is, he must nationalize all the properties belonging to Americans (or Britons or Turks or whatever is the dominating imperialist power).

The old economic and political order must give way to a drastically different order. Only then can there be a total integration of the population in the new nation.

I am not trying here to define a psychological rationalization for violent revolution. What I am maintaining is that if basic social revolutionary leadership wants an overhaul of society, if it wants to establish an equitable society, if it wants to install

[15] L. Vincett Padgett, *The Mexican Political System* (Boston: Houghton Mifflin, 1966).

[16] John Gerassi, *The Great Fear in Latin America* (rev. ed., New York: Macmillan, 1965). Also Richard W. Patch, "United States Assistance in a Revolutionary Setting," in Robert D. Tomasek (ed.), *Latin American Politics: Studies of the Contemporary Scene* (Garden City: Doubleday, 1966).

economic democracy — without which all the *political* democracy in heaven and Washington is meaningless — then it must be ready to go all the way. There are no short cuts to either truth or justice.

Besides, violence already exists in the Latin American continent today, but it is a negative violence, a counterrevolutionary violence. Most such violence there takes the form of dying of old age at twenty-eight in Brazil's northeast. Or it is the Bolivian woman who feeds only three of her four children because the fourth, as one told me, "is sickly and will probably die anyway and I have not enough food for all four."

Liberal reformers, of course, will argue that one can always approximate, compromise, defend the rule of law while working for better living conditions piece by piece. But the facts shatter such illusions. Latin America is poorer today than thirty years ago. Fewer people drink potable water now than then. One-third of the population lives in slums. Half never see a doctor. Besides, every compromise measure has either failed or been corrupted. Vargas gave Brazilian workingmen a class consciousness and launched a petroleum agency; his heirs filled their own pockets but tried to push Brazil along on the road to progress. They were smashed by the country's economic master, the United States. Perón, whatever his personal motivation, gave Argentinians new hopes and new slogans; his successors, pretending to despise him, bowed to pressure from the United States, kept their country under their boot and sold out its riches to United States companies.[17] In Guatemala, as we saw, Arévalo and then Arbenz tried to bring about social and agrarian reforms without arming the people, without violence. The United States destroyed them by force and, when the right-wing semidictatorship of Ydigoras Fuentes decided to allow free elections in which Arevalo might make a comeback, America's great liberal rhetoretician, President Kennedy, ordered Ydigoras' removal, as the *Miami Herald* reported.[18] In the Dominican Republic, a peo-

---

[17] Turcuato S. Di Tella, "Populism and Reform in Latin America," in Claudio Veliz (ed.), *Obstacles to Change in Latin America* (New York: Oxford University Press, 1965).
[18] December 24, 1966.

ple's spontaneous revulsion — after thirty-two years of Trujillo — was met by United States Marines. The list of comparable cases is very long.

Latin America's revolutionaries know from the experience of the Dominican Republic, of Guatemala, and of Vietnam that to break the structure is to invite United States retaliation. They also realize that United States retaliation will be so formidable that it may well succeed, at least under normal conditions. In Peru, in 1965, Apra Rebelde went into the mountains to launch guerrilla warfare against the United States puppet regime of Belaúnde. Gaining wide popular support from the disenfranchised masses, it believed that the revolution could go from phase #1 (hit and run tactics) to phase #2 (open confrontation with the local military). But it made a grievous mistake because United States leadership had also learned from its experience in Vietnam. It knew that it could not allow the local military to collapse or else it would have to send half a million men, as in so small a country as Vietnam. The United States cannot afford half a million men each for all the "Vietnams" — in the countries that may stage basic social revolutions. Thus, as soon as Apra Rebelde gathered on the mountain peaks of the Andes for that phase #2 confrontation, the United States hit it with napalm. Apra Rebelde was effectively, if only temporarily, destroyed. Its leaders, including Luis de la Puente Uceda and Guillermo Lobatón, were killed.

But the guerrillas have also learned from that mistake. Today, in Guatemala, Venezuela, Colombia, and Bolivia, strong guerrilla forces are keeping mobile and are creating such havoc that Washington is impelled to make the same mistake it made in Vietnam: It is sending Rangers and Special Forces into combat. In Guatemala, as of January 1, 1967, twenty-eight Rangers had been killed. The United States through its partners in Venezuela and Bolivia has again used napalm, but this time with no success. In Colombia, the United States is using Vietnam weapons as well as helicopters to combat the guerrillas, but again without noticeable success. New guerrilla uprisings were taking place, as of May, 1967, in Brazil, Peru, and Ecuador.

But, more important than that, a new attitude has developed. An attitude clearly enunciated by Che Guevara, and others. That attitude recognizes the fact that the United States cannot be militarily defeated in one isolated country at a time. It cannot, on the other hand, sustain two, three or five Vietnams simultaneously. If it tried to do so, its internal economy could crumble. Also, its necessarily increasing repressive measures at home, needed to quell rising internal dissent, would have to become so strong that, conceivably, the whole structure of the United States could be endangered from within.

The attitude further exclaims, with unhesitating logic, that imperialism never stops by itself. Like the man who has $100 and wants $200, the corporation that gets $1 million lusts for $2 million and the country that largely controls one continent seeks to control two. The only way to defeat it is to hit each of its imperialist tentacles simultaneously. Thus was Caesar defeated. Thus, also, was Alexander crushed. Thus, too, was the imperialism of France, of England, of Spain, of Germany eventually stopped.

Che Guevara had no illusions about what this would mean in Latin America. He recently wrote that,

The present moment may or may not be the proper one for starting the struggle, but we cannot harbor any illusions, we have no right to do so, that freedom can be obtained without fighting. And these battles shall not be mere street fights with stones against tear gas bombs, nor of pacific general strikes; neither shall it be the battle of a furious people destroying in two or three days the repressive scaffolds of the ruling oligarchies; the struggle shall be long, harsh, and its front shall be in the guerrilla's refuge, in the cities, in the homes of the fighters — where the repressive forces shall go seeking easy victims among their families — in the massacred rural populations, in the villages, or in cities destroyed by the bombardments of the enemy.

Nor shall it be a gentleman's war. We must carry the war into every corner the enemy happens to carry it: to his home, to his centers of entertainment; a total war. It is necessary to prevent him from having a moment of peace, a quiet moment outside his barracks, or even inside; we must attack him wherever he may be; make him feel like a cornered beast wherever he may move. Then his moral fiber shall begin to decline. He will even become more beastly and we shall notice how the signs of decadence appear to begin.[19]

This analysis is the inevitable and necessary conclusion of anyone who faces squarely the history of United States imperialism and its effect on the imperialized people. Latin America today is poorer and more suffering than it was ten years ago, ten years before that, and so on back through the decades. United States capital has not only taken away the Latin American people's hope for a better material future but their sense of dignity as well.

This is not to say that basic social revolution will come to Latin America because of *Fidelismo*, or Che Guevara. Nor will it come merely because of United States imperialism. Basic social revolution will come — when and as it comes — because of social and economic *conditions* in these areas, conditions which we perpetuate by virtue of our policy of economic penetration and control, in concert with local ruling-class oligarchies.

And, these areas may become Vietnams, because Washington is now "committed" to prevent or destroy basic social revolution whenever and wherever it exists.

This analysis will shock our liberal reformers and they will reject it. But they are measurably responsible for it, for United States foreign policy has long had the dominant support of our academicians and intellectuals.

---

[19] *Message to the Tricontinental*, 1967.

The United States in Asia:
A Century of Manipulation

C. S. BURCHILL

East-West Relations, 1500 to 1850: A Symbiotic Period

For some four and one-half centuries, regular, direct contact has been maintained between the Orient and the nations of the Western world. The basis of this contact has been trade. While other factors — missionary activity, strategic rivalry and, more recently, ideological conflicts — have been important, it is the economic factor which is most illuminating in any attempt to understand the changing character of our relations with the Far East.

During the first three and one-half centuries of contact, Westerners were active in the Far East chiefly as buyers. Oriental civilization had reached a level relatively higher than that of Europe. Oriental finished products — silks and spices; muslins and calicoes; ingenious metalwork; gems and carved objects of wood and ivory — all commanded a ready market in the West, but there was little demand in the East for the cruder products of Europe and America. There was a great excess of exports from the Orient over sales to the Orient, and the trade had to be balanced by transfers of gold and silver from Europe to the East. European bullionists denounced the Oriental trade as a sinkhole into which the treasure of the West was drained, and the trade would soon have strangled for lack of purchasing power in the West if new supplies of precious metal had not been obtained from the New World.

The effect of the trade on the East, then, was to provide to Oriental producers wider markets and better prices than would have been obtainable had the Western trade been interrupted. Much of the resultant prosperity was siphoned off into the treasuries of Eastern potentates or the hoards of Eastern merchants, but a fair amount sifted down to the village and artisan level.

So long as the Western trade brought increased prosperity, there was little violence in East-West relations. Western merchants were combined into national monopoly concerns, like the British and Dutch East India companies. These merchant concerns fought each other to secure control of segments of the Oriental trade, but military force was rarely used against the Orientals themselves. The latter were usually willing to let the Europeans fight each other, and then to make their bargains with the victor. The Western nations taxed the Oriental trade for what it would bear; they occasionally provided some support to their traders in European waters; but they left it to the traders themselves both to defend their own interests in the Far East, and to negotiate their own arrangements with Eastern rulers. The latter generally welcomed the Europeans, and only when Eastern pride was offended by Western attempts to subvert the basis of Oriental society, and to substitute foreign gods and foreign ideas for Oriental traditions, did friction arise. This was notably the case in Japan and China, where missionary activity led to the expulsion of Europeans and to the rigid restriction of trade with the West to a single port in each of those countries.

East-West Relations, 1850 to 1967: A Period of Exploitation

The Industrial Revolution ended the long period of symbiotic relations between East and West. Western finished goods, cheap, machine-made, and of increasingly higher quality, not only replaced Oriental luxuries in Western markets, but began to make serious inroads on the consumer trade in the Orient, bringing ruin first to the village textile workers and then to the urban craftsmen. The Western salesman replaced the Western buyer as the dominant figure in East-West trade, selling finished goods of all kinds, and seeking payment for them in cheap raw materials — raw cotton and jute, or in plantation products like tea and rubber, developed by Western capital and worked by cheap Oriental labor; or in "concessions," the right to levy a permanent toll on Oriental peoples through the ownership of railway and other public utilities; or in long-term loans, secured against Oriental taxes administered by Western agents.

The second stage in East-West relations required a considerable increase in violence. Oriental markets had to be opened or kept open to the Western goods by military force; Oriental governments had to be compelled by Western governmental military force to accept treaties limiting their right to tax imports, and compelling them to tax native industry to give undue advantage to the foreign trader, to grant concessions to foreign traders and public utility promoters, and to pay indemnities for the costs incurred by Western governments in military operations used to extort these concessions from Oriental governments. In a good many cases the Oriental governments themselves disappeared, to be replaced by colonial administrations set up by European states. After the Indian Mutiny in 1857, the sprawling, unorganized sphere-of-influence of the British East India Company was reorganized, with the native princes subordinated to a British viceroy, an adjustment that required the first considerable employment of British troops in the Far East after the Opium War of 1839–1842. At approximately the same stage, Russian forces extorted control of the Amur River Valley, French troops occupied Cochin China, and British troops occupied Burma — all former tributary kingdoms within the Chinese Empire. Exploitative relations between East and West involved progressively heavier doses of military force, and the progressive elimination of the independent political authority of the Oriental states, which in most cases — if they were allowed to survive — were compelled to act as the agents of the Western powers in the exploitation of their own peoples.

In 1858 and 1859, more British and French war-making on

China compelled further trade concessions and the opening of several new Chinese ports to Western trade. From 1860, China was at the mercy of Western corporate and governmental decisions.

America's Far East Policy in the Nineteenth Century

American policy in the Far East, since it developed out of the same objective conditions, parallels fairly closely the policy of the other Western nations, but generally lags a few decades behind European policy in its successive stages. American traders were late arrivals in the Far East, though even before the American Revolution New England smugglers were buying tea in the Canton market, and smuggling it into the colonies in defiance both of the legal monopoly of the East India Company and of the British tax collectors. Students of the American Revolution will remember that the Boston Tea Party, which ushered in that revolution, was closely connected with this activity.

Like all Western traders, the American smugglers were faced with a problem in paying for goods bought in the Chinese market, since they had little to sell that appealed to Chinese buyers. They pioneered in the use of opium as a trade good, buying their supplies in Turkey and carrying the narcotic halfway around the world to be smuggled to Chinese buyers in defiance of the official prohibition of the drug traffic. The British East India Company, being inhibited from breaking Chinese laws by its status as a semiofficial body, did not itself engage in the opium trade in Canton, but a number of Anglo-Indian firms, like Jardine, Matheson & Company had no such inhibitions. After 1833, when the East India Company lost its monopoly, the smuggling of Indian opium into China increased substantially. These traders seem to have been less astute in keeping out of trouble than their American rivals, and in 1839 the Chinese authorities arrested a number of offenders and confiscated their supplies of opium. This action precipitated a war between England and China,[1] and during

---

[1] A lively popular account of the early opium trade is given by M. Collis, *Foreign Mud* (London: Faber & Faber, 1946).

the war the American firm of Russel & Company obligingly acted as agent for Jardine, Matheson & Company in the Chinese trade until the restoration of peace. When the British secured the opening of several additional ports to their traders as a part of the peace settlement, they offered no objection to the American demand in 1844 that similar privileges should be extended to American traders.[2] American cooperation with England in the Far East was well under way more than a century ago.

As the European penetration of the Far East became progressively more exploitative during the remainder of the nineteenth century, the official United States policy was generally an unadventurous "me-tooism," rather than one of active intervention. The few American figures who appear in the history of the Far East during this period were usually private operators rather than government agents. Frederick T. Ward, for example, who helped to organize "The Ever-Victorious Army" to protect the Manchu Dynasty against the Taiping rebels in the 1860s, if he represented anything at all, represented the interest of the Western traders in Shanghai in preserving the rulers who had granted them generous concessions. Anson Burlingame, although he had been for a time the envoy of the United States in Peking, had resigned from the American service in 1867 and was actually employed by the Chinese government as diplomatic agent to several Western governments when he ironically negotiated with Washington a treaty, in 1868, admitting Chinese contract laborers to the United States. The trade in contract labor, known as "the pig trade," was profitable to the Chinese labor brokers who recruited, kidnapped or "shanghaied" their victims; to the Western intermediaries who marketed this modernized version of slave labor abroad; and to the mine operators and railway construction contractors who imported it. Burlingame's success in legalizing the trade can be ascribed to private enterprise rather than to government initiative. With one important exception, American policy in the Far East until almost the end of the century was restricted to insuring, by diplomatic pressure, that any

---

[2] By the Treaty of Wang H'sia, negotiated for the United States in 1844 by Caleb Williams.

privileges extorted by European armed intervention were also extended to American traders.

The exception, of course, is in the case of Japan. There Commodore Perry, backed by a powerful naval force, in 1854 secured the first tentative extension of Western trade in Japan since its almost complete suppression two centuries earlier. Townsend Harris, in the next few years, negotiating for the United States in the shadow of active armed intervention by European powers in China, was able to persuade the Japanese authorities to extend peacefully many of the concessions that were extorted from China by force — the right of residence in foreign concessions, the privilege of extraterritoriality, and the limitation of the Japanese tariff on imports to 5%.

These concessions were considerably less damaging to Japan than were those forced on China during the same period, and their effect was countered by the vigorous action of the Japanese government, through the Meiji Restoration, to free Japan from foreign exploitation and eventually to make of Japan one of the most ruthless exploiters in the Far East.

The Transition to an Aggressive American Policy in the Far East: 1895 to 1941

In the late 1890s American foreign policy underwent a dramatic change. Behind this change lay the fact, which Turner regarded as fundamental in modern American history, of the disappearance of the American land frontier. Until this occurred, American energies were absorbed, and American horizons were limited, by the tremendous opportunities open within their own continent. For a century after the Revolution, the American frontier of settlement, followed more slowly by American military occupation and American political organization, had spread across the map from the crest of the Appalachians to the Pacific. Settlement came first, with the penetration of American traders and farmers into Indian lands and into the weakly held Spanish-American areas of Florida, Texas, and California. During this stage, all that was needed was a North American version of the "open-door policy" assuring American pioneers free access to the frontier. Military intervention came next, to brush aside the feeble power of the Indian tribes and of the Spanish-American authorities. Last came political organization, with barriers erected against foreign products and foreign investments, with the natives pushed aside onto reservations, and with all the resources of each newly acquired territory in turn opened to full American exploitation. When the Pacific had been reached in this process, it was natural to think in terms of continuing the same process into other continents.

The prophet and rationalizer of the new dispensation was Alfred Thayer Mahan, whose *Influence of Sea Power upon History*, first published in 1890, soon became the textbook of the military and naval colleges, and exercised an enormous influence, both in shaping official policies and in forming the attitudes of the American elite.

Mahan brought to American politics the concepts of social Darwinism. Reasoning perilously from analogy, he was convinced that nations, like animal organisms, were locked in an inescapable struggle for existence. "Eat or be eaten" was the law of the international jungle, and war and conquest were the expression of a nation's will to live.

The first law of states, as of men, is self-preservation. . . . Growth is a property of healthful life.[3]

Not in universal harmony, nor in fond dreams of unbroken peace, rest now the best hopes of the world. . . . Rather in the competition of interests, in the reviving sense of nationality . . . in the jealous determination of each people to provide first for its own. . . . There is no immediate danger of the leading nations turning their swords into plowshares . . . decay has not touched yet the majestic fabric erected by so many centuries of conscious battling.[4]

---

[3] A. T. Mahan, *The Problem of Asia* (Boston: Little, Brown, 1900), p. 29.

[4] A. T. Mahan, *The Interest of America in Sea Power* (London: Sampson, Low, Marston, 1897), pp. 122–23.

Mahan was a crusader, fighting for the expansion of his beloved navy, for the annexation of Hawaii and the Philippines, for the construction of the Panama Canal and the acquisition of island bases to guard it. He was above all a man of his own generation, the generation of Cecil Rhodes, and Mackinder and Bernhardi. He would not have sensed the irony in the young Winston Churchill, who wrote in 1899:

> What enterprise that an enlightened community may attempt is more noble and more profitable than the reclamation from barbarism of fertile regions and large populations? What more beautiful ideal or more valuable reward can inspire human effort? The act is virtuous, the exercise invigorating, the result often extremely profitable.[5]

For Mahan was convinced that "the national interest," whether that interest was the expansion of power or of profits, was the sole criterion by which a nation's policy should be judged.

Like Mackinder and Haushofer, Mahan saw politics as a contest between land power and sea power. So far as Asia was concerned, and viewing the power constellation as it appeared in 1900, he was surprisingly oblivious of Japan. North China and Manchuria, he felt, would be logically conceded to Russia, as the dominant land power in the area. The region between lat. 30°N and lat. 40°N, which he called "the Chinese Mediterranean," should be the preserve of the "teutonic powers" — America, England and Germany — whose combined strength would balance that of Russia. Mahan's ideas admittedly strongly influenced both America's participation in the Boxer expedition and the terms imposed on China after that rebellion was suppressed.

By the annexation of the Philippines, "the United States had become an Asiatic power. . . . Indeed in the 1890s no other Occidental power had come into possession of so much land

---

[5] W. S. Churchill, *The River War* (London: Longmans, Green, 1899), I, 18.

in that region. Nor had Japan."[6] To all those nations with competing interests in the Far East, the Secretary of State, John Hay, in 1899 conveyed the United States policy which was to stand for the next forty-one years with regard to the still unappropriated region, the mainland of China. This policy embraced three essentials: *the "open-door" policy* — allowing all foreign nations equal access to the raw materials and markets of China; *the maintenance of existing treaties* — guaranteeing to foreigners very extensive privileges in China, including exemption from Chinese law and from most Chinese taxes, and very extensive property rights in real estate, mining concessions, public utility franchises and missionary privileges; and *"the integrity of China"* — the maintenance in China of a single government which would be held responsible for the carrying out of these treaties and for the repayment of the very large Chinese foreign debt arising partly from reparations imposed on China in successive peace treaties and partly from foreign loans which China had been compelled to accept.

"The real significance of the Hay action was that through it the United States committed herself to a policy in the Far East. . . . Unless she were to withdraw from the position so taken, the United States might find herself forced to implement it by the use of armed force. She alone of the powers had made herself responsible for the policy."[7]

United States action may have prevented the partition of China at the end of the century. It certainly moderated the Japanese demand for Chinese territory at the end of the Russo-Japanese War, and the dispatch of American troops to Siberia, 1918 to 1920, while it failed to establish an anti-Communist Russian state in Siberia, probably had some success in temporarily checking Japanese expansion in Manchuria.

The picture would be incomplete, however, without the injection of the fact that all these Washington spectaculars had the potent encouragement of British brains — for British advantages.[8]

---

[6] K. S. Latourette, *A Short History of the Far East* (4th ed., New York: Macmillan, 1964), p. 430.

[7] *Ibid.,* p. 431.

[8] See P. A. Varg, *Open Door Diplomat, the Life of W. W. Rockhill*

Ironically, the most ambitious — and the maddest — aspect
of the policy was the original Washington pretense of 1899
to "preserve Chinese *territorial and administrative entity*, and
to safeguard for the world the principle of equal and impartial
trade with all parts of the Chinese Empire,"[9] augmented by
Mr. Hay's pronouncement, in July, 1900, that the "open door"
should mean preservation of the "territorial integrity" of all
of China.[10]

In the jargon of eighteenth- and nineteenth-century power
policies, the Manchu Dynasty could be said to have forfeited
its moral authority through its failure to protect its territory
from foreign conquest and its subjects from foreign exploitation.[11] The Boxer Rebellion at the close of the century was
suppressed only by the intervention of a multinational foreign
army. In the first decade of this century another revolt, largely
the work of a small group of Westernized Chinese, with private
American business support, and inspired by the success of
Japan in modernizing its institutions and freeing itself from
foreign control, seemed about to succeed.[12] In its last stages,
the revolutionary movement was taken over by the Chinese
army, which arranged the retirement both of the young Emperor and of the popular leader, Sun Yat-sen, and installed an
army leader as President of a so-called Republic of China.

The army leadership proved no more effective than that of
the Manchus had been. It was unable to protect China from
the extortionate twenty-one demands presented by Japan while
the Western nations were preoccupied with the first world
war, and during the 1920s China degenerated into anarchy,
with various warlords ruthlessly exploiting whatever sections

---

(Urbana: University of Illinois Press, 1952); and Charles S. Campbell,
Jr., *Anglo-American Understanding, 1898–1903* (Baltimore: Johns Hopkins University Press, 1957).

[9] See *Foreign Relations,* 1899, p. 299.

[10] See Thomas A. Bailey, *A Diplomatic History of the American People* (5th ed., New York: Appleton-Century-Crofts, 1958), pp. 481–83.

[11] See Franz Schurmann and Orville Schell, *The China Reader: Imperial China* (New York: Vintage, 1967).

[12] See Julian Hart, "Americans' Plot for Chinese Revolt Revealed:
Letters at Hoover Tower Tell of 1908 Conspiracy," *Los Angeles Times,*
October 13, 1966.

of the old Empire they were able to control. So far as the Western powers were concerned, most of them recognized a dubious government having its capital at Nanking, and directed by a small group of Western-oriented Chinese who had enjoyed long and profitable connections with foreign interests in the lower Yangtze Valley. A number of this group had been educated in the United States, out of funds left over from the Boxer indemnity after all property claims had been paid in full. An American college president had urged in 1908 that the United States should try "controlling the development of China in the most satisfactory and subtle of all ways — through the intellectual and spiritual domination of its leaders."[13] It was possibly with this object in mind that the remainder of the fund had been diverted to the education of future Chinese leaders. From this nucleus of Americanized Chinese came many of the administrators who during the next decades attempted to carry out the incompatible tasks of creating in China a government that would serve simultaneously American and Chinese interests.

Two rivals appeared during the interwar period to contest American domination of China. The least formidable were the Chinese Communists, who for a time had considerable influence in South China, but whose power was broken by the Nanking government, the survivors escaping to the northwest, beyond the reach of Nanking. Much more effective were the Japanese, who had already converted the old tributary kingdom of Korea into a tightly controlled colony, and who had taken over much of the former Russian interest in Manchuria. During the 1930s Japan expanded her economic interest into political control, first with the military occupation of Manchuria, and subsequently with the seizure of Peking and North China. In each of these areas a puppet government was set up, that in Peking assuming the title of the Provisional Government of the Republic of China, in 1937.

There seems to have been an honest difference of opinion among patriotic Chinese as to the best way to end foreign

---

[13] Jessie A. Miller, *China in American Policy and Opinion, 1906–1909*, Ph.D. Thesis, Clark University, cited in Felix Greene, *A Curtain of Ignorance* (London: Johnathan Cape, 1965), p. 7.

domination. Some regarded the threat from the West, in the light of past experience, as the more dangerous, and a number of respected and able Chinese were willing to serve in Japan's puppet governments, feeling that Japanese assistance might lead to a restoration of independence. After all, Japan had freed itself successfully from foreign control, and Japan had led a determined fight to secure the inclusion of a "racial equality" clause in the Charter of the League of Nations, and appeared as a champion of the oppressed races of Asia. When President Wilson vetoed the inclusion of that clause, after it had been approved by the Preparatory Commission, the United States then appeared to be the leader in the continued attempt of the white races to dominate the Orient.[14]

As the fact of Japanese exploitation became more apparent, immediately before and during the Second World War, many Chinese who had at first been inclined to accept a Japanese solution of China's problem turned either to the Western-dominated government of Chiang Kai-shek or to the Russian-sponsored government in the northwest, particularly as white domination had withered away during the war years.

While circumstances had changed profoundly over forty years, and the European nations, preoccupied with problems nearer home, had accepted the obsolescence of the Far Eastern arrangements and refused to challenge Japan's unilateral revision of these in the 1930s, the United States policy at least had the virtue of consistency. Secretary of War Stimson's note to Japan of November 26, 1941, demanding the withdrawal of all Japanese forces from the mainland, and Japanese recognition of the fugitive government in Chungking as the sole legitimate regime in China, and refusing to recognize any revision of existing treaty rights in China, was in its essentials a reaffirmation of Hay's notes of 1899, and of Stimson's 1932 position.[15] The Japanese government denounced the 1941 demands as an American attempt "to maintain and strengthen

[14] See Thomas A. Bailey, *Woodrow Wilson and the Lost Peace* (New York: Macmillan, 1944).

[15] See Department of State Press Release, January 9, 1932; and *The New York Times,* January 28, 1932.

. . . its dominant position . . . not only in China but in other areas of East Asia," and launched the attack on Pearl Harbor.[16]

America's Far Eastern Policy in the Period of World Domination, 1942 to 1967

The Second World War, and the changes in the power constellation which would result from it, demanded an elaboration of American foreign policy beyond the simple expansionism of Mahan and Theodore Roosevelt. An influential reassessment came from a group associated with the Institute of International Studies at Yale University, whose director, N. J. Spykman published *America's Strategy in World Politics* in 1942, shortly after Pearl Harbor, and laid down principles which appear to have been persuasive since then in American foreign policy.

Spykman viewed the world with a geographer's eye, and saw it composed of a few — a very few — concentrations of natural resources capable of supporting major industrial complexes and serving as the bases of military power. America was the most favored of all such concentrations, and was fated to be the dominant power in the world. Western Europe was less favored, and the island concentrations of Britain and Japan still less well-endowed. Other possible areas capable of future growth existed in China and the Soviet Union.

---

[16] There was, of course, much more of U.S. provocation toward the Japanese "attacks on Pearl Harbor." For the U.S. "War Council's" consensus, as of November 25, 1941, that the major U.S. "problem was how to maneuver them [the Japanese] into the position of firing the first shot without suffering too much damage to ourselves," quoted from Stimson's Diary for November 25, 1941, see Relman Morin, *East Wind Rising* (New York: Knopf, 1960), p. 353. See also Forest C. Pogue, *George C. Marshall: The War Years* (New York: Viking, 1966), Chap. 2. For a full account of a move based upon a Presidential order designed to provoke that "first shot without suffering too much damage to ourselves," see Kemp Tolley, Rear Admiral, U.S. Navy (Ret.), "The Strange Assignment of the USS *Lanikai*," *U.S. Naval Institute Proceedings,* XXXVIII (September, 1962), pp. 11–83. See also *Report of the Joint Committee on the Investigation of the Pearl Harbor Attack* (Washington, D.C.: U.S. Government Printing Office, 1946), p. 266.

Although the United States was in the most favorable position to exercise world hegemony, she must guard against any tendency of the other centers of power to combine against her. Her strategy must be one of divide and rule. She must prevent the political union of any possible rival regions, and both a United States of Europe and a united China would be dangerous to her interests. Both these continental areas must be kept divided among a number of rival states, and the aid of America's natural allies, Britain and Japan, should be enlisted to maintain the division of the vast mainland areas. In each case, this would require admitting the dependent allies to some share of the benefits accruing to the world leader. Since no ally is absolutely dependable, it would be necessary for the United States to maintain, both in Europe and in Asia, substantial permanent garrisons after the war. The division of the two continents should be insured by forming in each a regional League of Nations, composed of approximately balanced rival states, with the United States, through its dependent allies and its own permanent garrisons, able in any crisis to tip the balance in its favor.[17]

It must have taken some courage for Spykman and his publishers, at a time when China was a great ally and Japan was a deadly enemy, to propose the dismemberment of China and the formation of an alliance with Japan. He was drawing a blueprint for world domination, and was quite unconcerned either with loyalty to allies or with any other ethical consideration. His work is refreshingly free from ideological overtones. "If the peace objective of the United States is the creation of a United Europe," he said, "she is fighting on the wrong side. All-out aid to Mr. Hitler would be the quickest way to achieve an integrated trans-Atlantic zone."[18]

There is no color in Spykman's diagram to distinguish good nations from bad, only to distinguish strong nations from weak ones. Only one strong one, the United States, should exist. The others should be made or kept weak, and should be played off

---

[17] Nicholas J. Spykman, *America's Strategy in World Politics,* Institute of International Studies, Yale University (New York: Harcourt, Brace, 1942), see especially pp. 134–37 and 468–71.

[18] *Ibid.,* p. 466.

against one another to insure the domination of the United States through what he regarded understandably, as "an improved Balance of Power." Like Mahan, he was convinced of both the inevitability and the desirability of conflict between nations, and he opposed the setting up, at least in other continents, of machinery to secure the rule of law and the peaceful settlement of disputes. His preference was for the rule of force, balanced and manipulated for the advantage of his own country.

Most of Spykman's objectives have been achieved. The United States is by far the most heavily armed country in the world. NATO in Europe and SEATO in Asia purport to preserve "an improved balance of power" on those continents; both Japan and Britain serve as preferred allies of the United States; the emergence of either a world government, or a United States of Europe or a united China have all been avoided (although there is certainly some prospect of a united China). The apparent stability of United States hegemony has been maintained by stationing huge garrisons on both continents, supported by overwhelming naval, air and missile power on the oceans and in continental United States.[19]

McGeorge Bundy, who probably knows as much about the reality of American power as any man, surveyed in a recent article the vastness of that power, how widely it will be exercised, and how rapidly the world's wealth is passing into American ownership.

> Our real and relative strength has continued to grow. The general performance of our economy has been excellent. . . . Our achievements at the edges of science and technology are still more startling. . . . More than four-fifths of all the foreign investing in the world is now done by Americans. . . . We no longer doubt that we should have extensive policies — and take extensive actions — in Europe, in South America, in Asia and in all oceans.

---

[19] D. W. Tarr, "The Military Abroad," in the *Annals of the American Academy of Political and Social Science, March,* 1966, gives the figures for that date as: Europe — 358,000; Asia — 595,000; naval, afloat and mobile — 132,264; en route — 13,227.

. . . We must put troops where they are most needed.[20]

There is no question in the minds of America's leaders that the end sought — American world domination — is good, and that any means to that end are justified. The average citizen may feel a little queasy when confronted with what this actually means in practice: the subversion of foreign governments by American agents, like that of Mossadeq in Iran and Arbenz in Guatemala; the attempts, only rarely frustrated or exposed, to bribe foreign politicians, as in Singapore; the spectacular betrayals, as in the surrender of Ngo Din Diem to be murdered by his rivals; the millions of dead noncombatants in Korea or Vietnam, who got in the way of America's drive to gain and hold control over still more of the earth's resources and peoples.

These distasteful incidents are explained — and dominantly accepted in the States — as inseparable from power politics, and the playing of power politics as the inescapable burden of a great power. There is a measure of truth in these contentions. The concerned citizen may still ask "How have we acquired this power?" and "How wisely do we exercise it?"

To the first question the answer is fairly simple. Spykman's geographic analysis was correct, and the United States can and does support the mightiest concentration of industrial power on earth. Much of that potential has been diverted into military power, because America's leaders have deliberately chosen this use, and they have frightened and manipulated the American public into endorsing their choice. The technique was outlined by John Foster Dulles in 1939:

> The creation of a vast armament in itself calls for a condition midway between war and peace. Mass emotion on a substantial scale is a prerequisite. The willingness to sacrifice must be engendered. A sense of peril from abroad must be created.[21]

[20] McGeorge Bundy, "The End of Either/Or," in *Foreign Affairs,* January, 1967.

[21] John Foster Dulles, *War, Peace and Change* (London: Macmillan, 1939), p. 90. Later in the same work (p. 92) he insists that "Armament is of little significance if there does not exist the willingness to use it. . . . The armed nations, if they would through their armament preserve peace, must be prepared to wage 'preventive wars.' "

The alleged Russian threat, the more generalized threat of the Communist menace, the myth of "traitors in our midst," and most recently, the Chinese threat, have all been invoked to maintain this sense of "peril from abroad," and to induce the American public to accept what their leaders have chosen as the nation's destiny.

To the question, "How are we using this power?" the stock answer is "To preserve Freedom." But Freedom from what? and Freedom for whom? Again, the answer might be to cite the Four Freedoms of the Atlantic Charter, but over much of the "free world" several of these freedoms are rather rigidly suppressed. Even Freedom from Fear can hardly be invoked since in those areas where American power is actively exercised, such as Vietnam, the fear inspired by massive bombing, by overwhelming firepower, by the poisoning of vegetation, and by the latent threat of America's nuclear arsenal, clearly overshadows any fear that can be inspired by the primitive military equipment of America's enemies.

The official line now is to concentrate on Freedom from Want as a major American objective. At the Hawaii Conference, in February of 1966, this was the theme presented to the American Cabinet ministers, the other 125 American and Vietnamese officials and the 234 newsmen who attended.

"We are here to talk especially of the works of peace," the President told the conference, "We will leave here determined, not only to achieve victory over aggression, but also to win victory over hunger, disease and despair." And to Barry Zorthian, the U.S. Public Affairs Chief in Saigon, he said, "Barry, every time I see a picture of a battle in the papers, I want to see a picture of a pig."[22]

This is the image which is most assiduously presented, of a benevolent United States using its power paternally for the benefit of what used to be referred to, when the British had the same kind of problem in projecting a kindly image, as their "little brown brothers." It is a false image, though most Americans would wish it to be true, and it is an image that probably could never coincide with reality.

---

[22] *Time,* February 18, 1966.

The Failure of the American Crusade for Freedom

The Republic of Korea provides an ideal laboratory for testing the validity of the American crusade for "Freedom." This state has been the protégé of the United States since its government was set up by that country after the Second World War. The Republic was briefly overrun by invaders from the North for a few months in 1950, but was secured again by a vast expenditure of American lives and treasure. The war was continued in North Korea for another three years, and resulted in almost total destruction of that area. Postwar aid to North Korea from China and Russia was only a fraction of the six billion American dollars poured into South Korea.[23] A tabulation by an anti-Communist South Korean scholar, comparing the performance of the two economies in 1963, shows that, on a per capita basis, the North was producing twice the tonnage of food grains, three times the tonnage of fish, four times the yardage of cloth, four times the tonnage of coal, eight times the output of cement, twelve times as much electric power, and fourteen times the tonnage of steel. The next year, when South Korea was suffering an acute shortage of food and basic raw materials, and had some two million unemployed workers, North Korea offered to the South 300,000 tons of rice, 100,000 tons of structural steel, 10,000 tons of synthetic fiber and large amounts of cement, timber and machinery, and offered as well to provide employment for as many South Koreans as would be permitted to migrate to the North. Doubtless this offer was made in the knowledge that it would be rejected, but even so the offer does not appear to have been in excess of what North Korea could have provided.[24]

Certainly North Korea seems to have solved the problem of Freedom from Want more satisfactorily than the free Republic of Korea, but the contrast may not reflect any inherent

---

[23] *U.S. Overseas Loans and Grants. . . . ,* A.I.D. Statistics and Reports Division, Washington, D. C., 1966.

[24] Soon Sung Cho, "The Politics of North Korea's Unification Policy," *World Politics,* January, 1967, pp. 222–36. See Joan Robinson, "Korean Miracle," *Monthly Review,* January, 1965, p. 150.

superiority in Communist ability to organize and develop the resources of the country. It also depends on the fact that North Korea enjoyed a much greater degree of political independence than its southern neighbor. Its government was not constrained to shape its policies in accordance with pressures emanating from Peking or Moscow, since those pressures largely canceled each other out. Like Japan during the Meiji Restoration, the government of North Korea was able to operate under the two conditions laid down by W. W. Rostow as indispensable for the modernization of a backward country: "The formation of an effective, modern, central government capable of exercising fiscal power . . . and the emergence of a group . . . with vested interests in the development of an effective national government, and the technical talents and motivation to operate the modern sections of the economy."[25]

Rostow's brilliance as an economic historian has been somewhat dimmed by his less than brilliant performance as a policy-maker in Washington, but his analysis is still valid. The extent to which his two essential preconditions are lacking in South Korea is set out by another anti-Communist South Korean scholar:

> South Korea lacks nationalism and . . . also a revolutionary ideology. Political development demands both of them. . . . Since 1945 the history of South Korea can be written as the story of an emergent nationalism being emasculated almost consciously by a policy aimed at keeping the friendship of the United States.[26]

The Westernized top layer of South Korean society, he feels, is alienated from the mass of the population, and is distrusted for its close links with the foreigners. In itself, this top layer is united by no shared convictions; "its political struggles are undisciplined and almost predatory contests" of individuals,

---

[25] W. W. Rostow, *The Process of Economic Growth* (2nd ed., Oxford: Clarendon Press, 1962), pp. 346–47.

[26] K. W. Kim, "Ideology and Political Development in South Korea," *Pacific Affairs*, XXXVIII (Summer, 1966), 164–73.

whose survival depends on gaining and holding the favor of those who have the ear of Washington.

This condition is probably inescapable in any dependent nation set up by a foreign power, and dependent on the continued support of its great protector. On the one hand, the government selected and maintained by foreign influence is able neither to enlist popular enthusiasm nor to organize and operate the resources of the nation; on the other hand, the dominant elements in the dependent society see their greatest advantage as lying not in the development of internal possibilities in their own country, but in exploiting their connection with the protecting power. In North Korea, where circumstances favored the development of Rostow's prerequisite of an independent national government, we find Kim Il-sung able to issue, as early as 1955, almost immediately after the end of the Korean War, his own declaration of independence:

> Although some people say that the Soviet way is best or that the Chinese way is best, have we not reached the point where we can construct our own way?[27]

The same vigorous independence in North Korea, and the rejection of pressure from outside, has continued. An article in the August 12, 1966, issue of *Rodong Shinmoon*, the official organ of the Communist Party in North Korea, under the title "Let Us Defend Independence," declares that an independent economy and national pride are absolutely essential to modernization — precisely as Rostow argued. "Flunkeyism towards big powers," the article asserts, "is an obstacle . . . big parties or parties with long experience have no monopoly of guidance." "There can be no leading party" nor can there be "a single center of the world revolution."

In contrast to North Korea's success in maintaining an effective and independent national government, and in entrusting control to an elite "with the technical talents and motivation to operate the modern sections of the economy," we have

---

[27] Readers in countries effectively excluding North Korean publications will find this article summarized under the title "The End of Flunkeyism" in the Indian Journal, *China Report,* II, No. 6, 23.

expert testimony that "flunkeyism towards the big powers" is built into the American system of benevolent paternalism. Thomas L. Hughes, Director of Intelligence and Research in the Department of State, notes that:

> Requests from foreign governments for military and economic aid often bear an expert's touch in their drafting, as though the receiver were not the first American through whose hands they had passed . . . officially, we are called upon to act more and more in the shadow of an elaborate series of prompting by Americans, through foreigners, back to Americans.[28]

If this is true, both military and economic aid are increasingly becoming devices through which wily American promoters, and equally wily politicians in dependent countries, join forces to swindle the United States government, with scant regard for the interest of the subject peoples, of the American taxpayer, or of the American servicemen who will be called in to suppress the next outburst of exasperation in the dependent state.

What has been overlooked in United States foreign policy is the Fifth Freedom, not mentioned in the Atlantic Charter, barely present in the consciousness of the average American, but more keenly prized than all the others in the underdeveloped countries of Asia — Freedom from Contempt. To treat these people as objects, to be manipulated for our strategic or economic interest; to be made over into our idea of what they ought to be; to improve them, educate them and Westernize them, is to offer then the ultimate affront. It provoked violent rejection three centuries ago in Japan and China; it still provokes rejection, whether the interference comes from capitalist Americans or from Communist Russians; it will continue to provoke violent rejection wherever the affront is offered.

---

[28] Quoted by Thomas L. Hughes in *Foreign Affairs,* January, 1967, p. 211.

Toward a Rational View of China: The Vietnam War

YOUNG HUM KIM

There may or may not be a distinctive "Oriental mind," as Westerners so often infer. And, though Oriental "face" may not mean all that Westerners may impute to that word, both concepts may serve as starting points from which to explore what Kipling must have meant to suggest in his "East is East and West is West." Certainly, Sino-American difficulties of today stem partly from the lack of mutual understanding. The deeprooted attitudes of both peoples impede enlightened policy changes. Limited knowledge of China has bred among Americans the view that the Chinese are a mysterious people with strange names, feelings, and behavior, who invariably look alike and whose approach to life is antithetical to Western ways. Thus, the Oriental's virtues are grossly mistaken for Occidental vices: his quality of patience for laziness; thoughtfulness for timidity; courtesy and humility for subserviency and sycophancy. His sense of devotion and sacrifice is looked upon as the degradation of individual worth, and his respect for and homage to his elders is construed to be the propensity toward servitude and the manifestation of authoritarian personality.

The Chinese, on the other hand, have their misapprehensions. Proud, in their long cultural heritage and aware of their civilizing achievements, intelligent and industrious, and endowed with formidable talents, the Chinese know they are one of the great peoples of the world. But they were ruthlessly subjugated by Western power from the 1840s to the 1940s. So, for a century, much of what they saw of Western performance they had little occasion to admire. Western values are misinterpreted as Eastern vulgarities: the concept of freedom as license for anarchy, self-reliance as selfishness, gentlemanliness as effeminacy, the principle of human equality as defiance to ordered society, and public expression of affection as undisciplined display of bestial instinct.

The variations of the China myth seem infinite. The mysterious China of yesteryear was harmless, but the misunderstood China of today is dangerous. In recent decades the American image of China has changed to one of a monstrous society of human insects, destined to take over the world under the banner of Communism. The American obsessive and groundless fear that the Chinese will devastate the earth with their nuclear bombs and that the surviving Chinese will emerge from atomic ashes like the phoenix to inherit this troubled world is driving the United States to the brink of war with the Chinese through escalation of the war in Vietnam.

The deadly conflict in Vietnam is a tragic example of the continuous struggle which has spanned both World War II and the cold war. As it stands, the painful problem of the war in Vietnam will undoubtedly take one of three courses: (1) maintenance of the status quo; (2) de-escalation; or (3) escalation. Should the status quo prevail, the war, with an elusive hope for a negotiated settlement and heightened severity of military operations occurring simultaneously, would continue with no immediate, or even proximate, prospect of a satisfactory solution. The struggle has already become a twenty-eight year war. Its beginning can be traced back to the landing of the Japanese Imperial troops in Indochina in the summer of 1940. Ultimately, Indochinese nationalists — not Communists — opened a war of national liberation against their Japanese occupiers. As the Japanese were ousted, the French imperialists returned to resume their prewar colonial occupation of the area. And the Indochinese nationalists — still not basically Communists — continued their war for independence against the French. The Vietminh — whose leadership came increasingly to have Communist support and influence — ultimately succeeded in driving the French from the area by 1954.

What had been French Indochina came to be divided into new nationalistic areas, one of which was Vietnam. In 1954 Vietnam was, in turn, subdivided, temporarily, into two parts — North Vietnam and South Vietnam — pending national elections to be held by 1956 to determine the final political status of the nation. The Vietminh — by that time dominantly Communist — under the leadership of Ho Chi Minh, took over North Vietnam. They confidently expected the 1956 elections to result in a unified Vietnam, combining North and South under Ho Chi Minh's presidency.

The United States got into the picture when it provided enormous financial and logistic support for the French attempt to hang on to colonial control of the area — stopping just short of entering the war militarily.

South Vietnam had — and has — a typical traditional Asian upper-class feudalistic and corrupt government, with the masses of peasant people wholly subjugated and exploited by the ruling class. Naturally, that ruling class did not — and does not — want to lose control of what has been a satisfactory situation for itself. With Washington's support, it refused to let the national elections be held in 1956.

The National Liberation Front resumed in South Vietnam its civil war, to take control of the government, to consummate a basic social revolution — a *human welfare revolution* — and to unity an *independent nation* of Vietnam. The hope was that a new kind of government in a unified nation, free from all outside control, might be effectively dedicated to improving the lot of the masses of poor and distressed people in that independent nation.

Professor Arthur Larson, emphasizing that the "real world revolution of today and tomorrow" may be "the unfinished revolution of human rights," observes that the revolution in Vietnam may be — currently — a "unique" one. It is, he points out, a double revolution — a combination of a prolonged *nationalistic* revolution against Japanese, French, and

American control, successively, and a basic *human rights* revolution.[1]

And that is the kind of revolution which United States leadership is committed to thwart by war-making — under the guise of stopping "external aggression" against, and protecting the "freedom" of the "people of South Vietnam." That is the war-making which may run on and on indefinitely, and which — with or without further escalation by the United States — promises to bring utter destruction of that Georgia-sized area in Southeast Asia. This is the war of which the only practicable termination is by way of de-escalation.

De-escalation requires that all belligerents realize the futility of a protracted struggle which may ultimately entail the immense destruction of lives and property. It further requires wisdom and sagacity to effect the termination of senseless carnage.

Escalation, on the other hand, may be described in various terms. First, in terms of the number of United States military personnel in South Vietnam: the dispatch of a Military Assistance Advisory Group of thirty-five men to Vietnam in August, 1950, to advise on the use of American military equipment, was the beginning. (Ironically this is the same number of men with which General Vo Nguyen Giap, Deputy Premier and Defense Minister of the Democratic Republic of Vietnam, had organized his guerrilla army in the jungles of South China a decade earlier.) By February, 1962, American "advisers" numbered 4,000; by November 15, 1963, two weeks after the tragic fall of the Diem regime, the number reached 16,575; by February, 1965, United States forces totaled 23,000; by November of the same year, 160,000; and at the present time, half a million. The increase in the number of Vietcong guerrillas and North Vietnam army paralleled, or even exceeded, that of United States forces.

Secondly, in terms of weapons used: the Vietcong started with bamboo spikes, homemade bombs, and rifles of World War II or Korean War vintage. In the course of escalation,

---

[1] Arthur Larson, "The Real Nature of the World Revolution," *Saturday Review*, June 3, 1967.

modern weapons such as supersonic jet fighters and bombers, helicopters, napalm, chemicals, rockets, and missiles have been introduced. Consequently, Vietnam may well have become a testing ground for modern military technologies.

Thirdly, in terms of intensity, scope, and scale of the war: the fighting was at first limited to the engagement of ground forces in South Vietnam. But in August, 1964, when United States destroyers were "attacked" off the coast of Tonkin by North Vietnamese torpedo boats, President Johnson "directed air action against gunboats and supporting facilities used in these hostile operations."[2] Then in February, 1965, Vietcong guerrillas attacked a United States compound at Pleiku, and United States forces retaliated by bombing military targets in North Vietnam. This was the beginning of the United States air assaults on the North.

Both the city of Hanoi and the port of Haiphong were excluded from the *official* list of targets. But subsequent escalation has eliminated such sanctuaries and certainly a United States military invasion of North Vietnam cannot be ruled out. The response to an invasion might well take the form of direct military assistance to North Vietnam by an external power or powers, presumably China, the Soviet Union, or both.

Finally, in terms of the identities of the belligerents involved either directly or indirectly, the struggle resembles the Korean War. The war in Vietnam is often regarded as another war between the Big Powers. The Korean War, in a real sense, was a conflict between the United States and the Soviet Union using a number of proxies — South Korea and several United Nations member nations on the side of the United States; North Korea and China on the Soviet side. The argument proceeds to identify the war in Vietnam as a proxy war between the United States and China — South Vietnam representing the former; the Vietcong and North Vietnam fighting for the benefit of the latter. In this sense, escalation simply

---

[2] Furthermore, President Johnson urged Congress to adopt a joint resolution, which was subsequently passed by Congress and signed by the President on August 9. For the text of the joint resolution, see *Department of State Bulletin,* August 24, 1964, p. 268.

amounts to the process of absorbing or bypassing these proxies.

Initially playing the role of "advisers" and "supporting units," the United States military personnel in South Vietnam have now taken over the war and are actively engaged in combat. Similarly, the North Vietnamese army has assumed combat responsibility in close coordination and cooperation with the Vietcong guerrillas who are under the political leadership of the National Liberation Front. The logical conclusion is that the United States and China will inevitably come to a direct military confrontation.

Is the United States really on a collision course with the People's Republic of China? If so, how can the United States avoid it? What course of action or policy should the United States take or formulate to rectify the present unhealthy state of affairs?

Some of the guidelines, if not answers, to these crucial questions may be found in the pages of history. A realistic and sober reexamination and reevaluation of some of the fundamental issues and attitudes in United States-Chinese relations in the past two decades may provide helpful clues and insights into the immediate problems confronting the two countries. In formulating a foreign policy, a nation should look back upon the road it has trodden in order to chart a new route for the future.

The end of World War II left the United States in a position to assume unilaterally a stance of "free world leadership." In Europe, Britain, France and Italy were exhausted. Russia was no longer in that "free world." And Germany, having been put through the wringer of "unconditional surrender," was again supposed not to "come back" within the predictable future. And however that might turn out, Germany was partly under the "joint occupation" of non-"free world" Russia.

So, Washington underwrote the economic and political recovery of Western Europe through the Marshall Plan. Designed to be a military bulwark to contain an imaginary threat of Soviet expansion, the formation of the North Atlantic Treaty Organization followed the Marshall Plan. The extension of power and influence of the United States in Europe was only blocked by the power of the USSR at the direct line of contact.

In the Near East, effectuation of the Truman Doctrine is said to have thwarted Communist subversion and infiltration. In the Middle East, Soviet occupation of part of Iran was abandoned through a combination of factors.

In the Far East, the United States did not encounter much difficulty in filling the military power vacuum left by the fall of the Japanese Empire. The only major obstacle lay in China — a huge land mass of Asia larger in area than the United States with a population of over 600 million, more than three times that of the United States.

Unfortunately, China was torn by a titanic civil war between the Nationalists and the Communists, a situation which presented the United States with four possible alternatives: (1) complete withdrawal from China; (2) military intervention on a major scale to aid the Nationalists to destroy the Communists; (3) efforts to avoid a civil war by working for a compromise between the two sides; and (4) wholehearted acceptance of the new Communist China.

In its adoption of the third alternative policy, the United States government was influenced by certain obvious realities: (1) the Nationalists had been unable either to destroy or to win over the Communists during the ten years preceding the war; (2) after the war the Nationalists were weak, demoralized, and corrupt, lacking popular support and prestige; (3) the Communists, in contrast, had strengthened their power, militarily and politically, and were in control of most of the rural areas; (4) because of the ineffectiveness of the Nationalist forces, the Communists probably could have been dislodged only by United States armed forces; (5) the American people might not have endorsed such a colossal commitment of their armies in China; and finally, (6) official and intellectual leadership in the States had launched an all-out cold war against Communism, as incarnate evil.

At first the United States understandably attempted to influence the course of events in favor of the Nationalists. Later, as the fortunes of war were turning in the Communists' favor, Washington endeavored to establish a Nationalist-Communist coalition government. Failing in this, the United States dream of a friendly and unified capitalistic China as the basis for Far Eastern stability — and a place for profitable private corporate operations — was shattered.

By the summer of 1949, the Chinese Communists had swept the country and achieved victory. Americans were astounded; it was a frustrating reality for them to admit defeat. Critics called the United States China policy "a tragic failure" and a "crime." In the midst of charges and countercharges, the Department of State issued a "China White Paper" in August, 1949, in an effort to clear the air. In the letter of transmittal, Secretary of State Dean Acheson stated frankly:

> The unfortunate but inescapable fact is that the ominous result of the civil war in China was beyond the control of the government of the United States. Nothing that this country did or could have done within the reasonable limits of its capabilities could have changed that result; nothing that was left undone by this country has contributed to it. It was the product of internal Chinese forces, forces which this country tried to influence but could not.[3]

Many Americans agreed, but some did not.

In Vietnam the United States again faced the problem of making a fateful choice from available alternatives. The domestic situation in South Vietnam in the 1960s was somewhat comparable to that of China in the years immediately following World War II. The Diem regime, like Chiang Kai-shek's, was autocratic, undemocratic, and oppressive. It did not have a foundation of popular support and had been unable to destroy or check the rising influence and prestige of the Vietcong.

After the fall of the Diem government, the successive military coups further destroyed all vestiges of political stability

---

[3] Department of State, *United States Relations with China: With Special Reference to the Period 1944–1949* [China White Paper] (Washington, D.C.: U.S. Government Printing Office, 1949), Letter of Transmittal, XVI.

in South Vietnam. On the other hand, like the Chinese Communists, the Vietcong steadily increased their power and ultimately controlled two-thirds of the area. They were inspired to the point of fanaticism by the revolutionary zeal of national independence and of liberation from colonial rule. To them, the presence of foreign troops, friendly or otherwise, on their soil symbolized the return of imperialism in the form of "neo-colonialism." Against this background the United States determined to pursue the second alternative course — *military intervention on a major scale to assist the Saigon government and to destroy the Vietcong and their supporters.*

The United States choice of this alternative seems to have been based upon five possible fallacies which should be carefully scrutinized.

The first was the misapplication of the containment policy to Southeast Asia. The United States had made the halting of Communist expansion, regardless of time, place, character, methods, and tactics, the supreme goal of its foreign policy. In the words of Secretary of State Dean Rusk:

What we are seeking to achieve in South Vietnam is part of a process that has continued for a long time — a process of preventing the expansion and extension of Communist domination by the use of force against the weaker nations on the perimeter of Communist power.[4]

With sweeping generalizations the United States extended the policy of so-called containment, erroneously considered successful in Europe, to Southeast Asia where Communist influence has direct appeal in these underdeveloped societies. To be sure, with the inauguration of the Southeast Asia Treaty Organization in 1954 as a military countermeasure to balance political settlements at Geneva, and the formation of the Baghdad Pact (which later became the Central Treaty Organization), the United States had created a superficial wall

---

[4] Statement made before the Senate Committee on Foreign Relations; Press Release, February 18, 1966. See also, *Supplemental Foreign Assistance Fiscal Year 1966 — Vietnam* (Washington, D.C.: U.S. Government Printing Office, 1966), p. 564.

of containment of Communism, stretching from the Atlantic to the Pacific through Western Europe and the Middle East. But, it was destined to be ineffective.

The second fallacy was the underestimation of Vietcong and North Vietnamese strength, on several accounts: namely, their military capability to carry on the protracted war, their sense of dedication to what they believe to be a sacred cause, the potent force of their nationalism, their pride and stamina, and the cohesive strength of national unity. Believing that its industrial, technological, and military power was insurmountable, the United States naively expected the Communists to fall to their knees as soon as its power was introduced in the struggle. Washington's massive military operation, it was hoped, would so demoralize the revolutionary Asians as to force them to capitulate or disintegrate. It was assumed that they could neither endure the stresses and strains nor stand the attrition and drain of manpower and resources over a substantial period of time. It should have been recalled, however, that the Russo-Japanese War in 1904–1905 ended in a victory for Japan, whose power had been grossly underestimated by Czarist Russia.

One illustrative example of United States underestimation of the Vietnam situation is the statement made by Secretary of Defense Robert McNamara on December 12, 1963: "We have every reason to believe that United States military plans will be successful in 1964."[5] Time and again United States officials have displayed the same unwarranted optimism; yet the war has kept escalating.

For the Communists, conversely, this might be deemed their "finest hour." On April 10, 1965, Ho Chi Minh declared: "The people of our country are living in an historical moment of heroism and sacrifice. Our country is an outpost of the socialist camp and of the peoples of the world engaged in the struggle against imperialism, colonialism, and neocolonialism. To us, this is a great honor."[6]

The third oversight was the failure to recognize the chang-

[5] *Department of State Bulletin,* January 13, 1964, p. 46.

[6] *Solemn Pledge of the Thirty Million Vietnamese People* (Peking: Foreign Language Press, 1965), p. 36.

ing character of Communism. As the cold war crystallized in the wake of World War II, both the United States and the Soviet Union abandoned the spirit of cooperation and mutual understanding and sought to promote their respective interests, while assuming that a gain by one was ipso facto a loss to the other.

With the outbreak of the Korean War and through the subsequent years, United States leadership hardened in its conviction that Communism, as a monolithic and invincible force spearheaded in Asia by Communist China, was bent on a conquest of the entire world. A number of Americans failed to exercise reason and came to look upon any settlement, compromise, or ordinary diplomatic dealings with Communist nations as "evil" and "immoral."

The United States poured money, manpower, and military hardware into the poor and unstable countries of the world so long as they professed to be anti-Communist. It justified alignment with any dictatorial, totalitarian, antidemocratic — even corrupt — regime of dubious color so long as it was not Red. Taking the attitude that "if you are not with us, you are against us," the United States neither tolerated neutralism nor recognized nationalistic anticolonialism, thus alienating many Jeffersonian nationalists in Asia and Africa. It talked so much of great crusades against Communism that it mesmerized itself into recklessly undertaking what were considered to be "messianic missions."

The United States should recognize that Communism comes in many shades and colors. There is no monolithic Communist world any more than there is a unified "free world." Yugoslavia, Albania, and Rumania are definitely defiant of the Soviet Union; North Korea has taken a neutral stance; Poland, Hungary, and Czechoslovakia have gained greater freedom of action than most Central American republics. The Sino-Soviet rift is so obvious and well known that it requires no elaboration. The prophetic statement of Dean Acheson in 1949 has now become a reality. He said:

We continue to believe that, however tragic may be the immediate future of China and however ruthlessly a major portion of this great people may be exploited by a party in the interest of foreign imperialism, ultimately the profound civilization and the democratic individualism in China will reassert themselves and she will throw off the foreign yoke.[7]

In the light of contemporary history there is always a possibility that Ho Chi Minh might become another Tito or Ceausescu. In the contest for "winning the minds" of the people, Nationalism may be far stronger than Communism.

The fourth error was the attempt to bridge what may be called the "reliability gap." One of the principal arguments of the United States in justifying its presence in Vietnam is the contention that if Washington fails to honor its commitments, most Asian allies will lose confidence in the United States and will give second thoughts to their alignment with it. The truth is that, throughout the cold war period, the United States has created an immense "reliability gap" in its relations with those nations which have been placed under its protective assistance treaties. In the course of remaking these nations in its own image, and with anxiety and impatience, the United States has unilaterally assumed a leadership which was paternalistic and meddlesome as well as indifferent to the initiative of indigenous leaders and to the needs of the people. The United States has demanded their absolute loyalty and mistaken their self-assertion for anti-American posture. It fostered a sense of doubt and suspicion instead of one of trust and confidence in the minds of the leaders. To them, the American attitude has been frequently arrogant and domineering, but they dare not express their feelings overtly lest they incur American displeasure and anger.

When the Korean War broke out, the United States took up arms to repel the alleged aggressors. This action was based on the assumption that if the open aggression was unchecked and if South Korea's pleas for help went unanswered, the United States would demonstrate to the world that it was indeed a "paper tiger" unconcerned with the safety of its allies. Thus the United States returned to rescue the country which it had

---

[7] Department of State [China White Paper], *op. cit.*

recently left unprotected. The pattern of United States diplomacy in its worst aspect may therefore be categorized as follows: (1) empty promises and slogans; (2) indecision and vacillation; and (3) impulsive reaction to the positive action taken by its adversaries.

The "reliability gap" was further widened after America's alliance partners witnessed the performance, or sometimes the nonperformance, of the United States with respect to such crucial issues as the East European uprisings in 1953, the Geneva Accords of 1954, the Anglo-French-Israeli invasion of Egypt, the Hungarian Revolution of 1956, the Laotian conflict of 1960, the Congo crisis, the handling of the U-2 incident, the Bay of Pigs, and the Dominican intervention, to name a few. From the standpoint of many Afro-Asian peoples, the "reliability gap" is so great that a single stroke of military operation in Vietnam will not be able to bridge it. On the contrary, it may have an adverse effect because they believe that rather than righting the wrongs committed in the 1950s, the American military campaign in Vietnam serves only to double the wrong. The United States must not entertain the illusion that military power is a panacea for all the political, social, and economic ills of a nation. Power demonstrated without humility is arrogance; power used without prudence is affront; and power mobilized without discretion is aggression.

Another aspect of the "reliability gap" concerns the future of the divided nations, Vietnam included. United States officials have reiterated that one of the major objectives of the United States intervention in Vietnam "is to bring about a restoration of the conditions contemplated by the accords of 1954 . . . , to restore the integrity of the settlement made between the *French government* and the Communist force under Ho Chi Minh"[8] — a settlement which the United States refused to endorse. To Asian nationalists such a policy not only is clearly self-contradictory and self-defeating, but also gives rise to the credence that the United States favors a perpetual division of the nation.

---

[8] *Supplemental Foreign Assistance Fiscal Year 1966 — Vietnam, op. cit.*, p. 571. *Italics* are mine to emphasize that the South Vietnamese were not party to the accords.

The irredentism of nineteenth-century Europe has found its way into the nationalism of today and manifests itself in the form of fervent aspirations for national unification wherever a nation is divided. Washington's stated cold war policy, restoration and maintenance of a status quo often static and sterile, runs counter to the desires and designs of those nationalists who attempt to unify their countries one way or another. It gives the world the impression that the United States is less concerned for the plights of the divided peoples (Berliners, Germans, Koreans, Vietnamese) than for its own interests of "not upsetting the applecart of complacency and prosperity."

Fifth, and finally, the concept of Communist China as the ultimate enemy has certain pitfalls. In clarifying the purpose of America's involvement in Vietnam, Secretary of Defense Robert McNamara stated: "The choice is not simply whether to continue our efforts to keep South Vietnam free and independent, but rather, whether to continue our struggle to halt Communist expansion in Asia."[9] He did not say that we *will* have a war with Communist China, but the implication is clear that the United States is determined to carry on the struggle, so long as Communism exists in Asia. It means that peripheral military campaigns, such as in Vietnam, are meaningless unless the heart of the Communist power is destroyed. General Maxwell Taylor, who played a leading part in United States military intervention in Vietnam, recognized the prospect of a land war with China. In February, 1966, when he was asked about the danger of a military confrontation with Communist China, he replied, "One cannot write off the possibility."[10] The following month Secretary Rusk stated that the United States would continue its efforts "to reassure Peiping that the United States does not intend to attack mainland China." He

---

[9] Annual "military posture" statement by the Secretary of Defense to the House of Representatives Armed Services Committee on February 18, 1965. Department of State, *Foreign Policy Briefs*, March 1, 1965.

[10] *Supplemental Foreign Assistance Fiscal Year 1966 — Vietnam, op. cit.*, p. 485.

added, however, that there were, of course, "risks of war with China."[11]

No sane leader would contemplate sending millions of American troops to fight on the mainland of China. President Eisenhower expressed his conviction that there could be "no greater tragedy than for the United States to become involved in an all-out war in Indochina," let alone in China. General MacArthur advised President Kennedy not to send American soldiers to the Asian mainland to combat the Chinese. China has proved to be Asia's "quicksand" for foreign invaders, for no nation or people has ever really conquered China. The Mongols invaded China and established the Yuan Dynasty; yet, eventually they were absorbed into the Chinese culture, lost their own identity, and they themselves became "Chinese." The Manchus replaced the Ming Dynasty, but as with the Mongols, they were assimilated into the Chinese civilization. Beginning with the Sino-Japanese War of 1894–1895 and ending with World War II in 1945, Japan had never come close to defeating China. The sources of Chinese power lie in the vast territories, enormous population, and inexhaustible patience, none of which can be destroyed by bombs, bullets, or bayonets.

Should the United States get itself entangled in hostilities with China, which is no longer a "paper tiger," but a "baby dragon with thermonuclear teeth," the tragic consequences are too horrendous to contemplate.

In view of these analyses, the United States China policy should be reformulated on the basis of certain immediate essentials, including (1) de escalation of the war in Vietnam, (2) and a normalization of Sino-American relations.

The first recommendation to be considered is de-escalation. As pointed out, since one of the most important features of escalation in the Vietnam war has been the process of eliminating the proxies, the first step toward de-escalation lies in reversing that process. Through a positive and imaginative diplomacy, means can be found to disengage the United States and North Vietnam forces from combat. A cessation of United

---

[11] Statement made before the Subcommittee on the Far East and the Pacific of the House Committee on Foreign Affairs on March 16, 1966. See *Department of State Bulletin,* May 2, 1966.

States bombing of North Vietnam may be a beginning toward that goal, followed by gradual reduction or withdrawal of both forces from South Vietnam. The parties involved must come to believe that what they have failed to achieve on the battle-field can be achieved at the conference table. As a prominent Japanese scholar has pointed out, the most important question is "whether the United States, backed by its military superior-ity, will be wise enough to make political concessions to the Vietcong. If America has that wisdom, there can be an early end to the Vietnam war."[12]

In the same vein, United Nations Secretary General U Thant said:

This impasse can be broken and a halt put to the increas-ingly horrible slaughter and destruction of the Vietnam war only if one side or the other shows the wisdom and the courage and the compassion for humanity to take the initiative on a first step — that is to say undertaking militarily to put the standstill truce into effect, and there-after to fire only if fired upon. The United States, with power and wealth unprecedented in human history, is in a position to take this initiative.[13]

The United States should cast off the old habits of thought and rhetoric, and should introduce the virtues of flexibility and sophistication into the conduct of its foreign policy, espe-cially with respect to the Communist world. It should realize that the independence and security of a nation do not always require Washington's protection or intervention.

Secondly, the short-range policy must be intelligently formu-lated. At the moment, China is in a great turmoil exemplified by the Red Guards under the banner of the "Great Proletarian Cultural Revolution." The United States may be tempted to capitalize on the Chinese internal upheaval by: (1) a delib-erate expansion of the war in Vietnam, involving military in-vasion of the North with the belief that China cannot afford to intervene militarily on behalf of the Ho regime, or (2)

---

[12] *The Christian Science Monitor,* February 20, 1967.
[13] *The New York Times,* April 2, 1967, p. 3.

"unleashing" Chiang Kai-shek's armies to invade the Chinese mainland to aid the anti-Mao factions and to overthrow ultimately the Communist regime. None of these measures is practical or desirable. Such an adventure could precipitate a Sino-American military confrontation which, presumably, neither side has planned nor desired, certainly not China. Now is the time for the United States to adopt, at least, the Taoist principle — *wu wei* (do everything by doing nothing) — to modify its China policy. It is imperative for the United States to adopt and follow a constructive Asian policy with patience and prudence.

Thirdly, the long-term policy requires careful and thoughtful formulation. Irrespective of the outcome of the current power struggle in China, the United States should prepare, politically and psychologically, for a normalization of Sino-American relations in the near future. It could adopt a policy of "open door in reverse" so that the Chinese could enjoy the opportunity in trade and commerce corresponding to what the United States enjoys throughout the world. The United States must come to the realization that competitive coexistence with China is no more difficult than with the Soviet Union. Recognizing China's great power status, the United States should allow China to participate in major international parleys, and at the opportune moment, extend to it de jure recognition, admit its representatives to United Nations organs and processes, lift its embargo, and institute an exchange of personnel.

In conclusion, in this age of multirevolutions, the United States — "a nation conceived in liberty and dedicated to the proposition that all men are created equal" — should preach *and practice* the blessings of that liberty at home and abroad, and should respect and honor the principle of "sovereign equality," that all nations are equal.

Containing Communism in Asia: Theory and Practice

ROY BENNETT

Analysts have defined postwar United States foreign policy in, roughly, three different ways. One group sees this policy as fundamentally correct, even brilliant. It was, as they saw it, a creative response to Soviet expansionist aggression. The Truman Doctrine, the Marshall Plan, NATO (Europe), Cento (Middle East), and SEATO (Southeast Asia), characterized its strategically defensive, highly "successful" containment policy which, today, is being even more successfully implemented in Southeast Asia. Vietnam, to this group, is only part of the success story. Indonesia, the collapse of all China's positions in Africa and the internal upheavals on the mainland are all attributed to the "positions of strength" aggressive containment policy.

A second group — today a significant one (Kennedy, Schlesinger, Galbraith, Reischauer, Morganthau, Fulbright, Kennan) — pays tribute to the Truman Doctrine, the Marshall Plan and NATO as policies consistent with their times, but condemns present policies, almost totally, as utterly out of date. Most critics in this group would agree with Hans Morganthau that, "these policies have become obsolete" and that:

> the United States has been unable to devise new policies capable of dealing successfully with the issues of a new period. . . . Instinctive opposition . . . [to Communism]

has become today not only intellectually untenable but also politically useless and even counterproductive. The first postwar decade was marked by two factors: the unchallenged supremacy of the United States, on the one hand, the limitations of its military commitments to Europe and their hesitant extension to Asia on the other. The second postwar decade . . . receives its political character from the decline of the relative power of the United States, *coincident with a global extension of its military commitments. The Truman Doctrine and the Marshall Plan, originally limited in their practical applications to Europe, are now transformed into global commitments. These commitments have outpaced the power available to support them.*

Morganthau has elsewhere charged that United States policy has made our Secretaries of State the Metternichs of a new reactionary Holy Alliance, committed to preventing social and revolutionary change anywhere in the world, and likely to suffer the same fate as their predecessor.

A third group holds that the European containment doctrine — I will treat Asia later — owes its "success" to its being a defense against a nonthreat. By setting up a scenario with a self-fulfilling prophecy — a defense against an attack on Greece and Turkey (Truman Doctrine) and a defense against an attack on Western Europe (NATO) — it was assured of success. (We know today from reliable documents that Stalin, himself, blocked a forceful seizure of Greece; and the Soviet Union urgently pressed the Italian and French Communist parties not to take advantage of their temporary ability to seize power immediately after the war, on the grounds that it could not be retained.)

At this stage, with important basic information still classified by both sides, it is impossible to prove mathematically that European aggression was never Soviet postwar foreign policy. But the new material now being made available suggests that the critics of America's second-decade policy should review the evidence of the first. Containment may not have been as successful as was thought. Indeed, it may not have been successful at all. (The newest work by Martin F. Hertz, a diplomat serving in Iran, *Beginnings of the Cold War*, supplies data which suggests that a negotiated settlement, beyond a détente, was possible in 1945 and 1947. Walter Lippmann's little-known work published in 1947, *The Cold War*, argues the same thesis. The brilliant dissection of the events of 1945–1946 by the State Department's ex-employee Gar Alperovitz, together with Bernstein and Matusow's 1966 *The Truman Administration: A Documentary History*, provide sufficient material for a searching reappraisal of this period.)

The Shaping of American Postwar Foreign Policy

The first stage of America's postwar policy was fashioned in the early years after World War II — specifically the years from 1945 to 1950.

Stateside perception of this new world — a product of the most destructive war in history, and a war fought in association with a large and powerful Communist country — was one to which it could not adjust.

Formidable changes in the world balance of power resulted from three transcendent new factors:

(1) The extension of Socialist power to Eastern and Central Europe, reaching the outermost line of the Soviet army's Western perimeter. (1945–1948. The West's prewar *cordon sanitaire*.)

(2) The emergence of China (1949) from a warlord-ridden, Japanese-occupied, negligible power to the status of a nuclear country with the potential of a major unified world state.

(3) The national and colonial liberation revolution, sparked by the 1947 British withdrawal from India, a movement which marked the beginning of the end of 150 years of colonial and semicolonial *political* rule in the world.

Washington's response to these unexpected developments was to recoil in horror; to seek the cause in demonology and in a unitary concept of an international conspiracy of Communism.

Soviet reaction to Washington, more particularly to the statesmen who took over from Roosevelt — President Harry Truman; Defense Secretary James Forrestal; State Department Europeanist James Byrnes; and Joseph Grew, East Asia ideologist — was almost a mirror image of America's syndrome. In reciprocal fashion, the Soviet government held that:

(1) Western capitalism was inherently expansionist and impelled by inexorable and unchangeable economic contradictions.

(2) Western capitalism was internally and profoundly weak. Its internal contradictions — mitigated for a very short period by war shortages — would shortly produce a devastating world economic crisis of 1929 proportions which would engulf the whole of the capitalistic world, its dependencies and colonies.

(3) Only the application of equivalent countervailing force — military and political — could contain a new attempt to destroy the "New Democracies" and, with the help of a revived revanchist Germany, the Soviet Union.

(4) In keeping with the 1917 concept of the general crisis of capitalism, Soviet ideology held that: if there was resistance by the peoples of capitalist countries; if the Western European nations — especially France and Italy — revolted against the role of American satellites; and if the colonial world gained its independence, imperialism, economically and strategically dependent on colonialism, would be critically shaken and, at key points, crushed.

The United States alleged nonideological perception of Russian Communism had a curious and almost symmetrically reciprocal character, holding that:

(1) Russian Communism was inherently expansionist (for ideological reasons).

(2) Russian Communism was internally weak.

(3) Its expansion could be stopped only by the exercise of power (containment).

(4) Stopping it would cause its internal decay by the explosion of inner contradictions (Kennan, 1945).

If the Russian people resisted;
If the Eastern satellites rose in revolt;
If the Western parties no longer acted as agents;
Communism would be crushed.

The result had to be and was: Exacerbation of the Cold War in the Two-Camp World. In the first five postwar years not only the rhetoric, but also political and military actions, on both sides, contributed to the polarization.

As early as May 11, 1945, Churchill, bordering on hysteria, in a telegram to Truman, had this to say:

> I fear terrible things have happened during the Russian advance through Germany to the Elbe. . . . The Russian frontier would run from North Cape to Norway along the Finnish-Swedish frontier across the Baltic . . . east of Lubeck . . . to the frontiers of Austria. Thus the territories under Russian control would include . . . all Czechoslovakia, a large part of Austria, the whole of Yugoslavia, Hungary, Rumania, Bulgaria. . . . It would include all the great capitals of middle Europe including Berlin, Vienna, Budapest, Belgrade, Bucharest and Sofia. *This constitutes an event in the history of Europe to which there has been no parallel.*

It is more than passing strange that every action Truman and Churchill took assured that the horror they foresaw would take place. Alperovitz and Hertz believe there was a period between 1945 and 1947 when, had a different policy been pursued, an Eastern Europe more on the model of Finland might have been possible. No one can know, looking backward, what might have been. But what did take place formed the basis for twenty years of mindless anti-Communism as one of the main pillars of United States foreign policy.

In 1946 the Soviet Union cut off a long, fruitless discussion on Poland and established a Lublin, not a London, regime. In 1947 the issue of a Hungarian government was settled. ("Truman Calls Hungary Coup Outrage" headlined *The New York*

Times on June 6, 1947.) In 1948 (due to a Western blunder which hoped to expel the one-third Communist representation in the government), Czechoslovakia moved into the Eastern camp — and without the presence of any Soviet troops. ("London and Paris Shocked by Coup in Czechoslovakia" headlined *The New York Times* on February 26, 1948.) In 1949 the greatest blow of all fell: Red China, in an astonishing — almost nonmilitary — campaign, took power in Peking. It took great ability at fantasy to attribute this to Russian expansionism. The State Department was, however, equal to the task.

NATO, SEATO, Cento, Anzus, military bases throughout the world, economic isolation of the Soviet Union — the last starting almost the day of Roosevelt's death — were Washington's answers to these developments which World War II, not Stalin, produced.

The mirror-image effect — each side's action and reaction reinforcing the preconceived perception — colored the first ten years of American and Soviet policy.

It is beyond the scope of this paper to trace the period further, but Henry Steele Commager's comments at the 1967 Senate Foreign Relations hearing effectively sum up, in a general way, contemporary American policy.

There have been in the long course of history many nations that regarded themselves, and always with some justification, as world powers, but there has never been a nation that could, in fact, exercise power everywhere on the globe.

It has remained for the statesmen of this decade to insist that we are an Asian power and have the same kind of responsibility for Asia that we have for Europe.

It is my feeling that we do not have the resources, material, intellectual or moral to be, at once, an American power, a European power, and an Asian power. . . . It is not our duty to keep peace throughout the globe, to put down aggression wherever it starts up, to stop the advance of Communism or other isms of which we may disapprove.

United States War Aims in Southeast Asia

Mr. Commager's realistic analysis notwithstanding, it is the assumption of the declarers of United States policy that the only basis of political coexistence is a balance of forces in East and Southeast Asia preponderantly on the side of the United States. It is their further assumption that China is inherently expansionist and, if contained, will collapse. It is the assumption of some — Secretary Rusk in particular — that the future of civilization will be decided in Asia and not in Europe. Thus, they reason, military domination, political control and Southeast Asia's economic exploitation by the United States are essential to a "peaceful" world.

The keystone arch of American policy in Southeast Asia (eliminating the bromidic "securing for the South Vietnamese people the right to choose their own form of government") has two facets, the second serving the first:

> *(1) To prevent any alteration in a United States-dominated, stable balance of power in Southeast Asia by any change in regime or social system in that area, and*
> *(2) Toward that end, to establish a pro-American, non-Communist, Saigon-based regime in South Vietnam, with the 17th parallel the borderline of Chinese containment.*

The Manila meeting of 1966 was a first step in establishing a new juridical security system which eventually aims to replace the internally inconsistent SEATO treaty.

The United States ultimate aim is to establish American power in the vacuum it perceives to have been left by the French withdrawal from Indochina and the Dutch withdrawal from Indonesia. The entire position historically held by the British, French and Dutch is to be assumed by the United States, in anticipation of the British withdrawal from "East of Suez" (Singapore to Aden).

From the United States point of view what has taken place is historic. Washington's commitments run to Latin America; to Western Europe; and now, with Johnson's Asian Doctrine, along a line in East Asia stretching from the Aleutians to the

Philippines; and in Southeast Asia from the South China Sea to the Indian Ocean.

Never before has any nation (King Canute was a piker) regardless of size and power, ever guaranteed the status quo, the security of incumbent regimes, and provided economic assistance on so vast a scale.

The United States is the "Moral Messiah." This is "Manifest Destiny" and Populist hyperbole run wild. In foreign policy it is Globalism unleashed without regard to the nation's capacity to meet its commitments; or, more important, consideration of the desirability of doing so, even if the capacity existed.

Vietnam Today

It is possible to take a simple position; legally, morally and politically the United States has no business in South Vietnam and, in its own interest, should get out.

The first part of the proposition is certainly true; the second, unfortunately, may not be true. If one is interested first in ending the war and second in indicting and changing the fundamental basis of American policy, the oversimple answer is not really an answer at all.

Nor, on the other hand, is the passive policy — deescalation, watchful waiting, and long-term normalization of Sino-American relations — which seems to be essentially the "enclave" position of Gavin, Ridgway, Kennan, and Fulbright.

Today the facts indicate that Hanoi and the NLF are pursuing a flexible policy and that negotiations are possible. More important, the outline of a compromise settlement fully acceptable to the NLF and Hanoi is known to Washington officials. It is a formula which is realistically based on today's balance of forces; it is politically feasible for the United States to accept; and it in no way compromises the principles of the Front or of the North Vietnamese, or of the United States.

How to get there is the problem. In general, U Thant's three points (cessation of bombing, deescalation and negotiation directly with the NLF) are regarded by diplomats everywhere, including Hanoi, as a sensible first step — everywhere, that is, except in the United States.

It is now beyond doubt that Hanoi and the NLF will accept a quid pro quo: negotiations in exchange for a halt to the bombings. Hanoi's representative in Paris, Mai Van Bo, last week informed Sanford Gottlieb, an official representative of the Committee for a Sane Nuclear Policy, that the North Vietnamese Foreign Minister's statement of February 28 set this out, without any restricting conditions. Kosygin's speech in London, he indicated, was intended to reinforce this position. It contained no mention of "unconditional" or "permanent." Mai Van Bo's own luncheon speech during the Lunar New Year halt was a further signal.

The Johnson administration, after a year of tearful pleas for "unconditional negotiations," subtly shifted ground on September 21, 1966, at the United Nations. It raised a new demand for a *major prior military concession* as a quid pro quo for a halt to the bombing.

Former Ambassador Maxwell Taylor saw Hanoi's acceptance of negotiations (hitherto all that Johnson had asked) as part of an "orchestrated Communist drive to get us to pay the price of giving up bombing as a ticket to get negotiations."

Secretary Rusk, speaking on the second day of the truce, referred to "a systematic campaign by the Communist side to bring about an unconditional cessation of bombing without any corresponding *military* action on their part."

It is hardly necessary to point out why this new demand is unacceptable. It makes Hanoi confirm its own "aggression," thereby legalizing America's naked intervention. "Hanoi would be accepting the American version of the war," said *The New York Times*, "and coming to the talks in the role of outlaw who is bringing in his weapons to the American sheriff."

In short, we have a situation in which Hanoi has softened its terms for negotiation and Washington has toughened its terms.

A relative change of this kind usually means the military tide has turned. But there is little evidence to support this view. Thus, most observers conclude that the one new element in the Asian picture, Mao's Great Proletarian Cultural Revolution, is probably the main basis for Washington's military

arrogance, and for the consequent hardening of its terms.
It seems to be a fact that, for the moment, Mao has effectively destabilized Hanoi's rear. The administration is banking
on the possibility that China's upheaval will physically isolate
Hanoi and the NLF, leaving only a 6,000-mile difficult sea
supply line with the Soviet Union.

(Although it is this writer's view that the internal struggle
in China is serious, it, in fact, concerns only which *regime*
and which *policies* will govern China. Washington's notion
that it will result in the dissolution of the State of China is
wishful thinking of the grossest sort.)

Whichever faction finally prevails in Peking, the attitude
toward continuing commitments in North Vietnam will be the
same.

It is my judgment that a resolution in China which brings
it into a reorientation with the Soviet Union will make an
American victory in Vietnam hopeless. This view is shared
by a number of hard-nosed Sinologists who, paradoxically
enough, announced at a recent Michigan University Conference that it would be in the American interest if Mao and his
anti-Soviet policy prevailed.

Hanoi's recent statements have reemphasized the "unconditional," "permanent" character of the halt to the bombings
before they would accept negotiations.

Diplomats — including some who have talked to Hanoi
representatives — point to the symmetrical nature of the conditions. If the United States were to drop its military reciprocal
demand, Hanoi could easily overlook the lack of a formal
statement on "unconditional and permanent."

The exchange would then be back to the simple halt for
negotiations.

Although at present there appears to be no give in the
American position, this might be mutable. Escalation, so dear
to the hearts of the Joint Chiefs of Staff and the congressional
Hawks, is by no means diplomatically, politically, or militarily
easy to justify. The Joint Chiefs have had a sympathetic audience for two years, but it takes a good case, not subjective
sympathy, to produce consent to such an apocalyptic course.

An alternative to escalation (where — and what do you

do after you have escalated, especially if it includes China?) is a proposal outlined in part in a recent interview given by Hanoi's Foreign Minister to Wilfred Burchett (February 28, 1967).

The same information was given, with Hanoi's approval, through formal channels to Secretary Rusk last fall by Hungary's Foreign Minister.

The proposal was to set up a neutralized coalition government representative of *all* points of view (the North Vietnamese single exception was to Ky, but they did not exclude the possibility of other rightist generals). South Vietnam would be nonaligned, and United States troops would be withdrawn.

The NLF did not claim sole authority. On the contrary, the model was apparently the Laotian pattern (one-third NLF, one-third Neutralist, one-third Rightist). Both North and South agreed that unification is a long way off and, in any case, is something for the Vietnamese to solve themselves.

This does not now meet Washington's aims outlined earlier — that is, a pro-United States, client state in Saigon. This is the specific aim that the United States must jettison. Once it is prepared to do that, the problem of achieving negotiations will be simple.

Not only does this paper disagree that Washington is ready for this decision; it suggests the harder evidence is that, in full possession of the facts, Washington is still seeking its maximum aims. *Its decision not to negotiate is not a blunder nor a misunderstanding.*

I do suggest, however, that the "enclave," "watchful waiting" proposal puts the situation backward.

It is not Hanoi and the Front which have to change; it is Washington. Watchful waiting will not accomplish that.

The Use and Abuse of
International Law

CLIFTON E. WILSON

This paper will consider both the application and unilateral interpretation of international law in relation to selected aspects of United States foreign policy and the methods and means by which the United States has utilized and circumvented United Nations processes in pursuit of American policy goals. These approaches are observable also in the policy pursuits of other nations. But the United States, because of its rapid emergence as a global power and recent assumption of "free world leadership" has been particularly addicted to these tendencies.

Moreover, Americans are supposed to believe strongly in a "rule of law," at home and in world affairs, whether or not they fully understand these rules. This American belief pattern strengthens our proclivity to cloak policy pursuits in a legal garb.

Of course, international law in itself is not an independent instrument of order and change. Rather, it is an integrated aspect of a functioning political system. Thus, national decisions and political actions do alter rules of law.

However, if national foreign policy decisions defy accepted international legal norms, they must be acceptable to other members of the international community.[1] Law is not changed

---

[1] The State Department Legal Adviser wrote in connection with the Cuban quarantine as follows: "The employment of force, the appeal for world support, to say nothing of the ultimate judgment of history, all

by *fiat* or by foreign office declarations. In other words, a viable system of law develops by consensual — not unilateral — action.

A basic problem arises when a nation takes a political action for political or security reasons which is not compatible with accepted rules of law, and then attempts to justify the act by legal arguments. In all fairness, it is important to note that this is a dilemma common to all nations whether it be the United States in Vietnam, the Soviet Union in Hungary, or France and Britain in the Suez. This situation stems from the fact that national decision-makers like to view the world as two systems — one of world order based on rules of law, the other of world order based on national interest and security.[2]

Action in many cases flows from the latter but is publicly justified by the former. For example, the United States did just this in attempting to justify new concepts such as the naval "quarantine" and anticipatory self-defense.[3] The Cuban "quarantine" of 1962, recent intervention in Latin American internal affairs, and the Vietnamese war will be discussed below as examples of this use and misuse of concepts of international law.[4]

---

depend in some significant degree on the reality and coherence of the case in law for our action." Abram Chayes, "The Legal Case for U.S. Action on Cuba," *Department of State Bulletin,* XLVII (November 19, 1962), 763. See also Leonard C. Meeker, "Defensive Quarantine and the Law," *American Journal of International Law,* LVII (July, 1963), 516.

[2] When discussing United States involvement in the Cuban crisis, G. S. Windass spoke of the two rival order systems which helped to explain American motives. These systems were the "sacrosanct hemispheric empire" and nuclear balance. G. S. Windass, "The Cuban Crisis and World Order," *International Relations,* III (April, 1966), 10–15.

[3] See also R. T. Bohan, "The Dominican Case: Unilateral Intervention," *American Journal of International Law,* LX (October, 1966), 809. In reference to the Dominican case, Bohan said the United States used international law as an "instrument for the self-righteous justification of illegal acts."

[4] Many other issues no doubt should be analyzed in a study of this nature. Examples include the violation of rules of the free sea by nuclear bomb testing and the interdiction of ships during the Cuban "quarantine," overflights and intrusions into the air space of Cuba,

Much of what has already been said also would apply to organization. National governments like to view the United Nations, for example, within the spectrum of two order systems. Examples discussed in this category will be cases in which the United States has either used or bypassed the United Nations, often in violation of the concept of universalism. In other words, United States policy has been more compatible with an American order system than with a universal order system.

Involvements and Implications

Cuban "Quarantine." The Cuban "quarantine" was a case involving a number of rules of international law. It also illustrates the dilemmas faced by a nation in its attempts to cloak with legal trappings political action perceived as essential to the national security. During the Cuban crisis, the United States government was concerned about hemispheric control, and viewed with apprehension what it saw as an unfavorable shift in its nuclear balance with the Soviet Union. Virtually all official statements referred to the so-called "quarantine" as necessary for "hemispheric protection," and pointed to a need for "hemispheric solidarity." The Russians were accused, in the words of two supporters of Washington policy, of seeking "to achieve a flagrant and deliberate modification of the existing world power structure" through sending missiles to Cuba.[5]

Although United States concern over any distortion of the power balance or the installation of missiles close to its shores

China, and the Soviet Union, and unilateral economic blockades. However, the writer believes that the problems of misusing international law are well illustrated through the cases included in this paper.

[5] Carl Q. Christol and Charles I. Davis, "Maritime Quarantine: The Naval Interdiction of Offensive Weapons and Associated Material to Cuba," *American Journal of International Law,* LVII (July, 1963), 526. Charles Fenwick went further in charging the Soviet Union with a violation of Article 2(4) of the United Nations Charter by "attempting to upset the balance of nuclear power." C. G. Fenwick, "Quarantine Against Cuba: Legal or Illegal?" *American Journal of International Law,* LVII (July, 1963), 591.

is understandable, no rule of international law prevents a
nation (USSR and/or Cuba) from attempting to change this
balance in its favor.[6] However, legalists have made out an
argument in support of the Cuban quarantine. First, the new
concept of "quarantine" was substituted for the traditional —
but rarely used — pacific blockade; second, the USSR was
accused of "deception" in the installation of "offensive missiles"; and third, our action was justified on the grounds of
both collective regional action and self-defense.

President Kennedy in his Proclamation referred to the interdiction of specified materials being sent into Cuba as a "strict
quarantine."[7] This was the official line. However, this unilateral redesignation of an older concept did not ipso facto
create a new rule of international law. Both the Soviet Union
and Cuba still viewed the "quarantine" as a naval blockade.[8]
The action, not the label, must be judged. And even one of
the stoutest defenders of the United States action, Charles G.
Fenwick, referred to the so-called quarantine as "a striking
instance of resort by the United States to pacific blockade."[9]

The idea of pacific blockade developed during the early
part of the nineteenth century and it was on occasion used by

---

[6] See F. B. Schick, "Cuba and the Rule of Law," *International Affairs*
[Moscow] (September, 1963), p. 61, and "Cuba: Role of the UN,"
New Statesman, October 12, 1962, p. 475. Raymond Aron also argues
that "the practical basis" for United States action in the Cuban crisis
rests on a "traditional and cynical prerogative of the major powers to
impose limits on the action of the lesser powers." Raymond Aron, "International Law — Reality and Fiction," *New Republic*, CXLVII (December 1, 1962), 14.

[7] *Department of State Bulletin*, XLVII (1962), 716. As defined by one
supporter of United States policy, "Maritime quarantine is a collective
peaceful process involving limited coercive measures interdicting the
unreasonable movement of certain types of offensive military weapons
and associated material by one state into the territory of another."
Christol and Davis, *op. cit.*, p. 527.

[8] In a statement before the Security Council, Dr. Mario García-
Inchaustegui, Cuban representative, declared that "the naval blockade
unilaterally decreed by the United States is an act of war against the
sovereignty and independence of our country." *United Nations Review*,
IX (November, 1962), 82.

[9] Fenwick, *op. cit.*, p. 642.

stronger powers as a device to coerce weaker nations.[10] Although at present no agreement exists among international lawyers that pacific blockade is compatible with the accepted rules of international law, and virtually all agree that the blockading state has no right to seize and sequestrate ships of a third state, strong protests have been registered by nations involved as victims in such action. In the postwar period, for example, West Germany and Yugoslavia objected when France interdicted vessels bound for Algeria.[11] The United States also has consistently opposed the halting of American vessels.[12] In fact, Secretary of State Rusk informed a con-

---

[10] Herbert W. Briggs, *The Law of Nations,* (2nd ed., New York: Appleton-Century-Crofts, 1952), p. 959. Unilateral intervention is now presumably outlawed by the United States Charter, Article 2(5), and, at best, a blockade must conform to the rules of reprisal. These would include the securing of a remedy for injury resulting from an illegal action and attempts to find peaceful methods of settlement. The United States was hard-pressed to show that the Soviet-Cuban action was illegal, and the normal procedures of pacific settlement did not fail because they were not utilized.

[11] In January, 1958, a Yugoslav ship, the *Slovenija,* was halted by a French vessel on the high seas off the coast of Casablanca. The French seized arms which they said were consigned to the FLN in Algeria. The Yugoslav Ambassador in Paris called the interdiction and seizure of the cargo a "flagrant violation of liberty of the seas." The following year, a German freighter, the *Bilbao,* suspected of gun-running to the Algerian rebels, was intercepted by the French in the English Channel and escorted into Cherbourg harbor. The Federal Republic of Germany protested the action as a violation of international maritime law. See Whiteman, *Digest of International Law,* IV, 513.

[12] Briggs notes that the United States "has consistently opposed the application of pacific blockades to American vessels and denied the legitimacy of such action." Briggs, *op. cit.,* p. 959. This conclusion is supported by both legislative and executive actions. A Senate resolution in 1858 stated that "American vessels on the high seas are not subject to search in time of peace." Moore, *Digest of International Law,* II, 956. "The United States objected vigorously when third state ships were stopped during the 1902 blockade of Venezuela by Great Britain, Germany and Italy." *Ibid.,* VII, 140. "In 1916, Secretary of State Lansing declared that 'the United States . . . does not acquiesce in any extending of the doctrine of pacific blockade which may adversely affect the rights of states not parties to the controversy or discriminating against the commerce of neutral nations. . . .' " Hyde, *International Law,* (2nd ed), II, 1669.

gressional hearing on September 17, 1962, prior to the October crisis, that "the use of force against ships going into a country so blockaded could be interpreted by the country who was stopped as an act of force, to proceed on the basis of an act of war."[13]

It is true that only two Soviet ships were stopped during the Cuban crisis and force was not used. However, United States naval units were authorized by President Kennedy to interdict ships of any nation and to use force "to the extent necessary."[14]

The United States would seem to contend, however, that the rules of blockade do not apply to so-called "quarantine." And the Cuban crisis invoked a quarantine and not a blockade action because of the nature of the military buildup in Cuba. The Soviet Union had, it was said, "voluntarily embarked upon the risky experiment of establishing a series of offensive missile sites in Cuba."[15] Simply stated, we created a new doctrine — quarantine — allegedly because the missiles were "offensive," not defensive. Official statements make this point clear.[16] But they are not legally convincing.

---

[13] U.S. Senate Hearings, *Situation in Cuba,* 87th Congress, 2nd Session, September 17, 1962, p. 60. Early in the same month that the "quarantine" was declared, Vice-President Lyndon B. Johnson told a Democratic dinner meeting that stopping a Russian ship during a blockade of Cuba would be an "act of war" and added, in reference to the blockade, that "some advocates . . . have more guts than brains and some don't have either." *Arizona Daily Star,* October 7, 1962, p. 1A.

[14] The President's Proclamation reads: "Any vessel or craft which may be proceeding toward Cuba may be intercepted and may be directed to identify itself, its cargo, equipment and stores and its ports of call, to stop, to lie to, to submit to visit and search, or to proceed as directed." *Department of State Bulletin,* XLVII (1962), p. 717.

[15] Christol and Davis, *op. cit.,* p. 526.

[16] President Kennedy, in his public notification of the crisis, stressed the presence of "these large, long-range, and clearly offensive weapons of sudden mass destruction . . ." He specifically referred to both the medium-range and intermediate-range ballistic missiles as well as to jet bombers capable of carrying nuclear weapons. *Department of State Bulletin,* XLVII (1962), 175. This added up to what Secretary Rusk termed an "offensive capability . . . of such a nature that it can reach into the far corners of our Hemisphere with its destructive force." Statement of October 23, 1962, in David L. Larson (ed.), *The "Cuban Crisis" of 1962* (Boston: Houghton Mifflin, 1963), p. 61.

What is an offensive weapon of war? Obviously a missile itself is neither offensive nor defensive.[17] The question can be answered only by determining how the weapons are used or what the plans are for their use. Can the United States unilaterally determine, to use the words of the Cuban United Nations Ambassador, "when a rocket is good and when a rocket is naughty, when a base is good and when a base is naughty"?[18]

Many respected authorities on international law have concluded that the missiles were not "naughty." Typical of these publicists is a British writer who notes that from Cuba's viewpoint the missiles were not "anything but a defensive measure."[19] Others, including Quincy Wright and Frans B. Schick, agree.[20]

Cuban leadership may have believed, on the basis of the American attempt to strangle them economically, the abortive Bay of Pigs invasion, and the rumblings of potential armed invasion, that they needed defensive weapons.[21]

If an offensive-defensive rule is to emerge in international law, the global commitments of all nations must be considered. The Soviets might well have viewed the United States alliances with forty-plus nations and the missile sites in Turkey and Italy, which were capable of striking almost any area of the Soviet Union, as potentially offensive. Ambassador Stevenson argued that these missile sites were not offensive because they were not of a recent date and because they re-

---

[17] Quincy Wright, "The Cuban Quarantine," *American Journal of International Law,* LVII (July, 1963), 551.

[18] Ambassador Mario García-Inchaustegui before the Security Council, *United Nations Review,* IX (September, 1962), 81.

[19] Windass, *op. cit.,* p. 2.

[20] Wright, *op. cit.,* pp. 548–49; Schick finds the Soviet Union's statement that "armaments and military material sent to Cuba" were "designed exclusively for defensive purposes" as "regrettably true." Schick, *op. cit.,* p. 60.

[21] For example, the Joint Congressional Resolution of September 26, 1962, reads that the United States "is determined . . . to prevent by whatever means may be necessary, including the use of arms, the Marxist-Leninist regime in Cuba from extending by force or threat of force, its aggressive or subversive activities to any part of this hemisphere." *Department of State Bulletin,* XLVII (1962), 597.

sulted from agreements "freely negotiated and publicly declared."[22] This in itself is not enough to determine their legal status.

Furthermore, did the missiles in Cuba constitute a greater danger to the United States than the vastly more destructive intercontinental missiles stationed on Soviet territory and presumably aimed toward the United States, the long-range nuclear Soviet bombers, or the fleet of Soviet nuclear submarines?[23] A Soviet spokesman noted, in this regard, that his country possesses an ample supply of rocket and missile carriers and "did not need to relocate in any other country — for instance, in Cuba — the means available for it for repelling aggression and for a retaliatory blow."[24]

Furthermore, in shipping the missiles to Cuba, the Soviet Union was accused of "unashamedly attempting to deceive the United States."[25] This accusation of deceit runs throughout official U.S. and Soviet statements.[26] Yet there is no accepted rule of international law which requires nations to publicize their military agreements. For that matter, the United States practiced deception in the U-2 flights over the Soviet Union. Also the United States, and other nations no doubt, believe that secrecy is necessary when national security is involved.[27]

---

[22] Quoted in Larson, *op. cit.*, p. 73.

[23] Question posed by Schick, *op. cit.*, p. 60.

[24] UN Ambassador Zorin, quoting a September 11, 1962, statement in *Tass. United Nations Review*, IX (September, 1962), 83.

[25] Fenwick, *op. cit.*, p. 591.

[26] See, for example, President Kennedy's address to the nation, *Department of State Bulletin*, XLVII (1962), 716; Stevenson's statement to the Security Council, *United Nations Review*, IX (September, 1962), 80; and resolution adopted by the OAS, October 23, 1962, in Larson, *op. cit.*, p. 66.

[27] Concern over U.S. informational policy has also been expressed in other situations. Morley Safer accused Arthur Sylvester, Assistant Secretary of Defense for Public Affairs, of telling correspondents in Saigon that "if you think any American official is going to tell you the truth, then you're stupid." Sylvester denied making the remark but another correspondent, Malcolm W. Browne, noted that Sylvester had earlier remarked that it is inherent in a government's right "to lie to save itself when it's going up into nuclear war." U.S. Senate, Hearings, *News*

Beyond these arguments, it is pertinent to note that neither the Soviet Union nor the United States is party to a treaty which bans trade in armaments. The Soviet Union, as well as Cuba and the United States, has defensive arrangements under international law.[28]

Beyond this challenge to Washington's interpretation of the concept of pacific blockade, two other basic legal reasons given to justify the United States action must also be questioned: (1) that it was a collective "regional" act authorized by the United Nations Charter; and (2) that it was legally justified under the doctrine of self-defense. The State Department clearly opted in favor of the regional argument.[29] The Department's brief centered on Article 53 of the Charter which reads:

> The Security Council shall, where appropriate, utilize such regional arrangements or agencies for enforcement action under its authority. But no enforcement action shall be taken under regional arrangements or by regional agencies without the authorization of the Security Council. . . .

Clearly "enforcement action" requires "authorization" of the Security Council. The State Department attempted to circumvent Article 53 by claiming that recommendations of the regional Organization of American States (OAS) were not enforcement actions.[30] As one observer tartly noted, this is

---

Policies in Vietnam, 89th Congress, 2nd Session, August 17 and 31, 1966, pp. 71, 91, 94. Also see comments on managed news by the United States in "The Ethics of Lying," *Worldview*, VI (January, 1963), 1, and Schick, *op. cit.*, pp. 57–58.

[28] "It is difficult," as Quincy Wright observes, "to support the allegation that the Soviet Union violated international obligations in sending and installing missiles in Cuba." Wright, *op. cit.*, pp. 548–49.

[29] "Our quarantine," said the Department's legal adviser, "was imposed in accordance with the recommendations of the Organization of American States acting under the Rio Treaty of 1947. . . . The President . . . did not invoke Article 51 (of the UN Charter) or the right of self-defense." *Department of State Bulletin*, XLVII (1962), 764.

[30] The Department argued that "since state signatories of the Rio Treaty were not obligated to carry out the resolution recommending

not "interpreting" the article; in fact it is "destroying" it.[31] A parallel is drawn between the OAS "recommendation" in this case and the General Assembly recommendations in the Suez and Congo peacekeeping operations which did not require Security Council endorsement in order to legalize the financial assessment.

The two cases can be easily distinguished. The International Court of Justice specifically held that the General Assembly recommendations, in the latter case under Article 11(2), were not enforcement actions since they were taken "at the request, or with the consent, of the States concerned."[32] Thus for the assessment rule to be controlling in the case of the quarantine, the USSR and Cuba must either have made a request for the action or have given their consent. The claim that the *state* of Cuba as a member of the Inter-American system (even though the *government* of Cuba was excluded at Punta del Este) was bound by its constructive consent is farfetched. And the USSR certainly did not willingly consent to the quarantine.

Finally, although the quarantine did not formally go into effect until after the OAS Resolution, the consultative organ of the OAS actually was faced by a fait accompli. The United States announced the quarantine decision to the public through President Kennedy's television and radio address on October 22, 1962.[33] The OAS endorsement was dutifully supplied a day later.[34]

For these reasons, even the most ardent supporters of the

---

quarantine, it should not be held to constitute 'enforcement action' under Article 53(1) requiring Security Council authorization." Meeker, *op. cit.*, p. 522.

[31] "It could be said that the need for Security Council authorization was already a dead letter of international law, or, if not already dead, fair game. This was no doubt the real attitude of the State Department lawyers; for they could have had no illusions that what they were doing was not 'interpreting' the second sentence of Article 53, but destroying it." Windass, *op. cit.*, p. 14.

[32] Advisory Opinion of the International Court of Justice on Certain Expenses of the United Nations (July 20, 1962), *International Court of Justice Reports*, pp. 151, 164, digested in *American Journal of International Law*, LVI (1962), 1053.

[33] *Department of State Bulletin*, XLVII (1962), 715–20.

[34] *Ibid.*, pp. 722–23.

U.S. policy in Cuba find the idea of regional justification difficult to accept. One of these writers observes, quite correctly:

> The world community has yet to recognize the Cuban
> crisis as standing for the proposition that regional agen-
> cies are free to use armed force to maintain the peace
> in the absence of Security Council authorities when
> conditions justifying self-defense are not present.[35]

Were conditions justifying self-defense present in Cuba? A
substantial number of writers who rallied to defend the U.S.
action think so. They based their arguments, not on the OAS
regional pact, but on Article 51 of the United Nations Charter
which provides for measures of self-defense.[36] In addition,
despite the denials, official Washington also appeared to view
the quarantine as a defensive measure.[37] For example, President Kennedy in his address of October 22, 1962, said the
United States was acting "in the defense of our own security
and of the entire Western Hemisphere. . . ."[38] The OAS Reso-

---

[35] James S. Campbell, "The Cuban Crisis and the U.N. Charter: An
Analysis of the United States Position," *Stanford Law Review*, XVI
(December, 1963), 176.

[36] See *ibid.*, pp. 160–76; Christol and Davis, *op. cit.*, pp. 525–45; John
W. Halderman, "Regional Enforcement Measures and the United Na-
tions," *Georgetown Law Journal*, LII (Fall, 1963), 89–118; Myres S.
McDougal, "Soviet-Cuban Quarantine and Self-Defense," *American
Journal of International Law*, LVII (July, 1963), 597–604; W. T. Malli-
son, Jr., "Limited Naval Blockade or Quarantine–Interdiction," *George
Washington Law Review*, XXXI (December, 1962), 335–98; and Eustace
Seligman, "The Legality of U.S. Quarantine Action Under the United
Nations Charter," *American Bar Association Journal*, XLIX (February,
1963), 142–45.

[37] See Christol and Davis, *op. cit.*, p. 534.

[38] *Department of State Bulletin*, XLVII (1962), 716. At the end of the
crisis, the President informed a press conference that "we, of course,
keep to ourselves and hold to ourselves, under the United States Constitution and under the laws of international law, the right to defend our
security." *The New York Times*, November 21, 1962. The U.S. Proclamation ordered interdictory measures in order to "defend the security
of the United States." *Department of State Bulletin*, XLVII (1962), 717.
Ambassador Stevenson at an October 23, 1962, press conference said the
measures were necessary to defend the U.S., the hemisphere and our
other allies. *Ibid.*, p. 734. Abram Chayes, Legal Adviser to the Depart-

lution of October 23, 1962, on the quarantine also used the term self-defense.[39]

The pertinent part of Article 51 reads:

Nothing in the present Charter shall impair the inherent right of individual or collective self-defense if an armed attack occurs against a Member of the United Nations, until the Security Council has taken measures necessary to maintain international peace and security.

Self-defense, like "offensive" weapons, is subject to varied interpretations. As a concept in international law, its most widely quoted definition is that of Secretary of State Webster in the Caroline case.[40] Forceful action in self-defense will apply only if the need is, in Webster's words written in 1842, "instant, overwhelming, and leaving no choice of means, and no moment for deliberation."

Article 51 inserts a new restriction: armed attack. And a restriction it is, according to many experts including Philip Jessup, now a member of the World Court. He contends that not even "alarming military preparations by a neighboring state" would justify "resort to anticipatory force by the state which believes itself threatened."[41]

This anticipatory self-defense provides the basic rationale for those supporting the quarantine. Anticipatory self-defense may have been acceptable as a legal basis for forceful action before World War I. However, by 1945, when Article 51 was approved, forceful action in "self-defense was understood to be justified only in case of an attack by the forces of a State."[42] This conclusion was supported by the International Military

---

ment of State, said the action was "designed to deal with an imminent threat to our security." *Ibid.*, p. 764.

[39] *Ibid.*, p. 722.

[40] Moore, *op. cit.*, II, pp. 409–14.

[41] Philip Jessup, *A Modern Law of Nations* (New York: Macmillan, 1952), p. 166.

[42] Ian Brownlie, "The Use of Force in Self-Defense," *British Yearbook of International Law*, XXXVII (1961), 246.

Tribunal which rejected the doctrine of anticipatory self-defense in the Nuremberg trials.[43] The concept also was denied by France in connection with its bombing raids in Tunisia.[44]

Thus, since the installation of missiles was not an armed attack, the quarantine violated Article 51.[45] It is doubtful if the concept of self-defense can ever be legally stretched to equate situations such as the shipment of missiles to Cuba with armed attack.[46]

However, pro-State Department legalists agree that because of the nature of modern weapons and their fantastic destructive power, atomic warheads in the hands of a potential foe might be regarded as a constructive armed attack, thus justifying forceful acts in anticipatory self-defense.[47] This is the so-called "sitting duck" theory — a nation should not be a "sitting duck" for possible destruction.[48]

However, it would appear that the real danger of an escalating nuclear war is to be found in the use of force in anticipatory self-defense by one of these so-called "sitting ducks."

---

[43] The right of self-defense was invoked in the Erich Raeder trial. The German invasion of Norway was offered as a defensive act to forestall imminent British invasion of Norway. But the Tribunal held that the attack was designed to prevent a possible future allied invasion. The Tribunal thus reverted in its decision to Webster's instant and overwhelming *dicta*. International Military Tribunal in German Major War Criminals Case, 1946, pp. 171, 207. As discussed by William L. Standard, "United States Quarantine of Cuba and the Rule of Law," *American Bar Association Journal*, XLIX (August, 1963), 747.

[44] Was the bombing and violence at Sakiet-Sidi-Youssef by the French, which was more aggressive than the missile installation, an armed attack under Article 51? The French delegates to the Security Council claimed that the right of self-defense was available only when there was *armed aggression* (emphasis added) and that the bombing was not in this category. Security Council Official Reports, United Nations Document S/4013, May 29, 1958 (819th meeting).

[45] Standard, *op. cit.*, p. 748.

[46] Windass, *op. cit.*, p. 7.

[47] Fenwick, *op. cit.*, p. 589. See also Christol and Davis, *op. cit.*, p. 532; Brunson MacChesney, "Some Comments on the Quarantine of Cuba," *American Journal of International Law*, LVII (July, 1963), 595; McDougal, *op. cit.*, p. 599.

[48] Windass, *op. cit.*, p. 6.

Driven to the extreme, a sufficiently loose interpretation of Article 51 could precipitate an all-out war.[49]

The United States action in the Cuban case may have established what has been called an "ominous precedent," since the line between self-defense and aggression is a thin one.[50] The precedent also is ominous because of the similarity of self-defense, unilaterally declared and not in the face of armed attack, with two other fearsome doctrines: preventive war[51] and preemptive strike, the latter doctrine supposedly abandoned by both superpowers because of the risks involved.[52] U Thant may have had these dangers in mind when he said the Cuban crisis involved "the very fate of mankind."[53]

The United States also was obligated under UN Charter Article 2(4) to refrain from the threat of force or the use of force against the territorial integrity or political independence of another state. If we considered the missiles a threat to the peace or an act of aggression, recourse could have been sought through the Security Council. Or the U.S. could have sought a peaceful settlement under the terms of Article 33. The United States did submit the question to the Council but not until after it had acted unilaterally and set the interdiction machinery in motion.[54]

Intervention.   Although the Cuban quarantine/blockade has been the most dramatic single legal-political cold war incident in the Latin American area, United States foreign policy has often challenged another doctrine of international law — nonintervention. Three cases of intervention will be reviewed: the overthrow of the Arbenz regime in Guatemala

---

[49] Philip Jessup expresses the hopeful wish "that the occasion will not arise for individual states to resort to their individual interpretations in some great crisis." Jessup, *op. cit.,* p. 167. Unfortunately nations have often resorted to their own interpretations.

[50] Standard, *op. cit.,* pp. 747–48.

[51] *Ibid.,* p. 748.

[52] Windass, *op. cit.,* p. 6.

[53] *United Nations Review, op. cit.,* p. 7.

[54] See Wright, *op. cit.,* pp. 560–61. The fact that a solution was soon reached indicated that the confrontation could have been settled without the military confrontation. Standard, *op. cit.,* p. 747.

in 1954, the Bay of Pigs invasion in 1961, and the occupation of territory in the Dominican Republic in 1965.

Intervention is a "dictatorial interference" in the domestic affairs of a state or in its relations with other states.[55] It is nondictatorial, or permissible, only when the danger "is real and immediate and can be averted by no other means."[56] The occupation of Santo Domingo and the invasions of Guatemala and Cuba were hardly justified by a "real and immediate" threat to the security of the United States. And "other means" were available through the machinery of the United Nations.

United States involvements in the three incidents were similar in principle but differed in degree. Unquestionably, the United States government and its Ambassador John Peurifoy had more than a passing interest in the aggression launched against Guatemala from Honduras and Nicaragua. Our involvement especially through the CIA was even more direct and widely known in the abortive invasion of Cuba by Cuban refugees launched from Guatemala and Florida.[57] Even though the U.S. justified action under anti-Communist resolutions adopted by the Organization of American States,[58] unilateral military intervention is prohibited both by the United Nations and the OAS Charters.

The United States went a step further and physically landed

---

[55] Quincy Wright, "Intervention and Cuba in 1961," *Proceedings, American Society of International Law*, 1961, p. 7.

[56] Oscar Svarlien, *An Introduction to the Law of Nations* (New York: McGraw-Hill, 1955), p. 124.

[57] As Tad Szulc reported in *The New York Times*, April 22, 1961, "It has been an open secret in Florida and Central America for months, the CIA planned, coordinated and directed the operations that ended in the defeat" at the Bay of Pigs. For the summary of the detailed reports of Szulc for that period, see Wright, *Proceedings*, 1961, p. 61, fn.

[58] See the Caracas Declaration of 1954, *American Journal of International Law*, XLVIII (1954), 127 ff.; The Resolution of the Fifth Meeting of OAS Foreign Ministers at Santiago in 1959, *American Journal of International Law*, LV (1961), 537–38; and the Resolution of the Eighth Meeting of the Foreign Ministers at Punta del Este in 1962, *American Journal of International Law*, LVI (1962) 604–5. Also, see *The New York Times,* April 4, 1961, p. 14, for accusation by the State Department that Castro was building a Communist bridgehead in the hemisphere.

its own troops in the Dominican Republic during the governmental crisis in that country in 1965. The action was allegedly justified under the traditional rule of self-defense.[59] The pretext was defense of the United States and other nationals. The real reason was a defense against what was alleged to be the possible establishment of a pro-Communist government.[60]

The alleged Communist threat does not provide a legal escape route for the United States. In the words of Senator Fulbright, "the United States acted on the premise that the revolution was *controlled* by the Communists — a premise which it failed to establish at the time and has not established since."[61]

The point is not that there was no Communist influence but

---

[59] See C. G. Fenwick, "The Dominican Republic: Intervention or Collective Self-Defense," *American Journal of International Law*, LX (January, 1966), 64, for an example of reliance on the self-defense concept.

[60] This action in alleged self-defense was based on (a) the protection of nations and (b) an effort to halt the hemispheric spread of Communism. President Johnson told a news conference that "99 per cent of our reason for going in there was to try to provide protection for these American lives and the lives of other nationals." *The New York Times*, June 2, 1965, p. 16. Senator Fulbright called this "more of a pretext than a reason for the massive U.S. intervention" and added: "In fact, no American lives were lost in Santo Domingo until the Marines began exchanging fire with the rebels after April 28; reports of widespread shooting that endangered American lives turned out to be exaggerated." J. W. Fulbright, "The Situation in the Dominican Republic," *Vital Speeches*, XXXI (October 1, 1965), 750. The 99 per cent reason was expressed in the so-called Johnson Doctrine: "The American nation cannot, must not, and will not permit the establishment of another Communist government in the Western Hemisphere." *The New York Times*, May 9, 1965, Sec. 4, p. 1. The words are those of the President. Fulbright reaches the same conclusion: "The United States intervened in the Dominican Republic for the purpose of preventing the victory of a revolutionary force which was judged to be Communist dominated." Fulbright, *op. cit.*, p. 751.

[61] *U.S. News & World Report*, LIX (September 27, 1965), 20. One student of international law claims that the United States did not have any more legal right to send the Marines into Santo Domingo in an anticipatory action against the creation of another Cuban-styled government than did Hitler in overwhelming Belgium to head off a French invasion. Bohan, *op. cit.*, p. 810.

rather that the revolution was not Communist dominated.[62]

But more to the point, *the United States has no right under international law to dictate the form of government for a hemispheric neighbor* — not in Guatemala, Cuba, or the Dominican Republic. President Eisenhower made this abundantly clear in 1953, before any of the three incidents occurred. He said:

Any nation's right to form a government and an economic system of its own choosing is inalienable. Any nation's attempt to dictate to other nations their form of government is indefensible.[63]

The United States, in "heading toward the unenviable self-righteous and self-defeating position of world policeman,"[64] also clearly bypasses Article 15 of the Charter of the Organization of American States (ratified by the United States) which says:

No State or group of States has the right to intervene, directly or indirectly, for any reason whatever, in the internal or external affairs of any other State. The foregoing principle prohibits not only armed force but also any other form of interference or attempted threat against the personality of the State or against its political, economic and cultural elements.

It also skirted Article 17 of the OAS Charter which reads:

The territory of a State is inviolable; it may not be the object, even temporarily, of military occupation, or of other measures of force taken by another State, directly or indirectly, on any grounds whatever.

Numerous other treaties also bar the United States from

---

[62] It is true that the CIA did list fifty-five Communists in Santo Domingo, some of them dead or in jail at the time of the uprising, but this hardly justified the Marine invasion.

[63] *Department of State Bulletin*, XXVIII (1953), p. 599.

[64] *The New York Times,* Editorial, May 6, 1965, p. 36.

intervention — direct or indirect, military or diplomatic — and from mounting an invasion from its territory.[65] Attempts by the United States to deny the doctrine of nonintervention[66] or by the Congress to authorize military intervention[67] do not automatically destroy venerable international rules. Nor did the U.S. actions fit into any of the accepted exceptions to nonintervention.[68] Insofar as intervention relates to the kind of military action taken by the United States in the Dominican Republic, the doctrine is "very much alive."[69]

The World Court also has denounced what it called the "alleged rule of intervention" as providing a potential weapon

---

[65] The Havana Convention of 1928 on Rights and Duties of States in the Event of Civil Strife, ratified by the United States in 1931. It binds the parties "to use all means at their disposal to prevent the inhabitants of their territory, nationals or aliens, from participating in, gathering elements, crossing the boundary or sailing from their territory for the purpose of starting or promoting civil strife" (Article 1). *American Journal of International Law, Supp.*, XXII (1928), 159. The Saavedra Lamas Anti-War Treaty of 1933 to which both Cuba and the United States are parties, forbids "intervention either diplomatic or armed" subject to obligations of other treaties (Article 3). *American Journal of International Law, Supp.*, XXVIII (1934), 79. The Montevideo Convention of 1933 on the Rights and Duties of States, ratified by the United States with a reservation, declares that "no state has the right to intervene in the internal or external affairs of another" (Article 8). *American Journal of International Law, Supp.*, XXVIII (1934), 75. The Buenos Aires Protocol on Non-Intervention of 1936 declares "inadmissible the intervention of any of them, directly or indirectly, and for whatever reason, in the internal or external affairs of any other of the parties" (Article 1). *American Journal of International Law, Supp.*, XXXI (1937), 57. These treaties are summarized by Wright, *Proceedings*, 1961, 13.

[66] Averell Harriman was more than candid in defending the United States position when he argued that the principle of nonintervention is becoming obsolete. *The New York Times*, July 3, 1965, p. 18.

[67] The House on September 20, 1965, by a 312 to 52 margin, approved a resolution calling for the use of force by any American nation if necessary to prevent a Communist take-over in any hemispheric country. *Arizona Daily Star*, September 21, 1965, p. 3A. One opponent said the resolution would perpetuate an image of the United States as a nation favoring "clumsy, heavy-handed intervention" in other countries' affairs.

[68] These exceptions are self-defense, the remedy of a wrong, the alleviation of undue suffering, or intervening with the consent of the state where the intervention takes place.

[69] Herbert I. Matthews, *The New York Times*, May 10, 1965, p. 32.

for use by powerful states to pervert the very meaning of international law itself.[70]

Under international law, states may change their form of government, ideology, or economic system. They enjoy the right of internal revolution. They may divide, split or cede their territory. These changes are not subject to outside intervention as long as they do not violate treaties with other states or are not a threat to the peace, in which case the United Nations should act. Freedom from foreign interference is written into numerous Inter-American agreements. It also is a pillar of the United Nations as reflected in such Charter terms as "self-determination," respect for "territorial integrity and sovereign equality" and nonintervention in "domestic affairs" of other nations.[71] The American actions in Latin America were contrary to these basic rules.

The War in Vietnam. The legality of the war in Vietnam has been argued ably and extensively by many experts.[72]

---

[70] International Court of Justice, Corfu Channel Case (Merits), *International Court of Justice Reports*, IV (1949) 43; *American Journal of International Law* XLIII (1949), 558, 581–82. The Court rejected the right of the British to sweep the Corfu Channel of mines. It labeled intervention as "the manipulation of a policy of force" which had previously "given rise to most serious abuses" and as such finds "no place in international law." The Court was repelled by the British minesweeping because, if admitted, that would reserve the practice of intervention "for the most powerful States, and might easily lead to perverting the administration of international justice itself." These words, it would seem, apply appropriately to the trio of Caribbean interventions which, on face value, were at least as extreme as the removal of the mines by the British.

[71] See Wright, *Proceedings*, 1961, pp. 3–4.

[72] For studies on the illegality of the Vietnamese war see the Lawyers Committee on American Policy Toward Vietnam, "Memorandum of Law: American Policy Vis-à-Vis Vietnam," *Congressional Record*, CXI (September 23, 1965), 24010–18; Lawyers Committee, Reply to the State Department (A Statement: The Military Involvement of the United States in Vietnam is Illegal Under International Law), prepared for insertion as a newspaper advertisement, 1967; Lawyers Committee, *Vietnam and International Law* (Flanders, N.J.: O'Hare Books, 1967); and Quincy Wright, "Legal Aspects of the Viet-Nam Situation," *American Journal of International Law*, LX (October, 1966), 750–69. Defense of the United States action is found in *The Legality of U.S. Participation in the De-*

It is impossible within the confines of this paper to analyze this matter in detail, and the issues do not lend themselves to cursory treatment. I thus propose to discuss what now seems to be the main United States legal argument in support of the conflict and to deal with the conduct of the war itself, a problem which has not received adequate attention.

Washington's case now seems to rest upon a claim that by waging the war in Vietnam we are fulfilling our obligation under the Southeast Asia Collective Defense Treaty of 1954. This shift to SEATO appears almost as a recent afterthought, perhaps because of the serious questions raised over previous attempts to justify the massive military undertaking under the United Nations Charter and the Geneva Accords.[73] As late as 1965, the United States had not added SEATO to its collection of Vietnam legal claims.[74]

---

fense of Viet-Nam, Department of State Publication 8062 reprinted from *Department of State Bulletin* of March 28, 1966, and American Bar Association, "The Lawfulness of United States Assistance to the Republic of Vietnam," *Congressional Record,* LXII (July 14, 1966), 14943–89.

[73] The basic arguments have centered on charges that the United States violated the United Nations Charter and the Geneva Accords. They might be summarized as follows:

(1) The unilateral military intervention of the United States in Vietnam violates the United Nations Charter.

   a. The United States has used force against the territorial integrity and political independence of another state in violation of Article 2(4).

   b. There has been no armed attack on South Vietnam within the meaning of Article 51.

   c. The United States failed to seek a peaceful settlement under Article 33(1) or under traditional international law.

   d. The conflict in Vietnam is essentially a civil war, which is a matter within the domestic jurisdiction of a state under Article 2(7).

(2) The military presence of the United States in Vietnam violates the Geneva Accords of 1954.

   a. The South Vietnamese government, with the support of the United States, refused to hold nationwide elections.

   b. The United States introduced new troops and the infiltration of political and military advisers was not an "armed attack," the reason given by the U.S. for its heavy military involvement.

[74] "The argument is a late discovery. SEATO was not mentioned in the official United States announcements in February, 1965, when the

However, when Secretary of State Rusk appeared before the Senate Foreign Relations Committee in January of 1966, he surprised many observers by shifting the primary legal grounds to the alleged SEATO obligation.[75] President Johnson picked up the SEATO theme in his 1967 State of the Union address. He declared that we are in Vietnam because "the United States and our allies are committed by the SEATO Treaty to 'act to meet the common danger' of aggression in Southeast Asia." He did not even mention the United Nations Charter or the Geneva Accords.[76]

In his statement before the Foreign Relations Committee, Secretary Rusk leaned exclusively on Article 4(1) of the Treaty which states:

> Each party recognizes that aggression by means of armed attack . . . would endanger its own peace and safety, and agrees that it will in the event act to meet the common danger in accordance with its constitutional processes.

"It is this fundamental SEATO obligation," Rusk declared, "that has from the outset guided our actions in South Vietnam."[77] Obviously, it had not guided policy "from the outset" but SEATO at this point certainly became the basic, although belated, anchor argument.

Rusk's interpretation of the Treaty is not convincing. The State Department admits the need for an "armed attack" before self-defense can take place. But in claiming that infiltra-

---

bombing of North Vietnam commenced. In March, 1965, the State Department, in a Memorandum entitled 'Legal Basis for The United States Action Against North Vietnam,' did not refer to SEATO. Neither Secretary of State Rusk, in an address on Vietnam before the American Society of International Law in April, 1965, nor President Johnson, in a statement on July 28, 1965, explaining 'Why We Are in Vietnam' made any reference to SEATO." Lawyers Committee, *Reply, op. cit.*, note 72.

[75] *The New York Times,* February 19, 1966, p. 3.

[76] *Ibid.*, January 11, 1967, p. 16. Johnson gave two other legal arguments: (1) an "international agreement" signed by the United States, North Vietnam and others in 1962 (apparently the Declaration of Neutrality of Laos), and (2) the need to guarantee the right of the South Vietnamese to remain non-Communist.

[77] *The New York Times,* February 19, 1966, p. 2.

tion into the South before our extension of the war to North Vietnam constituted armed attack, the Department is blurring "the essential distinction between the broad and vague general concept of aggression and the narrow one of armed attack."[78]

Furthermore, Article 4(2) of the Treaty (not mentioned by Rusk in his testimony) stipulated that if South Vietnam (as a treaty protocol nation) was threatened "in any way other than by armed attack," the SEATO members "shall consult immediately in order to agree on the measures which should be taken for the common defense."

Also, it has been assumed that unanimity among all SEATO powers would be required before one would be authorized to supply military support.[79] Although resolutions condemning Communist activities have been passed, there has been no joint regional action. Some SEATO members, but not all, have supplied troops on an individual, not collective, basis. Two members, France and Pakistan, not only have abstained in SEATO resolutions on Vietnam, but have denounced the war. Further, the Treaty (Article 1) recognizes the supremacy of the United Nations in these situations. As has been previously noted, Article 53 of the Charter stipulated that the Security Council must authorize regional action.

It appears as if, in grasping at the SEATO straw, the United States really is still adhering doggedly to the discredited claim of self-defense. Obviously, the United States perception of its own national interests and security needs has taken precedence over legal obligations and commitments. This is not unusual in the case of international conflicts.[80] But as in the case of Cuba, national needs are not enough to justify twisting the rules of international law or distorting the meaning of treaty obligations.

Reprisal and CB Weapons.   The legality of United States war-making in Vietnam may be a moot point for those who

---

[78] Lawyers Committee, *Reply, op. cit.*, note 72.

[79] *Ibid.*

[80] Quincy Wright, *American Journal of International Law,* LX, 769, finds a similar pattern in his study of forty-five international conflicts since World War I.

are not concerned with the rational utilization and development of international law. However, two aspects of the actual conduct of the war are more immediate causes for concern. The first is the use of so-called "horror" or CB weapons; the second is the massive reprisal raids by American forces.

The United States apparently is not formally bound by any specific treaty banning gas, chemical and bacteriological warfare.[81] However, it is perhaps universally conceded — on legal principle — that the conduct of war should be within reasonable rules of humane procedures. The United States War Department's Rules of Land Warfare of 1940 include the *"principle of humanity"* which prohibits the "employment of any such kind or degree of violence as is not actually necessary for the purpose of the war."[82] And the Hague Convention IV of 1907 on Laws and Customs of War on Land (declaratory of accepted legal principle) stipulates that it is "especially forbidden to employ poison or poisoned weapons"; "to kill or wound treacherously individuals belonging to the hostile nations or army"; and "to employ arms, projectiles, or material calculated to cause unnecessary suffering."[83] And, of course, the human rights provisions of the United Nations Charter are not restricted to peacetime.

But "horror weapons" have been used in Vietnam. The col-

---

[81] United States Law of Land Warfare, Army FM 27–10 (1956), states in Section 38: "The United States is not a party to any treaty, now in force, that prohibits or restricts the use in warfare of toxic or nontoxic gases, of smoke or incendiary materials, or of bacteriological warfare." Cited in William W. Bishop, *International Law* (2nd ed., Boston: Little, Brown, 1962), pp. 807–8.

A treaty was signed in Washington in 1922 by representatives from the United States, the British Empire, France, Italy and Japan prohibiting "the use in war of asphyxiating, poisonous or other gases, and all analogous liquids, material or devices." Malloy, *Treaties*, III, 3116. The treaty was not ratified by all parties and thus did not come into force. The Geneva Protocol of 1925 prohibits the use in war "of asphyxiating, poisonous, or other gases, and of bacteriological methods of warfare." *League of Nations Treaty Series 65*. It was signed by the United States and many other powers and ratified by a considerable number. However, the United States Senate has not given its "advice and consent."

[82] Article 4. Basic Field Manual 27–10, 1940, cited in Bishop, *op. cit.,* p. 799.

[83] Article 23. 36 *U.S. Stat. at Large* 2277.

lection apparently includes nauseating tear gas, poison crop sprays, antipersonnel bombs which spin out hundreds of razor-sharp metal splinters, napalm and phosphorus bombs, cyanide and arsenic sprays, time bombs,[84] and magnesium bombs. Add to these the torturing of prisoners by South Vietnamese (and we share a responsibility even though the Viet Cong engages in similar practices) and the fact that we have dropped more tons of bombs on this tiny, beleaguered land than we dropped on Nazi Germany in World War II. The civilian casualty list has never been estimated, but apparently it is at least four times (some say ten) as large as that of the "enemy" troops.

A storm of protests, both within the United States and in other nations, followed the revelation in March of 1965 that the United States was giving the South Vietnamese some "disabling types of tear gas" for combat use against the National Liberation Front. Secretary of State Rusk described them as "police type" riot-control gases. However, an unidentified administration spokesman noted that they were not the simple forms of tear gas, but rather tear gases mixed with nauseating agents. The State Department contended that the use of "nauseous tear gases was not contrary to international law."[85]

Senator Wayne Morse of Oregon disagreed. He said the gases were among those "justly condemned by the general opinion of the civilized world." Further, he noted "how easy it is, once we depart from the principles of international law, to violate more and more of them."[86]

Another technique has been aerial spraying of trees in defoliation raids and the chemical destruction of rice crops. The poisoning of rice crops has been called worse than the bombing of civilians in World War II, "criminal in intent and execution," and an "act of total war."[87] As of November, 1966, it was estimated that poison had been sprayed on

---

[84] Listed by Diane Leonette, "The Horror Weapons," *Fellowship,* XXXII (November, 1966), p. 7.

[85] See *The New York Times,* March 23, 1965, pp. 1–2; March 24, pp. 1, 6; March 24, pp. 1, 13.

[86] *Ibid.,* March 23, 1965, p. 2; Leonette, *op. cit.,* p. 8.

[87] The Rev. Peter J. Riga, Professor of Theology of Notre Dame University, expressed this view in a letter to *The New York Times,* Dec. 27, 1965, p. 24.

104,000 acres of food-producing land. The program now is being accelerated to three times its former size.[88]

Another questionable weapon found in the American military arsenal is napalm. These widely used bombs are said to "scatter fire which sticks to the skin over the area of two football fields. It burns everything, combatants and noncombatants alike, fields, trees, houses — everything."[89] Napalm also has an ". . . awesome effect on personnel. When hurled into buildings it not only burns them but consumes oxygen so rapidly that the people inside may be asphyxiated even when untouched by flame."[90]

More recently a new device was reported in one newspaper under the headline "Magnesium Bombs Create Flaming Hell."[91] These firebombs were used in a raid to turn eighteen square miles of Vietnamese jungle into a "flaming hell" to destroy Vietcong hiding places, and all else presumably — living and unliving — in the area. And, according to *Time* magazine, the United States "intends to spend much of 1967 scorching the enemy's earth all over Vietnam."[92]

In a comprehensive article in the *Viet-Report*, Editor Carol Brightman leveled some serious charges against the United States, stating that: the use of gases and defoliants against civilians is a deliberate strategic policy; at least one "nerve gas" has been introduced into Vietnam; and there is some evidence to indicate that the United States may be planning to induce an epidemic of tularemia, an infectious disease with a high fatality rate, in South Vietnam.[93] At best, the chemical

---

[88] Leonette, *op. cit.*, p. 8.

[89] James Colaianni quoted in "Napalm Comes to Redwood City," *War/Peace Report*, VI (August–September, 1966), p. 23.

[90] Jack Raymond, *The New York Times,* March 20, 1965, p. 3.

[91] *Tucson Daily Citizen,* January 18, 1967, p .1.

[92] *Time,* LXXXIX (January 27, 1967), p. 33.

[93] See "The 'Weed Killers,' " *Viet-Report,* II (June–July, 1966), 9–14; 33–48. The main points made by Miss Brightman were:

1. Civilian casualties *are not an accidental by-product of the tactical* employment of gases and defoliants. On the contrary these civilian casualties are a *deliberately chosen strategic means* to weaken and destroy the Vietcong military effort.

2. In addition, these chemical attacks are predictably far more harmful to civilians — the very old, the very young, pregnant and nurs-

attacks are a far greater danger to the aged, the young, the infirm than to the Vietcong soldiers.

The introduction of these terrifying weapons demands an "agonizing reappraisal" of our moral and legal values. One respected professional newsman questioned "whether the United States or any nation has the right to inflict this suffering and degradation on another people for its own ends."[94] The seriousness of the problem is underscored by the frenzied activity to produce larger quantities and "improved versions" of CB weapons.[95]

The use of these weapons places the administration closer to the old axiom that all is fair in war than to the accepted doctrine banning inhumane weapons. Technically, gases, incendiary materials and bacteriological weapons are not banned by treaty insofar as the United States is concerned. But ap-

ing women, the ill — than to Vietcong soldiers. Many agents now in use are seriously and permanently disabling.

3. Lethal gases are being used in Vietnam in ways calculated to maximize their lethal effect.

4. Though its use has not been "authorized" (i.e., acknowledged) at least one "nerve gas," BZ, has been used in Vietnam.

5. It has been acknowledged that University (of Pennsylvania) scientists are carrying out operations field research on the effectiveness of chemical warfare in Vietnam.

6. There is probative evidence that the United States Government had planned, and may still be planning, to induce an epidemic of tularemia in South Vietnam. Tularemia is an acute infectious disease with a high fatality rate.

[94] Neil Sheehan, "Not a Dove, But No Longer a Hawk," *The New York Times Magazine,* October 9, 1966, excerpted by David Schoenbrun, "Vietnam: The Case for Extrication," *Columbia University Forum,* IX (1966), p. 4.

[95] Extensive biological warfare research is under way at more than fifty American colleges and universities. The Rocky Mountain Arsenal in Denver is stockpiling nerve gas. The same product is being turned out in quantity in a plant in Newport, Indiana. An $11-million plant to produce napalm is planned for Redwood City, California. The $75 million Government Center for Biological Warfare Research at Fort Detrick, Maryland, has top facilities for research in disease-causing germs. The latest indication is that some of these scientists are trying to adapt serious insect-born diseases so that they can be transmitted from person to person through the air. See *The New York Times,* January 14, 1967, p. 10. The death potential of this scheme staggers the imagination.

parently we have been the only nation to employ these devices in recent warfare.[96] It certainly would be difficult to support a claim that such weapons as napalm and magnesium bombs do not cause "unnecessary suffering." And, if it is true, as Miss Brightman claims, that there is a calculated extermination of civilians, the violation of international law is obvious.

Serious legal questions also were raised by the reprisal raids taken as a result of the Tonkin Bay incident of August, 1964, and the Pleiku incident of February, 1965. Under traditional international law, the first requisite for a reprisal is that an injury has been caused by the illegal act of another state. But, even if this condition is met, the reprisal is lawful only if it is preceded by an unsettled demand for repatriation and unsuccessful effort to achieve a peaceful settlement. Finally, the reprisal must be in proportion to the act which motivated it.[97] The United States military establishment concedes that "reprisals are never adopted merely for revenge, but only as an unavoidable last resort."[98] One might even question the legality of all reprisals since the United Nations denounced them in principle. The Security Council in April, 1964, in deploring a British air raid on Yemen territory, condemned reprisals as "incompatible with the purposes and principles of the United Nations."[99]

It is a sad fact of international life that "reprisals are usually taken against a comparatively weak state" and that a similar act taken against a more powerful state "would in all probability be regarded as the initiation of war."[100] Despite this practice, law cannot be based entirely on the domination of the weak by the strong.

In the Pleiku incident, the reprisal was extremely severe. On February 7, 1965, the National Liberation Front (*South*

---

[96] *Ibid.*, March 24, 1965, p. 38. According to unconfirmed reports, the United Arab Republic experimented with chemical warfare in Yemen. *Ibid.*, March 23, 1965, p. 5.

[97] Naulilaa Incident, Portuguese-German Arbitration Tribunal (1925), Bishop, *op. cit.*, p. 747.

[98] United States Department of the Army, *The Law of Land Warfare,* Basic Field Manual 27–10, 1956, Bishop, *op. cit.*, p. 801.

[99] *United Nations Monthly Chronicle*, I (May, 1964), 19.

[100] Bishop, *op. cit.*, p. 746.

Vietnamese) launched a ground attack on the United States airbase at Pleiku, 240 miles northeast of Saigon. Eight Americans were killed and 120 wounded. The United States retaliated the same day. About fifty American fighter-bombers struck the Donghoi area in *North* Vietnam. This was the beginning of the air war in the North. Further, as D. F. Fleming notes elsewhere in this volume, "The assumption that the North Vietnamese were responsible was totally unproved." If this is the case, the first requisite for a reprisal, mentioned above, was not met.

In the Tonkin Gulf incident, the response was even more out of proportion to the attack. The destroyer *Maddox* was attacked on August 1 by three North Vietnamese PT boats in the Gulf of Tonkin. In the counterattack, two PT boats were damaged and one was left dead in the water. On Tuesday, August 3, in a second North Vietnamese attack on the two United States destroyers, the *Maddox* and the *C. Turner Joy,* the PT boats were driven off and two were sunk.

We responded by sending sixty-four carrier-based planes to attack four North Vietnamese bases and an oil depot. Could anyone claim that the destruction of twenty-four PT boats (a substantial part of the tiny North Vietnamese navy), as well as shore installations, was punishment to suit the crime? More importantly, Senators Fulbright, Morse and others have indicated that the North Vietnamese attack may well have been provoked and that the official Washington account of the incident was a fabrication. United States ships were nearby on July 31 when South Vietnamese vessels shelled two islands on the North Vietnamese coast. Also, United States ships had penetrated the twelve-mile limit claimed by North Vietnam as territorial waters. Further, it also has been indicated that the PT boats were in hot pursuit of the United States destroyers within and away from North Vietnamese waters, when the attack took place in the Gulf of Tonkin.[101]

Even without hot pursuit from a claimed territorial security

---

[101] I. F. Stone, "International Law and the Tonkin Bay Incidents," *I. F. Stone's Weekly,* August 24, 1964, reprinted in Marcus G. Raskin and Bernard B. Fall, *The Viet-Nam Reader* (New York: Vintage, 1965), pp. 310–12.

zone, the reprisals did not meet the minimum requirements of international law stated above, were not an "unavoidable last resort," and certainly were contrary to the United Nations resolution.

The United States and the United Nations. During the first two decades of its existence the United Nations has been the arena for intensive political conflict, most of it spilling out into other areas of diplomatic, economic, and military maneuvering. Given the nature of the international political system this is to be expected. Both the Soviet Union and the United States have attempted to use and manipulate United Nations processes to serve the ends of their conceived national interests.[102]

To students of international affairs this conclusion appears obvious. However, rationalizing a myth has influenced the thinking of many Americans to the effect that the Soviet Union is utilizing the United Nations for its own ends while the United States is concerned only with the promotion of a system of world order. In the process, the more extreme rationalizers believe our freedom and sovereignty are being eroded. Typically, a speaker on the Manion Forum was most eloquent in expressing this point of view. He charged that "devotion to the solvency and sovereignty of the United States has been made to give way to the urgent necessities of the United Nations" as part of what he viewed as an "ominous drift into world government."[103]

In the remaining part of this paper, I would like to do no more than cite a few examples of how the United States, as a superpower, utilizes or bypasses the United Nations to achieve its policy ends. Admittedly, these ends may often coincide with those of a substantial number of other governments. But the

---

[102] John Stoessinger, *The United Nations and the Superpowers* (New York: Random House, 1965), p. ix. The writer has drawn heavily from this excellent study for material used in this section.

[103] Alvin Owsley, "United Nations — A Blight on America," in Charles A. McClelland, *The United Nations: The Continuing Debate* (San Francisco: Chandler, 1960), p. 18.

cold facts of national security and other needs are never far below the surface in the decision process.

1. The "Veto" in the Security Council. The Soviet Union has often been castigated for casting most of the Security Council veto votes, 104 of 110 through 1966. Yet Professor John Stoessinger found in his recent study that 79% of these vetoes were either circumvented or rendered less effective by other means.[104] Note also that the veto is being used only at the rate of about one a year at present, that the United States has often forced the Soviet Union to use the veto (for example, seven times on the Italian membership application) and that the Soviet Union tends most often to use the veto on issues concerning its national interest.

The United States veto score is zero. It would be strange if it were anything but that, since the United States has long enjoyed an automatic majority in the Council. It easily votes down Soviet resolutions through this majority of "hidden veto."[105] For example, Soviet attempts to condemn the United States as an aggressor in the U-2 incident and in the Dominican occupation were handled in this fashion. The increase in the size of the Council to fifteen members may reduce the effectiveness of the hidden veto. The United States was able to place the Vietnam issue on the Council agenda by a bare requisite vote, and this only after its friends, the Jordanians, agonized for a day before joining in support of the United States. However, the United States position still seems secure. Look at the 1967 membership. The five new members are Brazil, Canada, Ethiopia, Denmark, and India. Two of the holdovers are Argentina and Japan. Add to these the four Western permanent members. It should not be too difficult to rally the needed nine votes.

Washington also has a financial veto. United Nations organs are not anxious to rush into programs where Washington support is not expected since it contributes better than 40% of the budget. This financial veto was used for some time, for

---

[104] Stoessinger, *op. cit.*, pp. 10–11.
[105] *Ibid.*, p. 15.

example, in preventing the formation of the proposed Special United Nations Fund for Economic Development.

2. Voting in the General Assembly. Robert E. Riggs in his 1958 study noted: "The record reveals, with few exceptions, that the General Assembly has adopted resolutions approved by the United States at least in principle whenever the United States has chosen to exert strong influence."[106] The United States still dominates the body although this may be changing with the increasing membership of the Assembly. The State Department reported that in roll-call votes between 1954 and 1961, the United States had an 87% win record[107] — and it has never lost a vote considered to be vital.

3. The Secretariat. United States concern over Communism during the McCarthy period also left its mark on the United Nations. A number of United States nationals were fired as security risks, and the United Nations was investigated by a grand jury and two Senate committees, during the tenure of Trygve Lie. As a consequence, arrangements for security clearance were agreed upon by the United States government and pertinent United Nations agencies, despite the impartial, international Charter-required composition of the Secretariat. Further, when the Soviet Union rejected Trygve Lie, Washington was able to maneuver an extension of his term, an action which at least winked at the letter of Charter law.

4. Communist China. The United States has been successful in keeping China out of the world body. Although the United States has been losing ground in the voting and was forced in 1961 to abandon the moratorium device to keep the issue off the agenda, it persuaded the Assembly to treat Chinese representation as an "important" issue requiring a two-thirds vote. Washington has maintained its record of exclusion since it still wields more influence over the uncommitted nations than does the Soviet Union.

The United States also involved the United Nations in its crusade to brand the Chinese Communists as aggressors be-

---

[106] Robert E. Riggs, *Politics in the United Nations: A Study of United States Influence in the General Assembly* (Urbana: University of Illinois Press, 1958), p. 163.

[107] United States State Department, *Report*, 1963.

cause of their response to the United States drive toward the Yalu in the Korean War. Washington's unilateral condemnation was not enough; it wanted the United Nations seal of approval. Both the House and the Senate adopted resolutions demanding this branding and early in 1951 the General Assembly yielded. As James Reston noted, the forcing of our will on friendly and reluctant governments was a bit like sending a battleship up the East River with its guns trained on the United Nations building. As a result of the high-handed United States tactics, Reston observed in 1951, some other United Nations members would have enjoyed passing a resolution that the United States had been "undiplomatic, unwise, emotional, contradictory, and slightly hypocritical in its handling of the Chinese Communists for more than a year now."[108]

5. *The International Atomic Energy Agency.* Stoessinger also observed in 1965 that the IAEA "was born in an American cradle, but the policy of bypassing it almost buried it in an American grave."[109] Simply stated, Washington has considered it to be in its interest to provide atomic power through bilateral agreements, rather than through the agency which it was so instrumental in creating.

6. *The United Nations Loan to Cuba.* The United States strongly opposed, on stated economic — but obvious political — grounds, a Special Fund loan to Cuba in 1961. The project came before the Fund just a few weeks after the Bay of Pigs invasion and opposition in the United States to the loan, especially in Congress, was intense, despite the fact that politics was not supposed to play a part in this aid program.

When faced with obvious defeat in an attempt to bar the loan, the State Department did not press for a vote. However, the precedent at least was raised for a potential Communist negative attitude toward similar projects, for example, on Taiwan, South Korea, and Vietnam.

7. *Peacekeeping.* The United States has not been faced with difficult decisions in the area of peacekeeping since all such United Nations operations have been compatible with its foreign policy. Korea was not really a United Nations under-

---

[108] *The New York Times*, January 28, 1951, Sec. 6, p. 3.
[109] Stoessinger, *op. cit.*, p. 150.

taking, but the United States-South Korean operation did benefit from the Security Council endorsement. In the Suez crisis, the United States formed a strange alliance with the Soviet Union against France and Britain because of the need to take an anticolonial stance, keep the Soviets out of the area, protect United States oil operations, and otherwise. In the Congo, the United Nations operation prevented a potential Soviet move to fill a power vacuum. It would be another matter if the United Nations were to consider a peacekeeping program which was contrary to United States policy. This, no doubt, would not be permitted.

8. **The Financial Crisis.**   In the financial crisis, the United States was almost hoist with its own petard. As the *New Republic* aptly put it early in 1965: "Ever since 1962, the State Department has been spoiling for a showdown; and now it is wildly hunting for ways to avoid one."[110] The showdown of course was on Article 19 which, if invoked, would have stripped Russia, France, and a cluster of other nations of their vote in the Nineteenth General Assembly in 1965 for failure to pay peacekeeping assessments. The State Department had formulated a persuasive legal case supporting the contention that General Assembly recommendations for the Middle East and Congo peacekeeping operations were financially binding on members. The United States raised this legal issue of collective responsibility in the General Assembly, won an endorsement by the World Court and an acceptance of the Court's advisory opinion by the Assembly. It was apparently correct on the legal interpretation. However, when the Nineteenth Assembly met, the Russians refused to yield, and the United States did not press for a showdown. As we all know, that Assembly was otherwise largely a lost page of history.

Washington reversed its position in August of 1965, basically because it recognized that most United Nations members did not want to apply Article 19 to the nations in financial arrears. Ambassador Arthur L. Goldberg outlined the reasons before the Special Committee on Peacekeeping Operations. He referred to the general opinion in the Assembly which

---

[110] "The UN Abused," *The New Republic*, CLII (February 13, 1965), 5.

opposed the invocation of Article 19 and said the United States would not frustrate that consensus. But essentially, the United States also reserved "the option" not to financially support any peacekeeping operation which it may oppose.[111] This is a logical reaction and was the basis for the Soviet attitude toward the Congo operation. Perhaps Washington had really agreed with Moscow but apparently believed that it could force Moscow's hand in the Assembly. The abortive nineteenth session was ample evidence that most of the nations in the world body did not support the United States position. Its campaign to make an issue of Article 19 when indeed it recognized the political validity of the French-Soviet stand was a disservice to the world body.

9. The U.S., the UN, and the OAS. After analyzing United States policy in a series of Latin American cases, Inis L. Claude concluded:

> The cold war has prevailed over the Charter; the latest adaptation of the Monroe Doctrine has relegated Article 53 to the ash heap of politically charred legal provisions; the fear of the Soviet veto has taken precedence over the principle that regional agencies should be subordinated to the United Nations.[112]

The first ashes were piled on in 1954, after Guatemala had charged that it was the victim of aggressive attacks launched from Nicaragua and Honduras, on the instigation of the United Fruit Company and with the support of the United States. This was the initial application of the Charter provision concerning the role of regional agencies in relation to the United Nations. The Arbenz government, which the United States considered Communist, appealed to the Security Council. The Soviet Union vetoed a United States-supported resolution to leave the matter to the OAS. The Council then

---

[111] United States Mission to the United Nations, Press Release No. 4615, August 16, 1965, pp. 3–4.

[112] Inis L. Claude, Jr., "The OAS, the UN, and the United States," *International Conciliation,* No. 547 (March, 1964), 61. This fine analysis has been used as a basic source for this section.

passed a French resolution, calling for the end of violence and for abstention of members from lending support to either side. The OAS assumed that it continued to have jurisdiction, but before any significant action could be taken, the Arbenz government had been ousted and replaced by the military under the protective cover of the conservative Armas regime.

The political considerations in this matter were obvious. The Arbenz government did not want to entrust the problem to the United States-dominated regional organization, especially since the United States was actively promoting the overthrow. Washington officially denied complicity but news commentators came to take it for granted that this country, aided by Honduras and Nicaragua, financed and provided arms and CIA talent for the elimination of an unwanted regime. In 1958, C. L. Sulzberger flatly stated in *The New York Times* that "when a regime sympathetic to our opponents was installed in Guatemala, we ousted it."[113]

Since the United States was involved, it turned toward the OAS where it could win acquiescence of its actions, if not actual support, rather than to the Security Council which it could not control because of the veto.

The United States reluctance to have regional problems brought before organs of the United Nations is also seen in the Cuban case.[114] In July of 1960, the Cuban government requested the Security Council to deal with charges of intervention and aggression by the United States. It objected to the handling of the issue by an obedient OAS since this, in the Cuban view, would be "to allow ourselves meekly to be led away, like a docile beast, to the slaughterhouse."[115]

The Council did not deny its jurisdiction, but did hand

---

[113] Fellow Timesman James Reston stated in 1960 that "every official who knows anything about the fall of the Arbenz government . . . knows that the United States Government, through the Central Intelligence Agency, worked actively with, and financed, and made available the arms, with which the anti-Arbenz forces finally 'threw him out.'" *The New York Times,* July 28, 1958, and October 24, 1960; Claude, *op. cit.,* p. 52.

[114] Claude, *op. cit.,* pp. 34–43.

[115] *Security Council Official Reports,* 15th yr., 874th Meeting, July 18, 1960, p. 24; Claude, *op. cit.,* p. 35.

the case over to the OAS. However, Cuba later came back to the United Nations, this time to the General Assembly, after the OAS, meeting in San José, condemned the Russians for intervention in the hemisphere instead of censuring the United States. The Bay of Pigs invasion also took place while the issue was before the Assembly. Ultimately the Assembly exhorted United Nations members to promote peaceful settlement but did not recognize a special role for the OAS. In any event, the vague plea had little meaning in terms of hemispheric politics.

We have already noted that in the case of the Cuban "quarantine," the United States unilaterally announced its plans for interdiction of ships bound for Cuba before the OAS acted or before the issues were placed on the UN agenda. While it is true that the Secretary General played an important role in the settlement, neither the UN nor the OAS had the opportunity to act before being presented with a fait accompli by the United States.

In the Dominican crisis, the United States government apparently consulted with its Latin neighbors before landing troops, but Security Council and effective OAS action followed this decision. A British writer noted at the time that "OAS presence will give a façade of internationalism while the United States resolves the Dominican crisis to her own satisfaction."[116]

Other matters involving United States operations in this hemisphere could be mentioned. Observe, however, the United States is more prone to take unilateral action, then turn toward the OAS, where it predominates, than to use the peacekeeping authority and machinery of the United Nations. Article 53 provides for regional action under authorization of the Security Council. One must agree with Claude that it is in the "ash heap of politically charred legal provisions." These cases support the political reality that major powers will act unilaterally when they conceive their interests or security at stake. The Soviet Union's brutal repression of the

---

[116] Gordon Connell-Smith, "The OAS and the Dominican Crisis," *World Today*, XXI (June, 1965), 235.

uprising in Hungary and the unsuccessful British-French landings in Suez are other examples.

Legal and Organizational Implications. As noted in the introduction of this paper, international law changes within the consensual framework of the international community. Some of the unilateral actions by the United States may be harbingers of future international law. But the dictates of United States policy within the world political system do not automatically reshape the rules of a world legal order. Some of the more pertinent examples might be summarized as follows:

The Cuban "quarantine" is of questionable legality. Both regional and self-defense justification impinge upon the OAS and UN charters and the traditional rules of international law. The charges of emplacement of "offensive weapons" and "deceitful" practices were spurious, in view of accepted policies and traditional practices of other states, including the United States.

Intervention into the affairs of other nations is contrary to organizational and legal rules and commitments. The United States is hard-pressed to muster valid arguments to support the legality of the war or of its reprisals in Vietnam. And if the emerging practices of CB warfare are accepted, the humane rules of warfare will be grievously weakened.

In the United Nations, the United States is the richest and most influential member. It has used its power and money to achieve its ends. If this is to be expected in the traditional semianarchic nation-state system, let us admit it. Washington has matched the Soviet veto with its hidden veto; it has dominated Assembly voting; it has pushed its own policy in the Secretariat, in relation to China and in peacekeeping operations. It has opposed United Nations programs on political grounds and has bypassed UN processes where necessary, for example, in unilateral action followed by OAS endorsement in Western Hemispheric affairs.

This mixture of politics with law and organization may be a witch's brew for those of us who desire a more orderly and peaceful world. But an understanding of the power-security-national-interest syndrome of all major powers is a requisite to the promotion of more rational foreign policies which in turn should better accommodate a more viable system of world order.

Certainly, if we are to move toward "World Community" and/or "World Order under Law" in this age of global disorder, then there must come to be national respect for the utilization of such evolving rules of world law, and such organs and processes of international organization as have already been developed.

Can *Pax Americana* Succeed?[1]

D. F. FLEMING

During the past fifty years the United States has demonstrated a very expensive inability to become a responsible member of the community of nations. Driven out of political isolationism by World War I, she overrode the efforts of Woodrow Wilson to give her leadership in a League of Nations and rushed back into isolationism. Propelled in 1941 into a still greater and more ghastly world war, she abandoned Franklin Roosevelt's leadership toward world community and assumed for herself the role of world policeman.

We were swung all the way over from isolationism to globalism — ideological, political and economic — and this extreme role threatens to degenerate into a self-destructive world imperialism. We should become sharply alert when so responsible a statesman as Senator J. W. Fulbright can say, as he did on April 28, 1966: "America is showing some signs of that fatal presumption, that overextension of power and mission, which brought ruin to ancient Athens, to Napoleonic France and to Nazi Germany."

Mid-April, 1945, was the time when the present manifestation of this "overextension of power and mission" began. Up to April 12, the day of Roosevelt's death, our government was set not only to found and lead the United Nations but to do

---

[1] This article was published in a shorter version under the same title in *The Annals of the American Academy of Political and Social Science* in July, 1965.

271

so in cooperation with the Soviet Union. This was the only basis on which a successful UN could be built. Both Roosevelt and Hull knew that and they had labored all during the war, not only to retain Russia's mighty, decisive help in winning the war but to build the new UN in cooperation with her. Then suddenly Harry S. Truman was President. On June 23, 1941, the day after Germany attacked Russia, he had seen no difference between Nazi Fascism and Soviet Communism, urging that we should help first one and then the other "and in that way let them kill as many as possible." Therefore, it was easy for him to give his famous tongue-lashing to Soviet Foreign Minister Molotov in the White House on April 23, 1945 — eleven days after Roosevelt's death — about Poland, a country from which Russia had been invaded disastrously three times since 1913.

The Truman Doctrine.   The Cold War thus inaugurated was not proclaimed to the world until Churchill's Fulton address of March 5, 1946, and the Truman Doctrine address of March 12, 1947. Truman made up his mind in September, 1945, to issue his Doctrine,[2] but was frequently dissuaded until the British were compelled early in 1947 to abandon responsibility for suppressing a deep-seated social and political revolution in Greece which was Communist-led.

By power politics standards there was justification for keeping control of Greece in the hands of her unwanted monarchy, but Truman insisted on going far beyond that to issue a globe-shaking proscription of all future revolutions. In his *Memoirs* (II, 105) Mr. Truman relates that the first draft of the Doctrine prepared by the State Department was "not at all to my liking." The second draft was still "halfhearted," so he stiffened it himself to read that "I believe it *must* be the policy of the United States to support free peoples who are resisting attempted subjugation by armed minorities or by outside pressure." He insisted on the word *must* and declared to a grim and silent Congress, except for light applause on three occasions, that "nearly every nation must choose between alterna-

---

[2] Arthur Krock, *The New York Times*, March 23, 1947.

tive ways of life"; between free institutions and "terror and oppression."

As I wrote soon afterward, for us to declare that all revolution was finished was to kill the American dream at a time when a billion and a half people, nurtured in our revolutionary tradition, were determined to move upward into a better life; and to condemn us to the sterile and hopeless task of trying to forbid all possible social change everywhere.[3]

Beyond that the Truman Doctrine had three long-range, perilous consequences. First, it automatically put us in the business of playing God to all the less fortunate peoples. We would suppress all revolutions from the left and interfere in the affairs of other peoples to prevent social revolution. This was *Pax Americana.* Second, by proscribing Communism and implicitly proclaiming the encirclement of the Soviet Union, the Doctrine launched the world into a global power-ideological struggle and a vast arms race that ate up well over a trillion dollars of wealth, while social conditions festered and worsened in the vast underdeveloped world and even in our own rural and urban slums. Third, the Doctrine relegated the United Nations to near impotence by destroying the key assumption on which it was built: that Communism had proved its validity as a social system in Russia's great victory over Germany, and that the United States and the Soviet Union could cooperate in leading the new United Nations. Instead, the Truman Doctrine decreed that Communism was synonymous with "terror and oppression" and soon we were being taught, endlessly and monotonously, that the ruined and exhausted Soviet peoples were out to conquer the world.

Capitalist Fear of Socialism.   The role of Mr. Truman in pushing the United Nations aside, beginning with Greece, and in launching *Pax Americana* was crucial, but of course there were other powerful Americans who were ready to back his program. A great many of our conservatives had not wanted to fight Fascism — which, predatory as it was, did ally itself with the capitalists — and they had been very reluctant allies of the Soviet Union. In the early months of the German war

---

[3] D. F. Fleming, *The Cold War and Its Origins, 1917–1960*, I, 447.

on Russia they had, like the appeasers in Britain and France, confidently expected that Hitler would conquer Russia and destroy Communism. Accordingly, when this did not happen and Communist Russia became the main agent in destroying Fascism the result was fundamentally unpalatable to many people. Reluctant fighters against Fascism, they would go on to fight Communism with enthusiasm. Six days before Truman declared his Doctrine, he delivered a speech at Baylor University which was a virtual declaration of irreconcilable conflict against both Communism and democratic socialism. Freedom of enterprise was limited, he said, when governments conducted foreign trade or planned the economy. It was alleged that "unless we act, and act decisively," this kind of trade would be "the pattern of the next century."

It is very unlikely that Mr. Truman actually wrote this address, which represented the views of the great American corporations that had just received $306 billion of government-planned war orders, with the government taking all the responsibility, building plants, guaranteeing unlimited markets and immense profits. This military socialism had given our sixty-two largest manufacturing corporations enough liquid capital to buy up 90% of all the others. In 1947 many of these economic giants were more powerful than the entire national economies of dozens of nations, yet in their behalf war was declared against the regimented economies of the world.

Our Outthrust in the World

In the intervening twenty years the already vast power of our corporate enterprise has increased tremendously. Powered by enormous orders for defense and space exploration purposes, the end products of which are mostly sterile economically, and stimulated by Keynesian policies applied by the government, they have expanded into all the non-Communist world.

Today the economy of Canada has been substantially taken over, many Latin American states are largely our economic fiefs, Europe is organizing against our business take-overs and we fight long and exhausting wars in Asia in no small part to keep areas of investment open to our corporate enterprises.

This is a matter of deep concern, since our corporations earn huge profits each year which must be invested somewhere, and the greatest returns can often be found abroad. Then they must be reinvested and the new profits must find employment indefinitely into the future. The dynamism of our war-directed economy is so great that it needs the whole world as its province, certainly the non-Communist part of it. The same dynamism moves also, or tries to move, against any additional country, no matter how small, going Communist.

From this standpoint a Communist Cuba or Vietnam means two calamitous things: (1) it confiscates American corporate properties and (2) it closes the door to any future American economic expansion. A new and mutually beneficial trade could grow up, but there could be no new private investment for private profits. This is the mortal sin which Communism commits and there is no forgiving it.

A Huge Counterinsurgency Apparatus. It is universally known that our Cold War with Communism generated the mightiest arms race of all time with the Soviet Union, in all the big weapons that had ever been invented or that are even theoretically possible. But it is not so well known that it also created an American machine for suppressing revolt wherever it may occur in the so-called "free world." In it other freedoms may be permitted so long as they do not interfere with freedom of investment, but they do not include the basic irreplaceable right to change any hated system of social oppression by force. Having forbidden this, we most naturally went on to build a great counterinsurgency apparatus to go out into the world and stamp out guerrilla rebels. It centers on the Army's Special Forces which is "primarily a teaching corps of about 6,000 men."[4]

In his unforgettable report in *Viet-Report*, Roger Hagan explains that this corps not only teaches our own troops all the techniques of killing social dissenters abroad but teaches these tactics to other armies on the spot, as in Bolivia and

[4] Roger Hagan, "Counterinsurgency and the 'New' Foreign Relations," *Viet-Report*, August–September, 1965, pp. 24–27.

Thailand, and to foreigners in army schools both here and abroad. Our own schools are normally training about 24,000 foreign military men, about a tenth of them exclusively in counterinsurgency, while others are trained in three army schools abroad: a jungle warfare school in Panama, a counterinsurgency school in Okinawa, and one in Germany to train both Americans and Europeans to suppress revolt in Africa.

Thus we train forces around the world to put down men who might have Communist ideas about property or, more likely, nationalists who want social reform of various kinds. In addition, other lesser programs deal with counterinsurgency. "One, called Public Safety, trains police forces in a couple of dozen countries. There are two Inter-American Police Academies, in Panama and Washington, as well as much exporting of specialists to train on locale." All this is buttressed by special training programs for counterinsurgency in our Army, Navy, Air Force and Marine Corps, each of which has a research program in the CI field, as does the Defense Department separately.

Abroad "there is the vast and least visible effort of the CIA, which conducts what is called 'black' psychological warfare, infiltrating insurgent groups which might threaten established governments and feeding in false information." Since the Bay of Pigs fiasco the actual handling of subversive *operations* appears to have been transferred to the Defense Department, which may, for example, develop "guerrilla forces within a Communist state." Even the State Department runs a course for generals and ambassadors at the Foreign Service Institute. State prefers to call its CI activities "Overseas Internal Defense," a concealing newspeak title.

This entire program of counterinsurgency activity throughout the world is directed by a general staff of civilians called the Special Group, which meets every Thursday in Washington to coordinate the various CI activities. It is chaired by an Under Secretary of State and includes half a dozen of the highest officials in Washington, or their representatives, whom Hagan names. It surveys the world and assigns CI work to military or civilian agencies, since one side of the global campaign is concerned with civic action — every kind of activity designed to separate insurgent leaders from their followers or potential followers, and to forestall insurgency.

Reformist Governments Overthrown. It is well known that this global activity, largely clandestine, has already upset leftist nationalist governments in Iran, Guatemala and the Congo — all of which threatened foreign investments — to name only some of its main successes. To these one should now add Santo Domingo, where in May, 1965, a revolt to restore a democratically elected government was crushed by a swift American occupation, in painful violation of the most explicit provisions of the OAS and UN charters and other treaties. To exclude the bare possibility that weak Communist leadership might seize control of a powerful army movement, some 30,000 United States sea and land forces were quickly dispatched to the island to take control, as President Johnson declared on May 3, 1965: "We don't intend to sit here in our rocking chair with our hands folded and let the Communists set up any government in the Western Hemisphere."

The affirmation of our right to defeat any revolution that may break out in the "free world" is therefore complete, since at least a few Communists will infallibly be involved in, or join, any revolution (or we will say there are). The Truman and Johnson Doctrines are welded together, for all the world to see, as the guiding light and purpose of our national life. Our long-term purpose for living is summed up in the great negation: *There shall be no more revolutions, lest they turn Red.*

Less than a month earlier, on April 7, Johnson had declared his immutable will to prevail in Vietnam, saying: "We will not be defeated. We will not grow tired. We will not withdraw, either openly or under the cloak of a meaningless agreement."

He insisted that "Armed hostility is futile. Our resources are equal to any challenge. . . . Our patience and determination are unending. . . . We will use our power with restraint and with all the wisdom we can command. *But we will use it.*" (Italics added.)

There was not the faintest suggestion of conceding any right of self-determination by revolution in Vietnam; or any right to conduct a war of independence against Western, white control; or any right of one-half of Vietnam to be involved in the affairs of the other half. Indeed, these issues were begged in the sweeping affirmation: "we will always oppose the effort of one *nation* to conquer another" (italics added), implying that South Vietnam was already one nation and North Vietnam another, in the plainest violation of the Geneva Conference of 1954 which temporarily divided Vietnam only for the purpose of ending the French war of reconquest.

A Hegemony Covering the Free World. For his part, Secretary of State Rusk, who has become a veritable Democratic Dulles, has kept pace with his chief in expanding our world hegemony. In a Senate Foreign Relations Committee hearing in February, 1966, he held that armed action by us in Asia did not depend on the agreement of all the members of SEATO. On the contrary he discussed the "freedom" of South Vietnam, in James Reston's words, "as a vital American interest, essential to our own security and critical to all the other countries."[5]

In other words, the whole global chain of our commitments would come apart if Washington failed to assert its authority in Vietnam, a new doctrine that was further clinched by President Johnson in a speech on July 12 in which he declared: "Asia is now the crucial arena of man's striving for independence and order — and for life itself." It will be noted that this apocalyptic announcement puts us on the side of independence instead of against it.

Ten days later Senator Fulbright challenged "the emerging Asian doctrine" under which "Without reference to the United Nations and with only perfunctory reference to the nonfunctioning SEATO treaty the United States on its own has set out to win a victory for its protégés in the Vietnamese civil war. . . ." However, in another hearing on August 25, Rusk interpreted our anti-aggression role as a global one which did not exclude the use of our armed forces even "in the absence of a defense treaty, Congressional declaration or United States military presence." Though he again denied that we operated a *Pax Americana*, his statements left no limits upon the oper-

---

[5] *Arizona Daily Star*, February 20, 1966.

ation of the American President's world power. His writ runs in any part of the world where he chooses to exercise it. He is equipped with an infinitude of global "commitments" he alone will honor and enforce, as he and his advisers see fit. Rusk warned any "would-be aggressor," that the United States might have to use its armed forces in "collective self-defense," even if no clear-cut defense treaty ties existed. Beyond treaties the United States extended its protection through joint congressional resolutions, Presidential executive agreements and Presidential statements. Could any assertion of Presidential world authority be more sweeping?

Our President now stands above all law. He has ignored and violated all of the great treaties, United Nations and Pan American, as well as the oldest canons of international law, all of which forbid his intervention in the affairs of other states, and this is asserted to be his prerogative. Internally, the President also feels freed from congressional restraint by the three blank-check resolutions covering the critical areas of the world, the two which Dulles obtained in the early months of 1955 and 1957 and the third which Johnson got in August, 1964, covering Southeast Asia. This was well before the election that he won as the man who would not get us involved in a land war in Asia — an incredible deception.

Bombing Vietnam.   On February 7, 1965, soon after his inauguration, he suddenly attacked North Vietnam as "an aggressor." The occasion was a damaging raid by the Vietcong on our unguarded barracks and planes at Pleiku. The assumption that the North Vietnamese were responsible was totally unproved. There was a full-scale rebellion in the South because our appointed tyrant, Ngo Dinh Diem, had driven the whole countryside into revolt by sending his Catholic troops into the villages to restore the land to the landlords and reverse the social, national revolution which the Vietminh had won by defeating the French in nine years of fighting, ending in 1954. This was a true war of independence if there ever was one, yet Diem sought to undo its main results by brutal efforts to herd the people out of their ancient villages into new agrovilles and strategic hamlets which they had to build at rifle point, under the tutelage of the Americans. It was this shocking campaign which created a rebellion that the North Vietnamese were loathe to aid for a long time and then aided only in small measure.

Nevertheless, our leaders constructed a myth of aggression from the North to conceal the real reasons for the rapid fall of Diem's successors and the imminent collapse of Saigon rule in early 1965. Incessant repetition has sold this myth to conformist Americans, but to virtually no one else in the world, as our leaders have waged the most unequal war in all modern history. While daily calling the North Vietnamese "the aggressors," we have almost incessantly bombed them for two years. For example, 553 of our bombers flew against them in February, 1966 and 3,621 in September, attempting to destroy all allegedly "military" targets.[6]

In South Vietnam every kind of terrible firepower has been used on our real opponents, the peasants — bombs of every size, including great quantities of the big ones from B52s; napalm by the shipload, that maims for life if it does not kill, melting the flesh on people's faces, causing it to run down on their bodies where it sits and grows again[7]; phosphorus that keeps on burning until it eats to the bone, chemicals that kill foliage and crops and also old and young people; artillery fire of all types; naval gunfire reaching many miles inland; villages shot up at night with machine guns that pour out 18,000 rounds a minute, a one-second burst laying down "enough lead to cover a football field"; everything except atomic bombs — all propelled by the mightiest engines of war, the most efficient means of communication and the most scientific means of detection, even at night. Yet much of this incessant destruction is blind, killing far more civilians than peasant fighters. More than a million people have been driven out of their homes as pitiable refugees, some think 3,000,000.

What Our Conquest Means.   All the while the vast weight of our troops on the people, especially the women and children, and of avalanches of goods and money dumped on a primitive economy, is disintegrating the whole fabric of Viet-

---

[6] *U.S. News & World Report*, December 26, 1966, p. 26.

[7] War correspondent Martha Gellhorn, "Suffer the Little Children," *Ladies Home Journal*, January, 1967, p. 108.

namese society, which has had its own internal health, beauty and viability for many centuries. French officials who know Vietnam think that we will so destroy it that in the end there will be only ruins and refugees, and that the Americans will never be able to revive or run a Vietnamese state.

The Nazis called the Slavs of Europe *Untermenschen*, sub-human, and tried to exterminate them to make way for blond German humans. We have degraded our alleged enemies in Vietnam to the status of vermin, killing them both blindly and personally, and celebrating an alleged body count each day and week. We assume that the patriots fighting for their lives and homes are only Communists, or at least led by Communists. Doesn't that justify all? And in some vague way are we not containing China by killing Vietnamese?

Standing on this queasy terrain we must press on to conquer South Vietnam, inch by inch. "The war cannot be won," wrote R. W. Apple, Jr. to *The New York Times* on December 12, 1966, "until the Vietcong guerrillas are rooted out of the 11,000 rural hamlets of South Vietnam." We propose to train the South Vietnamese army to do this while we hold the ring, but since they have little stomach for the effort it will be up to us to go out into the jungles and rice paddies and execute the main thrust.

What it will mean was explained by our Ambassador Lodge in Saigon, on December 4, 1966. Pacification, he said, will involve elaborate peace precautions, a thorough census, identity cards and systematic curfews. In other words, we must establish the sternest and most elaborate police state over the whole of South Vietnam — in the name of freedom, liberty and anti-Communism.

Then we shall proceed to construct a new society in our own image. We have poured riches into the hands of a small new class in Saigon, perhaps gaining their loyalty. By inundating the few cities with goods we have also produced a huge black market, based on thefts of at least 20% of all arriving materials, and we have corrupted Vietnamese society in every way, up to the very top. However, after pacification we will continue to pour capital into Vietnam until an economic "takeoff" has been achieved. Until this point democracy is impossible; then it will take care of itself — so the story goes. This is the theory of Walt W. Rostow, "one of the initial architects of the paramilitary program" for Vietnam, who elaborated the capitalism first and democracy last program in his book *The Stages of Economic Growth* (Cambridge University Press, 1960). Fittingly enough, Rostow is now Chairman of the Policy Planning Council in the State Department, since his marriage of "military style" and capitalist theory "has had as great an impact as any other single intellectual endeavor we might think of in shaping the direction of United States policy in the sixties."[8]

The Balance-of-Power Defense. It is difficult to imagine a more elaborate system of imperial conquest and rule for the Vietnamese, on top of what has been for us an utterly cold-blooded war. Yet our policy has been defended in great detail by Professor Robert A. Scalapino in *The New York Times Magazine*, December 11, 1966, and elsewhere, basically on the old balance-of-power argument: "We face a challenge in Asia," as in Europe twenty years ago, and we must "recognize the critical importance of building some balance of power." Asserting that our enemy is Communism "dominated by the North," he describes the gulf between the Communists and ourselves as being "fundamentally whether Vietnam shall be a unified Communist state" or not. Separating himself from the majority "doom and gloom" school, he takes an optimistic view of our future in Asia and is firmly for holding "a military umbrella" over South Vietnam until we have built a new, clean nation. To win the war and accomplish this goal "no limit should be placed on the number of troops necessary" and the bombings of the North should be tailored accordingly. Our power must prevail, because "the peace of the world depends on establishing some political equilibrium in Asia."

This is the classic balance-of-power argument. It assumes that the world's greatest ocean must be totally an American lake, with China on the far side of it ringed around completely with heavily armed bastions of American power in South Korea, Japan, the Philippines, Okinawa, Formosa, South

[8] Roger Hagan, *op. cit.*, p. 25.

Vietnam and Thailand. This is because China has shaken off centuries of Western exploitation and is standing up in the world as a unified nation, one growing in economic and military power and one in which slowly growing wealth is fairly divided.

It cannot be too clearly understood that the Johnson team has deliberately decided not only to maintain this encirclement of China but to nail it down. Richard Wilson wrote in the *Los Angeles Times* on January 20, 1966, that "all those who took part in the President's decision" understood what it meant — "many years of armed intervention and economic aid." It meant also a reversal of the position of the Democratic political leadership, which had "consistently and over many years opposed a confrontation with China." That was the Republican line.

After seeing our enormous new military bases in Vietnam, Walter Cronkite reported on his CBS program from Saigon, on July 21, 1965, that "The United States government is preparing an Asian power base on a long-term basis in South Vietnam. It is prepared to fight a Korean-type war if it must and a world war if necessary." This was before we were permitted to know about the building of equally tremendous United States bases in Thailand.

In gambling on their power to maintain the military encirclement of China indefinitely, our leaders are inviting a world conflagration, in every sense of the word, as surely as the Chinese would be if they came over here and established huge bases in Hawaii, Mexico and Vancouver Island to restrain our dangerous propensities.

War with China? The new Chinese giant in the East must be expected to develop great power, even thermonuclear, and when it does — or well before — it must be expected to do what we or any other proud people would do, smash the American encirclement and take control of its own neighborhoods, including some of its own islands and harbors. When this happens we will have to accept a limited war that we could not win or a nuclear war that would involve our own devastation.

This easily foreseeable end to our military encirclement of

China argues powerfully, of course, for escalating the Vietnam war into China now, or within a few years, before China has too many nuclear ICBMs and submarines. But if we do this we will invite our own destruction. If we cannot bring little North Vietnam into submission after two years of almost incessant bombing, surpassing the scale of World War II, what hope could we have of subduing huge China with conventional bombs? If it takes half a million United States troops, and probably many more, to dig the South Vietnamese patriots out of their little country, what would our prospects be in sending troops to fight a well-armed army of 10 million men in China, backed by scores of millions of militiamen and women and a human sea of guerrillas?

This leaves us with the last precious resource in the armory of escalation, nuclear fire. If we apply that "discriminatingly," in the doses necessary, we could devastate Japan with our fallout, which the prevailing winds would also carry across our own country. We could probably kill some 300 million Chinese people, of all ages and kinds, but if we ourselves survived we would be pariahs on the face of the earth forever. Yet the alternative is to so exhaust our human and material resources in nonnuclear struggles with China that our own political and economic systems would be fatally undermined. The Chinese will never forget, and we should not, that the first two world wars ended private capitalism and entrenched Communism from East Berlin to Shanghai. This is the most stupendous fact in the history of the twentieth century, and we should do well to ponder it in staking our future on military control of the frontiers of China.

What Is Power?   The balance-of-power argument can be used to justify the most disgraceful kind of war, one which bombs villages filled with women and children and the old, from which the able-bodied men have been drafted by the war, on suspicion that there might be a few Vietcong in them; one which bombs the north end of a small country eternally because it responds to the call of nationality and racial kinship.

But what *is* power? Surveying our interment of law and apotheosis of power over the past five years, Arthur Larson denies that it is raw physical strength. "Power is the ability to produce a desired result," by some method of influencing people. He cites the "power" of the press, of advertising, or of public opinion to get results, whereas our use of raw strength in Santo Domingo produced "a shock-wave of anti-American indignation throughout all of Latin America," and our acts in Vietnam have made us seem to all the world like "a confused and unpredictable giant."[9]

How Many Vietnams? It has been argued cogently that, in spite of its stark brutality, our imperialism is different from the traditional, exploitative kind; it is welfare imperialism, which seeks to impose Americanism, economic and otherwise, on underdeveloped peoples, ignoring the peasant majorities and supporting the social classes and values that we approve. In this drive John McDermott sees United States economic interests growing "daily more intertwined with government policy and more committed to its objectives." But he expects "to see the bureaucratic power of the United States government more and more opposed by armed resistance as native peoples seek to control their own future." And as they see our "overwhelming influence and resources" compromise their independence we must expect to find ourselves creating Vietnams everywhere.[10]

If, too, the pulverization of Vietnam, and the giant bases we have built in Vietnam and Thailand, do not lead on into a war with China, our leaders will have, after the "war" is over, a great supply of troops trained to suppress rebellion. The *New Republic* noted with well-justified foreboding on September 10, 1966, that "The Pentagon has got so guerrilla-conscious that the world's mightiest military structure spends most of its time brooding on insurgency and counterinsurgency. What will this country do with the enormous numbers of men who are being trained in guerrilla warfare tactics?" Suspecting that the brass would be almost hoping for other places to use Vietnam tactics, the editor might have added that Rome in her heyday

---

[9] Arthur Larson, "Power and Law in World Affairs," a very significant article in *The Progressive,* November, 1966.

[10] John McDermott, "Welfare Imperialism in Vietnam," *The Nation,* July 25, 1966. A very thoughtful article.

was never more imperial minded. She, too, had a mission to tame the native barbarians, even if she had to make places like Britain into deserts — until her self-imposed debilitation finally enabled the barbarians to overwhelm her.

We may well continue along the same road of arousing increasing antagonism among the lesser peoples, since the effect of our capitalist embrace is to *decapitalize* the underdeveloped countries. Our great corporations act as huge suction pumps, drawing out great quantities of raw materials at low prices and selling back processed goods at their own prices. The result is, in the words of *The New York Times* editorial on January 18, 1966, that "The developing countries are burdened with huge debts and soaring interest rate payments," to which there is added the withdrawal of the dividends of our business. Indeed our investors take out each year twice as much profits as we grant in "loans," all of which ["loans"] are in the form of credits which must be spent in the United States. Even the operation of our foreign aid in Latin America is strongly imperialistic.[11]

The traditional, agrarian and underdeveloped societies accordingly remain poor while we grow steadily richer, and they are thus driven to some kind of revolt both to protect their independence and to stave off the inroads of hunger by pushing their own development.

Our response is that if they are to develop, it must be by our method and under our control which means, essentially, they will not develop. This is why, in Barrington Moore's memorable words, the American government is "quite literally trying to burn these revolutionary movements off the face of the earth." As exploding populations compel the peoples to rise against parasitic, political landlordism, the United States has emerged as "the military bastion of counterrevolution, willing and able to rain fire on those made impatient by hunger." In the process we are destroying Western democracy's

---

[11] Sidney Lens, "Failure in Latin America," *The Progressive*, January, 1967, pp. 29–32. Some of these countries have reached the sad plight of having to float new loans to pay the interest charges on the older ones. See also, Alonso Aguilar, *Latin America and the Alliance for Progress*, as translated (New York: Monthly Review Press, 1963).

clearest claim upon humanity's allegiance, "that it was no terrorist society." Rejecting the myth that we are fighting in Vietnam (and now in Thailand) to counter a Chinese out-thrust, he observes tellingly that "the United States is desperately trying to *establish* vital interests close to China rather than to defend interests it already has." (Italics added.) [12]

This is the military-industrial complex which President Eisenhower in his farewell address feared would take us over, operating full blast with the throttle wide open. The military need wars to keep their dominance over the national budget; the corporations must have foreign expansion indefinitely to employ swollen profits.

Arms to Everyone. To serve the interests of both, our militarized industry forces arms out to all the non-Communist world, allegedly to counter Communism, but actually to maintain all the oligarchic regimes in power, to help balance our perpetual and dangerous cold war international deficits, and simply for profit. Fighting to slash $100 million from the current $917 million budget for foreign military aid, Senator Frank Church of Idaho pointed out that whereas we sent military aid to fourteen countries in 1950 the number has now mushroomed to sixty-seven! Later, Senator Eugene McCarthy wrote that the United States "has given or sold $35 billion of military assistance, including recent sales of $9 billion in weapons at a profit to the munitions makers of nearly $1 billion." The Pentagon itself has become the nation's top arms peddler. [13]

An American Corporate State? This double-barreled out-thrust of American government and business has been accompanied by the collectivization of so much of our economy as to point toward the creation here of a corporate state on the Italian Fascist model. On December 22, 1966, the redoubtable Ralph Nader, of auto safety crusade fame, proposed the creation of a national commission to study the trend. By 1970, he estimated that 200 of our corporations will hold 75% of all manufacturing assets, with the bigger ones constantly ab-

---

[12] Barrington Moore, Jr., "Why We Fear Peasants in Revolt," *The Nation,* September 26, 1966, pp. 271–74.

[13] *The Progressive,* October, 1966, p. 5.

sorbing the lesser, misallocating our resources and polluting our air, water and soil. He urged action to counter "the deadening conformity of monopolistic power centers — be they private or governmental." (The *San Francisco Chronicle*.)

Indirectly, the onrush of a corporate state powered by the military-industrial complex was described by John K. Galbraith, in a December 18, 1966, Reith lecture in Great Britain. He warned that many big corporations are becoming so dependent on government orders and planning that they "will eventually become a part of the larger administrative complex with the state. In time the line between the two will disappear," he predicted, and he foresaw complete governmental domination of our intellectuals. Nor did he find any comfort in the early retirement of legions of military officers of all types into our big corporations.

Global Corporations. It will take the aroused labor of a great many Americans and the ending of *Pax Americana* wars to preserve here something like a free democratic society. It will be difficult enough to reduce the decisive role of the Pentagon in our national life, and we shall discover that it is already too late to control more than partially many of our corporate behemoths, since they have gone global. In a startling article in the *New Republic*, Richard J. Barber names six of them which already derive half or more of their income or earnings from foreign sales and six others that make from 30 to 50% of their sales abroad. One has research and manufacturing centers in twenty-three countries and does business in 150! Describing "an unprecedented outrush of U.S. firms" in the past two decades he finds that our direct investment abroad "has skyrocketed from $25 billion to nearly $50 billion," without allowing for another $20 billion in noncontrolling holdings, the kind of investments which foreigners make here. Our companies build plants overseas, sell from them — thus reducing our net trade surplus — and escape American regulation. Long in firm control of our domestic market — a fact which enabled our Big Three auto companies to earn "a nearly unbelievable 27% after-tax return on their net investment in 1965" — they are now moving abroad in a big way, creating consternation in Europe, where by comparison "even the biggest European companies generally look like midgets."[14]

The peril of American engulfment in which the rest of the non-Communist world lives may be measured by the statement of McGeorge Bundy in the January, 1967, *Foreign Affairs* that "more than four-fifths of all the foreign investing in the world is now done by Americans."

Barber finds that the big supranational companies have already gained control of world markets in the non-Communist world and that by 1975 "they will have eliminated such price competition as remains in the sale of manufactured goods." He sees no hope of controlling them except by "mutual action of the industrialized countries," action through a world organization such as the Organization for Economic Cooperation and Development.

Toward Fortress America

The European Wall.   The threatened European corporations are responding to the American invasion by trying to merge into lesser goliaths of their own, as our outlays for manufacturing plants in Europe were expected to rise in 1966 by a "striking 40%." Though the aggregate of our European investment is not overwhelming, it threatens European control of big industries, creates alarm and promotes the union of Europe against us. While different from Communist take-overs, our method is just as permanent. It has alarmed the West Germans, already resentful at our pressure on them to buy unwanted arms to offset our army costs in Germany. The Europeans know that our invasion does bring technological advantages, but Joseph C. Harsch came to the jarring conclusion, in *The Christian Science Monitor* on December 9, 1966, "That Western Europe is today more disturbed about American economic power than about Russian military power."

---

[14] Richard J. Barber, "Big, Bigger, Biggest, American Business Goes Global," *New Republic*, April 30, 1966, pp. 14–16. Barber is counsel for a Senate anti-trust and monopoly sub-committee.

There is shock for us in Prime Minister Wilson's renewed effort to take Britain into the Common Market, to build Europe into a "pillar of equal strength" with the United States and prevent American economic domination. Though he welcomed some United States investment, he declared that "there is no one on either side of the Channel who wants to see capital investment in Europe involve domination or, in the last resort, subjugation."[15]

The economic side of our outthrust into the world was bound to bring about a defensive consolidation of Europe against us. After two extensive tours of Europe, Arnaud de Borchgrave reported in *Newsweek*, on March 8 and May 3, 1965, that resentment against our many business take-overs in West Europe combines with other forces to turn Europe toward the East. The debate about Atlantic union with the United States, he said, was over. The real issue was on stretching the new European order to include the Soviet Union.

The impact of the Johnsonian *Pax Americana* greatly hastened the turning of Europe inward and Eastward. Walter Lippmann reported it in three mid-June articles in 1965, after many discussions with highly placed Europeans. He found "a swelling tide of dissent and doubt and anxiety about the wisdom and competence with which U.S. foreign policy is being conducted." Almost everywhere he heard that there had been "a radical change in the spirit of the U.S. government" since President Kennedy's death. Europeans had been "stupefied" to see President Johnson "doing in Vietnam what Goldwater recommended, and Mr. Johnson denounced, during the campaign." They were "shocked by the unlimited globalism and the rough unilateralism" to which the President had resorted, and alarmed by the messianic illusion that he can rough-handedly impose "our kind of peace on the rest of the world."

This is the natural and inevitable recoil from the double blow of Washington interventions on two continents in a short space of time.

In July, 1966, an American in Europe found that "our gov-

---

[15] *The New York Times*, December 1, 1966.

ernment is resented and hated." A few days later Richard M. Nixon, a redoubtable hawk, reported after meeting old friends in London and Paris that the United States was in a lonely position. Our aims in Vietnam were neither appreciated nor understood.

On August 10, anti-Americanism was increasing rapidly in Paris. The tone of the press, radio and television was angry. On September 1, a Gallup poll showed that even in Britain a small majority felt the United States should withdraw from Vietnam. On October 31, a poll in Britain and West Europe found 74% feeling that United States prestige was higher under President Kennedy, and on November 5, defense of our conduct in Vietnam lost in a debate at Oxford University by a vote of 642 to 161, though there were fewer "U.S. Equals Fascism" signs in Britain than across the Channel. Earlier, on August 7, two energetic protests by university students in West Berlin against our conduct in Vietnam were reported, and there were others in Munich and other German cities. On July 21 a group of American churchmen in Geneva found themselves "more keenly aware than ever before of church and world criticism and anguish over United States involvement and escalation of the conflict in Vietnam."[16]

In other words, the United States was isolating itself in Fortress America. The foundations for its Atlantic wall were already laid by the end of 1966. The turning away from us of Europe was in full swing. Our oldest friends and kinsmen, including the British, were drawing together — France and Russia, France and Germany, West Europe and East Europe, Europe and USSR, all weaving new ties to become independent of Washington and its hegemony, its economic encroachments and its brutally operated *Pax Americana.* Even West Germany had a new coalition government of its two huge parties to emancipate itself from United States protection and pressures. Europe was breaking out of the cold war straitjacket in which our leaders had locked her — politically, militarily and diplomatically. The huge NATO military machine lay in ruins and when Mr. Rusk went to a NATO meeting to beg a little

---

[16] *The New York Times*, July 17, August 1, 3, 7, and 10; *The Oregonian*, July 24, 30, and September 1, 1966.

help in Vietnam his briefing conference was half empty, but
the West German one was crowded. Our allies seemed intent
on using NATO to bring the Soviet Union into Europe, instead of to isolate and confine her. This was the fruit of
twenty years of obsessive anti-Communism on the part of our
leaders, and of the *Pax Americana* which Truman proclaimed
and Johnson made a flaming reality in the minds of people
everywhere.

Constructing the Asian Wall of the Fortress. Even in
Turkey some of our Peace Corps workers encountered hostility to our policies and resentment in the middle class against
our military presence. In Iran the war in Vietnam brought
press charges of aggression and brutality. Editorials deplored
United States interventionism, "citing examples from all over
the globe except, of course, Iran" and an anti-American book,
Inheritor of Colonialism, ran through several printings. President Nasser of Egypt called our raids on North Vietnam
"aggression which arouses the indignation of world opinion,"
and on December 20, 1966, some 10,000 people in Zagreb,
Yugoslavia, attacked the United States Consulate and broke
the windows while demonstrating against the war in Vietnam.
Even in famine-stricken India, dependent on our wheat, a
country which had lately been attacked by China, anger about
the bombing was so strong that Prime Minister Indira Gandhi
ran "a real risk of being drummed out of office" if she did not
take a stand against it. In Japan the war popularized anti-
Americanism. The press saw it as a war against indigenous internal revolution, not external aggression, intellectuals protested
our use of "nonlethal poisonous gases," ninety-three leaders demanded a stoppage of the air war, 60,000 people demonstrated
against it and former Premier Yoshida said openly that the
Americans considered themselves a superior race and acted
accordingly in Vietnam.[17]

Discussing the racial resentment the war has stirred, Royce
Brier said in the *San Francisco Chronicle* on July 6, 1966:

[17] *The New York Times*, August 17, 1966; Majid Tehranian, "Politics
of Anti-Americanism," *The Nation*, October 24, 1966; Drew Pearson,
San Francisco Chronicle, December 12, 1966; Yoshikazu Sakamoto,
"The Japanese and Vietnam," *New Republic*, September 4, 1965.

"There is nothing trifling about the pattern, or about many manifestations of it. We drop bombs on some yellow people in Indochina, and half the white peoples, including our own, dishonor our mumbling defense of it. Our Secretary of State is spirited out a back road from Osaka Airport. Throughout black Africa, across all Asia, the Americans have become a symbol of failing white dominion. We say we are trying to help the colored peoples, but no matter, animosity — when it isn't hatred — burns around the world."

President Johnson's Asian tour in October, 1966, had its triumphal aspects, especially in Australia, but everywhere he went there were hostile demonstrations, save only in South Korea, where hundreds of guards armed with machine guns insured a "peaceful" crowd. The expressions of support from his small peripheral allies did not obviate the harsh reality that in the minds of a billion and a half Asians another great invisible wall of Fortress America was rising. Prince Sihanouk of Cambodia, hard by the Vietnamese tragedy, welcomed President de Gaulle on August 31 as a fighter "trying to aid the unfortunate Vietnamese people stricken by the cruel, unequal and unjust war which is imposed upon it." In South Vietnam itself an American student delegation found "a high degree of animosity among the students" against us, and Neil Sheehan, after three years in Vietnam for *The New York Times*, wrote on April 24, 1966, about growing anti-Americanism in South Vietnam. He described widespread resentment against the "profound economic and cultural shockwave" of our impact on the little country. Students and intellectuals feared the destruction of their society and saw "the United States as a neo-imperialist power that is gradually eroding South Vietnam's independence with its military might."

One of the ablest of American commentators, Emmet John Hughes, visited Vietnam and wrote afterward that during all his travel around the world he never left Vietnam; "in the political sense, for the conflict in Southeast Asia excites the concern of all capitals and foreign offices, from Manila and Singapore to Paris and London. And with absolute unanimity, all ministers and diplomats — Asian or European, leftist or rightist — privately voiced a few unvarying sentiments. All

regretted the extent of U.S. involvement in Vietnam. . . . All
yearned for diplomatic negotiations and U.S. withdrawal, on
politically decent terms. All insisted that such terms would
have to accept a major Communist role in South Vietnam's
politics." Throughout Southeast Asia he found a refusal to
equate the military interventions of Hanoi and Washington.[18]
Only Americans can be deceived about that.

The Latin American Wall.   In Latin America, too, the
returns from *Pax Americana* are hardly more reassuring. On
May 3, 1965, a survey by the *Los Angeles Times* from Buenos
Aires found an angry anti-U.S. wave sweeping all of Latin
America. All types of political groups, from one end of the
continent to the other, joined in the cry of intervention, which
was a "violently emotional issue." Everywhere people were
saying: "This could happen to us." Nineteenth-century fears
of "The Colossus of the North" were back again in full force.

Commenting on the flood of critical comment in Latin
America after the Santo Domingo intervention, Herbert L.
Matthews wrote that a chasm had opened between us. "The
dominant political emotion in Latin America is nationalism,"
he said, and expressed his belief that a new relationship "can
never again be based on a United States hegemony."[19]

It seems probable that the armies, police forces and spies
we have trained may enable rightist governments in Argentina, Bolivia, Guatemala, Brazil and elsewhere to hold the lids
on the cauldrons of social discontent in Latin America, for a
time. Armies partly trained by us now control the bulk of
Latin America, mostly through recent coups. But in every
country there are strong political forces working to shake off
our domination and to stop the process of Americanization.
The left-wing Social Christian parties in ten countries, the
Christian Unions, the lower reaches of the Catholic clergy and
many other groups are merging into nationalist movements
aiming for real independence and control of their own national lives and social systems. Nationalism, continues Sidney
Lens, "is churning in Latin America and reaching the boiling

---

[18] *ADA World Magazine,* July, 1966, p. 2M.
[19] *The New York Times,* July 26, 1966.

point precisely because the 'American way' has not worked there."

When in the Santo Domingo case President Johnson violated all the treaties carefully constructed over decades to limit our interventions in Latin America, he began to construct a Latin American wall for Fortress America. Justice William O. Douglas, who has seen with his own eyes so much of the misery of the earth, has warned us that "we can be twice as strong as all the Great Powers combined and still witness Asia, Africa, and South America in the throes of revolutions that our armaments cannot stop."

For years one of the deep students and thinkers of our time, Professor Neal Houghton of the University of Arizona, has been telling us that we are living in a *great convulsive transition period*, which is powered by several kinds of interrelated revolutions — "demographic, appetitive, racial, ideological, nationalistic and scientific," and that this unprecedented world-wide convulsion is "unique in having as a major impelling force lower-class mass-humanity determination to better its lot."

As the ranks of the hungry ones swell, almost geometrically, what is foreseeable about peace-enforcing operations? Perhaps we can suppress genuine, popular uprisings against the immensely wealthy oligarchies in some small countries around the Caribbean, but what do we do if revolution erupts in the big ones? Can there be any real doubt that neither our will-power nor our military power can prevent social revolutions where conditions urgently demand them?

Instead of trying to repress all social revolution would it not be wiser to recognize that as the interrelated world revolutions advance, we will need the aid of all evolving social systems everywhere, in Houghton's terms, "to feed, service and even proximately to satisfy the prospective 6–12–24 billions of dominantly distressed human beings" whom the demographers project?

The Illusions of Military "Power."   Our current leaders are the victims of the new school of military and civilian militarists who convinced themselves that we can choose scientifically from an infinite wealth of weapon systems to enforce our will on lesser peoples, without sending the giant nuclear mushrooms into the sky.

This theory has been tried out now for two years in Vietnam. Daily doses of almost every kind of destructive fire have been applied on both the North Vietnamese and the South Vietnamese. Yet the application of our destructive "power" has turned out to be illusory.

Nevertheless, it may be that leaders who are dedicated to enforcing *Pax Americana* will stay in power in Washington. The fears and cupidities of powerful interests among us may carry us down the imperial way to our national destruction. For the first time in our national history this is a prospect that must be faced.

In the middle of World War I an Englishman named G. Lowes Dickinson published a great book, *The European Anarchy,*[20] in which he demonstrated — with the greatest detachment, fairness and wisdom — that the war grew out of "the pursuit of power and wealth" by all of the leading European States. Then he warned that other catastrophes would come unless the nations submitted to law, reserved force for the coercion of the lawbreaker and constructed "some kind of machinery for settling their disputes and organizing their common purposes."

The machinery was constructed in the League of Nations, but it was palsied from its birth by the abstention of the United States and by the refusal or inability of the remaining powers to coerce the important lawbreakers. The deluge did come again and the United States, still more the world giant than before, quickly asserted its own world sovereignty.

The moral is manifest. The history of this power-devastated century tells us that the leaders of the complex will pursue both power and wealth into the final world war. Senator Fulbright, Chairman of the Committee on Foreign Relations, was not a moment too soon when on April 28, 1966, he warned that a nation that is very powerful but lacking in self-confidence "begins to confuse great power with unlimited power and great responsibility with total responsibility: it can

---

[20] New York: Macmillan, 1916.

admit of no error; it must win every argument, no matter how trivial." Gradually, but unmistakably, he continued, "America is succumbing to that arrogance of power which has afflicted, weakened and in some cases destroyed great nations in the past."[21]

It was illusory to think after 1945 that we could deny Russia the political and military security in Eastern Europe which she had so tragically won, or that we could contain her influence in the world with vast rings of pacts and fortresses. The example of her internal success was bound to leap over all barriers that we could construct. It is a great illusion to think that we can do the same thing all over again to China. If she continues to build a society which distributes the necessities of life fairly and without corruption, all the world will know about it, especially if we support corrupt regimes, as in Saigon and elsewhere, interminably. Above all, it is a delusion to think that we can move into the shoes of all the defunct empires, from the Congo to Southeast Asia, restore the *Pax Britannica* and repress the social upheavals through which many of the world's peoples are fated to pass.[22] In the words of Arnold Toynbee, the leading historian of the rise and fall of empires, it is futile for the United States to challenge "a force stronger than either Communism or capitalism. She is challenging the Asian, African, and Latin American determination — the majority of mankind's determination — to recover equality with the Western minority."

On three occasions in 1965 Walter Lippmann warned that "Mr. Rusk does not know how to stop the revolution permanently and he never will know"; that "the conception of ourselves as the solitary policeman of mankind is a dangerous

---

[21] In the Mansfield Report, January 7, 1966, following the study tour of a Senate Committee to Vietnam, Mansfield, the Senate Majority Leader and certainly no "dove," cautioned that "The United States must guard with great care the basis for the war, that this is primarily a Vietnamese and not an American struggle. Any change in this concept would raise the danger of draining the war of purpose and meaning for the Vietnamese population." As this happened with increasing rapidity through the year, Mansfield steadily increased his opposition to the adventure.

[22] See David Horowitz, *Free World Colossus* (New York: Hill & Wang, 1965).

form of self-delusion"; and that a great accommodation between Asia and the West "is the only alternative to global
disaster." Then, after the anger of the world had steadily risen
against us for two years, Lippmann wrote this pregnant prophecy, on January 3, 1967: "The self-righteous use of military
power will be just as dangerous as it has proved to be before
in the history of nations." Referring to the "tough" ones "who
cannot find words scornful enough to express their contempt
for those who ask for a decent respect for the opinions of
mankind," he predicted that "If they have their way we too,
like the militarists of the past, shall find that fear of our power
and distrust of our purposes will bring about an alignment of
the nations against us."[23]

This is simple common sense, but our national future hinges
on enough of us comprehending the danger, and working to
avert it. Our place in the world will not be determined by our
ability to rule it, but by what we do here at home. If we can
master the menacing problems of air, water and soil pollution;
if we can regenerate our decaying, crime ridden, rebellious
cities; if we can really banish the scandal of permanent poverty for the bottom 25% of our society and fabulous riches
above; if we can deal with our own population problem — if
we can do these things and establish here a viable, long-term
society, all the peoples will believe again in the American way
and honor it. Success here in the United States would give us
a far greater place in the world than we can get by trying to
control it.

There are too many dynamic forces loose in the world, and
there is too much countervailing power already in it to permit
Pax Americana to succeed. In his *Russia and the West Under
Lenin and Stalin*, George F. Kennan says:

> There is no magic by which great nations are brought to
> obey for any length of time the will of a people very far
> away, who understand their problems poorly and with
> whom they feel no intimacy or understanding. . . . Uni-
> versal world dominion is a technological impossibility,

---

[23] *The Oregonian*, July 29, 1966; *Newsweek*, September 13 and 27, 1966;
San Francisco Chronicle, January 3, 1967.

and the effectiveness of the power radiated from one national center decreases in proportion to the distance involved — and to the degree of cultural disparity.

Since the attempt to enforce *Pax Americana* can only end, at best, in national exhaustion and the closing in of Fortress America, we must have a national decision to turn away from our present course, while there is still time.

Our Imperative Need to Return to World Organization

We are well into the second half of the twentieth century and our living in it has been largely in vain if we have not learned that the great issues and problems of the world can be coped with only by international means. In this century we have had two great leaders who have fully comprehended this major and obvious lesson of our time. Wilson and Roosevelt gave the last full measure of devotion to creating a world organization to deal with global problems, including the greatest problem of all — keeping the peace.

Rejecting the true vision and practical common sense of those great leaders, we have tried both isolationism and globalism, with calamitous results in both cases. Now it is time to return to the middle way of relying on international organization for the solution of world problems. This means: (1) that we accept the United Nations, at last, as our best hope of living in a tolerable world; (2) that we stop trying to use the Organization of American States as a cover for our efforts to protect our properties in this hemisphere and return peacekeeping operations in it to the United Nations; (3) that we cease our efforts to impose our will on Asia, begin relaxing our stranglehold on China and help to bring her fully into the international community; (4) that we return to widening the *détente* with the Soviet Union, which meant so much to so many people; and (5) that we work to make the United Nations a center for distributing and supervising aid to the underdeveloped South.

This course will bind all the peoples together in functional and fruitful labor to solve the many world problems that are otherwise due to become rapidly insoluble. Once more, too, there is a precious gain involved; we could have funds for the Great Society, which will otherwise soon be smothered by escalating military expenditures and by the economically stultifying effects of using so much of our resources for unproductive purposes.

There is nothing in these proposals to return to the mainstream of our century which is not genuinely conservative, but the return will not be made unless the true and powerful conservatives of our country assert themselves in favor of working with all peoples to build a viable world in which we can all live and grow, instead of drifting fitfully toward increasing and perhaps final chaos.

Pax Americana was foreordained to fail, after nationalism had become universal and colonialism almost swept from the earth. Fortress America would be an intolerable, suffocating end to the American dream. Only a world united to deal with its common problems can offer us a role of leadership that its peoples will accept and honor.

Coming to Terms with a Revolutionary World

MICHAEL EDWARDES

No one would deny the need to come to terms with the great fundamental problems — political, social and economic — of our times. Few would deny that how the United States comes to them is a matter of overriding importance for us all. This, at least, is the achievement of Vietnam. It has spotlighted America's leading role in the drama of human affairs. It has also exposed the helplessness of practically every other country. And this is one of the causes of that unease and apprehension among non-Americans which so frequently receive an outlet in criticism of United States action. But there is more to it than that. There is a feeling of hopelessness as well as helplessness. Not only can we not influence United States policy — we are also apprehensive that the policy will not change fundamentally, that its ineffectiveness (which is frighteningly obvious) will continue to endanger us in the future, whatever solution is achieved in Vietnam. This, of course, is not to say that the nature of the solution will not affect future American responses. It undoubtedly will. But the essential problems of the post-Vietnam era — and you will allow me, I hope, the belief that there *will* be an end to the war — the essential problems, I repeat, will be the same. I am convinced that there are many more potential Vietnams in Asia, in Africa, and in Latin America, because (and I shall discuss this later) the challenge which has been so perversely interpreted in Vietnam is organic to that process of economic and social change which we call development.

I need hardly labor the terrible irrelevance of America's interpretation of the challenge in Vietnam, but I must, at the risk of supererogation, restate it once more. The American interpretation is theological, I might say almost Miltonic. Good and Evil — those death-dealing theological absolutes — are enmeshed in it. Anti-Christ, in the guise of Mao Tse-tung, constantly threatens the world of light. This has, oddly enough, not only the tone of the medieval world, the world of the Crusades, but also of more recent times. In fact, the Crusades themselves hold a lesson or two. They were, in spite of (or perhaps because of) their ideological — I should say, theological — overtones, the first wars of colonial oppression, of that mutual and beneficial partnership between God and Mammon which played such a significant part in the expansion of the West.

But a more pertinent example is that of the British, for it is their apparent role which the United States has chosen to inherit. In the early nineteenth century, on the threshold of empire in Asia, Britain too saw herself faced by a demonstrable evil. She recognized it in the ideology of Hinduism. For William Wilberforce, the abolitionist, the Hindu gods were:

> . . . absolute masters of lust, injustice, wickedness and cruelty. In short, [he said] their religious system is one grand abomination.[1]

These words have a remarkably contemporary sound, even in the pomposity of the language. They formed one of the first statements of Britain's messianism. The British, too, had been given the tablets of the law on Mount Sinai. They knew that they were fighting Evil with Good, and they were supported in their belief by a sense of destiny, by a consciousness of possessing illimitable power. Their belief was entirely empirical. The Industrial Revolution in Britain produced, in those who were making it and profiting by it, a sort of constructive aggressiveness. They saw in the products of their looms and

---

[1] Speech of William Wilberforce in the House of Commons, London. June 22, 1813. *Hansard,* 1st Series, XXVI, 164.

ironworks the materials of a new Jerusalem. The new world
that emerged before them seemed a dispensation of Providence. They believed themselves to be the missionaries of a
better world and, not unnaturally, saw their own institutions
— and the civilization from which they had emerged — as
superior to all others. The British at first set out deliberately
to change their Indian subjects into good simulacra of liberal
Englishmen, convincing themselves, in the words of Thomas
Babington Macaulay, that Indians:

having been instructed in European knowledge . . . may
in a future age demand European institutions.[2]

When the Indians did choose English institutions in 1947, they
added another delusive element to the West's interpretation
of Asia.

The Indian Mutiny of 1857, which was an atavistic, traditionalist reaction to the Westernizing policies of the British,
convinced the British that ideological aggression was fundamentally unprofitable. They did not change their standards of
value, but they covered them with sugar and fed them only to
those who asked for them. Indeed, they even came to the conclusion that some of their institutions were not suitable for
Indians — that a strong central authority combined with modern administration was infinitely superior. The British never
abandoned the belief that they were right, that their civilization
was superior to everyone else's, but they reserved the right to
change their minds about the relevance of their institutions in
developing Asian societies. They responded to the demand of
an Indian minority for English institutions by resisting it, primarily for reasons of self-interest, but also because they were
convinced — and from experience — that they were unsuit-
able. (The British failed to see that the modernizing process
itself was revolutionary, that the operation of modes of administration, of law and of economics, had itself torn the web
of traditional social relationships. They were not prepared to

[2] Macaulay, speech in the East India Company Charter debate, House
of Commons, July 10, 1833. From Macaulay, *Complete Works*, London,
1898, XI, 585.

apply the lessons of their own history because they did not consider that there was any similarity between Britain and India.) In any case, by the second half of the nineteenth century, the British, though still convinced that they were right, no longer saw themselves *in practice* as paladins of absolute good.

Nevertheless, they were involved in controlling an empire, a British-Indian empire which stretched effectively from Aden to the treaty ports of China. The other European powers were expanding in Asia: the Dutch who, though they had been there before the British, did not begin their forward movement until after 1850 and the French, who existed only in the shadow of the British. They expanded because the British did not choose to stop them. The *Pax Britannica* was a conditional peace, a peace with flexible rules. It may seem, from a superficial reading of Asian history in the late nineteenth and early twentieth centuries, that the expansion of the West in Asia — the French, the Germans, the Russians *and* the Americans — provided a continuous challenge to Britain. In one sense it did, but Britain did not lose by it. On the contrary, her empire increased in area by one-third between 1885 and 1900.

Now, I have gone into Britain's position in Asia in some little detail, because it is her history which supplies analogues for today. The British undoubtedly believed that the maintenance of what Rudyard Kipling called the "Queen's Peace" was a duty that Providence had imposed upon them. One Englishman, Fitzjames Stephen, went so far as to compare the *Pax Britannica* with the universal peace announced at Christ's nativity, when, as Milton put it:

> Kings sate still with awful eye
> As if they surely knew their sovran Lord was by.

But it was not so in fact. The *Pax Britannica* did not bring peace to Asia — merely a prohibition on internecine conflicts between the Western powers and a limitation to aggression, not only by the West but also by Japan. The *Pax Britannica* can be seen functioning, not in the Royal Navy sweeping pirates from the Eastern seas or maintaining lonely lighthouses, but in the unstated contract between the Western powers to share the profits of the exploitation of China.

And what was the foundation of this British "peace"? Not the strength of the British army but the ubiquity of the British navy, the possession of territories strategically placed around the world from which it could operate, and the possession of the great land-mass of British India which cast an impressive shadow over all the marginal lands of Asia. The Western powers never seriously challenged Britain because *their* possessions were supplied by sea — and the seas were dominated by the British navy. The first breach in the *Pax Britannica* came not in 1947 when the British political presence in Asia declined with the transfer of power in India, nor in 1937 with the outbreak of the Sino-Japanese War. The breach came in 1891, with the beginning of work on the Trans-Siberian Railway. Its construction meant that, for the first time, Britain in Asia was faced by a land-based military power against which her naval supremacy could not be utilized. Britain therefore turned more and more toward Japan, which could supply an army to fight on the Asian mainland — and did so, though not in support of British interests or for the maintenance of the British peace.

Is it possible to draw a purposeful parallel between the position before 1914 and today? The answer, surely, is "no." Superficially, there may appear similarities between the United States presence in Asia, directed as it is against a land-based military power with alleged aggressive intentions, and that of Britain and Russia at the turn of the century. But the basic components of that situation do not exist. The *Pax Britannica*, such as it was, was a *colonial* peace, its purpose to control overt colonial expansion, and to protect the territorial integrity of the British Empire not against Asians but against Europeans. In the final analysis, the problems of Asia in the colonial period were settled, not in Asia, but in Europe.

It should be obvious to everyone that structurally there are no similarities between Asia today and the Asia of 1900. But is it? Apparently not, and we should not be surprised at this. Historical parallels — those illusions created by historians either purposely or by default — are fed upon and extended by politicians. History is abundant with excuses and justifications. It was, I think, Immanuel Kant who said that a nation without knowledge of its past does not exist. I would not go all the way with that, but it is difficult to envisage a nation's political life shorn of its wealth of historical metaphor and allusion. But when in our times such metaphors and allusions leave the rhetoric of electioneering and enter the structure of decision-making, it becomes a matter of international consequence.

There is little doubt that those who make the policy of the United States have accepted the modern validity of long-dead historical situations. The messianism of the British reformers of the early nineteenth century leaks out in the statements of those who seek to justify United States presence in Asia. That artificial — and, in its time, entirely purposeful — creation, the *Pax Britannica*, seems to have been considered a hereditable commodity. But the operative phrase is "in its time." As an historian, I would not willingly deny that the study of history is a valuable exercise. Experience, both real and vicarious, is an indispensable component of decision-making. But if there is one thing that history teaches us, it is that we cannot construct the future out of the *whole* cloth of the past, that we cannot rely on old, ready-made responses to new challenges, however much those new challenges may look like the old ones. A superficial study of history is likely to give us the response before the challenge, and it is often the desire — and the achievement — of governments to make the challenge fit their response. There is in fact no other way of simply defining the increasing United States involvement in Asia and the escalation of the American presence in Vietnam. The response was ready-made, culled from the history of postwar U.S.–Soviet relations, and based on the preconceived notion that Communism in itself is an absolute evil, and that those who believe in it are out to spread it by force.

The use of history — of the analogues of history — is a highly selective process. The problem, of course, is to select the right (or perhaps I should say, the most relevant) analogues, because they are there to be found. They do not, of course, supply a model for short-term problems, but they do, I think, offer a basis for attitudinal readjustments which in turn would encourage — or at least not inhibit — a more empirical approach to individual issues. The first area for relevant study is that of European society — and particularly Britain's — in the nineteenth century. I have already mentioned the avid acceptance by the new British industrial middle class in the first part of the century of a *mission civilisatrice*. For this, they had every excuse. The British were the first to experience the excitement of great technological power. Not unnaturally, in a society dominated by a Christian view of history, they accepted that they were a chosen people — and went off to convert the heathen with Lancashire cottons in one hand, and the Bible (in English, of course) in the other. But there was another side to the revolution. The traditional preindustrial society, rural-based, engaged in husbandry and handcrafts, was slowly atomized. Urban concentrations appeared. New social classes heaved themselves out of the mass and began the anguish of social adjustment to rapidly changing conditions. That adjustment was convulsive. There was repetitive social disturbance, skirmishes in a growing and virulent class struggle. Traditional leadership resisted, turned out the troops, manufactured martyrs, and either adapted themselves to new situations or were overthrown. And this process continued until the time when it became possible to accommodate dissent and the desire for social and economic change within the institutions of representative political democracy — as revolutionary an ideology to the traditionalist classes of nineteenth-century Europe as Communism is to the traditional-minded classes of the contemporary West.

My point — and it is a deceptively simple one — is that the countries which have now emerged from behind the imperialist curtain have done so in a nineteenth-century situation in some sectors, if not in others.[3] To the tensions and irritations of the process of modernization have been added the pressures of food shortages and population growth — a consequence, in

---

[3] For a functional historical account of the "development of under-development" see Andre Gunder Frank, *Capitalism and Underdevelopment in Latin America* (New York: Monthly Review Press, 1967).

part at least, of one aspect of modernization, that of preventive medicine. These factors increase the incidence of revolution and spread its seeds among a larger number of people. There have been rebellions of the hungry in the past — when, for example, the women of Les Halles marched off to Versailles in 1789, claiming on their return that they had brought back, not the king and queen and their son, but the baker, the baker's wife and the baker's boy. Tomorrow, it will not be a few thousand women marching on the palaces of the rulers, but millions. And their hunger will compound the intensity of social change, a change which even under less nightmarish conditions would be convulsive and violent anyway. The time-cycle of nineteenth-century industrial societies at least supplies us with a framework of recognition. The convulsive response is inevitable to the process of modernization, to the readjust-ment of social relationships, to the creation of new institu-tions, to the acceptance of new social values, and to an increasing awareness of the irrelevance of the old. Traditional societies do not take radical change peacefully, for there is no way of absorbing it peacefully. The fear of change sometimes overcomes the desire for change. But history shows that ac-commodation finally appears, a flexible and sometimes ill-defined accommodation which is even capable of operating within the framework of a rigid ideology. Indeed, if there is one thing that the history of the Soviet Union in the last twenty years can show us, it is that a Communist society may not be the end product of the modernizing process but a social device adopted for the period of transition from immobility to development.

There are going to be revolutionary upheavals of one sort or another throughout every part of the developing world, and it is likely that they will go on for the rest of this century. Some will undoubtedly be inspired by Communist ideas. Many will not. All will probably be anti-West, though that will really mean anti-have. I see nothing essentially evil in this — envy is a spur to action. What is important is that that action should not be deflected from creative ends. The highly developed nations of the world, among whom the United States is the most powerful force, have an important role to play in helping the developing nations to get through their periods of convulsive change as quickly as possible. Overt interference on grounds of ideology or calculations of national security can only delay the process of change, and compound and therefore intensify the destructive elements in that process. This is one of the lessons that history has to teach us.

Another is the fundamental role of national identification, that sense of being "special" which sometimes defies rational analysis. We know that nationalism — the concept of the nation-state — is itself a product of the growth of industrial societies in the West. Philosophers, both amateur and professional, have sought for some rationale for an international community and have, sometimes with regret, decided that it can only be founded on the association of nations so secure in their nationhood that they have no need to assert it aggressively. We have seen over the last few years the Communist countries of Eastern Europe, which used to be considered, accurately, as satellites of the Soviet Union, asserting their nationalism against the imperial power of Russia. Subjection, either ideological or by military force, produces a search for identity as a rallying point against the oppressors. It was an image of maturity in the struggle against the colonial powers, who themselves had given a special aura of superiority to the concept of the nation-state. The "white man's burden," that poetic expression of social Darwinism, was generally accepted by all white men, but — within the general terms of racial superiority — the British knew they were better than the French and other Europeans just because they were British. In the postwar world, it has been shown that, even where the majority of a country's population has no deep feeling of national identity, they are capable of finding one in times of threat — as, for example, when Indians responded (at least temporarily) to an appeal to feel like Indians at the time of the Chinese attack in 1962. Even though such feelings may evaporate when the threat is removed, the ruling elites continue to act as if the territorial frontiers contain a nation. Within those frontiers, there are at least some elements of ethnic and historical pride. That remembrance of some precolonial situation — of independent kings and virile traditional cultures which gave colonial nationalism its local relevances — is entrenched in the countries which have emerged from colonial or semicolonial domination. National independence is a real and living thing, if only to the rulers. They may ask for outside help to preserve it, but if that help is so overwhelming that local nationalism appears to be submerging under a new alien conquest, they will turn against the helpers and look for other support.

What conclusions can be drawn from the points I have made? Firstly, the basic irrelevance of historical parallels between the *Pax Britannica* and the United States present role in Asia — either as determinants of policy, or as justification of it. Secondly, that the British learned very quickly that consciously attempting to remake the world in their own image — on the proposition that Absolute Good and Absolute Evil were primary forces loose in society — was an activity that rebounded bloodily in their faces. Thirdly, that convulsive change is endemic in the development process, and that though it may not be particularly pleasant or result in regimes particularly friendly to the West, it is a process which moves toward the resolution of conflicts. Fourthly, that Communism is itself an *agent* of change, and that a Communist society is not the inevitable successor to a capitalism that must inevitably decay. And lastly, that nationalism in developing countries is essentially defensive.

I would not claim any profound insight in assembling these conclusions. They are sufficiently obvious to many people, though not, apparently, to the men who hold so much of the world's destiny in their hands. But how relevant are such conclusions to the future? Certainly, they offer material for the readjustment of attitudes, and they contain a qualified prevision of the trend of events. They cannot, however, predict those events. Historical analysis is not capable of doing that. Nor do they offer much in the way of a solution to Vietnam. What they do is confirm the need for systematic thinking about the legitimate uses and the inevitable limitations of power — and thinking based not upon the rhetoric of history but upon a reasoned analysis of all the factors of social change.

Can such thinking take place in the United States, or, indeed, in the lesser nations which have the interests of global peace at heart, while Vietnam poisons the national and the international atmosphere? As an Englishman, I share neither my government's uncritical support of United States action in Vietnam nor the emotionalism of those who condemn it without any genuine consideration of reality. For me, their condemnation has the same theological quality as some of the statements of members of the Washington administration. I want to see this terrible affair ended as quickly as possible, because, apart from the suffering which needs no underlining, it imperils the future. The Vietnam war is the great stumbling stone, for while it continues there is no coming to terms with those wider realities which will go on after the war is over.

I have mentioned some fundamental attitudinal readjustments. They add up to "stop playing God." But they apply not to the world today, but to the world *after* Vietnam. In general terms, that world can be envisaged — but only in general terms. Whatever the solution in Vietnam, it is not going to be clear cut. Its residues will haunt United States policy-makers for the next generation — at least, I hope so. And there will be physical residues, too. Even if some tolerably satisfactory negotiated peace can be arrived at in Vietnam, it will be a peace which, allowing for the massive emotional readjustments the United States will have to make, I cannot see including total American withdrawal from Asia, however desirable that may be. I repeat, an American withdrawal from Asia is desirable. I am not, however, concerned with ideal and theoretical situations, but with those that are possible. I cannot see a solution in Vietnam which does not involve some humiliation for the United States. In the world outside, it may be partly offset by the delighted recognition that at last the United States will not only have done the right thing, but the most intelligent. It will, however, bring to a head, if this has not already happened, the great debate inside the United States, out of which it is hoped changes of attitude and changes of policy will emerge. The problem then will be not how to end the Vietnam imbroglio, but at what level to sustain Washington's commitments elsewhere in Southeast Asia.

It is in such a situation that fundamental attitudes will be of overriding importance, for without a radical change in them, without indeed a rational and pragmatic approach to reality, other Vietnams are inevitable — and not only in Asia.

However, it is Asia that presents the dramatic polarization of United States problems. Will it still do so in 1990? It will depend a great deal on the delicacy of United States foreign policy. But it will also depend upon China's interpretation of that policy. For China, too, must make attitudinal adjustments and accommodations as radical in their way as those of the United States. China already has nuclear weapons and will undoubtedly attain the capability of delivering them. A false interpretation of some comparatively minor event, based upon faulty historical analogy, could produce some irrevocable response by the Chinese. This possibility is a further argument for a United States withdrawal from Asia as soon as practicable and certainly before China achieves missile capability.

But once we dispose of the theological interpretation of China's absolute evil, we find ourselves faced with other sources of danger. The upheavals of developing societies are obviously more intense and destructive in larger communities. One of the principal components of the Chinese "threat" is the size of its population. If the romantic and irrational Cultural Revolution is coming to an end and turns out to have been only an interruption in the progress of China's development, then the Communist idea will continue to exert social discipline during the process of modernization. This will not neutralize the possibility of irrational response, but it will help to get China through social disturbances until there emerges some sort of modern "consumer proletariat" economy and, with it, those civilizing restraints upon the actions of government which we have seen at work in the Soviet Union.

There is, however, another large developing country where the political system may not be able to exert social discipline — India; if it has not yet reached nuclear maturity, it is at least going through nuclear adolescence. The illusion about Indian democracy, a legacy of the special nature of British rule and of its immediate successor, could be just as dangerous as the anti-Christ syndrome in relation to Communism.

The case for coming to terms with a rapidly changing, revolutionary world cannot include the prevision of policies of immediate response. It does include the need for the abandonment, in the last third of the twentieth century, of theological attitudes of proved irrelevance and danger. It includes, too, the acceptance of situations offensive to the ideological structure of democratic societies. But within this scaffolding, desperate problems will remain, and they will need those flexible, informed responses which can only come from flexible and informed minds. It would therefore be sensible, during the debate about the nature and use of United States power abroad, to inquire into the nature and use of political power inside America itself. It may be that the democratic system is in need of overhaul in this multirevolutionary world.

If, like the conversation of children, this paper seems to have consisted almost entirely of questions, it is because I have no reassuring answers. Nevertheless, I believe there is fundamental value in defining the sort of questions that should be asked and for which answers will have to be found. However, if I may offer a suggestion from the history of the British Empire, there is, I think, some relevance in the attitude held by a mid-nineteenth-century viceroy of India, John Lawrence, to the then pressing problem of Afghanistan. The British, in irrational fear of Russian expansion in Central Asia, had fought a disastrous and unnecessary war in Afghanistan between 1839 and 1842. Lawrence did not see a Russian menace under every stone — he was no dreamer, not even a theologian. He took his view of neutrality-to-change to a logical conclusion. He was prepared to support any faction in Afghanistan which appeared capable of bringing stability to the country, but he would not raise a finger to help anyone to achieve the throne. In a letter to Afzal Khan, one of the many contenders for power, he blandly wrote:

My friend, the relations of this government are with the actual rulers of Afghanistan. If your Highness is able to consolidate your Highness's power, and is sincerely desirous of being the friend and ally of the British government, I shall be ready to accept your Highness as such.

Lawrence's policy was sneeringly described, as "masterly inactivity." To this Lawrence replied that "masterly inactivity" was for abroad and that at home he practiced "masterly activity." Perhaps this could be defined in a more contemporary phrase, as "constructive isolation." This I define as the withdrawal from unilateral involvement in alleged "peacekeeping" activities in favor of wholehearted support for international institutions and agencies operating under the aegis of the United Nations, and as a corollary, the creation in the United States itself, of — not, perhaps, the "Great Society" — but a better society for that domestic third world, the underprivileged America of the Negro and of the rural and urban poor.

Afterword
The Challenge Facing
American Statesmen

NEAL D. HOUGHTON

I

Cold War Mentality in the United States

It would not be adequate to say categorically that United States leadership — even in its dominantly cold war mentality — desires *merely* to preserve the status quo of old economic and political orders. Declaredly and demonstrably, that leadership has also been concerned with human welfare.

Yet, Britain's Professor J. W. Burton has emphasized the observable fact that:

> The consistency with which Western Powers . . . the United States and the United Kingdom in particular . . . have supported elites whose function it is to deny political participation and social justice to the peoples they govern, is one of the more remarkable aspects of post-1945 diplomacy. In China, in Korea and in Vietnam — as in Latin America — Western Powers have given support to elites known to be inefficient and corrupt, but otherwise to be relied upon in defending politically unacceptable institutions . . . given support to factions in whose interests it has been to prevent social revolution . . . and sought to impose solutions to problems in Asia, to prevent the operation of indigenous processes.[1]

---

[1] J. W. Burton, "Western Intervention in South-East Asia," *The Year Book of World Affairs 1966,* The London Institute of World Affairs, University of London (London: Stevens & Sons, 1966), pp. 1–22. Quotation from pp. 5 and 10.

And, certainly, official Washington does insist that any major improvement in the economic and social status of mass humanity must be sought within a basic framework of "free enterprise" — "freedom" — saith Washington.

From no higher source has that principle come more forcefully than from President Truman, very early in the emergence of the post-World War II cold war era.[2] It has been reiterated frequently by his successors. And that, in an era of "Multi-Revolution on all Continents," when, according to a number of competent students, private capitalism has never had less hope of coping with the overwhelming economic and social problems of humanity in the vast mass-poverty areas of the world.[3]

I have had occasion elsewhere to state that, as a matter of record, major industrialization by free enterprise has been largely confined to Britain, Western Europe, the United States, Canada, Australia, New Zealand, and Japan. All, except Britain and Japan, have started with a combination of uniquely favorable conditions and circumstances. (1) All have had available vast areas of fertile soil and adequate supplies of natural resources. (2) All have been vastly underpopulated.

---

[2] See President Truman's Baylor University speech, *The New York Times*, March 7, 1947. See also James P. Warburg, *Put Yourself in Marshall's Place* (New York: Simon & Schuster, 1948), pp. 12, 46.

[3] See Robert L. Heilbroner, *The Great Ascent* (New York: Harper & Row, 1963); O. Edmund Clubb, "The Second World Revolution," *The Progressive*, June, 1965; William A. Williams, *The Tragedy of American Diplomacy* (Cleveland: World Publishing Company, 1959); Gerald Clark, *The Coming Explosion in Latin America* (New York: McKay, 1963); Peter Ritner, *The Death of Africa* (New York: Macmillan, 1960); Walter Lippmann, *The Communist World and Ours* (New York: Little, Brown, 1958); John Gerassi, *The Great Fear* (New York: Macmillan, 1964); "The Necessity of Revolution," (ed.), *Monthly Review*, VII (December, 1965), 1–9; George C. Lodge, "Revolution in Latin America," *Foreign Affairs*, XLIV (January, 1966), 173–97; and Ronald Steel, "One Millionaire and Twenty Beggars: Why Violent Revolutions Probably Are Inevitable in Most of Latin America — In Spite of Anything the United States Can Do," *Harper's*, CCXXXIV (May, 1967), 81–87.

And for a new potent economic argument, see Andre Gunder Frank, "The Development of Underdevelopment," *Monthly Review*, September, 1966.

(3) All have been able to draw upon rapidly increasing amounts of profit-seeking investment capital from Britain and Western Europe. (4) All were unquestionably safe places for that foreign investment. (5) All were able to live comfortably on their own extractive economies, so that, for those areas, industrialization could *wait,* and accumulating domestic capital could be a sort of "moonlighting" operation.

But hardly any of the underdeveloped areas of the twentieth century has any of these advantages, and certainly no one area has all five. The mass-poverty areas simply have no prospect of receiving adequate traditional private investment capital.

Robert L. Heilbroner has said essentially, with persuasive reasoning, that democracy and private capitalism as they have developed in the West, are luxuries which the vast mass-poverty areas probably cannot afford. Nor is there the native patience or upper-class will to permit the time and basic social reforms required. And, deploring as impractical the utter intolerance in the United States for the development of new collectivistic, even Communistic, orders in those areas, he advises Washington that:

> Above all, an effective policy requires a change in the official attitude of America toward "socialism" in the underdeveloped world, widely. These areas [he warns], must receive the strongest possible encouragement — and not merely a grudging acquiescence — in finding independent solutions along indigenous socialist lines.[4]

It may well be, of course, as some demographers have pre-

---

[4] Heilbroner, *op cit.,* p. 175 and *passim.* See also Heilbroner, *The Limits of American Capitalism* (New York: Harper & Row, 1966).

Still, however, the basic notion persists that, somehow, in these vast mass-poverty areas, the remarkable development by *private entrepreneurs,* which has come in the United States, Western Europe, and a few other developed countries can also be induced. Says one apostle of that hope, "We must plant [there] ... the missing ingredients of private local initiative ... [so] the nationals of these countries [may] create their own enterprises ... communism in these developing countries will only be avoided by the creation of *indigenous private capitalism.*" See Aaron Scheinfeld, *A Plan for Accelerating Private Investment in Developing Countries.* Copies available free from the author at 211 East Chicago Avenue, Chicago.

dicted, that the masses of people in those vast areas may never eat well under any system. Some prominent geographers and economists are sadly but boldly warning that starvation, "dire famine," may well come widely and early to those peoples surely within the next two decades.[5]

But these conditions of life and death—*not Communism*—are the really basic impulsions to revolution among the increasingly distressed, impatient, racially and nationalistically oriented peoples. As Justice William O. Douglas said of the Asian situation in the mid-1950's, "there is not one ounce of Communism in the *issues* of those revolutions."

Yet, under whatever leadership, basic social revolutions perforce may be required to overthrow and displace the unyielding old ruling classes and obsolete social orders. And, from the record of history, basic social revolutions are almost necessarily just not even arguably nice social experiences.

> More often than not, [says Professor Schuman], they are horrible and hideous convulsions in human affairs . . . they testify to human cruelty and irrationality, even when they may have ultimately liberalizing and creative results . . . yet they are facts of life to which other governments are obliged to respond.

That response may be rational, involving acceptance of and adjustment to those facts of life, or it may be irrationally fearful and counterrevolutionary. And, though most such basic social revolutions in contemporary history have been provoked by the intransigence, arrogance, and corruption of

---

[5] For example, Dr. R. B. Sen, Director General of the UN's Food and Agriculture Organization, has predicted that some areas may experience "serious famine in five to ten years." See *The New York Times*, August 31, 1965. William H. Draper, Jr., National Chairman of the Population Crisis Committee in the United States, says, "in the coming decade." *Ibid.*, December 3, 1965. See also a series of six articles by Jean M. White on "This Crowded Earth" in the *Washington Post* and *Denver Post*, August 15–20, 1965; George B. Cressy, "How Rich Is the Earth?" Syracuse University, May, 1963; Sherwood Ross, "U.N. Report Indicates 10,000 Deaths Each Day: Half World's Population Suffers Chronic Hunger," *Arizona Daily Star*, September 14, 1964; and "C. P. Snow Warns of World Hunger," *The New York Times*, January 1, 1966.

obsolete traditional ruling upper classes, the open encouragement — and sometimes spectacular leadership — of some recent ones by Communists has provided United States leadership
with an excuse for refusing to come to rational terms with
history in the era of irrepressibly rapid social change.

Near-psychotic fear of Communism is, of course, basic to
our cold war mentality. That mentality, characterized by a
high degree of official and popular insensitivity to human welfare and social reality and expressed in much of our recent
foreign policy and cold war tactics, equates with an alarming
movement toward further *social blindness.*

Professor Burton alertly observes:

> The political struggle for independence in Asia is asso-
> ciated in Western minds with postwar *Communist* influ-
> ences . . . this is a misconception; it is not of such recent
> origin. What is recent is the translation of values into
> demands. It is wartime conditions that gave opportuni-
> ties to indigenous Nationalist movements to develop and
> to assert rights of independence.[6]

II

Manifestations of Social Blindness in the United States

Recent and prospective basic social revolutions — it is said
— defy and threaten "freedom," "human dignity," "democracy," and other traditional Western "values" and "principles."[7] To which U Thant, from the vantage point of acquain-
tance with Asian conditions and the so-called "Oriental mind"
has vainly replied, with respect to Asian peoples:

> To preach to them and tell them about the virtues of
> democracy, the virtues of human dignity, the virtues of

[6] See Burton, *op. cit.,* p. 4. See also Franz Schurmann and Orville
Schell, *Republican China: Nationalism, War, and the Rise of Communism 1911–1949* (New York: Vintage, 1967).

[7] For an excellent succinct statement of the stateside rationalizing line
for the irrational stateside reaction to those revolutions, see Burton,
op. cit., p. 10.

fundamental freedoms [including free enterprise] is not only irrelevant but comic . . . that is not the remedy. Their need is to have food, clothing, and houses. Those are their primary needs.[8]

So overwhelming are the immediate social and economic needs of 240 million Latin Americans and 1.25 billion Asians — and the predictable needs of the impending 1 billion Latin Americans and 4 billion Asians in only a few more decades — as to call for the maximum economic productive contributions of all social orders everywhere.[9] Each of the new ones seeking to serve segments of the vast underdeveloped regions is developing its own technological talent and its own ways of utilizing whatever of "capital equipment" may be available to it — including the sheer muscle power of hundreds of millions of men and women, which has been the major source of energy in all the traditional economies in history. And I know of no responsible evaluation of the evolving new systems in Russia or China which does not report relatively remarkable progress, in spite of almost indescribably great handicaps and disadvantages.[10]

---

[8] Excerpted from his speech on May 27, 1965, at the annual conference of nongovernmental organizations associated with the United Nations.

See also, James Reston, "Inscrutable Asian Mind Baffling to U.S. Statesmen," *Arizona Daily Star,* January 23, 1966, a masterful analysis, so headlined in that particular outlet for the Reston column on that day. It is, of course, readable in any of the newspapers which carry the column. And, see Reston, "Washington: McNamara's Nightmare China," *The New York Times,* March 2, 1966; and E. W. Kenworthy, "McNamara Denies U.S. Vietnam Role Threatens Peking: A Peaceful Red China 'Has No Reason to Fear Military Action,'" *ibid.,* March 4, 1966. But, see note 51.

[9] See Danilo Dolci, *A New World in the Making,* translated from the Italian by R. Monroe (New York: Monthly Review Press, 1965), and (Worcester and London: Trinity Press, 1965). See also Harrison Brown, James Bonner, and John Weir, *The Next Hundred Years* (New York: Viking Press, 1957 and 1963).

[10] On Chinese efforts, see Edgar Snow, *The Other Side of the River: Red China Today* (New York: Random House, 1962); Felix Greene, *Awakened China* (Garden City: Doubleday, 1961); *A Curtain of Ignorance: How the American Public Has Been Misinformed About China*

Certainly, no small handicap has been the desperate determination of official Washington as "leader" of the "free world," not only to discourage other nations from maintaining economic relations with these new regimes but also to undermine their internal stability. In January, 1954, the Department of State (through Walter S. Robertson, Assistant Secretary for Far Eastern Affairs) declared:

> The heart of the policy toward China and Formosa is that there is to be kept alive a constant threat to military action vis-à-vis Red China in the hope that at some point there will be an *internal breakdown* . . . a cold war waged under the leadership of the United States, with constant threat of attack against Red China, led by Formosa and other Far Eastern groups and militarily supported by the United States. We have a complete embargo on [United States] trade with the mainland. Our allies trade in [what they consider] non-strategic materials . . . Canada and Japan, next to the United States, exercise the strictest [embargo] controls of all.[11]

And, testifying before the House Appropriations Committee in February, 1955, Mr. Robertson repeated: "Our hope of solving the problem of China is . . . through action *which will promote disintegration from within.*"

Now, I pause to ask what degree of social blindness is required to plan cold-bloodedly to bring about the complete

---

(Garden City, Doubleday, 1964); and A. Doak Barnett, *Communist China in Perspective* (New York: Praeger, 1962). On North Korea, see Joan Robinson, "Korean Miracle," *Monthly Review*, January, 1965. See also James Charrerie, "Socialism in North Vietnam," *ibid.*, February, 1966. For some assessments and evaluations of developments in Eastern Europe, see Josef Korbel, *Tito's Communism* (Denver: University of Denver Press, 1951); Fred Warner Neal, *Titoism in Action* (Berkeley: University of California Press, 1958); Fred Warner Neal and George W. Hoffmann, *Yugoslavia and the New Communism* (New York: Twentieth Century Fund, 1962); and Arthur J. Olsen, "Since August 13 [1961] Everything's Been Different [East Germany]," *The New York Times Magazine,* September 19, 1965.

[11] Hearing Before the Subcommittee on Appropriations, House of Representatives, 83rd Congress, 2nd Session, 1954, pp. 124–25.

social, economic, and political "disintegration" of an area where more than half the people of Asia live? Is that a socially tolerable way to "solve the problem of China"?

What degree of social blindness is required not to see that such spectacular destruction could not help the Chinese people, or the other peoples of Asia — who altogether are expected to outnumber the entire present world population within some thirty years — and not to see that complete *social* chaos in Asia could not be followed by the "freedom," the "human dignity," "peace," or any other of the virtues of which Washington leadership prates?

Is "social blindness" an adequate expression to connote such proffered world "leadership"?

It is true, of course, that at the end of 1963 public statements by Roger Hilsman (successor to Walter Robertson) were eagerly and hopefully interpreted by some intellectuals as promising some possible softening of Washington's policy toward China.[12] But, Mr. Hilsman seems to have come to recognize that no really basic change in that policy was to be expected. He resigned his State Department post and wrote a book hailed editorially by *The Nation* just before its publication as "said to contain the most detailed, factual indictment of the Johnson administration war policy yet written by anybody with inside knowledge."[13] And, when the book appeared, it seemed partially to justify that advance billing.[14]

Editorially, the *Bulletin of the Atomic Scientists* has deplored, moderately enough, the fact that in the United States:

> political leadership has not yet advanced to the decision that health and prosperity everywhere in the world — not only among our allies and the uncommitted nations, but also in the countries under communist rule — is in our interest, . . . [and that we are] still inclined to see a

---

[12] See Roger Hilsman, "United States Policy Toward Communist China," *Department of State Bulletin,* January 6, 1964, pp. 11–17.

[13] See *The Nation* (ed.), March 27, 1967.

[14] See Hilsman, *To Move a Nation* (Garden City: Doubleday, 1967). See also Malcolm W. Browne's review, "Double the Effort and Square the Error," *The Nation,* June 3, 1967.

prolonged famine in China or a deepening economic crisis in Cuba as a "good thing," a welcome demonstration of the inadequacy of the communist system and a factor in weakening the communist side in the [cold war] power conflict . . . [whereas] in a world integrated by the scientific revolution, human miseries are calamities to all, not only from the humanitarian point of view, but also from that of the long-range interest of all nations.[15]

Yet, as of the spring of 1967, in efforts "to prevent all of Asia from falling to Communism," official Washington leadership — so urgently and so forcefully offered to the whole so-called "free world" — was devoting its foreign policy talents, energies, and military hardware to the increasingly systematic destruction of much of one Asian peninsular area. That talent, energy and literal firepower complex was blatantly and bloodily consecrated — with rhetorical overtones of Presidential Godliness — to impeding, restricting, and destroying economic productive capacity in that region, whose social order (like those of China and Cuba) Washington leadership does not approve. You will also be aware that — since military incursion No. 1 into Cuba in 1961[16] Washington has been officially engaged in the systematic economic starvation and strangulation of the people of that nearby island in an attempt to induce them to overthrow their government.

Why — all of it?

Certainly, not because Asian and Cuban peoples do not *need* the productive capacity that is being restricted and/or destroyed. Every road, every mile of railroad, every railway car, every motor truck, every bridge, every power plant, every steel mill, every hospital, every sampan, every tank of oil, every native hut is *needed* in South Asia. All are desperately

---

[15] Eugene Rabinowitz, "The Open Door," *Bulletin of the Atomic Scientists,* XVIII (June, 1962), 2–3, 24.

[16] See Neal D. Houghton, "The Cuban Invasion of 1961 and the U.S. Press in Retrospect," *Journalism Quarterly,* Summer, 1965. See also Victor Bernstein and Jesse Gordon, "The Press and the Bay of Pigs," *Columbia University Forum,* Fall, 1967.

needed *under whatever social system those people may come to live.*[17]

In Walter S. Robertson's testimony before a Congressional Committee in the mid-1950s (parts of which have been quoted earlier here), he also took occasion to restate: *"The United States is undertaking to maintain for an indefinite period of years American dominance in the Far East."*

When pressed by a committee member for the reason for such an ambitious policy, Mr. Robertson replied that:

I think the only possible justification for it could be the belief and conviction that it is necessary for our security; not for any other reason under the sun but that, the security of America, Americans, free institutions, and what we loosely call the free world.[18]

Not only was that truly an ambitious dogma, but one conceived, I submit, in unwarranted fear and social blindness, based on ignorance of the Asian experiences of other Western governments and the basic impelling forces at work in this great global upheaval. But it also was and is sheer cold war nonsense!

As early as 1942, before the atomic age, Professor Nathaniel Peffer warned:

The West must give up rule in the Far East politically, because it really has no choice. For the age of imperialism is done and the day of Western domination of the world must be committed to the dead past. This is history's decree, not our option.[19]

For one brief hour, in January, 1950, President Truman,

---

[17] See Dorothy Dunbar Bromley, *Washington and Vietnam: An Examination of the Moral and Political Issues* (Dobbs Ferry, N.Y.: Oceana, 1966). See also *The Conscience of the Senate on the Vietnam War* (excerpted short Senatorial quotes from the *Congressional Record*, largely in 1964–1965), (New York: Marzani and Munsell, 1965).

[18] See Hearings as cited in note 11, pp. 126–27.

[19] *Basis for Peace in the Far East* (New York: Harper & Row, 1942), p. 58.

in a speech before the National Press Club, warned that a "new day" had come in Asia:

> a day in which old relationships between East and West are gone, relationships which at their worst were exploitation, and which at their best were paternalism. That relationship is over, and relationships of East and West must now be one of mutual respect and mutual helpfulness.[20]

In 1955, after Hiroshima, Nagasaki, Korea, and Dien Bien Phu, Walter Lippmann declared: "Any more Western war-making is effectively outlawed in Asia by the massive popular opposition to any kind of Western military intervention on the Mainland of Asia."[21] In 1961, General Douglas MacArthur who had directed a lot of Asian war-making, advised President Kennedy to "keep U.S. troops off the mainland of Asia at all costs."[22] And in the same year Professor D. F. Fleming warned that "the double impact of the two world wars made the liberation of all Asia from Western control unavoidable."[23]

But in August, 1963 a badly confused President Kennedy deplored the persistent and prospective viability of the developing social structure of the New China — despite Washington's exertions toward its "disintegration from within." He anticipated a Chinese population of perhaps 700 million very soon, with a "Stalinist-type" leadership — no longer subject to white Western, capitalistic domination, as it had been for the century from the 1840s to the 1940s — and possessed of nuclear power. Then, he warned, "I would regard that combination, *if it is still in existence in the nineteen seventies . . .* as potentially a more dangerous situation than any we've faced since the end of the second world war."[24]

---

[20] Norman A. Graebner, *The New Isolationism* (New York: Ronald, 1956), p. 79.

[21] "Today, Tomorrow," January 14, 1955. That was just twelve days before Mr. Robertson's declaration on the U.S. policy purpose to dominate Asia.

[22] *New York Herald Tribune,* July 26, 1961.

[23] D. F. Fleming, *The Cold War and Its Origins 1917–1960* (Garden City: Doubleday, 1961), II, 661.

[24] *The New York Times,* August 2, 1963.

By 1964 and 1965 knowledgeable people were speaking frankly of Washington's allegedly obvious design to induce Chinese "provocation" (by escalating involvement in Vietnam) which might provide an excuse for all-out bombing of Chinese "nuclear bases," and even major cities, in order that the New China, so frightening for Mr. Kennedy, might not be "still in existence in the nineteen seventies."[25]

In the spring of 1967, Harrison Salisbury declared that:

Perhaps those generals were right [?] who believed that the only way to deal with China was to atomize it. But I thought that there must be another way. China was the world's most talented nation, the reservoir of more human skills than any other existent, a people of infinite capabilities, possessor of the world's longest history and most complex culture, inventor of so many of the great technologies of the human era. Was it true that we could not find a way to live with China? Must the Globe be turned into a poisonous desert because of China? I did not believe so. Surely, America's heritage, Yankee ingenuity, and the democratic imagination of our great people could devise a better course.[26]

---

[25] In late April, 1965, Barry Goldwater was quoted by *The New York Times* News Service as saying in Paris that, if he were President, he would "pray that Communist China give us provocation to attack their nuclear possibility." *Arizona Daily Star*, April 28, 1965. For pertinent clarifying matter, see Hans J. Morganthau, "War with China?" *New Republic*, April 3, 1965; George Mct. Kahins' Study Paper in *Council for a Livable World*, March, 1965; D. F. Fleming, "What Is Our Role in East Asia?" *Western Political Quarterly*, March, 1965; "God Help the Victor," (ed.), *The Nation*, March 1, 1965; John Roderick, "Bomb Gives China Truculence," *Arizona Daily Star*, December 20, 1964; George T. Harris, "The Chinese Bomb Menace," *Look*, December 1, 1964; "New Look at Arms Race," State Department *Foreign Policy Briefs*, March 1, 1965; William E. Griffith, "We Must Stop Red China Now!" *Reader's Digest*, February, 1965; and "Ky Urges Facing the Chinese Now," *The New York Times*, July 26, 1967.

[26] Harrison Salisbury, "Is There a Way Out of the Vietnam War?" *Saturday Review*, April 8, 1967, p. 96.

III

Challenge to the United States: Come to Rational Terms With Contemporary History

1. Internationally. Doubtless, men with impaired social vision who yield to the eighteenth-century temptation to use twentieth-century military firepower can, and may, destroy ancient civilizations in Asia.

But, *twenty-first-century social statesmanship should not permit that to be done.* From whom shall come effective demand for that grade of social statesmanship?

Professor Henry Steele Commager of Amherst has deplored the fact that:

> The arguments that were invoked to justify religious wars and religious persecution in past centuries are invoked now to justify sleepless hostility to Communism — even preventive war [and that] for years now we have heard, and not from extremists alone, that the struggle between democracy and communism is the struggle between Light and Darkness, Good and Evil, and that the moral distinction is an absolute one.[27]

In his very impressive testimony before the Senate Committee on Foreign Relations in February, 1967, Professor Commager elaborated upon this position, warning that the United States "is not God," that we do not have the "resources — material, intellectual, or moral" to play that role in the world, and that it is "not our duty to . . . stop the advance of Communism or other isms which we may not approve."[28]

Hannah Arendt has decried the fact that:

---

[27] "A Historian Looks at Our Political Morality," *Saturday Review,* July 10, 1965.

[28] See "Commager Declares U.S. Oversteps World Role," *The New York Times,* February 21, 1967. For the full Commager statement, see *Changing American Attitudes Toward Foreign Policy,* Hearing Before the Committee on Foreign Relations, United States Senate, 90th Congress 1st Session, February 20, 1967. (Washington, D.C.: U.S. Government Printing Office, 1967.)

Fear of revolution has been the hidden *Leitmotif* of postwar American foreign policy in so desperate attempts at stabilization of the *status quo*, as though it was wealth and power and abundance [and the profit-seeking pursuit thereof] which were at stake in the conflict between the "revolutionary" countries in the East, and the West.[29]

And Lippmann has declared himself to be, modestly:

In favor of learning to behave like a great power, of getting rid of the globalism which would not only entangle us everywhere but is based on the totally vain notion that, if we do not set the world in order — no matter what the price — we cannot live in that world safely.[30]

By just about any standard, Washington leadership has blindly involved itself — and all of mankind — in an untenable situation in Asia. It is tragically futile to demand that Chinese and other leadership in new social orders in the vast regions of mass poverty—with historical, racial and nationalistic complications — must abandon their pursuit of better ways of life by their new methods. Predictably, they can't and won't do that. Necessarily, any major adjustments toward human and social survival in this cold war business will have to be made by Washington. The so-called Communist "enemy" does not have to come diplomatically to terms — in areas of its strength — with *our* conceptions of what the future of *their* world ought to be.

Conceivably, the wreaking of sufficient destruction upon their peoples, area by area — Vietnam by Vietnam — may compel them to *accept, temporarily,* American-dictated terms.

---

[29] Hannah Arendt, *On Revolution* (New York: Viking, 1963), p. 219.

[30] "Today and Tomorrow," April 27, 1965. See also D. F. Fleming, "Can We Play God in Asia?" *The Progressive,* XXIX (June, 1965), 12–15; "Can Pax Americana Succeed?" *Annals of the American Academy of Political and Social Science,* CCCLX (July, 1965), 127–38; "Is Containment Moral?" *ibid.,* November, 1965, pp. 18–27; J. W. Fulbright, "America in an Age of Revolution," *The Progressive,* February, 1966; and Howard Zinn, "Vietnam: Setting the Moral Equation," *The Nation,* January 17, 1966.

But few if any such acquiescences can be expected to come in good faith. As a matter of fact, numbers of competent close observers of the almost indescribable suffering of the people in Vietnam from our overwhelmingly superior military power have come away with the impression that, as Bernard Fall quoted one Vietnamese soldier — a captain, with an advanced degree in physics and mathematics — who had been fighting continuously for thirteen years, "We will all die, but we will not surrender."[31]

And how long will the conscience of mankind tolerate the process?

Nothing short of recognition that *ultimately Asia will have to be run by Asians without Western strings* can enable Washington to develop an enlightened policy in this area.

Professor Hans Morganthau — in a brilliant and courageous "Teach-in" performance — in Madison Square Garden, June 8, 1965, called for frank recognition of Communist China's political and cultural predominance on the Asian mainland.[32]

That, I submit, was man-talk — not a typical professorial operation.

Dominantly, stateside professors — cold warriors, nearly all[33] — have not ventured far beyond asking for "debate," "dialogue," and "negotiation." They have looked for some easy way to get Washington away from the Vietnam quagmire,[34] and to get some sort of "international" operation to "neutral-

---

[31] See Bronson P. Clark, "With Bernard Fall in Saigon," *The Progressive*, May, 1967. See also *Harrison E. Salisbury's Trip to North Vietnam*, Hearing Before the Committee on Foreign Relations, United States Senate, 90th Congress, 1st Session, February 2, 1967. (Washington, D.C.: U.S. Government Printing Office, 1967.)

[32] *The New York Times,* June 9, 1965.

[33] See Neal D. Houghton, "The Challenge to Political Scientists in Recent American Foreign Policy: Scholarship or Indoctrination?" *American Political Science Review,* LII (September, 1958), 678–88.

[34] On the origins and nature of that involvement, see Victor Bator, *Vietnam: A Diplomatic Tragedy* (Dobbs Ferry, N.Y.: Oceana, 1965); Robert Scheer, *How the United States Got Involved in Vietnam* (Santa Barbara: Center for the Study of Democratic Institutions, 1965); Victor Perlo and Kunar Goshal, *Bitter End in Southeast Asia* (New York: Marzani and Munsell, 1964); Robin Moore, *The Green Berets* (New

ize" and "supervise" the Indochina area, so as to guarantee it
— official Washington says — against Chinese or local Communist take-over.

But that is not good enough! Just as Washington has
boasted that "Communism in the Western Hemisphere is not
negotiable" — so it seems only reasonable to assume that
United States or other long-term Western military occupation
of the Indochina region is not predictably negotiable with
Chinese or other strong Asian Communist spokesmen.

Since Walter Lippmann has been, on occasion, as he says,
"one of the small minority in the States who have been willing
to consider the question of whether our military presence on
the Asian mainland should be, needs to be, and can be made
permanent," it may be pertinent to know that, at the end of
1965, he was saying, "I am convinced, the fundamental conflict between China and the United States is over our military
presence on the Asian mainland. . . . It was an accidental and
unplanned consequence of the second world war. Making this
artificial and ramshackle debris of old empires permanent and
committing our lives and fortunes to its maintenance, means,
I believe, unending war in Asia."[35]

Neither the Communist government of a new strong China
nor any other kind of government of a strong unified China
that might have emerged, in mid-twentieth century, from a
century of Western subjugation, could have been expected to
accept continued — or new — Western imperialistic operations on the Chinese border.[36] Certainly, as Professor Morganthau has said, "a strong China will not countenance a ring
of United States bases around its borders from Taiwan to
Thailand."[37]

Yet very few competent students seem to see China as a
military threat to her Asian neighbors. Morganthau is quoted
as saying:

York: Crown Publishers, 1965); and Malcolm W. Browne, *The New
Face of War* (New York: Bobbs, Merrill, 1965).

[35] *South Bend Tribune,* December 29, 1965.

[36] See C. P. Fitzgerald, *The Chinese View of Their Place in the
World* (New York and Toronto: Oxford University Press, 1966).

[37] See Dick Thomas, "Far East Policy Called Risky," *Denver Post,*
June 29, 1967.

Communist China has no interest in conquest of the
smaller nations on her borders, but a continued United
States military presence in Asia might push the Peking
government into a third world war.[38]

Dr. Allen S. Whiting, while he was State Department Director
of the Office of Research and Analysis for the Far East, said
in 1965 that the Chinese "do not want to expand their territory, they want to expand their influence. And this ultimate
goal, of expanding their political power, acts as a restraint on
their use of military might."

Said *The Nation*, editorially, in 1967:

Whiting is probably on sound ground in his evaluation
of Chinese objectives. If so, their hydrogen bomb is not
a threat to world peace. The threat lies rather in our
much greater nuclear arsenal, and in our determination
to maintain a military position on the Chinese borders.[39]

And Professor Toynbee has assessed the situation similarly
on many occasions.

Perhaps nowhere else has the American proclivity for *talking down* to the Communist world — boasting of superior
"principles" and "values" — been less judicious than in the
haughty and repeated insults to Chinese and other Asian
Communist leaders in the cold war era. Unnecessarily — and
vitally — that affronts Asian "face." China had a great civilization long before Western "values" and "principles" became
objects of Western pride. "China was indeed at the top of the
known world for more than 3,000 years of its recorded history," says Professor Fairbank.[40]

Yet, from the 1840s to the 1940s, China, and much of Asia,
had been victims — and beneficiaries — of Western white
military and economic dominance.[41] So, when the new Com-

---

[38] *Ibid.*

[39] *The Nation*, July 3, 1967.

[40] See John King Fairbank, "How to Deal with the Chinese Revolution," *New York Review of Books*, February 17, 1966.

[41] See Michael Edwardes, *Asia in the European Age 1498–1955* (New
York: Praeger, 1962), and *The West in Asia 1850–1914* (London: B. T.

munist China emerged at midcentury, on its own steam, with early popular and intellectual support,[42] there were plenty of grievances against the West. And it was too late for Washington and London to talk down to China. Arrogantly threatening, official Washington's policy statements — basic and typical examples of which have been quoted earlier — have been, as I have had occasion to say elsewhere, "exercises in diplomatic bankruptcy and political irresponsibility."[43]

Reference has already been made here to some rash and irresponsible policy declarations regarding the new China made by the State Department in the mid-1950s. But long before Dean Rusk became Secretary of State, in a speech before the China Institute in New York in May of 1951, he declared:

> The independence of China is gravely threatened. . . . The peace and security of China are being sacrificed to the ambitions of the Communist conspiracy. . . . We can tell our friends in China that the United States will not acquiesce in the degradation which is being forced upon them. . . . The Peiping Regime may be a colonial Russian government — a Slavic Manchuquo on a larger scale. It is not the government of China. . . . We recognize the National Government of the Republic of China [Chiang Kai-shek on Formosa]. . . . It more authentically represents the views of the great body of the people of China.[44]

Botsford, Ltd., 1967); Franz Schurmann and Orville Schell, *Imperial China* (New York: Vintage Books, 1967), II and III; John King Fairbank, *The United States and China* (New York: Viking, 1962); Maribeth E. Cameron, Thomas H. D. Mahoney, and George E. McReynolds, *China, Japan and the Powers* (New York: Ronald, 1952); and Young Hum Kim, *East Asia's Turbulent Century* (New York: Appleton-Century-Crofts, 1966).

[42] See Jack Belden, *China Shakes the World* (New York: Harper & Row, 1949).

[43] See Neal D. Houghton, "The Challenge to Intellectual Leadership in Recent American Foreign Policy," *Social Science*, XXXVI (June, 1961), 167–76.

[44] *The New York Times*, May 19, 1951.

Any particular friction between the new China and the United States has been largely due to American arrogance and irresponsibility — Washington's peculiar capacity for operating in a state of persistent and perverse social blindness — without an understanding of Asian culture and the Asians' reaction to a century of Western white dominance.

Adoption, at this late date, of a rational attitude toward China would not, of course, make China a capitalistic good neighbor. *It would simply make sense.*[45]

Competent people have come forth, in recent years, with many specific constructive suggestions for a shift toward rationality in United States policy with respect to China and Asia. Perhaps none have been more basic than those proposed by the American Friends Service Committee in 1965,[46] and a 1966 discussion of the matter by Professor Fairbank.[47]

All such suggestions are made with some hope that they may have some impact upon Washington policy-making. So they are couched in language meant to seem both *positive* and *practicable* to the political mentality.[48] They do not call upon Washington to abandon its oft-declared purpose to "win" the cold war in Asia.[49] And they seem to call for only such mild

---

[45] See Franz Schurmann and Orville Schell, *Communist China* (New York: Vintage, 1967).

For a most rabid *contra* work, prepared for the Committee of One Million ("Against the Admission of Communist China to the United Nations"), see Edward Hunter, *The Black Book on Red China* (New York: The Bookmailer, 1958).

[46] *A New China Policy: Some Quaker Proposals* (New Haven, Conn.: Yale University Press, 1965).

[47] John King Fairbank, "How to Deal with the Chinese Revolution," *New York Review of Books,* February 17, 1966. See also Jean Lacouture, "Vietnam: The Lessons of War," *ibid.,* March 3, 1966.

[48] See, for example, Sir Richard Allen, "The Task of Western Diplomacy in Southeast Asia," Center for the Study of U.S. Foreign Policy, Department of Political Science, University of Cincinnati; "Four Perspectives on Vietnam," *War/Peace Report,* V (December, 1965), 3–11; John W. Finney, "Fulbright Asks China Pact on Neutral Southeast Asia," *The New York Times,* March 2, 1966; and Russell J. Leng, "Vietnam: What Role for the UN?" *The Nation,* February 28, 1966.

[49] For official 1965 Washington policy statements by the highest spokesman for the government, all published by the Department of State and available at nominal cost from the Superintendent of Docu-

Washington concessions as may well not be acceptable or adequate for the Chinese government: for example, recognition of the Chinese government; admission of the Chinese government to functioning United Nations operations, as one of "two Chinas" (the other being Formosa) and removal of Washington-imposed restrictions upon trade with China. All are proper proposals — but they are too mild to be adequate.

In the spring of 1967, even the "experts" on China could not know what was coming in China.[50] But even a weak China

---

ments, U.S. Government Printing Office, Washington, D.C., see Lyndon B. Johnson, *Pattern for Peace in Southeast Asia,* April 7, 1965; *Vietnam: The Third Face of the War,* May 13, 1965, *We Will Stand in Vietnam,* July 28, 1965; Dean Rusk, *Vietnam: Four Steps to Peace,* June 23, 1965; *Why Vietnam* (statements by Presidents Eisenhower, Kennedy, Johnson, Secretary Rusk, and Secretary McNamara), published August 20, 1965. For later official statements, see Lyndon B. Johnson, *Viet-Nam: The Struggle To Be Free,* Department of State Publication 8048, March 1966; Under Secretary of State, George W. Ball, "Toward an Understanding of the Vietnam Struggle," *Department of State News Letter,* February, 1966; U. Alexis Johnson, *Viet Nam Today,* Department of State Publication 8039, Far Eastern Series 139, February, 1966; and Secretary Rusk and General Taylor, "The Heart of the Problem," *Department of State Bulletin,* March 7, 1966, published also as Department of State Publication 8054, Far Eastern Series 146, March, 1966.

See also *Vietnam: Vital Issues in the Great Debate* (New York: Foreign Policy Association, 1966). "Basic Data on South Viet-Nam," *Viet-Nam Information Notes,* Office of Media Services, Department of State, No. 1, revised May, 1967; "The Search for Peace in Viet-Nam," *ibid.,* No. 2, February, 1967; "Communist-Directed Forces in South Viet-Nam," *ibid.,* No. 3; "Free World Assistance for South Viet-Nam," *ibid.,* No. 4, April, 1967; and "Political Development in South Viet-Nam," *ibid.,* No. 5, April, 1967.

See also *The Other War in Vietnam,* Department of State Publication 8151, November, 1966, reprinted from *Department of State Bulletin,* October 10 and 17, 1966.

On *legal aspects* of our war-making in Vietnam, see "The Legality of U.S. Participation in the Defense of Viet-Nam," *Department of State Bulletin,* March 28, 1966, for the *official* State Department line. Reprinted also in Department of State Publication 8062, released March, 1966. But, for the *contra* case by the Consultative Council of The Lawyers Committee on American Policy Towards Vietnam, see *Vietnam and International Law: An Analysis of the Legality of the U.S. Military Involvement* (New York: O'Hare Books, 1967).

50 See "China Today," *Bulletin of the Atomic Scientists* (Special Issue), June, 1966; Lee Olson, "Mao Idolized as Communist Confucius,"

— with nuclear potential — may just not be amenable to such terms.

At some risk of overplay upon Walter Lippmann — to whom American academics have so largely abdicated their proper intellectual leadership in cold war matters — I refer respectfully to his profound early-1966 admonition:

> President Johnson . . . is on the verge of making the kind of ruinous historical mistake which the Athenians made when they attacked Syracuse, which Napoleon and Hitler made when they attacked Russia. He is on the verge of engaging this country in a war which can grow into a great war lasting for many years and promising no rational solution . . . mainly because he has let himself be persuaded by bad advice. . . . Both Rusk and McNamara have committed themselves to the fallacy that South Viet Nam is the Armageddon of the conflict with communism.

This misconceived war has in fact boomeranged. Its effect has been quite the opposite from what it was sup-

---

Denver Post, July 17, 1966; Isaac Deutscher, "Mao at Bay," *The Nation,* October 31, 1966; Max Frankel, "Prestige of Red China Plummets," *The New York Times,* November 14, 1966, and "Further Upheaval in China Foreseen in Power Battle," *ibid.,* November 15, 1966; Franz Schurmann, "A Special Feature: What Is Happening in China?" *New York Review of Books,* October 20, 1966; Hugo Portisch, "China: Behind the Upheaval," *Saturday Review,* December 16, 1966; Charles Mohr, "The Outlook for Mao," *The New York Times,* January 16, 1967, and "Mao's Revolution," *ibid.,* March 7, 1967; "Counterattack in China," (ed.), *ibid.,* January 16, 1967; and " 'Economism' vs. Maoism," (ed.), *ibid.,* January 23, 1967; C. L. Sulzberger, "Foreign Affairs: Thunder on the Left," *ibid.,* January 27, 1967; and "The Confession of Liu Shao-Chi," *Atlas,* April, 1967.

Robert S. Elegant, "Maoist Rule Seen Tottering," *Star-Bulletin and Advertiser* (Honolulu), February 12, 1967; Morton H. Fried, "Those 'Mad' Chinese," *The Nation,* February 27, 1967; C. P. Fitzgerald, "Old Man in a Hurry," *ibid.,* March 13, 1967; Carl T. Rowan, "China's Nervous Breakdown," *Arizona Daily Star,* March 24, 1967; "China's Cultural Revolution," (ed.), *Monthly Review,* XIII (January, 1967), 1–17; Charles Taylor, *Reporter in Red China* (New York: Random House, 1967); and Roy Bennett and O. Edmund Clubb, "Behind China's Cultural Revolution: Who's Winning the Power Struggle?" *War/Peace Report,* March, 1967.

posed to be. . . . The United States cannot lose face by liquidating a miserable war. . . .

If the President is not prepared to make his terms of *peace* consistent with the reality in Southeast Asia, he is likely to find that United States friends and adversaries alike regard the whole spectacular business — not as the action of a statesman — but as the device of a showman.[51]

But even the liquidation of one "miserable" and "misconceived" Metternichean war in Asia would not assure humanity of a hopeful future.[52] So long as Washington (with intellectual and popular support at home, and prevalent acquiescence abroad) persists in its refusal to tolerate the establishment and functioning of great new (and harsh) social orders evolving toward meeting the social and economic needs of mankind, for that long are the full, and questionably adequate, capacities of mankind for serving the needs of mankind tragically and unnecessarily handicapped.

The cold war mentality, in defiance of the irrepressible forces impelling this global convulsive transition, has been obsolete from its inception, in the very nature of the world situation.[53] As Cambridge historian, Professor Geoffrey Barraclough has said: "There is no greater obstacle to sane political thinking than our obsession with the cold war . . . and the real question is whether our obsession with the cold war

---

[51] *Leader Post* (Regina, Canada), January 11, 1966. See also Edgar Snow, "Deeper into the Trap: A Christmas Message on Viet Nam," *New Republic,* CLIII (December 25, 1965), 13–18.

[52] For perhaps the strongest denunciations of the Johnson policies yet to come from a stateside columnist, see John Chancellor, "Is There No Alternative to Johnson's Bravado?" *Capital Times* (Madison, Wisc.), July 17, 1967, and "The Human Angle: Kennedy and Fulbright Must Beat Johnson," *ibid.,* July 24, 1967.

[53] See David Horowitz, *The Free World Colossus* (New York: Hill & Wang, 1965); Charles O. Lerche, *The Cold War and After* (Englewood Cliffs: Prentice-Hall, 1965); Evan Luard, (ed.), *The Cold War: A Reappraisal* (New York: Praeger, 1964); Frederick L. Schuman, *The Cold War in Retrospect and Prospect* (Baton Rouge: Louisiana State University Press, 1962); and Martin F. Hertz, *Beginnings of the Cold War* (Bloomington: Indiana University Press, 1966).

is not a total misjudgment of the current world situation, and whether the fundamental criticism of American foreign policy is that, by myopic concentration on the cold war, it has misread and fumbled the challenge of the twentieth century."[54]

By — or before — the mid-1960s, there was a noticeable proclivity among students of contemporary international politics to refer to the cold war in the past tense, as though that nightmarish experience had already been largely lived through, and survived.[55] In fact, as early as 1961, Professor Fleming, in his monumental *Cold War and Its Origins*, devoted a brilliant chapter to "Why the West Lost the Cold War."[56] In 1967, Thomas Schelling was quoted as saying, "The Cold War Is Dead."[57] And Britain's Elizabeth Young declared:

Cold War I and Cold War II are being waged simultaneously. Cold War I saw the free world wrestling with what appeared to be a "communist international conspiracy," nose to nose in Berlin, eye-ball to eye-ball in Cuba, left knee to right elbow in Korea. Cold War II is now shaping up between the rich white superpowers and China, with Europe perhaps or perhaps not in the third world.[58]

If the United States is to come to rational terms with this multi-revolutionary world, we must abandon what Barraclough calls our "myopic concentration on the cold war" — whether

---

[54] For a survey of his analysis of that challenge, see Geoffrey Barraclough, *An Introduction to Contemporary History* (New York: Basic Books, 1964).

[55] That was evident even in the titles of books and papers. See, for example, Charles O. Lerche, Jr., *The Cold War . . . and After* (Englewood Cliffs, N.J.: Prentice-Hall, 1965); Robert A. Goldwin, (ed.), *Beyond the Cold War* (Chicago: Rand McNally, 1965); and David S. McLellan, *The Cold War in Transition* (New York: Macmillan, 1966).

[56] D. F. Fleming, *The Cold War and Its Origins 1950–1960* (Garden City: Doubleday, 1961), II, Chap. xxxiv.

[57] See Jerome B. Wiesner, "The Cold War Is Dead, but the Arms Race Rumbles On," *Bulletin of the Atomic Scientists*, XXIII (June, 1967), 6–9.

[58] Elizabeth Young, "ABM: No Alternative to Politics," *ibid.*, pp. 47–49.

I or II. We must face "the challenge of the twentieth century" — and move constructively and peacefully forward and into the twenty-first century. We must abandon our arrogant cult of world power and our misguided, bloody pursuit of world empire. Admittedly, that will require more than a bit of doing. It will require a rapid development of a kind and degree of *social statesmanship* which has never guided the leadership of a great empire at the height of its imperial power and wealth.

This social statesmanship cannot be merely political. It will have to be basically *social* and *economic*. It must be focused on *human welfare*. Wherever the current 3.3 billion, the prospective 7 billion, and the potential 15 billion people may live — under whatever political systems — *they* are the real "challenges of the twentieth century," and of the twenty-first century.

We must direct our efforts *not* toward stopping the clock of history and *not* in any major degree, "to shape history in our favor."[59]

Rather, our enlightened concern must be directed toward *adjusting to* and *living in* this great convulsive — and normal — course of history, as helpfully and constructively as we may.

For the predictable future what are left of the so-called "Great Powers" — the United States, Russia, and China — may perhaps be expected to undertake to exercise influence in their respective regions. That could mean, as has been indicated here, that perhaps much of the Asian mainland may lie in the Chinese orbit of ambition. Central and South America may continue to lie in the "sphere of [some] influence" of United States ambition. The USSR may be expected to aspire to play a potent role in East Europe and — increasingly — in the Middle East.

Conceivably, that pattern could tend to keep all these Greats

---

[59] For one of the most significant analyses of our cold war mentality and some of its observable effects, see Robert G. Wesson, *The American Problem: The Cold War in Perspective* (New York, London and Toronto: Abelard-Schuman, 1963); and "The Vietnam War and American Life," *Newsweek* (Special Issue), July 10, 1967.

sufficiently busy and — relatively — out of the porridge pots of the others, at least away from nuclear incineration.[60] There are historical bases for that pattern.

One of the major myths of the international politics of this era has been the illusion in London and Washington, that the Soviet Union had to be — and has been — "contained," to prevent its military "attack" upon the West.[61] Yet, a very real — and very old — Russian ambition has been to have Russian-controlled Middle Eastern access to the outside world, by way of the Mediterranean Sea.

Under the guise of the Monroe Doctrine — after a century of continental imperialism — official Washington, in close cooperation with New York banking houses, completely and ruthlessly dominated Central America and the Caribbean area from 1910 to the mid-1930s.[62] In more recent decades, in the face of increasing Latin American animosity, a somewhat more subtle but no less effective scheme of things has developed.[63] We are getting confident predictions of impending basic social revolutions in Latin America — under Latin American leadership.[64] But stateside officials, liberals and intellectuals persist in hoping that a new and adequate economic development can come to Latin America "on its own terms, without cataclysmic

[60] See Amitai Etzioni, *Winning Without War* (Garden City: Doubleday, 1964).

[61] See George F. Kennan, *On Dealing with the Communist World* (New York: Harper & Row, 1964); and Neal D. Houghton, "NATO — Defense, or Delusion?" *International Yearbook 1958–59* of the *Cotton Trade Journal*. See also Fred Warner Neal, *U.S. Foreign Policy and the Soviet Union* (Santa Barbara, California Center for the Study of Democratic Institutions, 1961).

[62] For a cogent contemporary depiction of those operations, see Benjamin H. Williams, *Economic Foreign Policy of the United States* (New York: McGraw-Hill, 1929), especially Chaps. ix–xii.

[63] See later chapters in this volume by Ramón Ruiz and John Gerassi. See also Andre Gunder Frank, *Capitalism and Underdevelopment in Latin America: Historical Studies of Chile and Brazil* (New York and London: Monthly Review Press, 1967).

[64] See Regis Debray, "Revolution in the Revolution? — Armed Struggle and Political Struggle in Latin America," *Monthly Review*, XIX (July–August, 1967) (Special Issue), 7–126. See also Georgie Annie Geyer, "The Threat of 'Vietnams' in Latin America," *The Progressive*, XXI (August, 1967), 22–25.

upheaval."[65] In fact, the whole Alliance for Progress operation is based — warrantably or not — upon that hope.

Certainly, the major challenges to United States social statesmanship require us to be tolerant of conditions-based social revolution, and to be constructively helpful to the developing new orders, as Professor Heilbroner has so logically urged.[66]

2. *Domestically*

Understandably, it is especially difficult at this point to be receptive to even moderately adequate treatment of the forces shaping this era — domestically — within our own country. Yet these explosive conditions are far more important — even to our "national security" — than any or all the Vietnams which may be in prospect, if Washington persists in its military resistance to each and every prospective basic social revolution on other continents. Certainly, our domestic challenges are far too important to be left unmentioned here.

And, since I have suggested earlier the urgent need for social statesmanship, it seems imperative that our own grave social problems should be listed here.

Let me refer briefly to my earlier listing of the basic irrepressible human and technological forces, which are impelling the several kinds of interrelated revolutions on all continents, including: demographic, economic and social, racial and nationalistic, scientific and technological.

Observably, all of these sets of forces are actively — and, in varying degrees, alarmingly — operative inside our own country. In fact, it may well be that this country — whose official spokesmen have so gratuitously and so blatantly sought to impose their "leadership" upon the whole so-called "free world" — is, domestically, in the grip of some almost unique and serious public problems. And our official — and, too widely, our intellectual — leadership may not even be aware of either the complex causes or the impending gravity of those problems.

Surely, we have not had enough serious political or intellectual concern with these problems. Much as we have had considerable mouthing about the "population explosion," the

---

[65] See Charles W. Anderson, *Politics and Economic Change in Latin America* (Princeton, N.J.: Van Nostrand, 1967).

[66] See Heilbroner, *op. cit.*, and Chap. VIII of this volume.

"revolution of rising expectations," the "scientific revolution" — and occasionally, the oversimplified "triple revolution" — on the international scene, so we have had and are having a lot of talk-talk about our domestic "crime wave," "civil rights," "organized crime," "pollution," "poverty," "hunger," "water," "slums," "education," "riots," fear of "business recession," *et al.* But, on none of these domestic matters have we had leadership concern — or public spending — even remotely comparable to what we have had with respect to "defense," "national security," "foreign aid," the alleged menace of "International Communism," "putting a man on the moon," or even Korea and Cuba, not to mention Vietnam. Yet it could be argued that the only really serious menaces to our national security lie within our own country.

At the height of the acrimonious hassle about "cancellation" of the World War I allied war debts to our government, in the 1920s, a Paris editorial asked whether history might record that the United States was the only country whose people "passed directly from barbarism into decadence, without ever having known civilization." That may have been a rashly harsh castigation — it may, or may not, have been prophetic — but only history can evaluate it. Much depends upon what is connoted by the word "civilization."

Certainly, no other so-called "great" country is so crime-laden. It is not merely the headlined "Cosa Nostra," the Mafia, and other "organized" criminality.[67] Nor is it merely the "hoodlum" criminality of recent Negro "riots." It is all of that and much more. There is no safety from it in homes or apartments, or on streets, highways, in mountain campsites, urban parks, or even in school buildings. Local newspapers are full of it for all to read daily. But, what do we do about it? Each year we read reports that the "crime rate" rises. Not uncommonly, the rise has been 10% over the previous year.[68]

---

[67] For two excellent reports on organized crime, see Martin Mooney, *Crime, Incorporated* (New York: McGraw-Hill, 1935); and Gus Tyler, *Organized Crime in America* (Ann Arbor: University of Michigan Press, 1962).

[68] For an excellent recent study see *The Challenge of Crime in a Free Society,* A Report by the President's Commission on Law Enforcement and Administration of Justice (Washington, D.C.: U.S. Government

In no other "great" country is the gap between the operating capacity to "produce wealth" and the standard of living of its poor people wider than in the United States. Some one-fifth of our peoples are living in, or on the verge of, dire poverty,[69] many of them in rural areas.[70]

That it becomes increasingly difficult to deal separately with our major domestic problems may appear obvious, I assume, because all of them are inherently bound up together. Speaking of the world situation, Professor Arthur Larson has emphasized:

There remains the unfinished revolution of human rights. This is the real world revolution of today and tomorrow. The future of the United States — and of any other country — will turn on how well it learns to understand this revolution and to find the right solution to it.[71]

By the term, "human rights," Professor Larson means not only legal "civil rights," but also economic and social rights — rights to adequate education, rights to be employed at adequate pay, to live in decent homes, to have adequate health services. For some one-fifth of all our people, we have not yet arranged for these minimal "human rights." But still we boast of our "affluence."

Our intellectuals, with varying effectiveness and some con-

Printing Office, 1967). For sale by the Superintendent of Documents at $2.25.

[69] See Michael Harrington, *The Other America: Poverty in the United States* (New York: Macmillan, 1963); Gabriel Kolko, *Wealth and Power in the United States* (New York: Praeger, 1962); and "The Case for Higher Social Security Benefits," *AFL-CIO American Federationist,* January, 1967.

See also Seymour Melman, "American Needs and Limits on Resources: The Priorities Problem," *New University Thought* (Special Issue), V (1967), *Decision for America,* 3–8; and Terence McCarthy, "The Economic Consequences of Vietnam: Alternatives to the Garrison Economy," *ibid.,* pp. 8–16.

[70] See Tom Wicker, "In the Nation: The Rural Equivalent of Watts," *The New York Times,* June 13, 1967.

[71] Arthur Larson, "The Real Nature of the World Revolution," *Saturday Review,* June 3, 1967.

fusion, talk about what they called earlier "the shame of our cities," "slums," the mixed blessings of technology, the racial "riots" in increasing numbers of our cities.[72] And the truth is that perhaps no other "great" country faces the imminent possibility of major urban violence, which we may face. Mass media comment ranges all the way from rabid denunciation of the "lawlessness," "destructiveness," and social irresponsibility of riot "agitators," to pseudo-profound efforts to explain the causes of it all and to urge the necessity for public understanding and public responsibility for dealing with the *basic* causes of Negro agitation and violence.

In fact, among the causes of the riots and the Negro call for "Black Power" are:

(1) a century of Negro powerlessness and the social irresponsibility of white power,
(2) Negro and slum poverty and an inordinately high proportion of Negro joblessness,
(3) poor educational facilities for Negroes,
(4) rat-infested slum housing for Negro families,
(5) discrimination in public and business hiring policies,
(6) lack of adequate health services for Negro families,
(7) lack of community parks and recreation programs and facilities for Negro youth, and
(8) the consequent development of a peculiar — but avid — sense of "Negro nationalism."[73]

Among the logical — but oversimple — remedial measures, proposed in some understandable panic, are:

(1) immediate provision for "jobs for young Negroes,"
(2) "slum clearance,"
(3) "city beautification,"[74]

---

[72] See Percival Goodman, "The Decay of American Cities: Alternative Habitat for Man," *New University Thought, op. cit.,* pp. 19–29.

[73] See Louis E. Lomax, *The Negro Revolt* (New York: New American Library, 1964); and David Danzig, "The Racial Explosion in American Society," *New University Thought, op. cit.,* pp. 30–39.

[74] See a series of three articles by Nan Robertson, *The New York Times,* July 3–5, 1967.

(4) housing projects, health services and recreation programs,
(5) better educational facilities, and
(6) enormous federal aid for these developments.

Now, obviously, that would be a very large order, even if it involved only Negroes in revolt — and Congress in potential revulsion. But a great deal more is involved. The entire urban structure will also necessarily have to be drastically over-hauled.[75] And, some of the components listed here are mutually contradictory, basically.

For example, there is need for more and more jobs, not only for Negroes but also for a population which promises greatly to increase before the year 2000 A.D. But, the need for more jobs for more people comes just when private and public employers, who have traditionally provided the great bulk of jobs, are substituting automatic machinery for manpower — in the interest of greater "production" — at lower costs and for greater profits. In fact, year by year, and increasingly, about as many jobs are being automated out of existence as the newly available labor force needs. And there simply are not in prospect enough jobs for Negroes who will need jobs.[76]

There is imperative need for major systematic constructive attention to all aspects of the "Negro Revolt," comparable to that which produced the atomic bomb — for indescribably destructive purposes.[77]

Certainly, Presidential designation of a Sunday "day of prayer for racial peace" was not adequate to the occasion. Nor

---

[75] In 1958, Dr. Luther Gulick, President of the Institute of Public Administration, New York, told the National Conference on Metropolitan Growth, meeting in Washington, D.C., that: "In the next 20 years our urban areas must make a place for 72 million more people with all the urban services, schools and other facilities now regarded as standard equipment for city people." He estimated that the total cost may well run as high as 250 trillion dollars. Associated Press Dispatch, November 25, 1958.

[76] See Carl Dreher, *Automation: What It Is, How It Works, Who Can Use It* (New York: Marzani and Munsell, 1965).

[77] For a most timely and profoundly suggestive study, see Jeanne R. Lowe, *Cities in a Race with Time* (New York: Random House, 1967). See also "Proposing an American Negro Congress," *I. F. Stone's Weekly*, July 27, 1967.

was the hasty Detroit riots-triggered Presidential naming, in July, 1967, of an "Advisory Commission on Civil Disorders" to "investigate origins of urban riots and recommend solutions to the White House, Congress, state governors and mayors."[78]

The Commission did, however, meet its March, 1968, deadline by producing a serious and impressive *U.S. Riot Commission Report,* dealing with "What Happened?"; "Why Did It Happen?"; and "What Can Be Done?" Immediately, it became a popular best seller in paperback at $1.25. But White House response went not far beyond saying it was "worthy of study" — and immediately promoting the Chairman of the Commission, Governor Otto Kerner, off the Commission to a United States judgeship. Mass media response to the *Report* emphasized its "white racism" feature, though the *Report* suggested leads to much more than racism.

Much more is involved in the normal profits-motivated intrusion of automation into our "civilization." No academician would dare pose as an opponent of scientific and economic "progress." But, many recognizably serious social implications are involved, along with the respectably computerized unemployment impact. In fact, these implications constitute a whole set of major domestic social problems with which there is not space to deal here. But, those problems go directly to the very heart of our economic system. How can the traditional "good business" slogan, "Buy low and sell high" be reversed? How can business management be brought to operate on the smallest possible margin of profit — as it has traditionally claimed to be doing — so as to sell goods and services at prices people can afford to pay? How, otherwise, can the vast potential production of the system be sold — so the system can operate at full capacity in peacetime?

Or, shall we be destined to live on and on in a perpetual era of rising prices — which some Keynesian economists persist in refusing to recognize as inflation? Does management dare accept the dominant academic economists' advice that the

---

[78] Nor was that gesture strengthened by the Presidential assurance that, "The FBI will continue to exercise its full authority to investigate these riots, in accordance with my standing instructions, and to continue to search for evidence of conspiracy." *Denver Post,* July 28, 1967.

system can be made to operate without the stimulation of the "military-industrial complex" — and its attendant Vietnams? How does the nonaffluent majority of our population adjust to the ever-increasing pressure to adopt the standards of an affluent minority?[79] And how does a society reverse the consequent trend which, as stated by Dr. Jerome H. Halland, President of Hampton Institute, portends a ". . . decline in traditional moral and ethical standards . . . a family pattern of grasping for material comforts in an atmosphere of superficial affluence."[80]

These are the socially pregnant queries. And they reflect a situation that *demands* an answer.

---

[79] See Henryk Skolimowski, "The 'Monster' of Technology," *Center Diary: 18,* May–June, 1967; Pete Cowgill, "Unused Time Terrifying Prospect" (quoting Turner Catledge, Executive Editor, *The New York Times), Arizona Daily Star,* March 3, 1967; Lord Bowden, "How Much Science Can We Afford?" *The Nation,* January 2, 1967; Edward B. Fiske, "New 'Barbarian' Called a Threat," *The New York Times,* May 9, 1967; Sir Julian Huxley, "The Crisis in Man's Destiny," *Playboy,* January, 1967; Stephen Unger, "Humanizing Modern Technology," *New University Thought, op. cit.,* pp. 66–83; "Technology and Human Values," (Santa Barbara: Center for the Study of Democratic Institutions, 1966); and Aaron Levenstein, "Technological Change, Work, and Human Values," *Social Science,* April, 1967.

[80] *Arizona Daily Star* (ed.), July 26, 1967.

ABOUT THE AUTHORS

Neal D. Houghton has been Professor of Government at the University of Arizona since 1928. As a Visiting Professor of Political Science, he has taught at the universities of Missouri, Illinois, Washington, and Saskatchewan. Dr. Houghton is Past President of the Western Political Science Association and has served for some ten years as a member and Vice Chairman of the Arizona Power Authority. His numerous articles have appeared widely in law, history, political science, and economics journals — notably the *Yearbook of World Affairs*, the *American Political Science Review, Background*, the *Western Political Quarterly*, and *International Conciliation*.

Arnold J. Toynbee, world-renowned historian and author, is a member of the Royal Institute of International Affairs in London. During World War I he served with numerous governmental agencies and delegations. He has received degrees from Oxford, Cambridge, Princeton, and Columbia universities, and has been a visiting professor at a number of universities throughout the world. He is Professor Emeritus at the University of London and was Director of Studies at the Royal Institute from 1925 to 1955. Among his most important works are *The World and the West, Greek Civilization and Character*, and *A Study of History*.

William Appleman Williams is Professor of History at the University of Wisconsin. Dr. Williams has studied at Leeds University in England and received his Ph.D. from the University of Wisconsin. Among his publications on the development of foreign policy are *American-Russian Relations 1784-1947, The Tragedy of American Diplomacy, The United States, Cuba and Castro,* and *The Great Evasion.*

Fred Warner Neal is Professor of Government at the Claremont Graduate School and University Center in Claremont, California. Dr. Neal is a political scientist of considerable practical experience and broad academic background. He served as Washington correspondent for United Press and *The Wall Street Journal* from 1938 to 1943 and as Consultant on Russian Affairs and Chief of Foreign Research in the State Department from 1946 to 1948. He is the author of *Titoism in Action: The Reforms in Yugoslavia after 1948, U.S. Foreign Policy and the Soviet Union, War and Peace and Germany,* and, with George W. Hoffman, *Yugoslavia and the New Communism.*

John M. Swomley, Jr., is Professor of Christian Ethics at St. Paul School of Theology in Kansas City, Missouri. He received his Ph.D. in political science at the University of Colorado. Widely traveled in Europe, Southeast Asia, North Africa, and Central America, he has authored several works relating to his experiences and insights, of which perhaps the best known is *The Military Establishment.* He has served as Executive Secretary of the Fellowship of Reconciliation and currently holds offices in the Council on Religion and Race, the Council for Responsible Dialogue, the Kansas City Peace Council, and the American Civil Liberties Union.

Dallas W. Smythe is Professor of Economics and Chairman of the Division of Social Sciences at the University of Saskatchewan. From 1943 to 1948, he was Chief Economist for the

Federal Communications Commission and he has also served as Consultant to Royal Communication Broadcasting in Canada. He is the author of *The Television-Radio Audience and Religion, Canadian Television and Sound Radio Programmes: An Analysis*, and *The Structure and Policy of Electronic Communications.*

Hugh H. Wilson is Professor of Political Science at Princeton University. He has also taught at the University of Wisconsin, where he received his Ph.D. A contributor to *The Nation* and the *Monthly Review*, he is the author of *Congress: Corruption and Compromise, The Problem of Internal Security in Great Britain*, and *Pressure Group: Commercial Television in Great Britain.*

Jerome D. Frank is Professor of Psychiatry at the Johns Hopkins University School of Medicine and holds both Ph.D. and M.D. degrees from Harvard University. In addition to his clinical and academic responsibilities, he has served as President of the Society for the Psychological Study of Social Issues, Director of the Council for a Livable World, a fellow of the Center for Advanced Study of the Behavioral Sciences, and a member of the National Institute of Mental Health. He is on the board of directors of the National Committee for a Sane Nuclear Policy. Well versed and active in foreign affairs, he was recently a witness before the Senate Foreign Relations Committee. He has written numerous papers and articles on the psychological aspects of disarmament and is the author of *Persuasion and Healing: A Comparative Study of Psychotherapy.*

George B. Vetter is Professor Emeritus of Psychology at New York University. He received his Ph.D. from Syracuse University and served in the Morale Division of the U.S. Strategic Bombing Survey in 1945. He is the author of *Magic and Religion.*

Robert L. Heilbroner is Professor of Economics at the New School for Social Research, where he received his Ph.D. In World War II, he served as an intelligence officer. He has lectured before the National War College, university, business, and labor groups and has participated in many discussion programs on radio and television and published articles in numerous magazines and periodicals. Among his most important books are *The Worldly Philosophers*, *The Future as History*, *The Great Ascent*, and *The Limits of American Capitalism*.

Joan Robinson is Professor of Economics at Cambridge University. One of the world's foremost economists, she has written and lectured extensively throughout the world. Her writings include *The Accumulation of Capital*, *Essay on Marxian Economics*, *The New Mercantilism*, *Notes from China*, and *The Chinese Point of View*.

N. B. Miller (a pseudonym) is a political scientist whose extensive travels throughout the underdeveloped countries of the world have put him in close contact with a number of the people who are today in positions of leadership in the struggle against imperialism. Mr. Miller's articles have appeared in the *Monthly Review* and various foreign periodicals. He is presently at work on a book, *Revolution: Theory and Prospects*, to be published in 1969.

Ramón Eduardo Ruiz is Professor of Latin American History at Smith College. He has taught and lectured widely on Latin American, Mexican, and American history and was Fulbright Professor of Economics at the University of Nuevo León in Mexico for the academic year 1965-1966. Currently serving as Associate Editor of the *Sociology of Education Review*, he has edited *The Mexican War: Was It Manifest Destiny?* and authored *Mexico: The Challenge of Poverty and Illiteracy*.

John Gerassi has taught International Relations at San Francisco State College. He has also taught at the New School for Social Research and New York University. From 1960 to 1962 he was *The New York Times* correspondent in Uruguay, and he covered both Punta del Este conferences. He has also traveled in North Vietnam and Cambodia. Among his many publications are *The Boys of Boise* and *The Great Fear in Latin America.*

Charles Samuel Burchill has been head of the Department of History and Economics at Royal Roads Academy in Victoria, British Columbia, since 1949. He received his degrees in history and economics from Queen's University, Kingston, and the London School of Economics. After serving as squadron leader in the Royal Canadian Air Force during World War II, he resumed teaching at the University of Alberta. He has traveled extensively in the Soviet Union, China, and the developing countries of Africa and Asia. His articles have appeared in the *Canadian Historical Review, The Canadian Journal of Economics and Political Science, Queen's Quarterly, The Dalhousie Review,* and *The International Journal.*

Young Hum Kim is Professor and Chairman of the Department of History at California Western University. Educated in Korea, Japan, and the United States, he has served as Research Associate at the School of International Relations and Assistant Director of the Soviet-Asian Studies Center at the University of Southern California. His publications include *East Asia's Turbulent Century, Patterns of Competitive Coexistence: USA vs. USSR, Twenty Years of Crises: The Cold War Era,* and *The Central Intelligence Agency: Democracy vs. Secrecy.*

Roy Bennett is United Nations correspondent for the *London Tribune.* A graduate of Ohio State University, he is Contributing Editor to *The Correspondent* and *War/Peace Report.*

His articles on foreign policy appear regularly in a number of journals, including *International Affairs*, the foreign policy magazine of the Yugoslav Journalists Association (a Yugoslav government publication). He has served as National Chairman of the Foreign Policy Committee of Americans for Democratic Action and is presently on the national board of that organization. He is also on the board of directors of the National Committee for a Sane Nuclear Policy.

Clifton E. Wilson is Associate Professor of Government and Research Specialist at the University of Arizona. Prior to 1961, Dr. Wilson served as Assistant Director of the World Affairs Program at the University of Minnesota. He is the author of *Cold War Diplomacy: The Impact of International Conflicts on Diplomatic Communications and Travel* and *Diplomatic Privileges and Immunities: A Documentary Analysis*.

Denna Frank Fleming is Professor Emeritus of International Relations at Vanderbilt University, where he taught from 1928 to 1961. After World War II, he served as adviser to the atomic energy section of the State Department. From 1950 to 1955, he was Director of the Woodrow Wilson Foundation, and he is a member of the executive council of the American Association of University Professors. His many publications include *The United States and the League of Nations 1918-1920, The United States and World Organization 1920-1933, Can We Win the Peace?* (published in 1943), and *The Cold War and Its Origins 1917-1960.*

Michael Edwardes is a well-known author and commentator for the British Broadcasting Company. During World War II, he served in the Intelligence Service in the China/Burma/India theater. Since the war he has traveled extensively through Asia. His books include *The Last Years of British India, Asia in the European Age, A History of India,* and *A Biography of Jawaharlal Nehru.*

Index